BAUDELAIRE: A FIRE TO CONQUER DARKNESS

By the same author

LE SPECTRE DU GRIS

BAUDELAIRE
A Fire to Conquer Darkness

Nicole Ward Jouve

© Nicole Ward Jouve 1980

All rights reserved. No part of this publication may be reproduced or transmitted, in any form or by any means, without permission

First published 1980 by
THE MACMILLAN PRESS LTD
London and Basingstoke
Associated companies in Delhi
Dublin Hong Kong Johannesburg Lagos
Melbourne New York Singapore Tokyo

Filmset in Great Britain by
Vantage Photosetting Co. Ltd
Southampton and London

Printed in Hong Kong

British Library Cataloguing in Publication Data

Jouve, Nicole Ward
1. Baudelaire, Charles – Criticism and interpretation
841'.8   PQ2191.Z5

ISBN 0-333-27092-4

This book is sold subject
to the standard conditions
of the Net Book Agreement

This book is in memory of Auguste Valensin, s.j., my great uncle, whom I heard lecture on Dante's *Ulysses* when I was twelve, when the line 'e volta la nostra poppa nel mattino' was swept into my mind for ever; and for my father, who used to read 'L'Horloge' to me as a child.

Contents

	Page
Acknowledgements	viii
Abbreviations	ix
Introduction: A System of Contradictions	1
PART ONE BAUDELAIRE AND ROMANTICISM	11
A. *Nature*	12
1 Nature and Politics: the Fall	13
2 Wordsworth and Baudelaire: Versions of Nature	34
3 *A Rebours*: Nature, Economics, and the Problem of Knowledge	43
4 The Significance of Form	70
B. *Consciousness*	89
5 Reverie	91
6 'Auras'	105
7 Cure through the Disease	115
8 *The Waste Land* and *Les Fleurs du Mal*	137
PART TWO FORM AS TRANSCENDENCE	145
9 *Les Fleurs du Mal*	147
10 *Le Spleen de Paris*	186
PART THREE THE MORAL WORLD: BAUDELAIRE AND DE QUINCEY	197
11 Baudelaire and Translation	200
12 Solitude and Communication	224
13 The Voyage	241
14 Time	253
Conclusion: A Fire to Conquer Darkness	286
Notes	297
Bibliography	323
Index	340

Acknowledgements

I wish to express my deepest gratitude for Professor M. A. Ruff's help at an early stage in the writing of this book; for his most helpful corrections, for his illuminating suggestions; and for his generous encouragement throughout. My gratitude equally goes to Professor W. T. Bandy, that great bibliographer and patron of Baudelairians: I thank him most heartily for his help with my bibliography; for his comments on my text; for his kind and lively support. I also wish to pay tribute to Jean-Pierre Richard's inspired and delicate reading of part of this text, for his timely and incisive help on repeated occasions; to Martin Turnell, whose reading of Chapter 9 helped me clear up some errors; and to David Kelley, for his accurate, scholarly comments.

The publishers and I are much indebted to the F. R. Leavis Fund from US University of York, whose supporting grant has helped towards the publication of this book.

And last but not least, my warmest thanks go to Anthony Ward, whose stirring impatience has urged me on through a difficult pass; and who, dazzlingly, has exhibited for me, live, some Baudelairian-type contradictions, thus helping me on to many an insight I might not otherwise have reached.

Abbreviations

The following abbreviations for Baudelaire's works have been used:

PPP	*Petits poèmes en prose*
CG	*Correspondance générale*
CE	*Curiosités esthétiques*
AR	*Art romantique*
JOPR	*Juvenilia. Oeuvres posthumes. Reliquiae*
PA	*Paradis artificiels*
HE	*Histoires extraordinaires*
NHE	*Nouvelles Histoires extraordinaires*
HGS	*Histoires grotesques et sérieuses*

(All in the J. Crépet edition published by Conard)

FM	*Fleurs du Mal*, in the Crépet edition revised by G. Blin and C. Pichois, José Corti.
JI	*Journaux intimes*, ed. J. Crépet and G. Blin, José Corti.

For fuller references, see the Bibliography.

1

Non era lunga ancora la nostra via
di qua dal sommo, quand'io vidi un foco
ch'emisperio di tenebre vincía.
Di lungi v'eravamo ancora un poco,
ma non sí, ch'io non discernessi in parte
ch'orrevol gente possedea quel loco.
'O tu ch'onori scienza ed arte,
questi chi son c'hanno cotanta orranza
che dal modo delli altri li diparte?'
E quelli a me: 'L'onrata nominanza
che di lor suona su nella tua vita
grazia acquista nel ciel che sí li avanza.'

                Dante, *Inferno*, IV, 64–78 (Limbo)

Our way was not yet far since my slumber, when I saw a fire, which conquered a hemisphere of the darkness.
We were still a little distant from it; yet not so distant, that I did not in fact discern what honourable people occupied that place.
'O thou, that honourest every science and art; who are these, who have such honour, that it separates them from the manner of the rest?'
And he to me: 'the honoured name, which sounds of them, up in that life of thine, gains favour in heaven which thus advances them.'

Introduction: A System of Contradictions

It is beautiful to see how people who write about Baudelaire fall in love with him. There is something magnificent about his pride. His aloofness, the clear outline which the intentness of his concern draws around everything he writes, the impeccability of his stance, are, through a paradox which is at the core of his work, what enable the reader to feel so close to him. He offers himself to the world as irreducibly set apart: yet he creates an intimacy which thrills.

Indeed, if one contemplates the face that Nadar's photographs have preserved for us, it is difficult not to be drawn in. The eyes catch one's attention first; the words they suggest, range bizarrely: they seem to pierce, to burn, to attack; but they also exude infinite sadness; reveal a depth which is like that of a well. Their substance seems to have the softness of coal – and its glint. There start singing in the gazer's head the lines about the eyes of the little old women, who

> . . . ont des yeux perçants comme une vrille,
> Luisants comme ces trous où l'eau dort dans la nuit . . .
> – Ces yeux sont des puits faits d'un million de larmes,
> Des creusets qu'un métal refroidi pailleta . . .[1]

And one wonders from what Rembrandt-like interrogation of his own face – of his own heart – such lines may not have sprung.

These eyes, the forehead full of thought, the mouth, sensual, haughty, firm, sarcastic, the handsome regularity of the features, command passionate involvement. They seem to say that love is a more enlightened guide into Baudelaire than 'poised judgement'. There is perhaps more *justice*, as he himself would argue, in passion than neutrality. Passion comes closer to its object, becomes vitally engaged in it. Poise is an ideal which, like Jupiter's scales of justice which Joseph de Maistre sneers at, presuppose that the world is good. That face tells the world, for a start, that it has not found it so.

And the voice it speaks confirms this:

> La sottise, l'erreur, le péché, la lésine,
> Occupent nos esprits et travaillent nos corps,
> Et nous alimentons nos aimables remords,
> Comme les mendiants nourrissent leur vermine.[2]

This voice is slow, relentless. Above all, kingly in the ease and perfection with which it inhabits the alexandrines. The reader is taken possession of, and surrenders because there is such delight in the unerring solidity of its beat. The lines are full of echoing, memorable sound, like the nasals in 'Et nous alimentons nos aimables remordş/Comme les mendiants nourrissent leur vermine'. Yet a – mediaeval? seventeenth century, rather – homily is being preached. The awesome enumeration of sins of the first line is brought home to us dual creatures: 'nos esprits', 'nos corps'. We are also aware of a curious etymological incisiveness: 'occupent', as a beseiged city is occupied by the enemy, and preoccupy; 'travaillent', as one labours the earth and in the seventeenth-century sense of 'torturent'. Yet again, the voice is full of rounded, urbane irony: 'nos aimables remords'; then of vicious relish in its denunciation: 'comme les mendiants nourrissent leur vermine'. It unnervingly swings from a level of cultured sharpness to a kind of dandyism, then to an image that resurrects Jacques Callot's etchings or Murillo's beggars. There is, that is, a violent tension between the multiple directions into which tone and imagery are pulling the stanza (themselves an enactment of the ingenious swarming of sins) and what offers itself as a preacher's accusing voice, and this tension is kept in check only by the impeccable certainty of the verse.

Yet that the verse should maintain this assured height is amazing given the strains which are put upon it:

> Ainsi qu'un débauché pauvre qui baise et mange
> Le sein martyrisé d'une antique catin,
> Nous volons au passage un plaisir clandestin
> Que nous pressons bien fort comme une vieille orange.

The first line of this stanza limps. The caesura, instead of coming after the sixth foot, is put off till the eighth syllable, giving a kind of voracity to the last four, ('Ainsi qu'un débauché pauvre/qui baise et mange . . .'), partly because the voice has been famished of its expectation and forced to rush on to 'pauvre' before it could stop, and is further rushed by the run-on- line. The whole stanza exudes rapacity, it skirts the edge of the vulgar in 'catin', in the crudeness of 'qui baise et mange/Le sein martyrisé . . .' What makes it remain this side of it is the classical device of the 'noble' epithet, sustaining the noun which brutally points to the thing: 'Que des chiens *dévorants* se disputaient entre eux', Racine's Athalie says of the dogs fighting for the mangled remains of her mother's body. Thus 'catin' is preceded by 'antique', the wizened breast elevated to the status of martyrdom. In its perfect symmetry, the line plays with rise and fall, the noble and the vulgar, unwrapping itself with lucid sinuousness.

This was the time when Hugo, massive as always, was posing as the 'Robespierre' of literature, who had removed from the neck 'du chien stupéfait son collier d'épithètes', thus promoting a contemporary poetic idiom. Baudelaire achieves his modernisation of verse by far subtler (and more radical) means: such as the unpoetic, nasty 'Que nous pressons bien fort comme une vieille orange'. Did not Frederic of Prussia say of Voltaire, whose wit he had exploited and of whom he was tiring, 'On presse l'orange et on jette l'écorce'? But the triviality of the image is countered by the supercilious mockery of the voice holding up a mirror to us and contemplating its own state in it as a well. A grotesquely deforming mirror, like those of Mme de Beaumont whom Jarry describes in one of his prefaces to *Ubu-Roi*, in which the beholder sees a monstrous image of himself, revealing his secret nature.

And this 'reflexion' of the inner self expands in the next stanza:

> Serré, fourmillant, comme un million d'helminthes,
> Dans nos cerveaux ribote un peuple de Démons,
> Et, quand nous respirons, la Mort dans nos poumons
> Descend, fleuve invisible, avec de sourdes plaintes.

The opening line has the opposite effect to that in the previous stanza. The caesura comes early instead of late, after the fifth foot – which is rare in alexandrines. It delays the voice, enabling it to dwell on density, 'Serré, fourmillant', with the incipient image of ants which the second part of the line develops, a density which is such a threat, such a 'nameless thing' that nothing but adjectives will describe it. The crowding of this line is fantastic: one's mouth is full of rather repulsive, wet 'l's', till it feels its saliva itself is breeding ants. It then gives way to the riotous, Dante-like people of Demons, and the 'swarming' transfers itself to the brain. A bizarre awareness of the vast inside of one's body is thus being induced, further expanded by the next two lines, which transform the lungs into a landscape of hell, and breathing into the thick flowing of Acheron. There is the whistle of bronchitic breathing in the alternation of sibilants and labials: 'Descend, fleuve invisible, avec de sourdes plaintes . . .' and the pause of imitative inhalation, 'fleuve invisible', allows Death both to penetrate the lungs and to earn the majesty of its capital letter.

The voice indeed confirms what the face suggests. It combines an extraordinary strength and steadiness of presence with a dizzying range of suggestiveness. In three stanzas only it shifts from a seventeenth-century homily to Dantean hell through a modern prostitution scene; from the casuistical 'lésine' (as a particular branch of avarice) to the rare zoological 'helminthes' and the ancient 'ribote' (suggestive of Bosch or Breughel) through, in intervening stanzas, the colloquial 'payer grassement' and the crude 'ténèbres qui *puent*'. As well as this, the reader is subjected to various tensions. He shrinks from what the voice tells him he is, and yet that voice grips him so powerfully that he is fascinated and – enjoys hearing what it says, in a way free from personalities. Something in him – his aesthetic sense? – fully responds to what the verse is doing and that something is being divorced from the other something which hates being told that 'we' feed our remorses as beggars their vermin. 'Hypocrite lecteur' indeed, with a dual nature that loves and hates, identifies with and is alienated from, runs away and is pulled back by the hand of the poet till he becomes his very flesh and blood, 'frère', left facing an exclamation mark as the only adequate response to his condition – looking into the poet's eyes.

Such poetry induces extreme alertness in the reader – as well as enabling him to surrender blissfully, with an easy sense of power. It makes him feel that the world is at his bidding, since it can thus radiate in multiple directions, without ever ceasing to be, aurally, at the centre. Did Baudelaire not say that four or five miles of seascape are sufficient to give man the sensation of the infinite? From the compact nutshell of 'Au Lecteur' such striding energy expands that it makes one begin to count oneself a king of infinite space.

But how is this achieved, and what insights inform this power? It is clear from the sheer complexity that a glance at a few stanzas reveals, that 'practical criticism' will not discover the springs that activate this combination of unity and multiplicity that seems so characteristic of Baudelaire.

The contradictions and complexities at work inside the individual poems, such as 'Au Lecteur', reappear, magnified and expanded, in the relations between poems in the first section of the *Fleurs du Mal*,

INTRODUCTION: A SYSTEM OF CONTRADICTIONS

'Spleen et Idéal'. To the 'ennui' of the Prologue answers 'Bénédiction', and the few poems that follow it confirm its redemptiveness. The sixth, 'Phares', ends on a profession of faith uttered through a collective, 'humanistic' first person:

> Car c'est vraiment, Seigneur, le meilleur témoignage
> Que nous puissions donner de notre dignité
> Que cet ardent sanglot qui roule d'âge en âge
> Et vient mourir au bord de votre éternité![3]

Through the strangest anticlimax, this is immediately denied by the bleak *'mode mineur'* of a solitary 'I':

> Ma pauvre muse, hélas! qu'as-tu donc ce matin?
> Tes yeux creux sont peuplés de visions nocturnes,
> Et je vois tour à tour réfléchies sur ton teint
> La folie et l'horreur, froides et taciturnes.[4]

The four poems which follow this address to the sick Muse, 'La Muse vénale', 'Le Mauvais moine', 'L'Ennemi', and 'Le Guignon', each emphasise this desolation; there arises from them a sense of vileness, insuperable laziness, waste. But in XII the reader is bathed in a subconscious, Nervalian dream:

> J'ai longtemps habité sous de vastes portiques
> Que les soleils marins teignaient de mille feux,
> Et que leurs grands piliers, droits et majestueux,
> Rendaient pareils, le soir, aux grottes basaltiques.[5]

This is enough to see the difficulty. In what spirit should one approach the oppositions of mood and stance of the poems? Should one read them separately, without regard to the structure of the volume, (as Croce suggested one should read the 'poetic' passages of the *Divine Comedy*), forgetting about the framework? Should one say: 'some moods are deeper or truer than others; a poem like "Phares" being major, one should treasure it at the expense of depressed efforts like "L'Ennemi"? Or on the contrary that 'L'Ennemi' being more intimate, says more about Baudelaire himself – take the poems, that is, as confession. Should one then look for the subterranean continuity of the *Fleurs du Mal* by means of psychoanalysis[6] and hope that thus the surface contradictions may be explained?

The difficulty is much magnified if, reading extensively through

Baudelaire's prose as well as his verse, one comes to realise that the antithetical quality of the *Fleurs du Mal* is a constant quality of the writing. Thus the admirable editorship of the *Journals* makes clear that whatever Baudelaire may assert in one or the other of his *Fusées* can be pitted against diametrically opposite assertions in other contexts; that words like 'prostitution' or 'solitude' here represent an ideal, there are dismissive. And finding that Baudelaire listed his right to contradict himself as one of the Rights of Men[7] does not help one fathom whether he veers about from inconsequentiality, wilful paradox, because his thinking constantly evolves or because he has a dialectical frame of mind. Yet each statement is made with such tautness of concern that their self-contradictoriness cries out to be understood.

The *Correspondance* does not clarify the issue either: how do you reconcile Baudelaire's permanent state of subservience to his mother – to her he is always the little child – with his understanding of her limited intelligence, his sense that by creating the 'Conseil Judiciaire' she has put his life in the shadow of ever-growing debt, made him an eternal 'minor': 'L'aveuglement fait des fléaux plus grands que la méchanceté'.[8] And there is a jarring contrast between the dead certainty of the voice, the unerring artistic judgment, and the childish rages against a notary of a 'concierge': between the minute punctiliousness with which publishers are being pursued about a comma or the etymology of a word, and the airy prodigality with which princely presents (invariably called 'une bagatelle') are bestowed.

There is some comfort that the modern reader's perplexity about the real nature of Baudelaire's sensibility was shared by the poet's contemporaries. Some were struck by his taste for artifice, and viewed it as a sign of decadence. Jules Lemaitre writes:

> Le baudelairisme serait donc . . . le suprême effort de l'épicurisme intellectuel et sentimental. Il dédaigne les sentiments que suggère la simple nature. Car les plus délicieux, ce sont les plus inventés . . . Le fin du fin, ce sera la combinaison de la sensualité païenne et de la mysticité catholique, s'aiguisant l'une par l'autre . . . On arrive ainsi à quelque chose de merveilleusement artificiel . . .[9]

This image of Baudelaire prevails in the late nineteenth century, projected by Huysmans through his des Esseintes, by Barrès, Swinburne, Symons . . .[10] But at the same time, the opposite view was being offered. Banville often pleaded in the defence of Baudelaire: 'Seul, absolument seul, il a osé être sincère . . .'.[11] The highly imperceptive and egotistical Sainte-Beuve made the plea to his fellow Academicians that Baudelaire was 'un gentil garçon, fin de langage et tout à fait classique de formes'.[12] Laforgue celebrates the directness of his voice: 'Le premier, il se raconta sur un mode modéré de confessionnal et ne prit pas l'air inspiré'; and Rémy de Gourmont stresses his health: 'Jusque dans le malaise nerveux, Baudelaire garde quelque chose de sain . . .'[13] This is contradicted by Verlaine, who stresses his 'esprit douloureusement subtil, . . . cerveau saturé de tabac, . . . sang brûlé d'alcool, . . . individualité de sensitive',[14] and his photographer friend, Nadar, portrays him as outrageously unpredictable.[15] But his most trustworthy advocate and intimate friend, Asselineau, insists that Baudelaire was simple and loyal to those who knew him well; that his extravagance was a means of testing people, of keeping his mind in a state of alertness:

> . . . ces singularités . . . n'indiquaient-elles pas déjà le parti pris de révolte et d'hostilité contre les conventions vulgaires qui éclate dans les *Fleurs du Mal, un besoin de s'entretenir dans la lutte* en provoquant journellement et en permanence l'étonnement et l'irritation du plus grand nombre? . . .[16]

This sense of total commitment to living and to his work is supported by Baudelaire's famous admission to Ancelle:

> . . . dans ce livre *atroce* j'ai mis *tout mon coeur, toute ma tendresse, tout ma religion* (travestie), *toute ma haine* . . . Il est vrai que j'écrirai le contraire, que je jurerai mes grands dieux que c'est un livre d'*art pur, de singerie, de jonglerie*; et je mentirai comme un arracheur de dents.[17]

Should we believe, then, that the image that Baudelaire projected for his contemporaries was one thing, what he wrote 'seriously' another, and that we can confidently turn to the works to find out what they mean?

Even if we agreed with F. W. Leakey that many contradictions in Baudelaire can be explained chronologically, that he started life hopefully and ended it in despair, and looked at the *Fleurs du Mal* as a fall from grace – the general movement of the book at least is evident – this would not account for the brusque changes of mood on the level of the poems themselves. Professor Leakey has to resort to a less linear theory to explain why Baudelaire is always giving himself the lie:

> Such self-repudiations constitute . . . a recurrent pattern within his intellectual development, and indeed one is tempted to claim that the more positive and dogmatic the tone that Baudelaire assumes in any given situation, the more likely it is that he will be contradicting, as self-evidently fallacious, ideas that he had previously professed with quite equal confidence . . . [18]

The real problem is that while reading Baudelaire, one gains a powerful sense of unity from recurring themes, images and vocabulary. How can this co-exist with the self-contradictions?

Some commentators of Baudelaire are tempted to seek an answer in his temperament. Gide, who finds in him the dual tendencies he had explored through the complex of *La Porte étroite* and *L'Immoraliste*, suggests that 'l'antithèse'

> . . . éclôt spontanément dans ce coeur catholique, qui ne connaît pas une émotion dont les contours aussitôt ne s'effacent, que ne double aussitôt son contraire, comme une ombre, ou mieux: comme un reflet de la dualité de ce coeur.[19]

and Sartre thus comments on Baudelaire's remark that as a child he felt the two opposite pulsions, the horror of life and the ecstasy of life:

> Il ne faut pas envisager cette horreur et cette extase indépendamment l'une de l'autre. L'horreur de la vie, c'est l'horreur . . . de l'exubérance spontanée de la nature, l'horreur aussi des molles limbes vivantes de la conscience. Puis, c'est l'adhésion au conservatisme étriqué de Joseph de Maistre, avec son goût de contraintes et de catégories artificielles. Mais l'extase de la vie naît ensuite, bien abritée par toutes ces barrières . . .[20]

But others view this self-contradictoriness as the reflection, in the poet's sensibility, of tensions actually at work in the world he inhabits:

> . . . Trois hommes à la fois vivent dans cet homme . . . Ces trois hommes sont bien modernes, et plus moderne aussi est leur réunion. La crise d'une foi religieuse, la vie à Paris, et l'esprit scientifique du temps ont contribué à faconner, puis à fondre ces trois sortes de sensibilités, jadis séparées jusqu' à paraître irréductibles l'une à l'autre, et les voici liées jusqu' à paraître inséparables, au moins dans cette créature, sans analogue avant le XIXe siècle français, que fut Baudelaire.[21]

This claim has not been made often enough. Indeed, when we reflect on the degree of controlled complexity that a poem like 'Au Lecteur' achieves, and on the public nature of its tone, it is difficult to regard it as expressive of a self-centred temperament, or as the offspring of the Roquentin-like being, turned Tory and *salaud* at one move, whom Sartre portrays. Martin Turnell seems closer to the truth, when he states that the contradictions inside the *Fleurs du Mal* reflect a tense and divided world:

> ... The drama ... lies in the impact of a hostile environment on his (Baudelaire's) consciousness which continually cheats his dream of reaching a unity outside him, and in the sudden eruption of destructive impulses from the depths of the unconscious which destroys internal unity ...
> ... The habit of perpetually pitting words and images against one another is a further reflection of the insoluble conflict at the heart of the *Fleurs du Mal*. For every emotion and every sensation is balanced by its opposite or by the hope or fear of its opposite, and is undermined by it the moment it comes into being.[22]

This has the merit of relating the drama of consciousness to the pressures of the world at large, under the guidance of Laforgue's own preoccupation with the contemporary. The strength of Martin Turnell's book comes from its close touch with the text; its weakness from the myopia of such a scope, when dealing with a writer whose every work touches all the others, and also when trying to relate a man with a history which is only nominally there: Baudelaire is shown to be representative of a world which is largely absent from the book.

In order to respond in a full and informed way to Baudelaire's writing, one must start from a larger perspective than simply that which can be achieved through a close attention to the text – to the words on the page. The poetry may indeed make us kings of infinite space, but we must *earn* the right of reading it *justly*, finding out first what space it is that it thus concentrates, and how.

Baudelaire himself confirms us in this purpose. He acknowledges his own innate tendency to self-contradiction, which alone can explain his taste for Marceline Desbordes-Valmore's 'naturalness': ... J'aime cela; je l'aime, probablement à cause même de la violente contradiction qu'y trouve tout mon être ...[23] This tendency is the voice in him of the subterranean law of 'le monde, ce vaste système de contradictions'[24]: 'Ne saisissez-vous pas par l'imagination, que quelles que soient les transformations des races humaines, ... la nécessité de l'antagonisme doit subsister ... suivant une loi éternelle de nombres et de forces proportionnels.'[25]

For him there exists a great yet unexplained correspondence between some works of art and the events which they foreshadow or engender (or perhaps which produce them). It is only all the sciences together which might provide a means of evaluating these correspondences. Discussing the vogue of Pierre Dupont's poems during the 1848 Revolution, Baudelaire opens a question which the modern critic, examining Baudelaire's own vogue in the late nineteenth and in the twentieth century, is compelled also to ask:

> Ce chant était-il un de ces atomes volatils qui flottent dans l'air et dont l'agglomération devient orage, tempête, événement? Etait-ce un de ces symptômes précurseurs ...? Je ne sais; toujours est-il que ... très peu de temps après, cet hymne retentissant s'adaptait admirablement à une révolution générale dans la politique et dans les applications de la politique.[26]

Thus one might not be wrong in assuming that the way to a real understanding of Baudelaire's contradictory use of words and forms lies through the multiple impact of his historical situation upon him and his own efforts to understand and express it. The great man is 'préparé', is never 'aérolithe'.[27] We must apply this to Baudelaire himself; working from the simple, from words like 'nature' and 'artifice' which so challenged his contemporaries, towards the complexities of the *Fleurs du Mal* and the *Spleen de Paris*; hoping that, though the way of approaching the difficulty is discursive, at least some of the spirit of *imagination* in which Baudelaire demands that a critic should approach the foreign, will inhabit us:

> ... il faut ... que ... le spectateur ... par un phénomène de la volonté agissant sur l'imagination, ... apprenne de lui-même à participer au milieu qui a donné naissance à cette floraison insolite. Peu d'hommes ont, – au complet – cette grâce divine du cosmopolitisme: mais tous peuvent l'acquérir à des degrés divers.[28]

PART ONE

Baudelaire and Romanticism

A. *Nature*

> Read Nature; Nature is a friend to truth;
> Nature is christian; preaches to mankind;
> And bids dead matter aid us in our creed.
>
> Young, *Night Thoughts*, IV, 703–5

> Céder aux forces de la nature, c'est suivre le courant de la vie collective, c'est être esclave des causes secondes.
> Résister à la nature et la dompter, c'est se faire une vie impersonnelle et impérissable, c'est s'affranchir des vicissitudes de la vie et de la mort.
>
> Abbé Constant, *Dogme et Rituel de Haute Magie*, Paris, 1862; quoted by P. Mariel as a key-text to Villiers de l'Isle-Adam's *Axel*, Paris, La Colombe, 1960, p. 24

> ... toute poëte véritable doit être une incarnation ...
>
> Baudelaire, AR,185

1 Nature and Politics: the Fall

I

Baudelaire's sensibility is deeply rooted in the second half of the eighteenth and the early nineteenth centuries. This may seem obvious: after all, in cultural terms, a century's span is a 'normal' range. When Boileau wrote of poetry immediately relevant to his age the Pléiade was a good landmark, and Voltaire felt the need to situate himself in relation to Pascal. Yet it is important to stress Baudelaire's deep, specific involvement in his own immediate past and present. Evidence for this may be found in the orientation of his critical interest. True, he may have been a gifted writer of Latin verse at school; he may have had Racine's diction in his blood; had affinities with Agrippa d'Aubigné, with the authors of mediaeval 'Danses Macabres' and with the baroque style; but he is primarily involved in the literature and painting of the later eighteenth and of the nineteenth century. His critical vision is informed by Diderot and Stendahl. His theories come from, or are a reaction to those of Rousseau, Bernardin de Saint-Pierre, Laclos, Sade, Chateaubriand, Joseph de Maistre, Sainte-Beuve, Byron and his own contemporaries. The steadiness of this anchorage may be felt if we contrast the chronological consistency of his essays with the wide range of Eliot's or Pound's. One might even say that the two periods Baudelaire was involved with meet in his blood. His father, much older than his mother, lived most of his life in the eighteenth century. He can be regarded in many ways as embodying its spirit. A painter of arguable talent, his allegiance was to what Baudelaire will call 'le culte des images', and to a world of wit, enlightenment, 'savoir-vivre'. His mother, on the other hand, could have come out of a novel by Balzac. She is like those middle-class girls of the *Comédie Humaine*, with their touching mixture of deep sensibility, 'bêtise', goodness, catholicism and love of respectability. But the relationship Baudelaire had with his mother is closer to the end of the nineteenth century than to its beginning: close to Freud, that is. His private life is prophetic of much to come in that 'fin de siècle', as his poetry is.

The biographical and critical evidence is reassuring when what must be argued is, that Baudelaire's 'nature' has its source in the pre-Romantic and the Romantic period. The argument, however, will not take a linear form – nor will it rest on biographical or even textual data. Establishing what Baudelaire 'borrowed' or plagiarised from his pre-Romantic and Romantic predecessors is a labour which has been well done – most notably by Robert Vivier and Jean Pommier, as well as by Baudelaire's most distinguished dynasty of editors. And much excellent research has gone into the 'influences' at work on his poetry and thought. We are concerned with relations and contrasts, because we believe that such a procedure alone can do justice to the temper of Baudelaire's mind. Baudelaire therefore will have to be left aside from time to time while an attempt is made to establish what implications the term 'nature' had in the pre-Revolutionary and Revolutionary period – or, more specifically, in particular writers.

The word 'nature' is much more than an isolated concept. It is the barometer of the possibilities of life and hope in this period. The continuity of life and language must be asserted at this stage, for it is a vital 'Romantic' assertion, and one without which one cannot understand a writer like Baudelaire. This continuity does not of course work on a simple basis. But in the literature of a given period (in which the language of that period is used most significantly), the concretions of meaning around particular words and images are the form which the spirit of the age takes to express its realities. The strong value-judgments which gather round 'nature' in the Romantic period may be positive or negative, according to whether Rousseau or Sade is speaking. But the fact that they are making *value-judgments* is in itself significant. It means that the men in that period think they can be the masters of their own destiny – that the making of their future is in their hands – that they are becoming conscious of their own historicity.

We shall therefore start operating from what might be called a 'naive' view of language, which we believe to be a creative one. The assumption is not that there is such a thing as an 'innocent' language (to use Sartre's term), but that any language is historical. By which we do not mean 'dated', but continuous with, through being expressive of the realities of its age.

II

This assumption is in blatant contradiction with Lovejoy's famous essay, 'On the Discrimination of Romanticisms'.[1] To show that 'Romanticism' has no circumscribable, useful meaning, and that it would be wiser to speak of a 'plurality' of Romanticisms, he focusses on the term 'nature' to show how values fluctuate in the period. He argues that it has, in the late eighteenth, early nineteenth centuries, no outstanding, new or coherent meanings which we could use to isolate the category 'Romantic sensibility'. He stresses that the theme of the superiority of 'nature' to 'art', which is taken by some, to be an identifiable Romantic tenet, had been a theme for centuries before Warton (and Rousseau), that goes back to Rabelais's contrast of Physis and Antiphysis. It was the inspiration of some of the most famous passages of Montaigne, was to be found as well in Shakespeare as in Pope's *Essay on Man*. In that sense it meant what is 'most spontaneous, unpremeditated, untouched by reflection or design, and free from the bondage of social convention'.[2] But there had also been from the first a duality of meanings in the antithesis of 'nature' and 'art'. 'While the "natural" was on the one hand conceived as the wild and spontaneous and "irregular"', in connection with landscape gardens especially, but later on by implication in connection with the arts, it was also conceived 'as the simple, the naive, the unsophisticated. No two words were more fixedly associated in the mind of the sixteenth, seventeenth, and early eighteenth centuries than "Nature" and "simple"'.[3]

But the term which is already at least dual before its uses become multiplied in the 'Romantic' period, splinters further as the various German, French and English 'Romanticisms' go their separate ways. There is thus a strong contrast between Wordsworth's search for a 'return to nature' in the *Lyrical Ballads*, and Schiller's conviction that '"harmony with nature" (in any sense which implied an opposition to "culture", to "art", to reflection and self-conscious effort) was neither possible nor desirable for the modern man or the modern artist'.[4] Similarly, to what might be called the Wordsworthian quest for 'natural' oneness, Lovejoy opposes the connections established by Schlegel, Schiller, Richter, Novalis – and in their wake, Mme de Staël, between modernity and Christian *duality*. Nor is this proliferation and divisiveness of meanings simply the mark of different national tendencies. In the same writer sometimes insoluble contradictions are to be met with. Thus Chateaubriand, when writing the first part of *Atala*, represents in some sort 'the culmination of a naturalistic and primitivistic Romanticism.'⁵ But the Chateaubriand of 1801 burns the idols he had worshipped: 'Je ne suis point, comme M. Rousseau, un enthousiaste des sauvages; . . . je ne crois point que la *pure nature* soit la plus belle chose du monde. Je l'ai trouvée fort laide partout où j'ai eu l'occasion de la voir . . . Avec ce mot de nature on a tout perdu.'

The strength and clarity of Lovejoy's arguments, the solidity and breadth of his scholarship, make his onslaught on various definitions or coherences a powerful one. And recent critics of Romanticism would not have taken so much pains to refute him if the truth of his thesis were not so substantial. But while recognising the presence of that truth, and perhaps learning from Lovejoy's *Discriminations* to tread carefully on a ground which must prove a mine-field to the simple-minded, we must be allowed to follow his remarks to their conclusions. And those conclusions, to a certain extent, witness the rebirth of the very thesis they might be supposed to destroy.

The contrast between 'nature' and 'art' as Lovejoy defines them, is thematic in Western literature from Rabelais onwards. Indeed, one encounters this opposition well before that; one might have to go as far back as the Greeks to find its genesis. But what is unprecedented in the Romantic period is the degree of intensity and frequency of the opposition. The terms are suddenly made to bear an extraordinary 'moral' charge. The same is true of other Romantic terms. Marcel Raymond traces back the source of the term 'rêverie', to which Rousseau gave such prominence, to the seventeenth, then the sixteenth century, and eventually to Medieval Latin.⁶ Mario Praz sees the dawning of the Gothic not in *The Castles of Otranto* (1764), but in *Paradise Lost*, and further back, in Tasso, Spenser and Shakespeare.⁷ Terms, however, achieve the plenitude of their meaning only at particular historical moments, and those meanings inhere in, and are not separable from, the metaphors in art wihch embody them.

Stendahl's image of 'cristallisation' expresses this notion of real changes in time. A branch, left for a long period in the depths of Salzburg's salt mines, gradually becomes frosted over with salt crystals, so that when it is finally brought out, what was wood has become diamond-like. We may use that image to express our idea of what happens to a word like 'nature' in the course of its history. It is a simple pointer to 'man' when Philinte says to Alceste, in *Le Misanthrope*: 'Vous voulez un grand mal à la nature humaine'. It neutrally refers to the mechanical world as the 'vast assemblage of everything that exists' when one of the Encyclopedists, the Baron d'Holbach, says: '... whenever, in the course of this work, the expression occurs, that "Nature produces such or such an effect" there is no intention of personifying that nature, which is purely an abstract being ... it is to prevent circumlocution, to avoid tautology ...'.[8]

'Nature' there is simply a piece of wood. The term draws no special attention to itself. Nothing perhaps can show the contrast between this neutrality and the diamond branch that the term will become at Wordsworth's hands, better than Boyle's definitions of it. Dr Johnson quotes them in full in his Dictionary, finding them so apt, he says, that he thinks they deserve to be 'epitomised':

> *Nature* sometimes means the Author of Nature, or *natura naturans*; as, *nature* has made man partly corporeal and partly immaterial. For *nature* in this sense may be used the word *creator*.
>
> *Nature* sometimes means that on whose account a thing is what it is, and is called, as when we define the nature of an angle. For nature in this sense may be used *essence* or *quality*.
>
> *Nature* sometimes means what belongs to a living creature at its nativity, or accrues to it by birth, as when we say, a man is noble by *nature*, or a child is *naturally* forward. This may be expressed by saying, *the man was born, so*; or, *the thing was generated such*.
>
> *Nature* sometimes means an internal principle of local motion, as we say, the stone falls, or the flame rises by *nature*; for this we may say, that *the motion up or down is spontaneous*, or *produced by its proper cause*.
>
> *Nature* sometimes means the established course of things corporeal; as, *nature* makes the night succeed the day. This may be termed *established order*, or *settled course*.
>
> *Nature* means sometimes the aggregate of the powers belonging to a body, especially a living one; as when physicians say, that *nature* is strong, or *nature* left to herself, will do the cure. For it may be used, *constitution, temperament*, or *structure of the body*.
>
> *Nature* is put likewise for the system of the corporeal works of God; as there is no phoenix or chimera in *nature*. For *nature* thus applied, we may use *the world*, or *the universe*.
>
> *Nature* is sometimes indeed commonly taken for a kind of semi-deity. In this sense it is best not to use it at all.[9]

The refusal to grant 'nature' any kind of ethical status survives well into the 'Romantic' period. It finds a strong advocate in the Jane Austen of *Sense and Sensibility*. The very fact that one can call her attitude 'anti-Romantic' sanctions the wisdom of contending that there are distinctly 'Romantic' meanings of the word 'nature'.

But where is the wisdom in discussing English as well as French writers in this attempt to consider links between literary language and the realities of an age? After all, the languages and traditions are different. The political development of the two countries between the 1760s and the 1850s diverge violently. But here, as with 'Romanticism', it must be argued that although the faces which change wore in the two countries hardly have any likeness, the all-involving, deeply-upsetting pattern of change was similar. Sade saw this, when he claimed that the whole of Europe was feeling 'les secousses révolutionnaires'; so that novelists everywhere had to 'appeler l'enfer à (leur) secours pour se composer des titres à l'intérêt, et trouver dans le pays des chimères, ce qu'on savait couramment en ne fouillant que l'histoire de l'homme dans cet âge de fer'.[10] This thesis is amply borne out by the efflorescence of English Gothic novels and their extraordinary vogue in that period. But it was not simply that the eddies of the French Revolution touched the whole of Europe. The Industrial Revolution effected in English society as deep a change as that which the political revolutions brought about in France: 'As in France politics, so in England manufacture, and the movement of civil society in general drew into the whirl of history the last classes which had remained sunk in apathetic indifference to the universal interests of mankind.'[11]

It is in fact deeply appropriate to seek for what is most characteristic of Romanticism in its high tide in England rather than in France, where Romanticism never quite reached the peaks or the coherence it did in England and in Germany. The great poet of the French Revolution is Wordsworth, not Chénier. And Napoleon found more resonance in Byron, 'the grand Napoleon of the world of rhyme', than in Benjamin Constant or Chateaubriand. To perceive how feeling touches politics in that period, one must transcend the frontiers of language.

How nineteenth-century poets answer each other, take up from each other, can only be understood perhaps in an image similar to that of Stendhal's 'cristallisation'. In terms of Baudelaire's own 'Correspondances', that is: 'Comme de longs échos qui de loin se confondent/Dans une ténébreuse et profonde unité.'[12] The relations, one might say the fraternity of spirit is that which rings or shines through the dark spaces of the penultimate stanza of 'Phares':

> C'est un cri répété par mille sentinelles,
> Un ordre renvoyé par mille porte-voix;
> C'est un phare allumé sur mille citadelles,
> Un appel de chasseurs perdus dans les grands bois![13]

How these 'appels' travel through the intellectual, the spiritual air, is another problem. What matters is that the term 'nature', though differently used in each writer, yet works with remarkable consistency. It is made to point in all possible directions without ever losing its centrally stable position. And it becomes the operative focus for a revitalised myth of paradise and fall and a return to paradise. What gets defined as the Edenic and the fallen differs, but the Edenic always stands for some form of ideal unity. And there is a boundless faith in the possibility of its coming to pass.

III

> Montrer que le sentimentalisme (son développement depuis 1830) suit la politique et en reproduit les phases.
> Flaubert

> Few persons but those who have lived in it, can conceive or comprehend what the memory of the French Revolution was, nor what a visionary world seemed to open upon those who were just entering it. Old things seemed to be passing away, and nothing was dreamt of but the regeneration of the human race.
> Robert Southey[14]

These reminiscences of Southey's, added to statements by Hazlitt, J. S. Mill, Shelley, Francis Jeffrey and De Quincey, to the 'apocalyptic' expectations voiced by Volney, Condorcet and Godwin, are part of the massive evidence by means of which Professor Abrams supports his contention that the evolution of poets of the 'Romantic' era was strongly influenced by the evolution of politics. His suggestion that in the Revolutionary and post-Revolutionary period, such words as 'hope' and 'dejection', for instance, 'are used in a special application, as shorthand for the limitless faith in human and social possibility aroused by the Revolution, and its reflex, the nadir of feeling caused by its seeming failure'[15] confirms our nascent sense that there operates, at the centre of the 'Romantic' consciousness a myth of paradise, fall and redemption, which is the means of formulating a new perception of History, of the link between individual and collective experience.

In order to understand the experience of late Romantics, it is important first to feel the truly Edenic hopes raised by the French Revolution; to record how well the figure of Napoleon lent itself to 'associations of natural force, creative power and revolutionary outbreak'.[16] What is surprising is that one should have to turn to English rather than to French poets to find those energies, those hopes, expressed unambiguously, with consummate fineness. Rousseau's true heir is Wordsworth, and yet it is doubtful whether the poet of the *Prelude* had read the author of the *Confessions*, and when he uses his terms, as John Jones makes clear, he misunderstands them.[17]

But somehow, as Hazlitt recounts, the 'Lake School of Poetry' 'had its origin in the French Revolution, or rather in those sentiments and opinions which produced that revolution. . . . The change in the belles-lettres was as complete, and to many persons as startling, as the change in politics, with which it went hand in hand. There was a mighty ferment in the heads of statesmen and poets, kings and people. According to the prevailing notions, all was to be natural and new . . .'.[18]

Hazlitt's is a most perceptive mind, and one can glean much from its reapings. He explores those notions of novelty and naturalness:

. . . [Wordsworth's] poetry is founded on setting up an opposition (and pushing it to the utmost length) between the natural and the artificial; between the spirit of humanity, and the spirit of fashion and the world!

It is one of the innovations of the time. It partakes of, and is carried along with, the revolutionary movement of our age: the political changes of the day were the model on which he formed and conducted his poetical experiments. His Muse . . . is a levelling one. It proceeds on a principle of equality, and strives to reduce all things to the same standard.

. . . We begin *de novo*, on a *tabula rasa* of poetry.[19]

No other corpus of statements so speedily and incisively pinpoints Wordsworth's uniqueness. The way Hazlitt explores the opposition between the natural and the artificial reveals the range of operation of the terms as well as the immense ambition of Wordsworth's poetic enterprise. Nature means equality and freedom as against privilege and established rules, the eternally and basically 'human' as against the 'fashionable', the commonly and simply held as against the conventional: reality and language as a 'going concern' against 'poetic diction'.[20] Wordsworth's *'tabula rasa'* can be seen to have much in common, both with Robespierre's political attempt at a new start and with eighteenth-century empiricism.

Furthermore Hazlitt's 'We begin *de novo*' sharply summarises the purpose which was to animate *The Recluse*, in which, as Coleridge describes it,[21] Wordsworth was to show the need for 'the whole state of man and society being subject to, and illustrative of, a redemptive process in operation, showing how this idea reconciled all the anomalies, and promised future glory and restoration'. We may also find expressed in that '*de novo*', with the sense of a rebirth of language – no longer as in the vulgar eighteenth-century definition 'thought's dress, but its incarnation'[22] – and of that rebirth paralleling and reflecting a social and political rebirth, the Wordsworthian trust in the ideal innocence of childhood.

This provides another important insight into Wordsworth's extraordinary centrality – extraordinary, in that it may seem[23] more the result of temperament than history: it is true that many of the ideas were channelled by Coleridge, but Wordsworth, as every one of his critics from Hazlitt[24] onwards seems to agree, does not proceed in terms of ideas. For the Wordsworthian sense of nature, especially his sense of man as the potential redeemer of nature, offers striking analogies with the thought of the German 'philosophers of nature', Schelling, Franz von Baader, Johann Jakob Wagner, Passavant, Eschenmayer, Kieser, Steffens, Oken, Ritter,[25] in whom the 'naturalistic' and the 'mystical' element become reconciled. That the same poetic language could become the vehicle for a naturalistic understanding of the life of the senses as well as a mystical interpretation of man's destiny, is another respect in which Wordsworth bridges the seemingly unbridgeable.

It is in this 'bridging' that he represents an apex that no one else then, at least in France or in England (Goethe might be another matter) approaches. This is why one needs him, what he stands for, to perceive fully Baudelaire's own 'Romanticism'. It is not the smallest paradox Wordsworth offers to the imagination that he should thus tower above everyone else through the completeness of his committal to a 'levelling ideal'.[26] Thus, whereas faced with Wordsworth's 'exquisite adjustings' of Nature and Mind, Blake is reported[27] to have grumbled 'You shall not bring me down to believe such fitting and fitted', it is with a sense of deep exaltation that throughout the *Prelude*, the image of a flowing stream comes to stand for the course of consciousness and the course of history:

> . . . Inly I revolv'd . . .
> that there was
> One Nature as there is one Sun in heaven,
> . . . as an instinct among Men, a stream
> That gather'd up each petty straggling rill
> And vein of water . . .[28]

And the poet can use the same words, prolong the same image, to claim that at the height of the French Revolution it ought to have been possible for a 'paramount mind' to 'Have clear'd a passage for just government . . .'[29] and to render its due to Calvert's generosity:

> He clear'd a passage for me, and the stream
> Flow'd in the bent of Nature.[30]

It may well be because Wordsworth's sensibility is so 'naturalistic', operating so much on the level of, as it were, an extended body, sensations felt not only on the individual pulse but on that of surrounding 'nature', because he is so blissfully free from the analytical mind, because, in a word, he is so richly *prosaic*, that his poetry, in its turn, thus seems to gather 'each petty straggling rill and vein of water'. One is led to feel this when one meditates on that word 'levelling' which Hazlitt profoundly uses. It is a fruitful notion, if one considers how energies distribute themselves between prose and poetry around the revolutionary period, particularly when one compares French and English literary production. For in France, at least from Rousseau to Stendhal, it is through the medium of prose, and prose frequently organised around autobiography, that the major quest for values, both public and private, seems to be conducted. This is the period in which, according to the early Lukács, the novel assumes something of the ancient status of epic: and what he says might be extended to a work like Rousseau's *Confessions*:

> Le roman est l'épopée d'un temps où la totalité extensive de la vie n'est plus donnée de manière immédiate . . . mais qui, néanmoins, n'a pas cessé de viser à la totalité.
> . . . Le roman fait tenir l'essentiel même de sa totalité entre son début et sa fin et, par ce fait, il exhausse l'individu jusqu'à l'altitude infinie de celui qui doit créer tout un monde par son expérience vécue et maintenir cette création en équilibre . . .[31]

Prose is the medium through which this 'totality', at least in the early part of the nineteenth century, is being pursued in France, partly perhaps because it is free from all the presuppositions – social and other – of verse, but more importantly because it is then a much more adequate, much more *level* linguistic mode: because, that is, it seems so much closer to the rhythms of feelings, to the speed of action – if we think of Stendhal using the *Bulletins de la Grande Armée* and the *Civil Code* as his literary models.

The history of France between 1789 and 1815 is one of continuous turmoil. Thus, as Auerbach puts it, 'all the human figures and all the human events in (Stendhal's) work appear upon a ground socially and politically disturbed'.[32] There was, however, in the same period, relative political stability in England, where 'the novel figured forth a vision of permanence and perpetuity, consigning all the kinetic energies of life to a series of romantic episodes'.[33] But what Lukács attributes to the form of the novel could be said, with very little modification, essentially of the *Prelude*, but also of much of Byron's and Shelley's poetry – and, in a more fragmentary way, of Coleridge's. The more ambitious, more central, more 'revolutionary' energies in England seem to flow into poetry; the more conservatively social, or moral, into the novel – at least in the early part of the century. And this may well be, although no doubt it would require a much more complex explanation, because somehow, mainly through the agency of the authors of the *Lyrical Ballads*, poetry achieves an immediate, an active, a *level*, a new relationship with 'life'. The 'mystery of genius in the Fine Arts', which is 'to make the external internal, the internal external, to make nature thought and thought nature',[34] is accomplished through verse.

That term of Hazlitt's, 'levelling', may yet have another dimension. Is one entitled to read into it an allusion to those 'Levellers' who represented the extreme left wing of Cromwell's revolution, and whom one could regard as a prefiguration of Babeuf's 'communists'? The possibility is interesting, not simply because it gives a measure of the immense poetical revolution that the Lake School seemed to be accomplishing, of something absolute, extreme, in the authors of the *Lyrical Ballads*, but also because a relation is thus established between the French and the English Revolution – and through this Wordsworth and Milton. Recalling what a powerful model Milton was for Wordsworth, one may at first wonder that rhythms which in the poet of *Paradise Lost* were so frequently 'vertical' rhythms, could become 'horizontal' in the poet of the *Prelude* – could be made to flow forwards rather than scale upwards or be hurled downwards. But that is too complicated a question to be considered here without detriment to our main argument. What the thought of the strong bond between Wordsworth and Milton rather suggests is that the *Prelude* may be read as the last epic just as well as one of the first 'modern' novels. And that the theme of the epic of the French Revolution, like that of the epic of the English Revolution, is *Paradise Lost* and *Paradise Regained*. Only, the authorial, autobiographical voice of the poet becomes the focus of what, in the seventeenth century epic, was presented through the opposite poles of Adam and Christ – the old man and the new man.

Wordsworth is exceptional among the English Romantic poets through the sheer importance given to the earthly paradise, the stage before the fall, in his work. It is in him that one finds best exemplified Frye's notion that the Romantic poet has a sense of being united to a creative power greater than his own, which has a 'vehicular form', and carries him along, be it wind or current; and which manifests its might through 'huge' forms, that resist 'fragmentation': through a long continuous poem.[35] This may not be due only to temperament; it may be because the best years of his youth coincided with the finest, most 'apocalyptic' upsurge of the French Revolution. For the English poets whose youth was spent under Napoleon seem to taste disillusionment much more quickly, and more irreparably. They invest imagination and emotions in him who, as Blake who was older (and wiser) saw him, started as a Prometheus and became another tyrant. In a short but useful study of 'The Romantic Myth of Organic Energy',[36] Harold Bloom attributes the gall of Byron's 'Ode to Napoleon' to bitter disappointment: 'His overthrow, from the beginning, was a blow on the head to me. Since that period, we have been the slaves of fools'.[37] For Shelley, after the downfall of Napoleon, the tyranny of imperialism appears retrospectively less evil than the tyranny of 'old Custom'.[38] But the wrong orientation given by Napoleon to the French Revolution meant the splitting up of the ideal and the real: '... God made irreconcilable/Good and the means of good':[39] the means of good in the Romantic Age, that is, 'fell into the hands of Napoleon, and those hands could destroy and not create'.[40] But the result is terrifying, for it seems that the forces of establishment, 'Earth' as Shelley calls them, thrive on the defeat of fine energies: 'Earth', upon hearing the news of the death of Napoleon, tells the poet 'I feed on whom I fed', and 'the quick spring like weeds out of the dead'.[41]

This view of political doom is borne out, although from a very different standpoint, by both Balzac and Stendhal. One gathers from those of Balzac's novels that touch on the Napoleonic era[42] a sense of excitement, recklessness and brilliance: the social malleability which Bonaparte preserved as an inheritance from the Revolution, the possibility for young men of any class to reach the highest positions through skill and courage, produced a selection of the fittest which at least satisfied energies. Nothing better represents the splendid drive of the energies thus let loose than the famous opening sentence of Stendhal's *La Chartreuse de Parme*.[43] For Byron and Shelley the fall starts under Napoleon, though it is only consummated by his collapse from power. For Stendhal it is that collapse which constitutes the fall. A fall from the scarlet into the black, from energies directed outwards to energy preying upon itself, extravert violence turning into hypocrisy.

A divorce thus occurs, between man and nature, between consciousness and self-consciousness. We are talking as though this had happened 'historically' and could nearly be dated. It could be objected that such falls, in human experience, are always mythical, because they need to be measured against an ideal state which is invented retrospectively. Thus all poets who want to explore the fall have, like Milton, to pluck an earthly paradise out of thin air. Paradise can only exist retrospectively, and as Proust will discover, 'les seuls paradis sont les paradis qu'on a perdus'. This may be true, but the proliferation of myths of the fall at a given period must show that the historical climate was favourable to the formation of such myths. But it is, of course, in the very nature of the myth of the fall, that it should be expanded to infinite dimensions. The Romantics – the term is taken in its largest sense – grant it such importance in the history of the human psyche (perhaps because History on a collective basis invites them to do so) that they present it either as the cornerstone of the Christian consciousness – or as an integral agent in the making of consciousness. The first view is offered by Mme de Staël – she herself has borrowed it from the German Romantics:

> Il y a dans les poèmes épiques et dans les tragédies des anciens un genre de simplicité qui tient à ce que les hommes étaient identifiés à cette époque avec la nature . . . . . . cette réflexion inquiète, qui nous dévore souvent comme le vautour de Promethée, n'eût semblé que de la folie au milieu des rapports clairs et prononcés qui existoient dans l'état civil et social des anciens . . .[44]

Coleridge gives this 'divorce' even greater significance:

In the commencement of literature man remained for a time in that unity with nature which gladly concedes to nature the life, thought, and even purposes of men, and on the other hand gives man himself a disposition to regard himself as part of nature. Soon however he must have begun to detach himself; his dreams, the very delusions of his senses which he became acquainted with by experience, must have forced him to make a distinction between the object perceived and the percipient . . .[45]

In this, though he is impelled by different longings, Coleridge comes close to an extreme form of German Romanticism – that of the Hegel of the *Phenomenology of Mind*, for whom, as Merleau-Ponty puts it

> Avoir conscience de la mort et penser ou raisonner, c'est tout un, puisqu'on ne pense qu'en quittant les particularitiés de la vie, et donc en concevant la mort.
>
> On ne fera pas que l'homme ignore la mort. On ne l'obtiendrait qu'en le ramenant à l'animalité; encore serait-il un mauvais animal, s'il gardait conscience, puisque la conscience suppose le pouvoir de prendre recul à l'égard de toute chose donnée et de la nier. . . . Toute conscience est donc malheureuse, puisqu'elle se sait vie seconde et regrette l'innocence d'où elle se sent issue.[46]

The 'fall' may be seen to occur 'in the commencement' of man's life (as a species and as an individual) or it may appear as the very condition of his humanity: but there is unanimity, beneath the multifarious ways in which it is explored, in the acknowledgement of a fall.

IV

In *Paradise Lost* and *The Prelude* the fall does not occur until Book X. It is true that the fall of Lucifer and his demons, in the first two books of *Paradise Lost*, acts as a dark prelude to the fall of Adam, that Satan's presence throughout the other books is a constant reminder of the certainty of that fall. Nonetheless, one remains impressed with the vast scope given to innocence in Milton's and Wordsworth's epics, when one compares them with the *Fleurs de Mal*: a new Satan, *l'Ennui*, stands at the gate, as certain of his power to swallow the world in one yawn as Milton's Satan is of his bold attempt to conquer Eden. 'Bénédiction', the first of the six 'unfallen' poems of 'Spleen et Idéal' is already overshadowed by original sin. The child-poet is no sooner born than his mother curses him; his innocence is not sinlessness but the ability to absorb and transcend that curse. The one poem that states a belief in the underlying unity of all things, 'Correspondances' (which, precisely for this, has been made by some into the keystone of the whole volume, a statement of the 'ideal'), posits a world that is ahead, to be discovered, to be deciphered, rather than a state of vibrant and joyful oneness with nature. Its present tense dictates the possible rather than affirms a stable here and now: 'La Nature est un temple où de vivants piliers/Laissent parfois sortir de confuses paroles . . .'. These words have to be deciphered. Eden in *Les Fleurs du Mal* is a grave and threatened state, shot through by the actuality or the memory of suffering.

This contrast between Wordsworthian and Baudelairian innocence is much too simple. It ignores such readings of *The Prelude* as Harold Bloom's,[47] which makes it a sort of *Temps Retrouvé avant la lettre*, and disturbs any naive sense of the kinds of innocence it is dealing with. It is, however, with all its crudeness, a fairly sure way of establishing how much graver is the state of fall Baudelaire is dealing with than that of the early Romantics.

On one level, largely chronological, which has been excellently described by Professor Leakey, Baudelaire goes through the whole spectrum of 'Romantic' attitudes to Nature. He moves as it were from Wordsworth to Chateaubriand:[48] as if, but spread in time, his sensibility were a kind of prism with the power to attract whatever was significant, however contrasting, in the Romantic sensibility.

Early on in his life, at the time of the 1848 Revolution, his enthusiasm for Nature is an adhesion to natural force, creative power. His friend Asselineau, who spent much time with him in 1848, thus describes his attitude:

En vertu . . . de l'influence transmise de Rousseau et de Diderot, Baudelaire aimait la Révolution; plutôt, il est vrai, d'un amour d'artiste que d'un amour de citoyen. Ce qu'il en aimait . . . c'était l'enthousiasme, la fervente énergie qui bouillonnaient dans toutes les têtes et emphatisaient les écrits et les oeuvres de toutes sortes.[49]

In Baudelaire's *Correspondence*, one sees traces of a profound disillusionment about the 'coup d'état' which aborted republican hopes. The bitterness of the tone reminds one of Shelley's and Byron's own gall at the downfall of revolutionary energies: 'Vous ne m'avez pas vu au vote; c'est un parti pris chez moi. *Le 2 DECEMBRE m'a physique-*

ment dépolitiqué. Il n'y a plus d'idées générales. . . . Si j'avais voté, je n'aurais pu voter que pour moi.'[50] The passion for politics is still there, but unable to gear itself to any reality: 'Good and the means of Good' have become divorced, and individualism ensues: 'Je me suis vingt fois persuadé que je ne m'intéresserais plus à la politique, et à chaque question grave, je suis repris de curiosité et de passion.'[51]

Whatever the circumstances, public and private, which contributed to Baudelaire's growing pessimism, the striking fact is that within the twenty odd years of his life as a poet, he moves from the 'Rousseau–Diderot' allegiance mentioned by Asselineau to a bad-tempered conservative vision. What happens to the name 'Robespierre' in his scale of values shows this. Maxime Rude recounts how, having become an editor of a reactionary paper in Chateauroux in 1848, Baudelaire harangued the 'comité de rédaction'. Scandalised by the speech, they dismissed him on the spot: 'Messieurs, dans cette révolution dont on vient de parler, il y a un grand homme, – le plus grand homme de cette époque, – un des plus grands hommes de tous les temps: cet homme, c'est Robespierre.'[52] But in 'Mon Coeur mis à Nu', which most critics date around 1859–66, Robespierre has been demoted: 'Robespierre n'est estimable que parce qu'il a fait quelques belles phrases.'[53]

In a review published in 1861, the past revolutionary generation under the Second Empire is judged with airy contempt. Robespierre is exonerated from blame, not because he had anything valid to say, but because he said it in such 'pure' language:

> Il y a une troisième espèce de jeunes gens qui *aspirent à faire le bonheur du peuple*, et qui ont étudié la théologie et la politique dans le journal *Le Siècle*; c'est généralement de petits avocats, qui réussiront, comme tant d'autres, à se grimer pour la tribune, à singer le Robespierre et à *déclamer*, eux aussi, des choses *graves*, mais avec moins de pureté que lui, sans aucun doute . . .[54]

Similarly, Baudelaire's estimates of 'nature' and the 1848 Revolution undergo an extraordinary fall in a short period of years. There is a growing curtness, dryness and irony in the style. As the poet ages, his prose slashes across life and men with growing speed and bitterness.

In the years 1845–51, in Baudelaire's twenties, 'nature' is used as a synonym for *innocence*, naivety, primitivism – in one of the senses which prevailed in the late eighteenth century:

Ce qui fait le mérite particulier des *Contes Normands*, c'est une naïveté d'impressions toute fraîche, un amour sincère de la nature et un épicurisme d'honnête homme[55]

. . . Voilà ce que Champfleury osa pour ses débuts: se contenter de la nature et avoir en elle une confiance illimitée . . .[56]

The most original, the most fully thought out version of 'nature' as not only good, but *one*, is developed in 'De l'essence du rire' and in the essays that deal with caricature. The pure inventiveness of one of the forms of the comic that get defined, the grotesque, reverts to that state of 'anti-self-consciousness'[57] which Coleridge and Madame de Staël identified with the ancient world: 'Les créations fabuleuses, les êtres dont la raison, la légitimation ne peut être tirée du code du sens commun, excitent souvent en nous une hilarité folle, excessive, et qui se traduit en des déchirements et des pâmoisons interminables . . .'.[58] The grotesque is a departure from nature (in so far as the French seventeenth century would have equated it with 'sens commun') which in fact leads back to it: '. . . le (grotesque), se rapprochant beaucoup plus de la nature' (que le 'comique significatif', Molière's comic), 'se présente sous une espèce *une*, et qui veut être saisie par intuition. Il n'y a qu'une vérification du grotesque, c'est le rire, et le rire subit . . .'.[59] In this text, 'nature' is understood in a Rousseauist sense. Baudelaire adds that in the grotesque, laughter is the expression of the idea of superiority, no longer of man over man, but of man over nature. It is an innocent triumph, which makes one participate in what is being mastered instead of separating one from it: 'Le grotesque a en soi quelque chose de profond, d'axiomatique et de primitif qui se rapproche beaucoup plus de la vie innocente et de la joie . . .'.[60]

This ideal of *joy* in 'De l'essence du rire' defines all unfallen states of being. Baudelaire offers a vision of the great age of Greece which is analogous to Nietzsche's in *The Birth of Tragedy*: the destroyers were the introducers of duality, the apostles of the Apollonian spirit, philosophers like Plato:

Quant aux figures grotesques que nous a laissées l'antiquité, . . . les petits Priapes . . . tout en cervelet et en phallus, . . . je crois que toutes ces choses sont pleines de sérieux. Vénus, Pan, Hercule, n'étaient pas des personnages risibles. On en a ri après la venue de Jésus, Platon et Sénèque aidant . . .[61]

Not only the child's, but the superior man's immunity to laughter reveal a nature totally at one with itself: Jesus, the Word incarnate, never laughed, and even in excessively civilised nations, if a man of superior intelligence like the author of those lines were willing to boldly soar towards pure poetry, 'dans cette poésie, limpide et profonde comme la nature, le rire fera défaut comme dans l'âme du Sage.'[62]

Implied in this is a near-Wordsworthian sense of the naturalness of great verse. And echoes of Wordsworth's republicanism, and of his trust in the redemptive power of nature can be heard in this early text of Baudelaire's:

> ... [le] grand secret [de Dupont] ... est dans l'amour de la vertu et de l'humanité, et dans ce je ne sais quoi qui s'exhale incessamment de sa poésie, que j'appellerais volontiers le goût infini de la République ... ... la nature est si belle, et l'homme est si grand, qu'il est difficile, en se mettant à un point de vue supérieur, de concevoir le sens du mot: irréparable.[63]

But this relish for 'nature' is short-lived – like the hopes of the 1848 revolution. In the years to come Baudelaire was to conceive so well the meaning of words like 'irréparable' and 'irrémédiable' that they would signpost the descent into Spleen of the *Fleurs du Mal*.[64] In a later article on Dupont (1861) he is much more lukewarm in his appreciation of the republican poet's optimism. That optimism now seems due more to the blindness of a generous temperament than to what was called earlier 'un grand esprit de sagesse':

> Il y a dans son esprit une certaine force qui implique toujours la bonté; et sa nature, peu propre à se résigner aux lois éternelles de la destruction, ne veut accepter que les idées consolantes où elle peut trouver les éléments qui lui soient analogues ...[65]

Baudelaire here is being gentle to Dupont, as to a youthful love. There isn't a hint of gentleness in the judgements passed on the Revolution by the *Journaux Intimes*. The best that is claimed for it is that it exalted a perverse side of men's imaginations:

> Mon ivresse en 1848.
> De quelle nature était cette ivresse?
> Goût de la vengeance. Plaisir *naturel* de la démolition.[66]

1848 ne fut amusant que parceque chacun y faisait des utopies comme des châteaux en Espagne.
1848 ne fut charmant que par l'excès même du ridicule.[67]

Le canon tonne, les membres volent.... Des gémissements de victimes et des hurlements de sacrificateurs se font entendre... C'est l'Humanité qui cherche le bonheur.[68]

It is from Sade that this late use of the word 'nature' is derived – no longer from Rousseau or Diderot, let alone Wordsworth. 'Il faut toujours en revenir à de Sade, c'est-à-dire à *l'homme naturel* pour expliquer le mal.'[69] The gloom reaches apocalyptic violence in *Pauvre Belgique*, notes for a vast satire which was never completed (1864–8):

... Moi, quand je consens à être républicain, *je fais le mal le sachant*...
... je dis *Vive la Révolution*! comme je dirais: *Vive la Destruction*! *Vive l'Expiation*! *Vive le Châtiment*! *Vive la Mort*! ...
Nous avons tous l'esprit républicain dans les veines comme la vérole dans les os, nous sommes démocratisés et syphilisés.[70]

What had been to the early Romantics an apocalypse of hope becomes an apocalypse of destruction. And the cause which had seemed to Wordsworth, in the first flush of revolutionary fervour, 'good', and such that no one could stand up against it 'who was not lost, abandon'd, selfish, proud... Hater perverse of equity and truth',[71] turns into a pox in the blood. Innocence is not only out of reach, it becomes inconceivable, undateable. Manicheanism prevails, and creation is seen, in the extremity of despair, as the fall of God:

Qu'est-ce que la chute?
Si c'est l'unité devenue dualité, c'est Dieu qui a chuté.
En d'autres termes, la création ne serait-elle pas la chute de Dieu?[72]

The cycle of nature, like the faculty of hope, goes full circle in Baudelaire.

That the fall, for him, should ultimately be seen as 'preceding existence' singles him out among the Romantics.

The 'Romantics' of the first and second generations see paradise as being lost, as it were, earlier and earlier on, as they become more dejected about the prospects of the French Revolution: but it still can be somehow placed in the history of the human consciousness, related to infancy or to some primitive stage in the history of civilisation. This may not be quite so true in Germany, where Hegel's dialectic of the master and the bondsman endows the myth with an 'eternal' and universal dimension, and where those whom Albert Béguin calls 'les penseurs romantiques' seek to explain 'cosmic becoming' as a return to a lost unity, thus making of the myth of the fall a fundamental law of modern consciousness.[73] However this may be, in Baudelaire the fall antedates history, antedates consciousness. He believes, in other words, in original sin.

Joseph de Maistre, one of the fiercest enemies of the French Revolution, seems to have breathed his passionate suspicion of 'nature' into Baudelaire. Maistre belonged, like Sade, to the old aristocratic class, was exiled from France until 1815, and from exile scathingly attacked the various revolutionary regimes. The author of, among others, *Considérations sur la France*, a work akin in its bias and vehemence to Burke's *Reflections on the Revolution in France*, and the more metaphysical *Soirées de Saint-Pétersbourg,* he became, along with Bonald, one of the apostles of 'Légitimisme' in Restoration France. His historical predicament may have made him, in many ways (as Sartre rather unfairly stressed) the spokesman for a doomed class. But his voice, unlike Sade's, transcends his situation. Baudelaire calls him a seer, 'un voyant'. It may be because in Baudelaire's opinion events proved him right – or because his diagnosis of man as a being at war with himself seemed true to the two generations which followed him. Also, the righteous energy of his stance made him vivifying in an age of weakness and confusion.

All one discovers in 'nature' for Maistre, is the law of our common corruption:

> ... le mal a tout souillé, *et l'homme entier n'est qu'une maladie* ...
> ... Qui pourrait croire qu'un tel être ait pu sortir dans cet état des mains du Créateur? Cette idée est si révoltante, que la philosophie seule, j'entends la philosophie païenne, a deviné le péché originel.[74]

This is echoed, with a sense of the oddity of such a position in the 1860s, by Baudelaire's confession to Flaubert:

> ... de tout temps, j'ai été obsédé par l'impossibilité de me rendre compte de certaines actions ou pensées soundaines de l'homme, sans

l'hypothèse d'une force méchante, extérieure à lui. Voilà un gros aveu dont tout le XIXe siècle conjuré ne me fera pas rougir.'[75]

Like Maistre, it is Voltaire and Rousseau, and their nineteenth century republican or 'optimistic' heirs whom Baudelaire is attacking, when he claims that the negation of original sin has much to do with eighteenth century blindness to real beauty:

> . . . Tout ce qui est beau et noble est le résultat de la raison et du calcul. Le crime, dont l'animal humain a puisé le goût dans le ventre de sa mère, est originellement naturel. La vertu, au contraire, est *artificielle*, surnaturelle . . . Le mal se fait sans effort, naturellement, par fatalité; le bien est toujours le produit d'un art.[76]

2 Wordsworth and Baudelaire: Versions of Nature

I

This exaltation of artifice at the expense of nature is so pervasive in Baudelaire – although it may not be consistent – that on many levels he may be seen as the perfect opposite of Wordsworth – or Rousseau. It is so radical an opposition that it cannot be simply reduced, for the sake of bracketing the two kinds of attitudes under the same 'Romantic' label, as Frye does, to 'conservative' as against 'progressive' leanings.[1]

There is a 'Romantic' current of belief that a harmonious relation can be established between man and 'nature' (meaning the country, the unsophisticated, the primitive); as such this nature is opposed to the artifice of modern civilisation.

Cowper states this view of 'nature' with pedestrian clarity:

> God made the country and man made the town.
> What wonder then that health and virtue, gifts
> That can alone make sweet the bitter draught
> That life holds out to all, should most abound
> And least be threatened in the fields and groves?[2]

In France, after Rousseau, this kind of reverence for landscape never quite attains the scope it has in England in the Romantic period. Lamartine is perhaps the poet who comes closest to a belief in the gently recreative power of nature:

> Mais la nature est là qui t'invite et qui t'aime;
> Plonge-toi dans son sein qu'elle t'ouvre toujours;
> Quand tout change pour toi, la nature est la même . . .[3]

Baudelaire's denial of this ethos is both acid and passionate: 'J'ai toujours pensé qu'il y avait dans la *Nature*, florissante et rajeunie, quelque chose d'affligeant, de dur, de cruel, – un je ne sais quoi qui frise l'impudence.'[4] How much this contradicts an important Romantic strain can be shown by one suggestive example. Wordsworth thus addresses the daisy:

> Yet like a star, with glittering crest,
> Self-poised in air thou seem'st to rest; –
> May peace never come to his nest
> Who shall reprove thee![5]

To this delicate assertion of contemplative respect we may oppose Baudelaire's

> Autrefois dans un beau jardin
> Où je traînais mon atonie,
> J'ai senti comme une ironie
> Le soleil déchirer mon sein;
>
> Et le printemps et la verdure
> Ont tant humilié mon coeur,
> Que j'ai puni sur une fleur
> L'insolence de la Nature.[6]

The French cult of pantheism exasperates Baudelaire. He regards it as a 'sentimentalisme matérialiste', a drug against the real problems of modern society. He thus harangues the 'neo-Pagans': 'Vous avez sans doute perdu votre âme quelque part, dans quelque mauvais endroit, pour que vous couriez ainsi à travers le passé comme des corps vides pour en ramasser une de rencontre dans les détritus anciens?'[7] The very verve of his attacks reveals that the pantheistic fashion threatens something vital to him. What that is he most explicitly states in his letter to Desnoyers:

> ... vous savez bien que je suis incapable de m'attendrir sur les végétaux et que mon âme est rebelle à cette singulière religion nouvelle qui aura toujours, ce me semble, pour tout être spirituel, je ne sais quoi de *shocking*. Je ne croirai jamais que *l'âme des dieux habite dans les plantes*, et, quand bien même elle y habiterait, je m'en soucierais médiocrement, et considérerais la mienne comme d'un bien plus haut prix que celle des légumes sanctifiés.[8]

Baudelaire rebels with equal irony against belief in the goodness of 'natural man'.

The strongest exponent of this belief in France is Rousseau. Early on in the *Confessions* he describes a happy episode of his childhood, when as a child of twelve he was sent with his cousin to the country. There, he felt blissfully at one with nature. This oneness led him on to man, as Wordsworth would put it: it enabled him to feel trust and love for people:

> ... La simplicité de cette vie champêtre me fit un bien d'un prix inestimable en ouvrant mon coeur à l'amitié ... Tout nourrissoit dans mon coeur les dispositions qu'il receut de la nature ... Je ne connoissois rien d'aussi charmant que de voir tout le monde content de moi et de toute chose.[9]

For Rousseau, the child in this his 'natural' state is devoid of *amour-propre*, that is, of the desire to *appear* good or clever to others. But he is full of *amour de soi*, simple self-esteem, serenity. As Rousseau grows up, the injustice of society estranges him from nature and from himself. A false self grows, which feeds on his *amour-propre'*. He struggles to make this image conform to his own sense of himself, embarks on endless self-justifications, such as the *Confessions*. The *Dialogues de Rousseau et de Jean-Jacques,* in which Rousseau seeks to convince a 'Frenchman' that Jean-Jacques is innocent and good, mark a climax in what is becoming paranoia. Then a reversal occurs, which is described in the *Huitième Promenade.* Healed by a renewed intercourse with the countryside, Rousseau decides to return to his *real* childish self, to *amour de soi,* and to stop caring about the false self which society has forged:

> ... en se repliant sur mon âme et en coupant les relations extérieures qui le rendent exigeant, en renonçant aux comparaisons et aux préférences [mon amour propre] s'est contenté que je fusse bon pour moi; alors redevenant amour de moi même il est rentré dans l'ordre de la nature et m'a délivré du joug de l'opinion.[10]

But the reconciliation effected with nature does not extend to human fellowship. The paradise of childhood is only partially regained. Yet the main idea which passes on from Rousseau to the nineteenth century is that the child, and the unsophisticated man, are closer to goodness, being closer to nature than the adult or the city-dweller – or the intellectual. This assumption pervades George Sand's rural novels, or Millet's pictures. Certainly Baudelaire regards the eighteenth century in general, and Rousseau in particular, as the source of it.

Wordsworth also believes that the close contact of the child with nature is a force for good. Nature left to her own workings would be a superb tutoress. It is polished society which warps the child, develops his *amour-propre* – 'vanity' is Wordsworth's term, not having La Rochefoucauld but the Bible as a possible seed-bed for his vocabulary. The narrator of *The Prelude* is blessed in being protected against the glitter of vain appearances:

> The surfaces of artificial life
> And manners finely spun, . . .
> This wily interchange of snaky hues,
> Willingly and unwillingly reveal'd
> I had not learn'd to watch . . .[11]

There could be no more violent contradiction of this belief than Baudelaire's assertion of the child's innate wickedness: 'Je me souviens fort bien, – disait (Delacroix) parfois, – que quand j'étais enfant, *j'étais un monstre.*'[12] In Rousseau, it is punishment unjustly meted out by the adult which perverts the child. In Wordsworth, it is the over-cultivation of rational faculties, the temptation of 'vanity' which deforms and limits him. These 'too industrious times' have engender'd a 'dwarf Man', who lives a 'life of lies', 'locked in the pinfold of his own conceit', sadly estrang'd from 'old Grandame Earth'[13] cut off from his 'filial bond with nature'.

But for Baudelaire nature teaches nothing, or next to nothing: appetites, and appetites which have been defined much better by Sade than Rousseau, since it is 'nature' which urges man 'à tuer son semblable, à le séquestrer, à le torturer'. In correlation with this, it is precisely what corrupts in Rousseau and Wordsworth which redresses in Baudelaire:

> La connaissance du devoir ne s'acquiert que très-lentement, et ce n'est que par la douleur, le châtiment et par l'exercice progressif de la raison, que l'homme diminue peu à peu sa méchanceté naturelle.[14]

Quite characteristically, of course, Baudelaire seems to contradict himself. He does argue that '. . . l'enfant, en général, est, relativement à l'homme, en général, beaucoup plus rapproché du péché originel.'[15] But he also presents a quite different view: 'Le rire des enfants est comme un épanouissement de fleur. C'est la joie de recevoir, ... la joie de contempler, de vivre, de grandir. C'est une joie de plante ... La joie est une.'[16]

This, of a piece with the thinking about the 'grotesque' which was discussed earlier on, is close to Wordsworth's sense that the child is connected with the world by a 'filial bond', a strange umbilical cord which time severs but which, while it exists, ensures a perfect reciprocity:

> From nature largely he receives; nor so
> It satisfied, but largely gives again, ...[17]

The resemblance is all the more striking as this view of the child's absolute receptivity to nature is not an isolated example of Baudelaire. This is interesting, because it complicates the pattern so far established, according to which it seemed that Baudelaire started from an 'early-Romantic' optimism, and as time passed, moved towards a blacker pessimism than any to be found in Romanticism. Be this as it may, Baudelaire often states that not only the child, but the adolescent (the weaning, or the severing of the cord, seems to be dated as in the *Immortality Ode*), perceives the world with an immediacy which will ever after be remembered with nostalgia by the adult: '... C'est alors que les objets enfoncent profondément leurs empreintes dans l'esprit tendre et facile; c'est alors que les couleurs sont voyantes, et que les sens parlent une langue mystérieuse.'[18] This is stated in more detail in *La Peintre de la vie moderne*:

> Rien ne ressemble plus à ... l'inspiration, que la joie avec laquelle l'enfant absorbe la forme et la couleur ... C'est à cette curiosité profonde et joyeuse qu'il faut attribuer l'oeil fixe et animalement extatique des enfants devant le *nouveau*, quel qu'il soit, visage ou paysage, lumière, dorure, couleurs, étoffes châtoyantes ... .[19]

What Baudelaire, with obvious delight, calls 'châtoyant', would have been damned as 'snaky hues' by Wordsworth. But otherwise, there is no incompatibility between the sense offered by this text, that nothing resembles inspiration more than the joy with which the child absorbs forms and colours, and his own view of the child's creativity: except that his emphasis is on 'power' rather than on 'animal ecstasy':

> And powerful in all sentiments of grief,
> Of exultation, fear and joy, his mind,
> Even as an agent of the one great mind,
> Creates, creator and receiver both, . . .[20]

But the contradiction in Baudelaire has its coherence. What he celebrates about the child's 'naturalness' is in fact his creative potential. The stress is not moral, but an artistic (an artificial) one. Also, though in some instances he denounces the child's proximity to original sin – his duality, that is – and at other times he celebrates the 'oneness' of his joy, he always assumes, unlike Wordsworth, that the world the child is born into is fallen. The child-poet of 'Bénédiction' is a 'disinherited' child. He recreates rather than discovers nature, 'mends', 'reinvents' and 'spiritualises' it in the very act of perceiving it:[21]

> Pourtant, sous la tutelle invisible d'un Ange,
> L'Enfant deshérité s'enivre de soleil,
> Et dans tout ce qu'il boit et dans tout ce qu'il mange
> Retrouve l'ambroisie et le nectar vermeil.

Thus this oneness is not so much innocence as conquered duality – Paradise, as it were, naively regained.

This indeed seems to be the only acceptable form of 'oneness' to Baudelaire. Simple naturalness is anathema to him, and brings forth from him curt gall:

La jeune fille, ce qu'elle est en réalité.
Une petite sotte et une petite salope; la plus grande imbécillité unie à la plus grande dépravation.[22]

One could, of course, make Baudelaire give himself the lie and shatter the coherence we had just arrived at by remembering that, again in *De l'essence du rire*, one of the 'purest' creations of the eighteenth century idealisation of woman, Bernardin de Saint-Pierre's Virginie, becomes a touchstone by which to judge the element of evil implied in laughter:

> Essayons, puisque le comique est un élément damnable et d'origine diabolique, de mettre en face une âme absolument primitive et sortant, pour ainsi dire, des mains de la nature. Prenons pour example la grande et typique figure de Virginie, qui symbolise la pureté et la naïveté absolues . . .[23]

But this is not only an exception, it is also hypothetical. Virginie is seen as a 'symbol' for the way men conceive 'absolute' innocence, and the confrontation is between the ideal (purity) and the real (caricature), with a view to ferreting out something about the nature of real laughter. Indeed, when he is dealing with real womanhood Baudelaire is quite consequent with the view he offers elsewhere about the *redeeming* quality of the child's vision: '... je pense à tout jamais, que la femme qui a souffert et fait un enfant est la seule qui soit l'égale de l'homme. Engendrer est la seule chose qui donne à la femelle l'intelligence morale.'[24] In all other respects, Baudelaire's distaste of natural oneness can be seen as the very reverse of Rousseau's and Wordsworth's quest for it. One could pit text against text to show this:

> La femme ne sait pas séparer l'âme du corps. Elle est simpliste, comme les animaux. – Un satirique dirait que c'est parce qu'elle n'a que le corps.[25]
> La femme est *naturelle*, c'est-à-dire abominable.[26]

But that simplicity is praiseworthy 'artlessness' in Mary of Windermere:

> Her just opinions, delicate reserve,
> Her patience and humility of mind
> Unspoiled by commendation and the excess
> Of public notice ...[27]

all amount to virtue, not animality. This would be a red rag to Baudelaire's ferocious distaste for the rural and the idyllic:

> ... George Sand ... est surtout ... une grosse bête; mais elle est *possédée*. C'est le Diable qui lui a persuadé de se fier à *son bon coeur* et à *son bon sens*, afin qu'elle persuadât toutes les autres grosses bêtes de se fier à leur bon coeur et à leur bon sens.
> ... Si je la rencontrais, je ne pourrais m'empêcher de lui jeter un bénitier à la tête.[28]

II

This opposition of views extends to politics. Wordsworth's attack on privilege is fundamental to his work, to that 'levelling' intention which so fascinated Hazlitt:

> . . . Books mislead us, looking for their fame
> To judgments of the wealthy Few, who see
> By artificial lights . . .
> . . . flattering . . . our self-conceit
> With pictures that ambitiously set forth
> The differences, the outside marks by which
> Society has parted man from man
> Neglectful of the universal heart.[29]

Indeed, looked at in the light of this, the term 'levelling' yet achieves another meaning, the Biblical one of a God levelling the mountains and making high the plains. So that Wordsworth's attempt to discover an 'aristocracy' of nature is just as much part of an attempt to elevate the humble and humiliate the proud as is his pursuit of a diction based on universal language. The ground on which he defends the *Lyrical Ballads*, explaining why they have met with such opposition, is most revealing: 'For when Christianity, the religion of humility, is founded upon the proudest faculty of our nature [Imagination, that is,] what can be expected but contradictions?'[30]

At first sight, Baudelaire's ideal of the dandy who must 'live and die in front of a mirror': his sense that man is so 'naturally depraved' that he suffers less from universal debasement than from the establishment of a rational hierarchy; that the only valid form of government is aristocratic, might seem to be the denial of Wordsworth's whole system of values. The two poets are as opposed to each other as the positive and the negative poles of a magnet.

But of the same magnet perhaps. For a second glance at Wordsworth's defence of the *Lyrical Ballads*, the sheer passing memory that his nature is a nature of mountains, not of plains, suggest that, as Hazlitt so perceptively detected, this leveller is prouder than the proudest aristocrat. One thus becomes aware of a kinship, in tone and temperament if not in ideas, between Wordsworth the democrat, the progressist, and Baudelaire the aristocratic dandy, the reactionary. Their attack against 'dwarf man' engendered by 'these industrious times', or against *bon coeur* and *bon sens* have in common a passionate intensity of sarcasm, sprung from a real and strong concern for the forces of life. Wordsworth is loftier than Baudelaire; Baudelaire's wit is keener than Wordsworth's: he did not admire Swift for nothing. But each casts on his world what Yeats, talking of Blake, calls a 'bounding', a 'wiry' 'outline'.[31]

This is where contrasts which threatened to become static become dynamic. One suspects that the two poets are so fundamentally different, not because their values or outlooks are irreconcilable, as they at first seem to be, but because they are writing from, and about, very different worlds. Baudelaire rejects the Wordsworthian nature, but with a Wordsworthian passion for what he takes nature now to be. What *used to be* 'unnatural' has by 1850 become the norm. We may feel the force and energy of the reversal in these notes on trade:

> Le commerce est, par son essence, *satanique*.
> Le commerce, c'est le prêté-rendu, c'est le prêt avec le sous-entendu: *Rends-moi plus que je ne te donne*.
> – Le commerce est *naturel, donc* il est *infâme*.[32]

It is a fundamental reversal and one which seems to be at the very base and centre of Baudelaire's art. England was changing fast even in Wordsworth's youth, under the impact of the Industrial Revolution, but many areas – such as presumably the Lake District – remained virtually untouched. But by Baudelaire's time capitalism is so far developed that it is no longer possible to extradite as 'unnatural' what has come to permeate life. Capitalism or 'commerce' have become 'natural', in the sense that they constitute the fundamental bed-rock of the reality the poet must deal with. The 'natural' is the given condition, the norm, and this by 1850 is 'commerce'. The marrow in the bone has changed its nature. The world is upside down and its evil has become perverse: thus the terms 'nature' and 'artifice' change places. 'En réalité le Satanisme a gagné. Satan s'est fait ingénu. Le mal se connaissant était moins affreux et plus près de la guérison que la mal s'ignorant. George Sand inférieure à de Sade.'[33]

3 *A Rebours*: Nature, Economics, and the Problem of Knowledge

I

The 1848 Revolution focuses this reversal. Its reality was such that it undermined all idealistic pursuits of unity. It rendered them unsubstantial, 'ghostly', to use Marx's term: 'Si jamais période historique fut peinte en grisaille, c'est bien celle-ci. Hommes et événements paraissent comme des Schlemihl à rebours, comme des ombres qui ont perdu leur corps.'[1] Peter Schlemihl, the protagonist of a story by the German romantic writer Chamisso, loses his shadow through an evil pact. Using words which in French were to have such significant fortune at the hands of Huysmans, *à rebours* ('against nature' is the English translation), Marx brilliantly catches the feel of those days. It is the other way round from Romanticism and the French Revolution, it is the *shadows* which have lost their bodies, and restlessly seek them without finding them. As early as 1837, Stendhal had detected those 'absurd desires' stirred up in nineteenth century French imaginations by memories of Carnot, Dumouriez, and the glory of Napoleon: instead of 'inventing' its destiny, France wishes to '*copy* it'.[2]

Walter Benjamin draws the most revealing parallel between the ever-failing Republican conspirator, Auguste Blanqui, and Baudelaire: he points to their obstinacy and impatience, as well as to the 'impotence' which was their common lot.[3] That impotence seems, from all accounts, to have then been the universal lot. A divorce seemed to have occurred, not simply between 'good and the means of good', nor between 'action' and 'dream', but inside good itself, inside the dream itself:

> Passions sans vérités, vérités sans passion; héros sans héroïsme, histoire sans événements; développement dont la seule force motrice semble être le *calendrier*, fatigant par la répétition constante des mêmes tensions et des mêmes détentes . . .[4]

That greyness, that time *à rebours*, are the central theme of much of Flaubert's work, just as the 'reality' which his characters reach, be it Romanticism for Emma Bovary, or knowledge for Bouvard and Pécuchet, always is somehow *second-hand*. They go for the thing itself and only encounter its clichés. And the other way round. The shadows never find their bodies. And the Frédéric of *l'Education Sentimentale*, full of hope and ambition at the beginning of the book, can see, did he but understand it, the 'calendrier' to which the 'durée' of his life, his attempt at experience, is going to become reduced, prefigured in the illusion of perspective which makes the boat on which he is travelling appear motionless, while the banks of the river slowly move past him, backwards.

The course which the 1848 Revolution took symbolises the rise to power of the bourgeoisie. Politics in France made strangely clear changes which in England wore a more hushed social and economic face. 'Et le véritable lieu de naissance de la République bourgeoise n'est pas la "victoire de Février", c'est la "défaite de Juin"'.[5] Working-class and middle-class had acted in unison in February to overthrow the monarchy: they fight against each other in June, and the bourgeoisie wins. For bourgeois 'idealists' like Flaubert and Baudelaire, that victory entailed a split of consciousness, and worse still, as it were, because they were writers, a split between the forms and the realities of language:

> La révolution de Février fut la *belle* révolution, la révolution de la sympathie générale ... parce que la lutte sociale qui formait son arrière-plan n'avait acquis qu'une existence vaporeuse, l'existence de la phrase, du verbe. La révolution de Juin est la révolution *haïssable*, la révolution répugnante, parce que la chose a pris la place de la phrase.[6]

L'Education Sentimentale epitomises this split between 'la chose' and 'la phrase'. It tells the experience of Baudelaire's generation, of the young men who had to live through the third failure, in fifty years, of a revolution. And as such, it tells us a great deal about Baudelaire. Flaubert and Baudelaire always did 'fraternally' understand each other, as Du Bos says; and Flaubert's works illumine what in Baudelaire may remain hidden.

Flaubert shows how, when 'nature' as a collective moral force fails, the individual loses touch, not only with the countryside, but with his own heart. The account is of course reversible, like movement of water and boat. Perhaps it is the lack of faith, the lack of feeling and energy, which bring about the overall failure. It may be, that is, because the 'phrase' has no body to start with, that is is doomed to remain 'vaporeuse'. The 'fatality' in human actions may mirror the necessity not of 'natural' laws, as in the Greek world interpreted by Mme de Staël, but of economic laws.

Frédéric and Deslauriers, the two protagonists, start life with the ambition to succeed, the one in love, the other in politics. Like the Julien Sorel of *Le Rouge*, Frédéric is looking for a Mme de Rênal; like Napoleon, Deslauriers is waiting for an 18 Brumaire. Marx too saw the – as it turned out, grotesquely – imitative character of this revolution and its sequels: 'Louis Napoleon, with the emperor's hat and the eagle, parodied the old Napoleon no more miserably than the *Montagne*, with its phrases borrowed from 1793 and its demogogic poses, parodied the old *Montagne*.'[7]

Frédéric and Deslauriers live through amorous encounters or days of riot, trying to create opportunities which never come or which they never catch; never able to identify completely, without irony, calculation or second thoughts, with anything. Their 'sentimental' education is an education in failure.

The climax of the book comes when Sénécal, formerly an idealistic and rigid republican, now a 'gendarme', a defender of order', kills Dussardier, once his friend, a man of the people and still a passionate republican, on the last June barricade. This killing of a friend by a friend, of a Republican by a Republican, is for Frédéric, connected, through the complex intermeshing of events, with the wreckage of his sentimental life. He whose weak will and literary sensibility are always being paralysed by egotism and lust for respectability, but whose temperament, too fine for the brutal game of the day, will not permit him to succeed, is also, in some ways, both the killer and the killed. Or to use the words from the *Communist Manifesto*, the 'sentimentalist' and the 'egotistical calculator', the latter drowning the first in his 'icy water'. He is his own destroyer, as the 1848 movement was of itself.

Perhaps also, if Marx is right, the real forces at work in the movement, bringing the bourgeoisie to power, had little to do with the surface agitation which led people to enthuse over the dawning of a new era, or the possibility of brotherhood. What people *felt* had little to do with what was happening. What they strove for led to something else. Frédéric makes his room look beautiful to receive Mme Arnoux, and it is Rosanette he gets. The storming of the Tuileries ends in the success of a Martinon. No wonder that the consciousness which attempts to confront such a split and gutted reality cannot nurse monolithic ideas about the goodness or substantiality of 'nature'.

This twin failure of both feeling and politics is itself expressed by Frédéric's inability to take from Fontainebleau forest anything but sensations. The prose, with its strange moments of emptiness, clichés gaping beneath the lyrical momentum of the syntax, acts out the 'échec' of sentimentalism. Frédéric cannot 'commune' with nature for the same diffuse reasons that he cannot get the woman he wants, or love the woman he gets; as the 1848 Revolutionaries cannot establish a viable republic. And perhaps this bankruptcy of Republican idealism comes from the realisation that 'natural man', the man of the people, was no better than the bourgeois: there was in both, as the riot scenes in the novel show, a brutal taste for violence; and beside that, ineffective generosity or a ruthless cynicism. The *bonnet de coton* turned out of course to be no less hideous than the *bonnet rouge*. Natural law was evil. The 'bent of Nature' led to disaster. The century, as Vautrin had diagnosed in *Le Père Goriot*, was limp. Degenerate and shadowy, throwing up 'produits avariés' and 'beautés de vignettes'.

Little wonder, then, that the flowers of Baudelaire's verse should be 'fleurs maladives', flowers of evil, inversions of organic growth; or that 'Spleen et Idéal' should be a descent into the maelstrom of a 'héautontimorouménos' – self-tormenting – state. Like Frédéric, the protagonist of *Les Fleurs du Mal* starts his career under the 'limp' shadow of *Ennui*, the undoer, the self-defeating dreamer who, his eyes dimmed by involuntary tears and his brain by Eastern clichés, 'rêve d'échafauds en fumant son houka'. Like Frédéric again, like the 1848 Revolution, Baudelaire's 'hero', in the first part of the *Fleurs du Mal*, ends as the killer and the killed, 'la plaie et le couteau/Et la victime et le bourreau'. His career is a process of loss instead of a process of growth.

Late on in life, at the end of the novel, when they have failed, Frédéric and Deslauriers longingly evoke an incident of their adolescence, which set the pattern for their later enterprises, political or amorous: they went on a Sunday afternoon, while everyone was at vespers, to a brothel, with a bunch of flowers. The women laugh at these innocents, with their flowers. Frédéric, ashamed, runs away – and as he has the money, Deslauriers is forced to follow. This nostalgia for a past, which in fact was not fundamentally different from its future, but which seemed so because of its remoteness, has its – admittedly, much more lyrical – equivalent in Baudelaire. Within the span of 'Spleen et Idéal', the 'vert paradis des amours enfantines' turns out to have been, as

Deslauriers and Frédéric put it 'ce que nous avons eu de meilleur'. Experience becomes retrospective; worse, what follows only *repeats* what came first, *copies* it, but in an ever-darkening way. The scale of values, as well as the time-scale existing in Wordsworth, are, through force of circumstance, reversed in Baudelaire. His nature is, inexorably, a nature *à rebours*.

Indeed, whatever the level at which one considers it, one finds that the reality which Baudelaire's poetry is dealing with is 'ghostly', second-rate.

Marx perceptively analysed the combined degradations of the peasantry and the army under the Second Empire. Under Napoleon I the army had been 'the *point d'honneur* of farmers working a plot of land who were transformed into heroes'.[8] Now, however, under Napoleon III the army 'no longer is the flower of farm youth, but the swamp flower of the peasant *lumpenproletariat*. It consists largely of *remplaçants* . . . just as the second Bonaparte is himself a *remplaçant*, a substitute for Napoleon.' Walter Benjamin shows how this fallen heroism is recorded in Baudelaire's 'Les Petites Vieilles'. This occurs in the stanzas that describe how an old woman goes to sit in a public park to listen to

> . . . un de ces concerts, riches de cuivre,
> Dont les soldats parfois inondent nos jardins,
> Et qui, dans ces soirs d'or où l'on se sent revivre,
> Versent quelque héroïsme au coeur des citadins.

Benjamin comments: 'The brass bands staffed by the sons of impoverished peasants which play their melodies for the poor city population – they represent the heroism that shyly hides its threadbare quality in the word *quelque* and is in this very gesture genuine and the only kind that is still produced by this society.'[9] Measuring the tentativeness of this 'quelque' with the stentorian aggression of Byron's 'Ode to Napoleon'. or the drive of Stendhal's '. . . cette jeune armée qui venait . . . d'apprendre au monde qu'après tant de siècles César et Alexandre avaient un successeur', one realises how threadbare nature as a source of values has become in Baudelaire's lifetime.

This fading is the result of social and economic changes occurring in the forties and fifties. Again following Marx, Benjamin shows how the history of Lamartine's poetry is bound to the situation of the peasant with a plot of land. The 'rustic optimism' which breathes in the *Méditations* and the *Harmonies*, is 'the basis of the transfiguring view of nature which is characteristic of Lamartine's poetry. But in the 1840s the same peasant is in debt, his plot lies no longer, as Marx puts it, "in the fatherland, but in the register of mortgages"',[10] as a result of the process which Balzac so acutely portrays in *Les Paysans*. While the newly-created smallholding, 'in its accord with society, in its dependence on natural forces and its submission to the authority which protected it from above . . . was naturally religious, the smallholding that is ruined by debts, at odds with society and authority and driven beyond its own limitations, naturally becomes irreligious.'[11] Lamartine, who helped prepare the vote of the French peasants for Napoleon III, brought down the very heavens he had wanted to keep 'spread' over the landscape. This is one level at which, by Baudelaire's time, 'nature' has become emptied of any ideal meaning.

II

There are other, more pervasive, more intricate levels at which the term 'nature' is made to lose the status which it occupied in early Romanticism. They are the economic and epistemological levels which both Lukács[12] and Cassirer[13] attempt to describe in depth and detail. We can but briefly follow them, in the hope of illuminating the crisis of reality which confronts Baudelaire's generation.

The reason for drawing on both Lukács and Cassirer is that their theoretical or ideological viewpoints are entirely different: Lukács is attempting to extract from Marx's more diffuse analysis a coherent reading of the process of 'reification'. Cassirer is writing from a nearly Comtian viewpoint, he is an heir of the Enlightenment, a man who passionately deplores the splitting up of the sciences and the growing impossibility of a coherent theory of knowledge in the nineteenth century. Yet, though their diagnoses and values greatly differ, the two men, one feels, are confronting the same reality, and, while describing it from opposite angles, give it great solidity of presence.

Thus the two men read a fall into the History of the early nineteenth century, but the explanations they offer are very different. For Cassirer, the villain of the story is a weird combination of Christianity (fatally revived by the German Romantics especially) and Kant. He is close to Mme de Staël in his sense that the Greeks created the possibility of knowledge – therefore of unity of being – by opposing the religious pessimism that feels that the possession of absolute truth is denied to man. Thanks to this affirmation, 'There was no longer that sense of a "fall" of man and of an estrangement from the ultimate ground of things, but on the contrary a conviction that knowledge is the one power which can sustain and unite man forever with the ultimate being.'[14]

Throughout the ages, and with many vicissitudes, up to the end of the eighteenth century, 'Philosophy *directed* scientific knowledge toward new goals and opened new paths'.[15] 'The ideal of Science, as conceived by Plato and maintained and developed by Aristotle, was that of a true "organic" whole.'[16] Kant and some of the Romantics are seen as dealing this view a severe blow, but Hegel, and Comte after him, still maintain a universalistic way of thinking.[17] It is only in the second half of the nineteenth century that the problem of knowledge loses 'the stable foundations that it had preserved despite all the incessant struggle during the centuries past'.[18] A fragmentation of knowledge ensues. One of its effects is to isolate poetry from science, as is clear to another observer of the same phenomenon, Northrop Frye: 'with the hindsight of another century and a half, one century of which has been after Darwin, we can see that the scientific vision of nature was inexorably splitting away from the poetic and existential vision of Romantic mythology'.[19] Both Cassirer and Frye are discussing a process which in their eyes might have only partly affected a poet living in the early part of the century, but could not fail to depress one living in its later half.

Lukács's fable of the Hindu who, knowing that the world rested upon an elephant, had his curiosity satisfied by being told that the elephant rested on a tortoise, is probably applicable to Cassirer. Whatever tinges of heresy there may be to his interpretation of 'reification', Lukács's orthodoxy is unimpeachable in so far as his villain will not be the tortoise – be it Kant, Mill or Romantic nostalgia for the Christian Middle Ages – but the ultimate foundation for a Marxist: economic necessity. It is the development of commodity exchange to the point when it becomes the dominant form in society, that is, the advent of modern capitalism, which brought about some sort of a fall from an earlier, cleaner 'nature'.

The fall, or process of 'reification', rests upon a false, an alienating mystery: that of the commodity, in which 'the social character of men's labour appears to them as an objective character stamped upon the product of that labour'.[20] 'A definite social relation between men' 'assumes, in their eyes, the fantastic form of a relation between things'. In this process, both object and subject undergo complicated changes. The object becomes prey to increasing specialisation: 'The mathematical analysis of work-processes denotes a break with the organic, irrational and qualitatively determined unity of the product.'[21] But also,

> this fragmentation of the object of production necessarily entails the fragmentation of its subject. In consequence of the rationalization of the work-process the human qualities and idiosyncrasies of the worker appear increasingly as *mere sources of error* when contrasted with these abstract special laws functioning according to rational predictions.[22]

Lukács, still closely following Marx, believes that this reification spreads to all levels of man's existence.

> The transformation of the commodity relation into a thing of 'ghostly objectivity' . . . stamps its imprint upon the whole consciousness of man; his qualities and abilities are no longer an organic part of his personality, they are things which he can 'own' or 'dispose of' like the various subjects of the external world.[23]

It is difficult not to feel at this stage that one would like to be told *how* this happens – how the contagion spreads from the work-processes to the whole of man's consciousness. Perhaps, the only adequate account one can find, or for that matter, provide of it, is one which conveys both its mysterious character and its inescapability, that of a 'peste sous-jacente', the plague which affects all the infernal circles of the Paris of Balzac's *La Fille aux Yeux d'Or*, from the working-class suburbs to the centre of the aristocratic Quartier de Saint-Germain. Or one can see another 'image' of this process in the smallpox of *Bleak House*, which through its evil and invisible contagion affects both Joe and Lady Dedlock's daughter, connects, that is, the slums of Tom-all-Alone with the falsely remote upper classes.

Whatever the way in which reification penetrates 'the very depths of man's physical and psychic nature',[24] its traces can be clearly seen in the texture of the verbal universe which Baudelaire both inhabits and projects. Several of the 'Spleen' poems could be read as, among other things, the expression of the state of fragmentation which Marx describes in other, analytic, terms. Instead of representing an organic unit, the 'je' splits up into a random juxtaposition of 'things':

> Un gros meuble à tiroirs encombré de bilans,
> De vers, de billets doux, de procès, de romances,

Avec de lourds cheveux roulés dans des quittances,
Cache moins de secrets que mon triste cerveau . . .
Je suis un cimetière abhorré de la lune . . .
Je suis un vieux boudoir plein de roses fanées . . .[25]

Looked at in this light, the 'hero's', if not the poet's, gradual loss of power, which the movement of 'Spleen et Idéal' enacts, is an enquiry into the loss of human 'organic' connections. One must of course marvel at that other power which creates coherence out of disjunction and, as in Spleen IV, makes deeper metaphor out of the loss of metaphor. But the overt theme is the desiccation of consciousness. The 'I can connect/Nothing with nothing' of *The Waste Land* could sum up its paralysed condition.

Fragmentation and isolation indeed permanently overshadow the *first section* of *Les Fleurs de Mal*, though formally and, at the beginning, thematically, they are shown to be overcome. If 'Au Lecteur' is both startling and exciting, it is because the voice is organising the blatant disparity of the experiences it is gathering, it is also because through the sheer power of its assertiveness it creates a 'nous', a meeting-ground of speaker and reader. As 'Spleen et Idéal' proceeds, the voice goes on implicating the reader: its lyrical pull is so strong, its splenetic moods are so pervasive, its aggression and viciousness so stirring. And the accusation of hypocrisy cunningly circumvents all attempts to evade the 'brotherhood'. It spreads the contagion of its own bad conscience. 'Nous' is hateful therefore; it means acknowledging the common experience of 'ennui'. It is exhilarating too, and in that divisiveness extends to the relation between poet and reader that spirit of self-contradiction which is so much the poet's own.

Exhilarating: because it promises a 'je'. But a 'je', it soon becomes clear, which exists as something ahead. Something to be conquered through self-denial and pain. In 'Bénédiction', suffering, the 'divin remède à *nos* impuretés', helps the poet both discover and transcend his own identity. In 'Phares', the 'ardent sanglot' which voices through the ages the brotherhood of artists becomes

. . . le meilleur témoignage
Que nous puissions donner de *notre* dignité . . .[26]

In both poems, that is, what Marx might call an 'organic subjectivity' is conquered through its immersion in a 'nous', through a near-mystical form of subjectivity. It is through belonging and living the *common* experience at its peak that the self of the poet plucks itself out, not of thin air, but of Spleen.

Indeed, it soon becomes clear, with the '*Ma* pauvre Muse, hélas . . .' of 'La Muse Malade', that when 'je' attempts to speak its singleness, it speaks a sickly, threatened, corruptible state. So that one of the dilemmas which the opening of 'Spleen et Idéal' poses, is whether the poet's voice is going to achieve an organic – therefore universal – identity, or whether it is going to crumble into fragments – to be crushed by the 'barriers erected by a formalism that has degenerated into a state of complete fragmentation.'[27] The 'cracked soul' which, like a forgotten wounded man, at the end of 'La Cloche Fêlée', horrifyingly fails to lift up the weight of dead bodies under which it has been buried, eloquently bespeaks the failure of the self as an isolated entity:

> Moi, mon âme est fêlée, et lorsqu'en ses ennuis
> Elle veut de ses chants peupler l'air froid des nuits,
> Il arrive souvent que sa voix affaiblie
>
> Semble le râle épais d'un blessé qu'on oublie
> Au bord d'un lac de sang, sous un grand tas de morts,
> Et qui meurt, sans bouger, dans d'immenses efforts.[28]

What is tragic in *Les Fleurs du Mal*, of course, is that the book moves from the possibility of a communal to the inescapability of a fragmented state. From the hopefulness of a 'nous', however tormented, to a series of solitary 'je'.

One can certainly pit the precariousness of the poet's '*je*', in Baudelaire, against the splendid solidity of Wordsworth's 'I'. That is certainly a major difference in the temper of the reality each poet is prodding. But one could add that what is thus identified is more a difference of degrees than a difference in kind. Wordsworth's 'I', too, has to be conquered, and the conquest involves a radical questioning of the self. One could even argue that, far from being un- or post-Romantic, the absolute questioning of identity in *Les Fleurs du Mal* puts it into the best Romantic tradition. In an examination of *Sartor Resartus*, Robert Langbaum argues that 'in describing through the thin disguise of Teufelsdrockh's autobiography his own intellectual transition from the eighteenth to the nineteenth century, Carlyle shows how the *romantic quality of mind* grows through a total crisis of personality'.[29] However, and this is a crucial difference, the speaking consciousness of *Les Fleurs du Mal* does not *grow*, but is defeated, through its crisis of personality. The crisis may be inherited from Romanticism – but its effects are tragically reversed.

Fragmentation, indeed, affects Baudelaire the poet in a way which makes him a poet fundamentally different from Wordsworth, what we might venture to call a 'modern' poet, a poet for whom capitalism has become an inescapable and integral fact: in the *form* of the poetry he can write. *Les Fleurs du Mal* are in many ways 'l'histoire d'une âme', like *The Prelude*. But *The Prelude*, whatever the order in which its books were actually composed, arranges them *chronologically* in its final form: so that they are made to appear absolutely continuous with each other. Furthermore, the creation of an organic, unbroken continuity with 'natural' pauses, for breath, for meditation, for time passing, is one of the major and significant achievements of the poem. But *Les Fleurs du Mal* consist of the most apparently disparate, often clashing, collection of poems of a great range of forms and rhythms and meters. If the self that they express is continuous, it is in despite of, not through, its fragmentation.

III

Yet again the argument must be reversed: for the poetic world Baudelaire created is fragmented, not because he was giving form to a fragmented world (or consciousness), but because continuity to him was anathema – because it seemed to contain the essence of the state of reality which he was trying to escape from.

In this respect too, his 'nature' is the very reverse of Wordsworth's and Rousseau's. For the author of *L'Emile* there was continuity in nature in that it enforced a blessed, *just* necessity. The consistency of nature was contrasted with the caprice – the inconsistency – of men. It became a model for education:

> ... Qu'il (Emile) sente de bonne heure sur sa tête altière le dur joug que la nature impose à l'homme, le pesant joug de la nécessité, sous lequel il faut que tout être fini ploie; qu'il voie cette nécessité dans les choses, jamais dans le caprice des hommes; que le frein qui le retient soit la force, et non l'autorité.[30]

This necessity was also to provide a model for law-giving. Rousseau thought that men would give up their individual wills to the body politic only if they found in it the same impartial compulsion as primitive men encountered in nature.

But for Baudelaire, the necessity in nature only amounts to the lowest instincts: . . . la nature n'enseigne rien, ou presque rien, c'est-à-dire qu'elle *contraint* l'homme à dormir, à boire, à manger . . . c'est elle aussi qui pousse l'homme à tuer son semblable, à le séquestrer, à le torturer . . .'[31] The nature Baudelaire is talking about, whose continuity strangely co-exists with fragmentation, is the one brought about by the triumph of capitalism, and here again Marxist analyses provide insight into its contradictions. In fact, the contradiction is only apparent: fragmentation exists on the level of the individual, as a direct result of the 'abstract special laws'[32] which express the rationalisation of production:

> The atomisation of the individual is . . . only the reflex in consciousness of the fact that the 'natural laws' of capitalist production have been extended to cover every manifestation of life in society; that – for the first time in history – the whole of society is subjected, or tends to be subjected, to a unified economic process, and that the fate of every member of society is determined by unified laws.[33]

These new 'natural laws' are the very reverse of the flexible, 'organic' natural laws that in different ways Rousseau and Wordsworth were celebrating. Lukács underlines the paradox whereby the 'law' of primitive societies – which in many respects holds good well into the eighteenth century – while scarcely altering in hundreds or sometimes even thousands of years, could be flexible and irrational in character, renewing itself with every legal decision, while modern law, caught up in the continuous turmoil of change, appears 'rigid, static and fixed'. This is because 'the face turned towards the individual producer' by the 'ceaselessly revolutionary techniques of modern production' is 'rigid and immobile'.[34]

One measures the degree of flexibility of the 'old' nature by discovering that the surface antagonism of the versions of it which are offered conceal much compatibility between them – that entirely different accounts of 'natural law' can result in the same attitude – that a deep ideological opposition can lead to the same active alignments. Thus there is a pre-revolutionary and revolutionary attack on government, privileges, the Divine Right of Kings, which is conducted in the name of an ideal rationality – which calls itself 'natural law':

> The conflict revolving around natural law, and the whole revolutionary period of the bourgeoisie was based on the assumption

that the formal equality and universality of the law (and hence its rationality) was able at the same time to determine its content . . . The revolutionary bourgeois class refused to admit that a legal relationship had a *valid* foundation merely because it existed in fact.[35]

This idea is most strikingly expressed in *La Loi naturelle, ou Catéchisme du citoyen français* (1793), meant to propagate and make available the Montagnard creed in popular religious form. It claims that the social order can be based on the 'natural' order and thus become universal: and reason is the source and sanction of this universality:

D. Qu'est-ce que la loi naturelle?
R. C'est l'ordre régulier et constant des faits, par lequel Dieu régit l'univers; ordre que sa sagesse présente aux sens et à la raison des hommes, pour servir à leurs actions de règle égale et commune . . .[36]

But it is not enough to say, as Lukács does, that this ideal of natural law was so powerful that it could only be opposed by yet another natural law by the enemies of the French Revolution – he mentions Burke and Stahl. The contradictions go further, for precursors and supporters of the French Revolution uphold an ideal of natural law which rests on an attack on reason – proposes, that is, a version of society and consciousness radically opposed to the one offered by Voltaire, Volney or Saint-Just, but equally vehement in its pursuit of 'equality' and 'universality', in its search for a synthesis. Here the instinctual, the voice of the heart, becomes associated with the primitive law of nature, which in its turn assumes the radiance and authority of a lost paradise. By contrast, the 'real' world – or, and this is what very much complicates the issue – the rational, even the legalistic world, is seen as the agency or the embodiment of the fall. So that writers who are as profoundly inimical to each other as Rousseau and Burke may yet pursue strikingly similar visions of nature:

. . . J'essayerais de montrer . . . que par la raison seule, indépendamment de la conscience, on ne peut établir aucune loi naturelle; et que tout le droit de la nature n'est qu'une chimère, s'il n'est fondé sur un besoin naturel au coeur humain.[37]

. . . we have implanted in us by Providence, ideas, axioms, rules, of what is pious, just, fair, honest, which no political craft, nor learned sophistry, can entirely expel from our breasts.[38]

... unhappily for us, in proportion as we have deviated from the plain rule of our nature, and turned our reason against itself, in that proportion have we increased the follies and miseries of mankind.[39]

One can go even further, and argue that when Robespierre, at the height of the Terror, was trying to cleanse and revitalise the body politic, which, to use Rousseau's image, was like the statue of Glaucus that time and storms had so disfigured that it resembled more a ferocious beast than a God,[40] he was, in his way, trying to rid society from that 'learned sophistry' which had made men deviate from the 'plain rule' of their nature – pursuing, that is, the same end as Burke ...

This has another dimension. Burke and Joseph de Maistre, who in many ways is close to him, think of their relation to nature in terms of 'life', of 'blood', against 'reason', of 'organic' against 'mechanistic', just as much as Wordsworth – and Burke. On this plane, conservatives and revolutionaries are defending the same ethos. Thus Burke condemns the French Revolution as a deviation from Nature: 'Everything seems out of nature in this strange chaos of levity and ferocity ...'[41] But for Wordsworth, it is the failure of the Revolution which is the deviation:

> The blame is ours, not Nature's. When a taunt
> Was taken up by Scoffers in their pride,
> Saying, 'behold the harvest which we reap
> From popular Government and Equality',
> I saw that it was neither these, nor aught
> Of wild belief engrafted on their names
> By false philosophy, that caus'd the woe,
> But that it was a reservoir of guilt
> And ignorance, fill'd up from age to age,
> That could no longer hold its loathsome charge,
> But burst and spread in deluge through the land.[42]

Of course, what for Wordsworth is a 'reservoir of guilt and ignorance' is for Burke a saving tradition through which we hear the voice of nature. He would very much agree with Maistre's identification of 'nature' and 'order': 'Mais lorsque l'homme travaille pour rétablir l'ordre, il s'associe avec l'auteur de l'ordre, il est favorisé par la *Nature*, c'est-à-dire par l'ensemble des choses secondes, qui sont les ministres de la Divinité.'[43] Indeed, it is in these terms that Burke sees the policy of England, which shows 'the happy effect of following nature, which is wisdom without reflection, and above it: 'Our political system is placed in a just correspondence and symmetry with the order of the world . . . In this choice of inheritance we have given to our frame of polity the image of a relation in blood . . .'[44] Wordsworth would certainly not have accepted this vision of order. But he might have agreed to the values which inform that vision – would have recognised the ethos of a 'relation in blood'. In some of Burke's oratorical flights one even sees traces of a Wordsworthian vocabulary already at work:

> . . . In England we have not yet been completely disembowelled of our natural entrails; we still feel within us, and we cherish and cultivate, those inbred sentiments which are the faithful guardians, the active monitors of our duty, the true supporters of all liberal and manly morals . . . We preserve the whole of our feelings still native and entire, unsophisticated by pedantry and infidelity . . .[45]

The contradictions which the force of the appeal of 'nature' succeeds in overcoming, in the Romantic period, are even greater than this. At the same time as political opponents define an ideal nature in similar terms, people who sympathise with the same moral values attribute to 'nature' and 'artifice' quite opposite parts. Thus, a wise return to Nature is for Wordsworth the means of a new life after the crisis of the French Revolution; but for Rousseau an absolute surrender of 'nature' in favour of 'artifice' is the only way there is for creating a new man:

> Celui qui ose entreprendre d'instituer un peuple doit se sentir en état de changer pour ainsi dire la nature humaine . . . de substituer une existence partielle et morale à l'existence physique et indépendante que nous avons tous reçue de la nature. Il faut . . . qu'il ôte à l'homme ses propres forces pour lui en donner qui lui soient étrangères . . . Plus ces forces naturelles sont mortes et anéanties, . . . plus aussi l'institution est solide et parfaite . . .[46]

Lukács analyses those various clusters of meaning of nature. He discovers, besides those that have just been described, another conception of nature, in which it becomes, in Schiller's words, 'what we once were' and 'what we should once more become':[47]

> 'Nature' here refers to authentic humanity, the true essence of man liberated from the false, mechanising forms of society: man as a perfected whole who has inwardly overcome, or is in the process of

overcoming, the dichotomy of theory and practice, reason and the senses, form and content . . . man for whom freedom and necessity are identical.[48]

This value is the one which recent critics of Romanticism – Northrop Frye, M. R. Abrams, René Wellek, Geoffrey Hartman – see as most essentially, most typically 'Romantic'. But by Baudelaire's time, not only the hopefulness which this view implies, but the very situation which allowed 'nature' to embrace and transcend all the contradictions, no longer exist. The process of reification has advanced too far. One kind of nature has been replaced by another, and that is what has to be expressed.

> . . . on the one hand, men are constantly smashing, replacing and leaving behind them the 'natural', irrational and actually existing bonds, while, on the other hand, they erect around themselves in the reality they have created and 'made', a kind of second nature which evolves with exactly the same inexorable necessity as was the case earlier on with irrational forces of nature . . .[49]

Thus the nature which Baudelaire encounters in the economic and legal fabric of the Second Empire is 'rigid, static and fixed'. It defines itself as pure *constraint*. Irrational fate, which was compatible with faith, and with action, has been replaced by a necessity 'which cannot ultimately and wholly be grasped, as was indeed recognised by the critical philosophers'[50] – Kant foremost among them – but which can be predicted. The mechanical impersonality of this necessity makes it inhuman. Values can only exist in despite of it. Thus whereas for Wordsworth the image of a flowing river, embodied in its urge forward by the dynamic progress of the verse, could become an image of the progress of History, experienced through the growth of a soul, in Baudelaire 'progress' is circular and morally evil – or rather, its predictability makes it immoral. The 'progress' of *Les Fleurs du Mal* is a fall into a degraded state – at least on one, explicit, level.

Indeed, Baudelaire's reaction to that aspect of capitalism is one of violent distaste. The Second Empire was a period of unprecedented economic expansion, and the ethos of 'progress' was then a powerful one.[51] But for Baudelaire, the man who believes in 'progress' and sets store by the material world, sells his soul to the devil. He damns himself on earth by entering an infernal circle of new desires, bred out of the latest invention, which the progressive society eventually satisfies but which are immediately replaced by other desires, bred out of a new fabricated offer. The material circle is doomed to endless escalation, and ever more rapid parody. It is caught – and the individual with it – in the fatal compulsion to rush forward, as though forward were towards somewhere else, which is the modern form of the 'voyage'. Of the poem which bears this title, the last of the *Fleurs du Mal*, Baudelaire said that it ought to make 'nature, and above all the amateurs of progress' shiver. The 'voyage' is the endless escalation of modern economy, the desire to set oneself outside it, the need to exert imagination away from what is, the fear to face oneself, to be still. It is man's longing for what he calls the infinite. For Baudelaire, the movement it accomplishes is circular, pointless, self-contradictory; though he insists on the greatness of its pathos:

> Nous imitons, horreur! la toupie et la boule
> Dans leur valse et leurs bonds; même dans nos sommeils
> La Curiosité nous tourmente et nous roule,
> Comme un Ange cruel qui fouette des soleils.
>
> . . .
> . . . l'Homme, dont jamais l'espérance n'est lasse,
> Pour trouver le repos, court toujours comme un fou!

Pascal spoke of the universe as being 'un cercle dont le centre est partout, et la circonférence nulle part'. It was an image of how man, because of scientific discoveries, of political, social and religious changes, was suddenly lost in a burst universe, which no longer made sense, and of which he no longer was the microcosm. But when Baudelaire remoulds that image to:

> Singulière fortune où le but se déplace,
> Et n'étant nulle part, peut être n'importe où . . .

he is saying that it is the 'modern' compulsion to move 'forward', which is now endangering – sanity, values, the possibility to fulfil oneself. The image expresses the perpetual pursuit of a goal forever evanescent, perfect efficiency or perfect knowledge or perfect comfort; a search for inner satisfaction which can never be reached, because it is being sought through flight, and flight is a disease generated precisely by the world of spleen from which one is trying to run away:

> Faut-il partir? rester? Si tu peux rester, reste;
> Pars, s'il le faut. L'un court, et l'autre se tapit
> Pour tromper l'ennemi vigilant et funeste,
> Le Temps! Il est, hélas, des coureurs sans répit
>
> Comme le Juif errant et comme les apôtres,
> A qui rien ne suffit, ni wagon, ni vaisseau
> Pour fuir ce rétiaire infâme . . .

The modern means of travelling swiftly, trains, steamers, have been devised in order to gain time, to defeat the vigilant and wakeful enemy. But the effect is the opposite. Baudelaire has been proved right 'statistically' of course, since now that travelling is so much swifter, people spend more *time* travelling than they used to. But what he means is that in order to 'fly' from time, which is movement, that is in order to overtake it, people try to move more swiftly than time. But all they do is increase time, which is flight.

The same, for Baudelaire, is true of all other aspects of progress. It is self-destructive. What it increases diminishes something which is more important.

> Ce fanal obscur . . . cette lanterne moderne jette des ténèbres sur tous les objets de la connaissance; la liberté s'évanouit, le châtiment disparait . . . Cette idée grotesque, qui a fleuri sur le terrain pourri de la fatuité moderne, a déchargé chacun de son devoir, délivré toute âme de sa responsabilité, dégagé la volonté de tous les liens que lui imposait l'amour du beau . . .[52]

We begin to read another impulse into the fragmentation of *Les Fleurs du Mal*. Only by a defiance of continuity, of predictability, does the poet escape from the *form* – the evil power – of 'progress', and so doing assert the possibility of values – artistic or ethical. Walter Benjamin most interestingly talks of Baudelaire having assigned himself a historic mission by deciding to write poetry that would fill gaps that other – Romantic – poets – Lamartine and Hugo – had left vacant.[53] But there is another reason why the poems in *Les Fleurs du Mal* all, as it were, occupy a series of gaps: because it is only in the chinks of the various continuities that the society of the Second Empire offers, that the spirit can breathe. The only freedom is that of the conspirator for more reasons than Walter Benjamin gives. Language, too, must be conspiratorial: paragraphs, sentences, stanzas, images, must, as it were, exist each in ignorance of the others' moves.

This profound hatred for the 'constraint' in nature is what impels Baudelaire to give such value to artifice. Gautier saw the how, if not the why:

> ... Ce goût excessif, baroque, anti-naturel ... était pour lui un signe de la volonté humaine corrigeant à son gré les formes et les couleurs fournies par la matière ... il y voyait une preuve de grandeur. La *dépravation* ... l'écart du type normal, est impossible à la bête, fatalement conduite par l'instinct immuable ...[54]

Seen thus, 'depravation', or, to use a word Baudelaire learnt to explore through Poe, 'perversity', becomes another gap through which the poet escapes from another materialistic circularity – that of 'l'instinct immuable'. 'Perversity' is often the theme of *Les Fleurs du Mal*: in 'A une Martyre', or 'A celle qui est trop gaie', or 'Les Bijoux' – the last two were 'condamnées' for immorality by the self-indicting justice of the Second Empire. But the most single-minded instance of an enquiry into 'depravation' in Baudelaire is his sketch of a play, 'L'Ivrogne', on which he was working at a time when he was also translating Poe's *Imp of the Perverse* and *The Tell-Tale Heart*. What is interesting about it is that he seems to be doing what a Naturalistic novelist like Zola will later do: show that depravation is a further instance of determinism, since he claims that the drunkard's killing of his wife is to be 'simplement le développement d'un vice, et des résultats successifs d'une situation.'[55] But he suggests the opposite. Describing how the drunkard attempts to plan a murder which – as in *Crime and Punishment* – happens as a series of surprises, he explores the ingenuity with which the mind under pressure surrenders to what was unbargained for: lusts, tenderness, cowardice, pity for one's victim, scrupulousness. And through these deviations from instinct, through the stage being kept empty for long minutes against all established theatrical rules, free spaces are created. One gathers a sense that for Baudelaire it is in the chinks of consciousness that the spirit breathes.

IV

Lukács makes it very clear that that is where it has to take refuge – though he would deny that such a refuge is valid – in a society in which determinism has become the norm. He argues that the development of the economic processes leads to growing codification. Rational calculation reigns supreme, and it is based upon 'the recognition and the inclusion in one's calculations of the inevitable chain of cause and effect in certain events – independently of individual "caprice". In consequence, man's activity does not go beyond the correct calculation of the possible outcome of the sequence of events.'[56] Baudelaire is reacting against this by making 'caprice' – 'perversity' – break the chain of cause and effect.

But – and this is the crux of Lukács's analysis – this rationalisation is reflected on all levels of life. For him, there is 'no qualitative difference in the structure of consciousness' of the worker faced by a particular machine, the entrepreneur faced with a given type of mechanical development, and the technologist faced with the state of science and the profitability of its application to technology. And again, 'the formal standardisation of justice, the state, the civil service, etc., signifies objectively and factually a comparable reduction of all social functions to their elements, a comparable search for the rational formal laws of the carefully segregated partial systems.'[57] This in turn affects the sciences. The more highly developed modern sciences become, the more they erect themselves into 'formally closed' systems of partial laws. They find that the world lying beyond their confines, and in particular the material bases which it is their task to understand, their own 'concrete underlying reality' lies 'methodologically and in principle', beyond their grasp.[58] Not only jurisprudence, but philosophy too, suffer from the same inability to reach an overall knowledge. 'Not that the desire for synthesis is absent; nor can it be maintained that the best people have welcomed with open arms a mechanical existence hostile to life and a scientific formalism alien to it'. But, Lukács goes on to assert, and it is an unpalatable statement, 'a radical change in outlook is not feasible on the soil of bourgeois society'.[59]

Cassirer agrees as to diagnosis, but offers a substantially different interpretation. Again and again when dealing with the evolution of history and biology in the nineteenth century, he notes that 'Science is not satisfied with sheer observation of particular phenomena or establishing general laws, but speaks in the name of a distinct 'interest of reason' which it has at heart and means to urge.' But, he goes on to admit, the two interests are not reconcilable. 'Controversies of this sort, as Kant emphasized, are incapable of being decided in such a way that one side is proved right or wrong. Critical philosophy must be content with understanding and safeguarding both the empirical and the rational interests instead of pronouncing a judgment in favor of either party.'[60] However, because the position he speaks from is that of the epistemologist, because, that is, he has no interest in relating the various crises in the sciences to the overall economic situation, he seems – although openly he refrains from 'taking sides' – to feel sympathy for nineteenth century thinkers who searched for a synthetic vision. Thus he speaks of Comte as one who strove to overcome possible cleavages in the idea of causality by seeing in *sociology* the science that would provide the real goal of knowledge. It could do so by ceasing to constitute 'a state within a state', and this would happen when it was realised that 'there was the same inviolable conformity to law here as in all natural events'.[61] 'I shall bring factual proof', wrote Comte, 'that there are just as definite laws for the development of the human race as there are for the fall of a stone.'[62] He believed one of these laws, and a fundamental one, was his 'law of the three stages'.

What makes Comte's philosophy distinctive, Cassirer argues, is that he believes in an absolute continuity between the laws governing mankind and the laws governing all other animate nature. True, as one advances from animal to human forms something new happens in the series, and in the transition from biology to sociology the idea of development assumes the form of historical thinking. But what matters is that there is no 'sudden jump, no complete transformation'.[63] An extreme form of this thinking is Taine's naturalism, his famous statement that vice and virtue are 'products' like sugar and vitriol, and his view of causes:

> There are causes for ambition, courage and truth just as there are causes for digestion, for muscular movement, for animal heat . . . Let us seek the simple phenomena for moral qualities, as we seek them for physical properties . . . There is a chain of general causes, and the general structure of things, and the great courses of events are their work.[64]

This is the extreme formulation of a belief in the absolute sway of the 'laws of nature' which pervades, at all sorts of levels, much nineteenth century thinking, and which had been given expression quite early on by Malthus. From Malthus it passed on to Darwin: 'Necessity, that impervious, all-pervading law of nature, restrains [the germs of existence] within the prescribed bounds. The race of plants and the race of animals shrink under this great restrictive law; and man cannot by any efforts of reason escape from it.'[65]

It is not within our scope to decide whether this deterministic vision of causes and effects is, as Cassirer suggests, an endeavour to regain epistemological coherence, or, as Lukács would have it, the result of, and the attempt to formalise, the laws at work in capitalist society. What concerns us is that this vision is extraordinarily pervasive – and that it is abhorrent to Baudelaire. This is felt at once by confronting what Comte says of the continuity of the laws that regulate animal *and* human life, with Gautier's statement that Baudelaire was attracted to depravation because it is 'impossible à la bête, fatalement conduite par l'instinct immuable'. Baudelaire is forever trying to break the chain of causes and effects. He responds to all forms of determinism as Stendhal's Henri Brulard reacted to all forms of imprisonment: with a feeling of 'mal au coeur', of nausea; with instinctive claustrophobia.

This is no doubt largely the source of the deep spiritual kinship he felt with Joseph de Maistre. The very quality of Maistre's prose, which proceeds in jumps, as it were, is forever on the attack, but attacks that come like a 'feu roulant' issuing from a series of separate guns,[66] must have made him attractive to Baudelaire. Thus he must have been delighted by Maistre's attack on the nineteenth-century concept of cause, which seemed to invalidate, as is clear from the statements from Comte, Taine and Malthus which have just been quoted, the notions of Providence and of free will:

> [Une cause physique] est une *cause naturelle,* si nous voulons nous borner à traduire le mot; mais dans l'acception moderne, c'est une *cause matérielle,* c'est-à-dire une cause qui n'est pas une cause: car matière et cause s'excluent mutuellement, comme *blanc, noir, cercle* et *carré.* La matière n'a d'action que par le mouvement: or, tout mouvement étant un effet, il s'ensuit qu'une *cause physique,* si l'on veut s'exprimer exactement, est un NON-SENS, et même une contradiction dans les termes . . . . . . tout moteur primitif est immatériel; *partout ce qui meut précède ce qui est mu, ce qui mène précède ce qui est mené, ce qui commande précède ce qui est commandé*: la matière ne peut rien, et même elle n'est rien que la preuve de l'esprit.[67]

The urge which informs Maistre's thoughts on the notion of 'cause' is to establish that it is 'l'esprit' which has precedence over the 'laws' of nature, and in more senses than one. It is both a response to a concrete situation and an assessment of the conditions under which spiritual life might be possible. One must believe that there is 'more' than there seems to be. And that 'more', which is where the spirit breathes, is given *absolute* value: Baudelaire sets form as much above matter as

Maistre the true cause above the *causa efficiens*: 'Toute Forme créée, même par l'homme, est immortelle. Car la forme est indépendante de la matière, et ce ne sont pas les molécules qui constituent la forme.'[68] And his sense that virtue is 'surnaturelle', totally irreducible to, and not deductible from, the 'cercle matériel' may be anchored in Maistre's defense of 'super-stition': the belief that for life to be whole, it must reach beyond what seems to be 'enough':

> ... qu'est-ce donc que la superstition? *Super* ne veut-il pas dire *par-delà*? Ce sera donc quelque chose qui est *par-delà* la croyance légitime...[69]

> Toutes les institutions imaginables reposent sur une idée religieuse, ou ne font que passer. Elles sont fortes et durables à mesure qu'elles sont *divinisées*... Non seulement la raison humaine... ne peut suppléer à ces bases qu'on appelle *superstitieuses*...; mais la philosophie est, au contraire, une puissance essentiellement désorganisatrice.[70]

One measures how much the idea of spirituality was displaced by determinism when one reflects that Maistre has to establish faith as a 'par-delà', something excessive and not demonstrable, whereas Coleridge could couch the same plea for religion in an image which makes internal appear essential: he says that the writings of the mystics

> gave [him] an indistinct, yet stirring and working presentiment, that all the products of the mere reflective faculty partook of death, and were as the rattling twigs and sprays in winter into which some sap was to be propelled from some root to which [he] had not penetrated, if they were to afford [his] soul either food or shelter.[71]

For Maistre, as for Baudelaire, man must continually reach *beyond*, if he is not to grow into a stunted being. Prayer is a source of power which saves man from 'the most perfidious temptation which could present itself to the human mind: to believe in the invariable laws of nature':

> ... à mesure que [les hommes] se sont rapprochés du déisme, qui n'est rien et ne peut rien, ils ont cessé de prier, et maintenant vous les voyez courbés vers la terre, uniquement occupés de lois et d'études physiques, et n'ayant plus le moindre sentiment de leur dignité naturelle.[72]

Maistre could have written this as a comment on Blake's *Newton*.

Baudelaire too believes that 'la superstition est le réservoir de toutes les vérités'. All his values have a dimension of excess or arbitrariness. Only people who cannot be inserted into series seem to him to be truly human:

> Il n'existe que trois êtres respectables.
> Le prêtre, le guerrier, le poète. Savoir, tuer et créer.
> Les autres hommes sont taillables et corvéables, faits pour l'écurie, c'est-à-dire pour exercer ce qu'on appelle des professions.[73]

And the great man's greatness is paradoxically demonstrated by the ostracism which the chain of being who are 'faits pour l'écurie' impose upon him:

> Les nations n'ont de grands hommes que malgré elles, – comme les familles. Elles font tous leurs efforts pour n'en pas avoir. Et ainsi, le grand homme a besoin, pour exister, de posséder une force d'attaque plus grande que la force de résistance développée par des millions d'individus.[74]

The effort, then, is to step outside the circle, to be translated outside the 'natural' series which spells death to the spirit. 'Etre un grand homme et un saint pour soi-même', Baudelaire prescribes to himself, endorsing as the only salvation the isolation to which he is condemned. His ideal of the dandy, who must 'live and die in front of a mirror', springs from the conviction that the only sources of spirituality which can exist in a materialistic age are those which are invented *ex nihilo*, which only the self can sanction.

This conception of the dandy keeps alive, in an age of growing decadence, the heroic freedom achieved by Stendhal's Julien Sorel, or by Balzac's Vautrin. Julien's sense that he owes a duty *to himself*, the way he trains his will, his attempt at self-control, his energy kept alive by the very limits within which he forces it to hide itself, coincide with Baudelaire's definition of dandyism:

> C'est avant tout le besoin ardent de se faire une originalité, contenu dans les limites extérieures des convenances.'[75]

> Le Dandy doit aspirer à être sublime sans interruption.[76]

The relation to Stendhal in this respect is a most interesting one. The author of *Henri Brulard* frequently expresses and through his characters projects a horror of imprisonment, of places and situations which bind the live spirit. Julien Sorel wants to get out of provincial Verrières because everything he sees in it 'freezes' his imagination. Yet both Julien and Fabrice eventually find freedom and fulfilment *in prison*. They reach a state in which the walls which enclose them, far from being experienced as the barrier separating them from that vast world which their sensibility requires to soar at ease, somehow become a protection against encroachment, the condition which allows them emotional and imaginative scope. Julien, battered by Mathilde's grand passion, complains that the one bad thing about prison is that you cannot deny your door. And Fabrice, freed from the charterhouse of Parma by the duchess's intricate plots, willingly surrenders to be recaptured.

There is something of this in Baudelaire's dandies. Their need to 'se faire une originalité' is not simply 'contenu' within the 'limites extérieures des convenances', but somehow made possible by them. It is as though freedom were achieved by turning the tables on what would deny it to you. Thus, Baudelaire argues, the superiority of painting over sculpture is that a painting is isolated from space by a barrier which gives it an exclusive and despotic point of view: 'aussi l'expression du peintre est-elle bien plus forte'.[77]

A *frame* cuts pictures away from surrounding nature. Make-up is similarly exalted for its power to separate the human from the natural. Samuel Cramer, the artist of *La Fanfarlo*, makes his mistress pose for him fully made up, in her actress's costume. His call to her when she goes to get dressed: 'N'oubliez pas le rouge!'[78] elevates the pursuit of artifice to the level of a rigorous idealism. The same spiritualising power is attributed to *poudre de riz* in the 'Eloge du maquillage', for it creates an 'abstract unity'[79] in the texture of the skin. And the arabesque is regarded as the most 'spiritualiste' of all designs in its complete freedom from natural forms.[80] The very elements which seem to be most unambiguously *matter*, which most evidently express our subservience to a materialistic society, that is, become at Baudelaire's hands the walls which keep it at bay. Thus it is a *frame* of jewels and furs which for a brief and uniquely tender moment, focuses and transmits with perfect luminosity the vanished splendour of Jeanne:

> Comme un beau cadre ajoute à la peinture,
> Bien qu'elle soit d'un pinceau très-vanté,

Je ne sais quoi d'étrange et d'enchanté
En l'isolant de l'immense nature,

Ainsi bijoux, meubles, métaux, dorure,
S'adaptaient juste à sa rare beauté;
Rien n'offusquait sa parfaite clarté,
Et tout semblait lui servir de bordure.[81]

Baudelaire's hatred for the laws of nature, and for the social and economic realities which they embodied, passes on to the next generation of French writers. Huysman's *A Rebours* and Villiers de l'Isle-Adam's *Äxel* are emphatic illustrations of the attempt to make artifice or perversity the means to recreate spiritual values. And in the late nineteenth century, the word 'artifice', largely under Baudelaire's influence, seems to occupy, in the intensity and representativeness of its occurrence, the position which was that of 'nature' in the Romantic era. Conversely, nature is thought to be 'bankrupt'. Referring to the terrible 'ransom' which must be paid for 'progress', to Russian nihilism, the excesses of the 1871 Commune, the bitter misanthropy of naturalistic novelists, Paul Bourget says: '[Tout cela] révèle ce même esprit de négation de la vie, qui, chaque jour, obscurcit davantage la civilisation occidentale ... Lentement, sûrement, une croyance à la banqueroute de la nature ne s'élabore-t-elle pas qui promet de devenir la foi sinistre du XXe siècle ...'[82] There is reason to think that Bourget was right, and that Baudelaire's sense of 'progress' reveals a predicament which is still with us today, and which makes his exploration of it still vital to us.

But there is another level, a more energising one, at which his handling of 'artifice' reveals something crucial. We have perceived that the fragmentation of his poetry not only gives form to a general state of social and epistemological fragmentation, but acts as a denial of determinism. We have seen that movement of reversal repeat itself with determinism. The limits of freedom, in Baudelaire, become the condition of freedom and the 'most absolute materialism' leads to the 'purest idealism'. A dialectical movement, that is, recreates the Romantic possibilities that seemed lost, through the very agency of what expressed or brought about this loss. We begin to gather a sense that the range and power of Baudelaire's poetry may have something to do, not only with his responsiveness to the realities of his age, but with the strength to struggle with them and change them. The word dialectical is indeed the right one. For the image of 'reversal' which springs to mind in contact with the dynamics of his verse is inescapably reminiscent of a complex of figures which recurs several times in Marx, and which he himself had inherited from Hegel.[83] Through the phenomenon of ideology, Marx argues, 'men and their circumstances appear upside down and in a *camera obscura*', and this arises 'just as much from their historical life-process as the inversion of objects on the retina does from their physical life-process'.[84] Things thus inverted must therefore be 'turned right side up again', and this will be done by ascending 'from earth to heaven', proceeding from 'real, active men' to their thinking instead of descending, as German philosophy has done, from heaven to earth. This is not simply a question of redressing a 'topsy-turvy' vision, any more than for Baudelaire rediscovering possibilities of freedom in and through determinism entails a licence to indulge in private perversity. What is at stake in each case, though within vastly differing perspectives, is the recreation of a future – that future which the early Romantics believed in and which became lost through the growth of capitalism.

4 The Significance of Form

I

Yet the neat sense of reversal of 'nature' and 'artifice' between the Romantic period and Baudelaire, though it has its truth, has been achieved at a cost. The vision of Romantic nature which has been offered in opposition to Baudelaire was an over-simplification (some readers may even have thought, a distortion), of Romantic attitudes. It may well be therefore that the sense of discontinuity which has been explored, masks important similarities, and that these similarities, in their turn, could illuminate Baudelaire's work.

Not that we want to fall into a limbo of complexities and half-truths. But the singularity of Baudelaire can only be discovered by a precise process of confrontations. These confrontations can only occur inside some clearly drawn outlines, and they are valid in those terms. One must then realise that the outlines are a means of discovery, not the basis of a permanent truth. Or that they can be truths only through their co-existence with other, conflicting, truths. If the boundaries of these truths eventually happen to overlap, there will then be a strong probability that a highly significant ground has been established.

Thus the idea expounded in the previous chapter that fragmentation becomes an active and perceptible phenomenon at a date which more or less falls between the early Romantics and Baudelaire may well be misguided in its definiteness. Baudelaire's 'ce ne sont pas les molécules qui constituent la forme' can be read as a continuation of Blake's 'an atom is a thing that does not exist'.[1] The resistance to all modes of atomisation, which this sentence forcefully voices, is pervasive in Romanticism. What Baudelaire calls 'form' is perhaps what Wordsworth (and Blake) identify as 'the life of things' in opposition to Newton's and Locke's view that 'the world of our ordinary perceptions is largely illusory, that the only objective reality consists of particles moving in space'.[2] The Romantic resistance to the implications of a mechanistic view of life is as strong as Baudelaire's, and almost universal. Indeed, it can be regarded as typical. One instantly recognises what Langbaum is pointing to when he connects Wordsworth's 'we murder to dissect' with Goethe's distrust of experimentation, as voiced here by Faust:

> The man who wants to know
> Organic truth and describe it well
> Seeks first to drive the living spirit out;
> he's got the parts in hand there,
> it's merely the breath of life that's lacking.[3]

Goethe's whole view of nature is permeated by a dynamic sense of life, and in his work on natural science he keeps insisting that to the analytical operation of the concept there must be joined the synthetic work of the imagination: 'What does all our communion with nature amount, to, indeed, if we busy ourselves with analyzing our simple material portions, and do not feel the breath of the spirit that dictates the role of every part and restrains or sanctions all excess through an immanent law?'[4]

This conception of imagination is close to Wordsworth's, and Blake's. It is also so congenial with Baudelaire's defence of form, that the word 'constituent' which Baudelaire uses, his denial that 'laws' should be determining (as the positivists assert), seem to be an echo of Goethe: '... we must not seek the model for all in any one. Classes, orders, species and individuals are related as cases are to a law; they are included under it, but do not *constitute* it.'[5]

The argument for spirituality, through terms such as 'imagination', 'life', 'model', 'organic', or 'form' is indeed so frequent among the early Romantics that Baudelaire's championing of it could be regarded as a sure indication of his own Romanticism. Also, poets like Wordsworth and Blake have insights which seem even more valid for the Victorian era (and for France in the mid-nineteenth century) than for Georgian England. They perceive forms of alienation with a lucidity which is much ahead of their time. And this makes them, in some ways, the spiritual contemporaries of Baudelaire:

> ... No officious slave
> Art thou of that false secondary power
> By which we multiply distinctions, then
> Deem that our puny boundaries are things
> That we perceive, and not that we have made.[6]

To find an equivalent for the account of reification which this compliment to Coleridge offers, one has to turn to Marxist analyses: 'Man in capitalist society confronts a reality "made" by himself (as a class) which appears to him to be a natural phenomenon alien to himself'.[7] Wordsworth's insight has its counterpart, a mythical and more clearly political one, in Blake's denunciation of Urizen:

> For Blake, the God who created the natural order is a projected God, an idol constructed out of the sky and reflecting its mindless mechanism. Such a God is a figment of man's alienation, for the tyranny of an absurd and meaningless nature suggests and guarantees the tyranny of exploiting ruling classes.[8]

The Industrial Revolution affected England on a large scale so much earlier than France that Blake and Wordsworth were already confronting the very changes which faced Baudelaire in the Second Empire. The crisis of rural values which anguished Lamartine around 1848–51, owing to the economic decline of the peasantry, was perceptible in England in the 1800s. Raymond Williams invokes Cobbett, and quotes from Owen's *Observations on the Effect of the Manufacturing System*, as proofs of this:

> The manufacturing system has already so far extended its influence over the British Empire as to effect an essential change in the general character of the mass of people. This alteration is still in rapid progress, and, ere long, the comparatively happy simplicity of the agricultural peasant will be wholly lost among us. It is even now scarcely anywhere to be found, without a mixture of those habits which are the offspring of trade, manufacture and commerce.[9]

In the wake of this, literature grew (or declined) into a commodity value. Baudelaire's and Flaubert's generation in France were the first to feel the chill of this transformation (though many precursor signs had been perceived by Balzac). It had much earlier blown its cold blast on the Romantic artist, as Raymond Williams shows conclusively.[10] Adam Smith's statement that knowledge was now 'purchased in the same manner as shoes or stockings' is a good thirty years ahead of the *Communist Manifesto*:

> The bourgeoisie, wherever it has got the upper hand, has put an end to all feudal, patriarchal, idyllic relations . . .

... [It] has stripped of its halo every occupation hitherto honoured and looked up to with reverend awe. It has converted the physician, the lawyer, the priest, the poet, the man of science, into its paid wage-labourers...[11]

Marx is describing a phenomenon that had been at work for some time. The victims of Jeffrey's reviews suffered from it. Even before, poets like Coleridge, going into opposition to the establishment, had felt ostracised and persecuted for it. Hazlitt thus summarises this evil of the age: 'It was a misfortune to any man of talent to be born in the latter end of the last century. Genius stopped the way of legitimacy, and therefore it was to be abated, crushed, or set aside as a nuisance...' 'Assailed by nicknames, lies, all the arts of malice and hypocrisy', poets like Coleridge, 'the creature of sympathy, could not stand the frowns both of king and people.'[12] Seen in this light, Coleridge's predicament heralds that of such members of the 'Bohême' as Baudelaire,[13] who were rejected both by the establishment and the revolution. The keen sense of exclusion which makes Wordsworth sit silent amidst the English Congregation who are praying for a defeat of revolutionary France, 'an uninvited Guest/Whom no one owned',[14] and which compels the Ancient Mariner to remain outside the wedding feast and involve another being in the purgatorial solitude of his tale, anticipates the exile imposed on Baudelaire's 'Poëte' by the fear and malice of men:

> Tous ceux qu'il veut aimer l'observent avec crainte ...
> ...
> Avec hypocrisie ils jettent ce qu'il touche,
> Et s'accusent d'avoir mis leurs pieds dans ses pas.[15]

What further invalidates clear-cut distinctions between Baudelaire and the Romantics is that some of the palpably 'modern' aspects of the *Fleur du Mal*, which will be seminal for Symbolist and Surrealistic poets, are derived from major Romantic themes. Thus 'Révolte', the last section but one of the *Fleurs du Mal*, whose 'cry' will be echoed by Rimbaud, Lautréamont and Breton, is full of the rebellious intonations of Byron, Shelley, and Hölderlin. 'Spleen', which will be the major mood of Laforgue's poetry and of T. S. Eliot's earlier work, has its acknowledged sources in Chateaubriand and Sainte-Beuve. Indeed, for Baudelaire, 'Satanism' and 'melancholy' are the marking features of *modern* poetry.[16] 'Paysage', the second poem of 'Tableaux parisiens', could be a re-writing of Keat's 'Fancy', just as 'Chant d'automne', in its longing for warmth, is suffused in a sensuousness akin to that of the 'Ode to Autumn'. This whole area of Baudelaire's indebtedness to his 'Romantic' predecessors (especially the French ones) is so well researched[17] that it would be pleonastic to enter into it: the research has even gone to the length of suggesting that there was hardly a line of Baudelaire's writing which was not lifted from somebody else – generally, somebody writing in the first half of the nineteenth century.

It is in some ways tempting to argue that the dividing line would fall more appropriately between the early and the late Romantics (Baudelaire being then regarded as one of the late Romantics) than between Romanticism and the post-1848 generation. The spirit of dejection which frequently overpowers Coleridge, or Byron is that which afflicts 'La Muse malade' and 'Le Vampire'. Baudelaire claimed to feel more kinship with Poe, who was 'malade' than with 'calm and virtuous' writers like Goethe and Walter Scott. The terms in which this preference is expressed may show blindness to the complexities of the writers thus labelled. They nonetheless reveal deep affinities. Goethe, Scott (and Wordsworth), whatever the vast differences between them, all have a stable and central abundance of spirit. Their immense susceptibility to the outside world is due to the solidity of their vitality, one might say its earthiness. Walter Scott and Wordsworth, in particular, have an extraordinarily tenacious and detailed grip over every inch of the ground they cover. Theirs is the knowledge of the man who *walks*. And there is in Goethe that peasant quality which Mann captures so well in *Lotte in Weimar*. By contrast, the various imbalances in Byron or Shelley or Keats of Hölderlin or Poe become manifest. They can in turn be seen as preludes to Baudelaire's albatross-like poet: the sailors have captured the bird, the king of the azure, which now, wings trailing, ungainly, hobbles along on deck:

> Exilé sur le sol, au milieu des huées,
> Ses ailes de géant l'empêchent de marcher.[18]

II

But this distinction too has its limits. For one of the most important senses of 'nature' in Baudelaire has its source, albeit a derived and surreptitious one, in *early* German Romanticism. Nature here is understood as 'that aspect of human inwardness which has remained natural, or at least tends or longs to become natural once more'.[19] 'They are what we once were', Schiller says of the forms of nature, 'they are what we should become once more'. 'Nature' in this sense refers to authentic humanity, the 'true essence of man liberated from the false, mechanising forces of society'.[20] In this perspective, as Béguin puts it, man for the German philosophers of nature becomes the *redeemer* of nature. For Baader and Schelling man has fallen, and the world has fallen with him. Nature is in a 'violent' state. But man has the power of rebecoming what he is already, and thus doing he becomes the agent of the regeneration of all things. He has that power, because he is the place where the Spirit can become conscious of itself: for the Spirit can only manifest itself and see itself in what is its image: man's consciousness.[21]

Baudelaire found access to that major 'Romantic' theory through Poe, or, which is more likely, found embodied in Poe's talès ideas which were already fundamental to him and to which he felt Poe had given perfect form.[22] Poe may, or may not, have inherited the idea from some Romantic source. What is certain is that it becomes transformed at his hands.

Two of his stories, *Landor's Cottage* and *The Domain of Arnheim*, strangely blend the 'Romantic' theme of man as a redeemer of nature with an 'anti-Romantic' exaltation of artifice. Baudelaire translated them at a time (1865) when his own interest in artifice was at its strongest. So that once again the comparative process will force us to change direction: Baudelaire's dissent from Romanticism seems about to reassert itself in the midst of an enquiry into his closeness to it.

The protagonist of Poe's *The Domain of Arnheim* wants to dedicate his huge fortune to the creation of beautiful landscapes. He has read, he explains, a treatise on landscape-gardening, which distinguishes two styles, the natural and the artificial. The 'natural' style is described in terms which are 'one of those mere vaguenesses of speech which serve to veil inaccuracy of thought', and it has only 'negative merit', and is 'better suited to the grovelling apprehensions of the herd than to the fervid dreams of the man of genius'.[23] Baudelaire's own attack on an 'inept and trivial' song which says that 'la nature embellit la beauté', in the 'Eloge du Maquillage', is in hearty agreement with Poe: 'Il est présumable que le poète, s'il avait su parler en français, aurait dit: *La simplicité embellit la beauté!* ce qui équivaut à cette *vérité*, d'un genre tout à fait inattendu: *Le rien embellit ce qui est.*'[24]

The surreptitious sliding of meanings through 'translation' of one term into another, here, is masterly. There is a provocative irony in that, equating the term 'nature' with the term 'rien', Baudelaire is invoking an anti-Romantic sense of the word; the one which it had for Johnson, for Boyle and for D'Holbach.

In the wake of this, the term 'beauty' becomes involved in a similar reversal of meaning. It becomes 'what is' – which suggests that nothing else *is*. Or rather, that the only things which graduate to 'essence' are things which are made artificially, *consciously*, significant.

We at last can see the dawning, on the level of the ideas which Baudelaire formulates, of a process of contradictions similar to that which the allusiveness of the verse was seen to be creating in poems such as 'Au Lecteur', at the beginning of this study. This new sense of nature as devoid of values, as best used as a shorthand for other, more precise, terms, as pure transparency, exists in a state of struggle against a sense of nature as 'fallen'. But it is the definition of nature as *nothing* which enables, by contrast, beauty to be defined as a positive brought about by the 'Spirit' of man. In other words, it is because nature ceases to be viewed in Romantic terms that it becomes possible to re-establish a Romantic view of nature.

Ellison spells this out quite clearly, though without the speed and range of Baudelaire. He argues that the artificial style of landscape-gardening is preferable to the natural because in it 'the art intervolved is made to assume the air of an intermediate or secondary nature – a nature which is not God, nor an emanation from God, but which still is nature in the sense of the handiwork of the angels that hover between man and God.'[25] Beauty, that is, only begins to *exist* once a landscape bears the sign of 'spiritual interference', once it is elevated from a first to a 'second' degree of naturalness. This is because Poe's Ellison believes, like Baader and Schelling, that the fall of nature followed the fall of man. In its first created state, Ellison argues, the earth's surface would have fulfilled man's sense of perfection 'in the beautiful, the sublime, or the picturesque': '. . . but the primitive intention (was) frustrated by the known geological disturbances – disturbances of form and color-grouping, in the correction or allaying of which lies the soul of art . . . Ellison suggested that (these disturbances) were prognostic of *death*.'[26]

Baudelaire fully shares this belief in the fallen condition of nature. The deterministic and fragmenting forces in the society around him, as we argued in the previous chapter, eloquently expressed that fall. In turn, the 'deathly' correspondence of mind and landscape which pervade the Winter cycle of 'Spleen et Idéal' are quite literally meant. If 'dans le suaire des nuages' the poet discovers 'un cadavre cher',[27] it is not only because Spleen projects its perverse gloom onto the landscape, it is also because nature itself is ailing. Baudelaire believes that the fall continues, that as History and individuals produce more evil, material signs of evil become visibly multiplied. Only this can explain the coming to form of Breughel's caricatures:

> ... souvent nous trouvons dans l'histoire ... la preuve de l'immense puissance des contagions, de l'empoisonnement par l'atmosphère morale, et je ne puis m'empêcher de remarquer ... que cette prodigieuse floraison de monstruosités coincide de la manière la plus singulière avec la fameuse et historique *épidémie des sorciers*.[28]

Toussenel's *Le Monde des oiseaux*, a book full of weird relations between birds and humans, was for Baudelaire the occasion to carry this thought even further:

> ... à propos de *péché originel* et de *forme moulée sur l'idée*, j'ai pensé bien souvent que les bêtes malfaisantes et dégoûtantes n'étaient peut-être que la vivification, corporification, éclosion à la vie matérielle des mauvaises pensées de l'homme. – Ainsi la *nature* entière participe du péché originel.[29]

But this deathly state of nature is reflected, for Baudelaire as for Poe, at a particular level. The 'component parts' of a landscape, as Ellison puts it, may be perfect. It is their 'arrangement' which 'will always be susceptible of improvement'. There is 'no part on the wide surface of the *natural* earth, from which an artistical eye' will not be offended by the 'composition' of the landscape.[30] This is a crucial word in Poe's vocabulary, the one that figures prominently in his major essay on the writing of poetry, *The Philosophy of Composition*. It is also a word which assumes great significance in Baudelaire's own critical writings on landscape-painting. Thus he criticises 'l'école moderne des paysagistes' for its 'culte niais de la nature': for not understanding that 'nature' must be purified and explained by imagination before it can become a work of art. They open a window, he says, and the space framed assumes for them the value of 'un poème tout fait'. But 'un poème ne se copie jamais: il veut être *composé*'.[31]

The role of the artist is thus to regenerate nature, by making it once more what it was before the fall. It becomes a rediscovery of paradise: '... un idéal ... c'est l'individu redressé par l'individu, reconstruit et rendu par le pinceau ou le ciseau à l'éclatante vérité de son harmonie native.'[32] But that rediscovery is effected through the injection into nature of a 'human' element. This is very close to Schelling's idea, as described by Béguin, that the spirit in man must be projected onto the natural world so that it can then contemplate its own re-created image outside as well as inside man's mind. If a landscape is beautiful, Baudelaire argues, it is not 'par lui-même, mais par moi, par ma grâce propre, par l'idée ou le sentiment que j'y attache'.[33] The mind, or the sensibility, become for Baudelaire the repository of the beautiful, because 'perception', as well as the sense of values, in man, remain relatively untouched by the fall, unlike will. There is a powerful Pauline tradition behind this, which may have passed on to Baudelaire through Maistre's passionate oratory:

> Toute intelligence est par sa nature même le résultat, à la fois ternaire et unique, d'une *perception* qui appréhende, d'une *raison* qui affirme, et d'une volonté qui agit. Les deux premières puissances ne sont qu'affaiblies dans l'homme mais la troisième est brisée, et semblable au serpent du Tasse, *elle se traîne après soi* . . .[34]

This sets the terms of man's power as a creator, and one grasps at this point how well the influences of de Maistre and Poe complemented each other, and why Baudelaire could write: 'De Maistre et Poe m'ont appris à raisonner'.[35] Also, Baudelaire's extraordinary mixture of agreement and disagreement with Romanticism can here be seen with some degree of completeness. For he attributes a redeeming power to the poet, which is quite in keeping with Schelling and Schiller.[36] But, like Poe, he makes that power entirely *a power of composition*. It is *form* which, for Baudelaire, regenerates. Returning once more to the phrase 'ce ne sont pas les molécules qui constituent la forme', one realises how vital the role which is here given to form is. Reality is richer than our means of reproducing it, and alien to them. 'Who shall presume to imitate the colors of the tulip, or to improve on the proportions of the lily of the valley?', Poe's Ellison asks. Language, paint, are clumsy tools, and participate in the materialness of the rest of nature. But reality is defective in expressiveness. The artist can give it that. He is not a maker of substance but a creator of forms and meanings. Baudelaire is here effecting a change that will be seminal for poets to come, especially for Mallarmé:

> Abolie, la prétention, esthétiquement une erreur, quoiqu' elle régit les chefs-d'oeuvre, d'inclure au papier subtil du volume autre chose que par exemple l'horreur de la forêt, ou le tonnerre muet épars au feuillage; non le bois intrinsèque et dense des arbres.[37]

Language must, as Ellison puts it, 'shrink from competition' with the 'dense' reality of nature. It has no accurate equivalents for objects. Sometimes even its own materiality contradicts theirs:

> A côté d'*ombre*, opaque, *ténèbres* se fonce peu; quelle déception, devant la perversité conférant à *jour* comme à *nuit*, contradictoirement, des timbres obscurs ici, là clair ... – *Seulement, sachons n'existerait pas le vers*: lui, philosophiquement rémunère le défaut des langues, complément supérieur.[38]

Poetry, 'complément supérieur', redeems the defectiveness of language. *Felix Culpa*. Thanks to the 'composing' power of verse, the world is recreated as meaningful as it should be.

The artefact of composition re-introduces not only spirit into the world, but immortality. 'Toute forme créée, même par l'homme, est immortelle, *comme une personne*.' Ellison argued that the unfallen state of nature reflected man's immortal, Edenic condition, and that the disturbances that followed his fall in turn expressed his 'deathly' state. Composition, through recreating the perfection of the primitive state, brings back a vision of immortality. It is conveyed by Baudelaire's dreamland: 'Pays singulier, supérieur aux autres, comme l'Art l'est à la Nature, où celle-ci est réformée par le rêve où elle est corrigée, embellie, refondue.'[39]

Baudelaire's 'Invitation au voyage' is also an invitation to poetry as a return to paradise: however 'fallen' the states which are the subject-matter of Baudelaire's poems, the power of the song sends them sailing to an ideal country where 'tout n'est qu'ordre et beauté,/Luxe, calme et volupté.' The cry of the utmost anguish dilates the lungs to a fullness of bliss:

> C'est grâce aux astres nonpareils,
> Qui tout au fond du ciel flamboient,
> Que mes yeux consumés ne voient
> Que des souvenirs de soleils.[40]

It was through Poe's own formulations that Baudelaire described what happens on contact with such poetry:

> ... quand un poème exquis amène les larmes au bord des yeux, ces larmes ne sont pas la preuve d'un excès de jouissance, elles sont bien plutôt le témoignage d'une mélancolie irritée, d'une postulation des

nerfs, d'une nature exilée dans l'imparfait et qui voudrait s'emparer immédiatement, sur cette terre méme, d'un paradis révélé.[41]

A paradise revealed, or rather regained, by the power of composition.

III

There is one respect in which Baudelaire seems even closer to the Romantics than in his vision of the poet as a redeemer of nature. It is in his contradictoriness. The antitheses which we earlier on attempted to draw between his and Wordsworth's visions of nature failed to take into account the fact that Wordsworth's poetry moves among contradictions whose intensity is not without analogies with Baudelaire's. The same point could be made about Blake. It should be added that the dynamics which, in each poet, organise and attempt or refuse to solve the contradictions, are dialectical.

We have, up to now, related the emergence of 'dialectics' in Baudelaire to Marx, or followers of Marx, and, more in passing, to Hegel. This is because one should render unto Caesar what belongs to Caesar. Because, that is, these writers have, in a more systematic and seminal way than anyone else in that period, discovered and pursued dynamic contradictions in history and in consciousness which were coming into being, or becoming more prominent, at that time, and because what their analyses have unearthed seems retrospectively so often true. When we use the term 'dialectical' about Baudelaire or Wordsworth, we are not pinning a decoration on their breast, nor giving them a free ticket to some ideological Olympus. We are drawing attention to the typicality of their readings of the situations in which they found themselves, as well as to their impulse to overcome contradictions – or, if they found those irreconcilable, to discover conditions under which life might still be possible.

Harold Bloom gives quite a good instance of the term 'dialectical' as we mean it when he says about Blake's *Marriage of Heaven and Hell*:

> In content, the *Marriage* compounds ethical and theological 'contraries'; in form, it mocks the categorical techniques that seek to make the contraries appear as 'negations'. The unity of the *Marriage* is itself dialectical, and cannot be grasped except by the mind in motion, moving between the Blakean contraries of discursive irony and mythical visualization.[42]

A similar sense of the dialectical nature of much of Wordsworth's poetry could be offered, and has been in various ways sketched by several of his more recent critics. Many of the *Lyrical Ballads*, especially poems like 'The Old Cumberland Beggar', 'Michael',[43] 'The Thorn' or 'Animal Tranquillity and Decay' owe the fineness of their tension to the number of levels at which they operate or to the paradoxical insights which make them up. Lionel Trilling's attitude to 'Intimations of Immortality' is also one of insistence on the quality of the energy which the poem generates: 'It is necessary to understand this contradiction (between resistance to, and acceptance of, growth), but it is not necessary to resolve it, for from the circuit between its two poles comes much of the power of the poem.'[44]

Indeed, one could argue that this attempt to integrate contradictions, not by endeavouring to solve them, but by making their tensions dynamic, is characteristically 'Romantic'. It may also be another way of 'redeeming' nature. History, public and more often private, becomes recuperated as its contradictions and losses are brought together by an overall form. That it should be through *form* that the dialectic is established, makes it very different from other, chronological dialectics. When Yeats – one of the 'last Romantics' – retorts to Hegel that the spring vegetables are not refuted because they are over, he is not simply propounding a cyclical view of existence, but asserting that various domains of reality may not be ruled by the same dynamics. What in 'historical' terms, in terms of 'praxis', may have to be seen as a chronological process to be dynamic may in poetry or painting take its impetus from such a circuit as the one Lionel Trilling describes. In a very real sense a man's present is his past as well as that one historical moment is made up of the infinity of pressures that brought it about and that it is a reaction to. This is a vital point, for it applies just as much to Baudelaire as to any of the early or late Romantics, and it is an integral part of what is entailed by applying the term 'dialectical' to literature or to art.

Even on a larger level than that of the 'Immortality Ode', in the *Prelude*, that is, Wordsworth undergoes crises of conscience, and even crises of identity, which drive him into areas that will become Baudelaire's haunts. England's opposition to the liberties of France throws him 'out of the pale of love', 'sours' and 'corrupts' his sentiments, to the point at which what we have argued to be a characteristically Baudelairian 'reversal' happens to him. Instead of feeling 'a swallowing up of lesser things in great', he is confronted by a 'change of them into their opposites'.[45] 'What had been a pride' becomes 'a shame'[46] for him, much as the triumphal beacon of Baudelaire's 'Phares' turns into 'un phare ironique, infernal' in the paralysed horror of 'L'Irrémédiable'. Wordsworth goes even further in his despair, indeed the *peversity* of some of his emotions is quite startling. As though wickedly inspired by a spirit of prophetic vindictiveness, the lover of liberty, the author of 'Lucy', at the height of the terror rejoices in the violence, sees it as a scourge meted out to the people, feels 'a kind of sympathy with power'.[47] He fraternises at this point, not only with Maistre, who regards war as the work of an exterminating angel, but with the late Baudelaire, the Baudelaire of *Pauvre Belgique,* who cries 'Vive la Révolution!' as he would say 'Vive la Destruction! Vive le Châtiment!'

But one must be aware of being deaf to the intonations and implications of Wordsworth's language. He is using one of his characteristic words: 'sympathy', even though he qualifies it by 'a kind of'. It has suggestions of harmony, it is part of the language of the heart. So that while the power with which the poet is identifying is ruthless, yet the language in which the necessity of its sway is being acknowledged, even celebrated, attempts to maintain the very values which that power is destroying. Or some higher power which is good is being abstracted from the evil power through which it works to its own end, and the survival of goodness thus ensured, both in history and in the poet's soul. In Baudelaire the emphasis is the reverse. There is a recognised 'sadistic' pleasure in the endorsement of revolutionary destruction. While, that is, Wordsworth is trying to keep alive, through the pressures of his vocabulary, the creative values that the speaker of the *Prelude* is making organically continuous, in the very moment he is 'sympathetically' espousing the forces which are threatening them, Baudelaire, is backing an 'order' based on 'disorder'. Or again, while Wordsworth is maintaining his identity through the process of seeming to lose it, Baudelaire is allowing his 'self' to be obliterated, to be the mere occasion for discovering what it is like to be in turns 'victime' and 'bourreau'. The 'Moi' that says 'Vive la Révolution!' is a nobody. It is an acting out, in which the author is forever in search of characters. Walter Benjamin's remark is profoundly true: 'Heroic modernism turns out to be a tragedy in which the hero's part is available'. When Wordsworth says, in the 'Immortality Ode', referring to the child, 'the little Actor cons his part', he is juxtaposing Shakespeare's vision of the fundamental theatricality of life with a secure affirmation of the rightness of its cycles. But when Baudelaire, in 'Les Sept Vieillards' discussing with his 'already weary soul', 'stiffens' his nerves 'comme un héros', he is pretending to play a part he doesn't believe in without even committing himself to the pretence. Wordsworth's sympathy with a destructive power is, in terms of the past and the future of the poem, part of that 'primal sympathy/Which having been must ever be'. It is stable and contains the seeds of a transcendence. In Baudelaire's 'Vive la Révolution!' we are faced with emptiness, and the impossibility of a transcendence.

Thus any effort to trace continuities between Baudelaire and Wordsworth as a major exponent of Romanticism ends in the delineation of differences. The difference which has just emerged is all the more significant as it confirms those that had appeared earlier, but shows even more strongly the importance of form. For indeed it seems to be in the overall composition of their poetry, in the impetus of their rhythms, in the continuities or discontinuities of their images that the two poets fundamentally differ, rather than in the intellectual or emotional quality of their vision of life. They both acutely experience and express the contradictory nature of reality. But much of the energy of *The Prelude* goes into transcending the contradictions. Lukács might have said that this is because Wordsworth still had the wind of the Enlightenment blowing into his sails; whereas Baudelaire belonged to an era in which the bourgeoisie had ceased to be the class at the spearhead of history, and could no longer solve its internal contradictions.

This may be true. But what it mainly signifies for us is that those contradictions express their quality through the *forms* of poetry. The form is the content in a larger sense than is generally claimed.

IV

There is something either compulsive or systematic in the way Baudelaire moves among contradictions. It is their extreme mobility more than anything else that characterises his 'nature' and his 'artifice'.

Thus side by side or alternating with the two senses of nature which we have found to be most coherent in his work, that of nature as fallen (opposed to artifice as saving), and that of nature as an ideal to be discovered ahead, through the redemptive power of poetry, there is a third, quite positive, version of nature as what is organically complete. It rests on the belief that form *is* content, that the natural world is the visible manifestation of this, and that it offers models to be imitated by the artist if he is to become great. This theme is most explicit in Baudelaire's art criticism.

He argues in the 1846 *Salon* that nature cannot be wrong in its arrangement of tones, for they express 'chemical affinities'. For nature, form and colour are one. Ruskin's idea that the leaf-shaped Gothic arch is beautiful because it directly imitates the forms of the natural world would have been nonsense to Baudelaire,[48] in that it ignores that form in nature is the expression of the identity of shape, colour and substance. The great artist can become as infallible as nature only by rivalling the complexity which faces him, and achieving oneness with it. Thus the true 'coloriste' instinctively knows the register of tones, the force of tone, the results to be achieved by mixing colours, the whole science of counterpoint, and can 'faire une harmonie de vingt rouges différents'.[49] The greatest painters, therefore, are those who have as it were immersed themselves in the materiality of the world, and come to understand it through the totality of their exposure to it. 'Cette canaille de Rembrandt' is a more powerful idealist than the 'pure' Raphael, because he is a 'canaille'.[50] Imagination can only work once it has at its disposal 'un immense magasin d'observations',[51] as well as technical mastery, a large and catholic range of gestures, a fanatic care for the tools of the craft: 'autrement l'idéal s'envole'.[52] Although Baudelaire admires Cruickshank's 'abondance inépuisable dans le grotesque', he criticises him for not always drawing in a conscientious enough manner, so that the limbs of his 'monde minuscule' are not always 'à leur place naturelle', and that Cruickshank's creatures 'ne sont pas toujours nées viables', are 'hypothèses' rather than live figures.[53] Conversely, Goya's great merit lies in having created 'le monstreaux vraisemblable'. His bestial or diabolical figures are 'pénétrées d'humanité'. The seam, the 'point de jonction' between reality and fantasy is impossible to grasp.[54]

In this perspective, the lover of pure form has less chance to create significant forms than a less perfect, but deeply committed artist.[55] By contrast, the 'puérile utopia of art for art's sake', which seems to be at work in the ideal of the dandy, or in the 'Eloge du maquillage' is judged as 'nécessairement stérile', because it excludes passion and morality.[56] And in an attack against 'l'Ecole païenne' Baudelaire denounces those 'insensés' who, like his own Samuel Cramer, 'ne voient dans la nature que des rythmes et des formes':

> Le goût immodéré de la forme pousse à des désordres monstrueux et inconnus . . . La folie de l'art est égale à l'abus de l'esprit . . .
> . . . Le temps n'est pas loin où l'on comprendra que toute littérature qui se refuse à marcher fraternellement entre la science et la philosophie est une littérature homicide et suicide.[57]

THE SIGNIFICANCE OF FORM

This is from a relatively early essay (1852): and those critics of Baudelaire who, like Professor F. W. Leakey, hold that there are not so much contradictions between Baudelaire's views of art and nature as an evolution towards pessimism, might say that a sense of contradictoriness is being engineered falsely, by mixing quotations from various epochs of Baudelaire's writing. The passage on the 'Ecole païenne' and on Pierre Dupont represent an early attitude of trust in life, they would say, which gradually changes towards the disenchantment at the root of the ideal of the Dandy or of the arabesque.

It is undeniable that Baudelaire's sense of reality darkens with time. But the *oscillation* between the valuing of artifice and/or nature is, as has been demonstrated, continuous.[58] It now becomes clear that Baudelaire is searching for a way of overcoming the simple opposition. This is where the *dialectic* begins to operate.

Even looking at the dates of the various passages quoted in the course of these chapters the continuous co-existent contradictions are manifest. Baudelaire's greatest enthusiasm for 'nature' comes in the first Pierre Dupont article – published in 1851, four years later than *La Fanfarlo*, where the focus is wholly on artifice. The celebration of the arabesque appears first in 1852, in the translation of Poe's *The Philosophy of Furniture* and recurs from time to time up to the *Journaux intimes* (1855–66). The ideal of the dandy is there in the young Baudelaire of 1844 and maintains itself to the last. In the thinking about the grotesque and caricature, the conviction appears that closeness to nature is the requisite condition for great art. This faith in nature pervades the attack on the *Prométhée délivré*, 1846; it triumphs in the essays on laughter, drafted in 1845, rehandled and published in 1855; it is still strongly there in the notes for an article on 'l'art philosophique' which he denigrates as 'artificial', contrasting it as an art form with 'l'esthétique involontaire, spontanée, fatale, vitale, du peuple'.[59] And this is in 1859, the year of 'L'Eloge du Maquillage' and *Les Paradis artificiels*. The contradiction is confirmed by an earlier remark in the *Correspondance*, following up on the 'condamnation' of the *Fleurs du Mal*, when he bitterly complains to his mother that he will now have to write some new pieces to replace the condemned ones, but write them 'artificiellement, par volonté'. The terms are intensely pejorative.

And this strange dialectical process goes on, right to the end of Baudelaire's life. It is most striking perhaps in the remarks on the baroque churches of Brussels which he celebrates both for their intense artificiality, the painted and dressed up Madonnas, the melodramatic crucifixes, the pulpits 'mondes d'emblèmes', 'style joujou', *and* for their total naturalness: 'C'est le gâchis naturel de l'histoire'.[60] And by 'histoire' he means something vast and organic and perpetually *moving*: '. . . Philosophie de l'histoire de l'architecture, selon *moi*. – Analogies avec les coraux, les madrépores, la formation des continents, et finalement avec la vie universelle. – Jamais de lacunes. – Etat permanent de transition.'[61]

Here at last, in some of his last writings, Baudelaire makes explicit what principle energises his thinking and organises the form of the volumes of poetry. The permanent state of transition, which is that of 'nature', a state which Darwin among others was then exploring, and which so deeply troubled Tennyson,[62] filled Baudelaire with a sense of exaltation. It somehow exactly fitted and expressed the temper of his own sensibility, and defined the form he had been working towards while *composing* the *Fleurs du Mal*. For in *Les Fleurs du Mal* Nature abundantly caters for its own perpetuation, through the various branches it pushes forth, through the strange vegetation of evil that calls itself not mammals or fishes but 'Spleen et Idéal', 'Tableaux parisiens' or 'Révolte'. But in the process, the evil which is itself an inversion of healthy growth is transformed into 'beauty', into a regained paradise. Also, this proliferation of species is never 'careless of the single life' as Tennyson would have said, since it exists only in so far as each life asserts itself in the fullness of its fused complexity – in so far as each is 'née viable'.

And the poet, in this perspective, is a 'voyant', as Rimbaud said of Baudelaire, he is he through whom the new forces of nature find a voice: '. . . Le poète, placé sur un des points de la circonférence de l'humanité, renvoie sur la même ligne en vibrations plus mélodieuses la pensée humaine qui lui fut transmise; tout poète véritable doit être une incarnation.'[63]

We can now see how Baudelaire is in fact salvaging the values of Romanticism by reversing or apparently denying them. The focus for this can be provided by Poe's contention that a long poem is a contradiction in terms, that only the short poem is a 'viable' lyric enterprise. Northrop Frye comments that this is a profoundly *anti-Romantic statement*. If this is true, and there are strong reasons for thinking that it is, since we have seen that organic continuity (dialectical or otherwise) was a characteristic feature of Romanticism, it places quite precisely Baudelaire's relation to it. *Les Fleurs du Mal* and *Le Spleen de Paris* are made up of short poems for reasons that would have been germane to Poe. But both constitute, through the interaction of these short poems, a long poem. The overall pattern remains Romantic in direction, but its Romanticism has little to do in its movement with previous forms of Romanticism.

It remains for us to question whether the sense of form as dialectical, at which we have arrived, is tenable. It is an important question, for our contention that Baudelaire is *the* modern poet through whom we gain an immediately relevant access to Romantic values, stands or falls by the answer to it.

The attack would come from Lukács. He does recognise that there are, in the Romantic and post-Romantic period, attempts to create 'a concrete totality that springs from a conception of form orientated towards the concrete content of its material substratum'.[64] In other words, attempts to effect, on an aesthetic level, the reconciliation that turns out to be impossible in reality. He pays homage to the 'magnitude of the enterprise' to build aesthetics into a life-saving principle in Fichte, Schiller and Hegel – in Schiller especially, whom he shows as pointing to the principle 'whereby *man having been socially destroyed, fragmented and divided between different partial systems is to be made whole again in thought*'.[65] But he claims that such enterprises are doomed to failure, that in the aesthetic mode, the contents of life can only be 'salvaged from the deadening effects of the mechanism of reification' '*in so far* as these contents become aesthetic'. And this he sees as an evasion of the 'real problem' and 'just another way in which to make the subject purely contemplative and to annihilate "action"'.[66]

In our enquiry into Baudelaire, we have been increasingly led to see the 'form' of *Les Fleurs du Mal* as both what 'incarnates' a fragmented and reified society, and what finds ways of transcending it. So that if that transcendence can be written off as pure 'contemplation' or evasion from reality, the ground vanishes under our feet.

It does not. The terms in which Lukács confronts 'form' and 'content' are not those which we have found to be operative. It was while we were trying to understand the 'contents' of the word 'nature' that we found ourselves continually directed towards 'form' as the only substantial answer. Lukács is arguing as though the two could be apprehended in a state of separation, and as though the way consciousness behaves towards language were not deeply analogous with the way a man behaves towards the world of praxis. This is what we must now enquire into, to be in a position to view with completeness what Baudelaire is doing in his poetry.

One must also reply to Lukács that although some of Baudelaire's spiritual heirs, Rimbaud notably, will attempt to make poetry no longer only 'ce qui rhythme l'action', but what is 'en avant', ahead of it, poetry nonetheless remains distinct from the material conditions out of which it springs. The ways in which 'Verbum' can be translated as 'Deed' (as Faust ultimately tries), hover around a mystery which involves the whole man. This mystery has to do with transubtantiation. In the domain of language, 'action' is not an exhortation to act, but describes the power of the verb to become yeast, or flesh.

B. Consciousness

> The antitheses which used to be expressed in terms of mind and matter, body and soul, faith and reason, freedom and necessity, etc. . . . became transformed as culture advanced into contrasts between reason and the senses, intelligence and nature, and in its most general form, between absolute subjectivity and absolute objectivity. To transcend such ossified antitheses is the sole concern of reason.
> Hegel[1]

It might have seemed to Hegel the sole concern of reason in that it loomed as its supreme task. But philosophy was not alone in being concerned with such transcendences. Romantic poetry is most distinctively involved, as many contemporary critics of Romanticism argue,[2] in attempts to bridge the gap between subject and object, consciousness and nature. To understand the dynamics of Baudelaire's own version of consciousness, to fathom how he tries in his turn to reconcile 'absolute subjectivity' and 'absolute objectivity', it is necessary once again to see how his Romantic predecessors dealt with the issue.

5 Reverie

I

The state of mind which effects to perfection a reconciliation of consciousness and nature is one to which Rousseau's writings gave vital status: reverie. In that state, as the author of the *Rêveries d'un promeneur solitaire* describes it, the ideal oneness of childhood days is brought back, the curse of the self's social and physical separateness is obliterated. Contemplating the movement of the waves on the lake of l'Ile Saint-Pierre, Rousseau surrenders his consciousness to the rhythms and spectacle of the natural world, and finds himself again through that very surrender:

> . . . là, le bruit des vagues et l'agitation de l'eau fixant mes sens et chassant de mon ame toute autre agitation la plongeoient dans une réverie delicieuse . . . Le flux et reflux de cette eau, son bruit continu mais renflé par intervalles frappant sans relache mon oreille et mes yeux suppléoient aux mouvements internes que la rêverie éteignoit en moi, et suffisoient pour me faire sentir avec plaisir mon existence, sans prendre la peine de penser . . .
> . . . s'il est un état où l'ame trouve une assiete assez solide pour s'y reposer tout entiére . . . où le tems ne soit rien pour elle . . . sans aucun autre sentiment . . . que celui seul de notre existence . . .; tant que cet état dure celui qui s'y trouve peut s'appeller heureux . . . d'un bonheur suffisant, parfait et plein . . .[3]

The state which for Rousseau has much regenerative power is most interesting in that the physical situation which gives it birth – a man idly contemplating the movement of the waves on a lake from the *bank* is a perfect emblem of the equipoise which it brings about. It could be seen as a perfect model of the democracy Rousseau is dreaming of, and which the French Revolution is going to pursue. The text is written in prose: but it is more musical than a great deal of verse, certainly than the French verse being written at the time. The language flows with great simplicity. But the terms which it carries along, terms such as 'azyle caché' which comes straight from seventeenth-century poetic diction, have a complicated cultural history. That is, a whole tradition is being integrated and transformed in the process, being shifted from an aristocratic to an equalitarian world. Astride poetry and prose, tradition and modernity, socially inherited values and the plainness of 'nature', the passage also inhabits the borders of consciousness and reality. Rousseau is on the edge of the water, *between* water and land, his eyes level with what he contemplates. The '*cogito* du rêveur'[4] which results from the contemplation of the waves makes nature the source of the feeling of existence, unlike Descartes's *cogito* which in its very formulation posited the alienness of mind and nature.

Also, Rousseau's 'sentiment précieux de contentement et de paix', retains the fullness and the overtones of mystical experience, especially of Fénelon's quietism. But again, the sentiment is attained not through ascesis, not through abstraction from reality, but through a complete exposure to it. And yet some mental discipline is required to reach the state, one in which a perfect balance is struck between consciousness and reality. For consciousness is spontaneously torn between evanescence and stance. Its mobility is both a response to, and the human form of, the temporality of all things: 'Tout est dans un flux continuel sur la terre: rien n'y garde une forme constante et arrêtée, et nos affections qui s'attachent aux choses extérieures passent et changent necessairement comme elles.' But his mobility is also a source of disharmony: the pace of consciousness never fits the pace of life: 'Toujours en avant ou en arriére de nous, elles rapellent le passé qui n'est plus ou previennent l'avenir qui souvent ne doit point être . . .' It is true that the rhythm by means of which Rousseau voices this disharmony is dictated by the remembered flow of the waves: 'Le flux et reflux de cette eau, son bruit continu mais renflé par intervalles frappant sans relache . . .' suggesting that in the rhythm of their occurrence, human emotions are better adjusted to the external world than in their substance. But this is because the lulling atmosphere of the reverie pervades Rousseau's thinking here, as he said once that the peaceful blue shade of the room in which he wrote *L'Emile* gave the book its serenity; not because he has become reconciled to the disharmony.

In fact, his life-long failure to find a satisfactory occupation, a peaceful dwelling-place, to establish a stable relationship, bears testimony to the deep conviction of what follows: '. . . il n'y a rien là de solide à quoi le coeur se puisse attacher. Aussi n'a-t-on guère ici-bas que du plaisir qui passe; pour le bonheur qui dure je doute qu'il y soit connu . . .' But 'branle', to use Montaigne's word, is not only in things. It is also in us. Even when happiness is willing to stay, we are not; when time is prepared to 'suspendre son vol', consciousness is not. We are dissatisfied because pleasure will not last; but we are also dissatisfied because even when it might, it fulfils us so little that we wish time to move on:

> A peine est-il dans nos plus vives jouissances un instant où le coeur puisse véritablement nous dire: *je voudrois que cet instant durât toujours*; et comment peut-on appeller bonheur un état fugitif qui nous laisse encor le coeur inquiet et vuide, qui nous fait regreter quelque chose avant, ou desirer encor quelque chose après?

A paradox is here at work. For here, exploring the disjunction of mind and nature, Rousseau is in fact showing them to be akin: since there is no better vehicle for conveying the movements of consciousness than the to and fro of the waves on the lake. The 'thinking' of the second paragraph has its solution in the reverie of the first:

> Le flux et reflux/de cette eau,/son bruit continu mais renflé par intervalles/frappant sans relache mon oreille et mes yeux/suppléoient aux movemens internes que la rêverie éteignait en moi/et suffisait pour me faire sentir avec plaisir mon existence,/sans prendre la peine de penser.

The prose here never wanders far from itself, but it never stops. Its flow is ever balanced by a gentle, steadying ebb. The piece creates a state, not of circularity, but of poise born out of the counter-movements. But this state is exactly that of consciousness, now thwarted by the fleetingness of time, now wishing it to move on. Only, in life, these counter-movements are a continuous source of misery. In reverie they create balance. It is this balance which Rousseau offers as a solution to the restlessness and isolation of living.

Consciousness, saturated and lulled by its object, loses its reflexiveness. It is no longer disruptive, maladjusted. By tasting of the tree of knowledge, the first man and woman, instead of becoming like Gods, acquired reflexive consciousness. They saw that they were naked, they discovered themselves to be separate from nature, perceivable by somebody else. In Rousseau's childhood experience, as we saw in an earlier chapter, there is a re-enactment of the first sin in the discovery of social injustice, which estranges him for a long time from nature. This is why reverie for him assumes such significance. It re-immerses his consciousness in nature. It frees him from the bondage of society. He thus becomes truly like a God: 'on se suffit à soi-même, comme Dieu'. The world outside now gives him his identity. He is the source of that world and that world creates his consciousness; becomes his consciousness. And the prose which conveys that experience, like the mind, like nature, remains inspired throughout by the initial 'flux et reflux': internal and primary like some slow motion beat of blood in the arteries.

The bliss of Rousseau's reverie is close to Wordsworth's 'serene and blessed mood':

> In which the burthen of the mystery,
> In which the heavy and the weary weight
> Of all this unintelligible world
> Is lightened.[5]

The state is more ambitious in Wordsworth, and carries larger implications. All that Rousseau asks is to feel at one with the world. Not so Wordsworth: the 'affections gently *lead us on*' in the state, towards the 'sublime gift' of seeing 'into the life of things'. Reverie for him is a form of insight, of man, by/into nature, of nature by/into man. The phrase from 'Tintern Abbey', 'both what they half create/ And what perceive', beautifully expresses this reciprocity of action, and echoes, on a mature level, the 'creator and receiver both' the child will be described as in the *Prelude*.

But already in Coleridge, contemplative states become ambiguous. 'Frost at Midnight' is a reverie strongly reminiscent, in its texture and vocabulary, of Rousseau's and Wordsworth's. But the 'correspondence' between mind and nature implies some fundamental separation between them. Rousseau's nature restored man to a true sense of himself: 'On se souvient de soi en oubliant tous ses maux'; in Wordsworth, the deeper spirit was being freed from the 'despotism' of the 'eye': 'We are laid asleep/ In body and become a living soul.' But Coleridge shows a sophisticated sense of the arbitrariness of the connection which is being brought about. 'Thought' may be, as in Rousseau and Wordsworth, dispelled by reverie. But intellect remains, as a form of subtle division. Sitting at night in his cottage in front of the fire, he is captivated by the 'film' that 'flutters in the grate':

> *Methinks*, its motion in this hush of nature
> Gives it dim sympathies with me who live,
> Making it a companionable form
> Whose puny flaps and freaks the idling Spirit
> By its own moods *interprets* . . .

As he goes on:

> . . . everywhere
> Echo or mirror seeking of itself –
> And makes a toy of Thought . . .[6]

he seems to manifest scepticism as to the value of reverie for an educated consciousness. Is reverie, which was supposed to open you up to the world, a subtle form of narcissism? It is certainly striking to contrast the irony, or reservation, of words like 'echo' and 'mirror', with Wordsworth's confidence that communing with nature brings about, not a monologue with one's own image, but a dialogue with an actual partner. Thus the Boy of Winander

> Blew *mimic* hootings to the silent owls
> That they might answer him . . .

That is, he tries to converse with nature by setting up an echo for it. Doing so, he puts himself in an attitude of openness which makes him intensely aware of the place he is in. He is educated both into a sense of reality and a recognition of the gap there is between his expectation and reality:

> And when it chanced
> That pauses of deep silence mocked his skill,
> Then sometimes, in that silence, while he hung
> Listening, a gentle shock of mild surprise
> Has carried far into his heart the voice
> Of mountain torrents . . .[7]

The void of vacancy, or availability, is created by the run-on-line: 'while he hung/Listening'. It has the superbly paradoxical quality of communicating a sense of power rather than a sense of suspense. It implicitly convinces that the growth into awareness that is being shown is not a privilege of childhood, but a gift that expands in the adult man into poetic power. But Coleridge's aim is more modest. What he demands from reverie is akin to Rousseau's '*cogito* du rêveur'. That 'le sentiment de l'existence', that is, should be given to him not through thinking, but through dreaming, or rather through being dreamt by the world of sense.

But Coleridge's 'I AM' has, unlike Rousseau's, a strange admixture of consciousness. 'Only in the self-consciousness of a spirit is there the required identity of objects and representation; for herein consists the essence of truth, that it is a self-representative'[8] says Thesis VII in *Biographia*. The 'idling Spirit' is indeed asserting its essence when it seeks the 'echo' or 'mirror' of itself in the vagaries of the smoke. Such a mode of self-consciousness is not 'intellectual', but emotional: 'By deep feeling we make our Ideas dim', Coleridge says, commenting on the lines from 'Tintern Abbey':

> . . . and the deep power of Joy
> We see into the life of Things . . .

adding that it is the occurrence of this which he calls 'I . . . identifying the Percipient and the Perceived'.

Even so, there is little doubt that this 'I AM', itself a form of the universal 'I AM' – that this kind of 'pantheism', more modest and philosophical than Wordsworth's – is not one which Coleridge experiences often or feels very confident about. He has inklings of it: '. . . I seem to myself to behold in the quiet objects on which I am gazing, more than arbitrary illustration, more than a mere *simile*, the work of my own fancy. I feel an awe, as if there was before my eyes the same power as that of reason . . .'[9] But more frequently and worryingly, he feels that perhaps after all it is his own fancy that is being projected on to the world: 'In looking at objects of nature while I am thinking, as at yonder moon, dim-glimmering through the window-pane, I seem rather to be seeking, as it were asking, a symbolical language for something within me, that already and forever exists, than observing anything new . . .'[10] Trust that the world outside can reflect 'in a lower dignity' the power within man, and therefore be as 'a symbol established in the truth of things' thus rests upon the occurrence of a particular state of mind. When that deserts the poet, he is left to the 'tyranny of the eye'. As in the 'Dejection Ode', which explores metaphorical impotency. Gazing to the 'peculiar tint of yellow green' of the sky, and the 'thin clouds above', the poet realises:

> I see them all so excellently fair,
> I see, not feel, how beautiful they are!
>
>> My genial spirits fail;
>> And what can these avail
> To lift the smothering weight from off my breast?
>> It were a vain endeavour
>> Though I should gaze forever
> On that green light that lingers in the west:
> I may not hope from outward forms to win
> The passion and the life, whose fountains are within.[11]

This would be inconceivable in Wordsworth, for whom Nature is always there, ready to welcome and heal him, after time at the university, after the harassment of politics. As Coleridge suggests, he inhabits that 'intermedium' of superior spirits, in which susceptibility to the outside world remains ever vibrant. This may be due to the extraordinary power of his own 'feeling of existence', which at times is so overwhelming as to question the existence of everything else: 'There was a time in my life when I had to push against something that resisted, to be sure that there was anything outside me. I was sure of my own mind; everything else fell away, and vanished into thought.'[12] That mind feels its power so intensely that it does not only have to convince itself of the existence of the outside world by pushing against it, or clasping it. It also believes that its power is a genuine alternative to the material world: 'Archimedes said that he could move the world if he had a point where to rest his machine. Who has not felt the same aspirations as regards the world of his own mind?'[13] As a result, solitude, 'differentiated existence', as John Jones puts it, 'is embraced by Wordsworth as the source of enlightenment and strength.'[14]

But Coleridge does not possess that almost physical power of mind which characterises Wordsworth. His mind seems to be antagonistic to nature, rather than some sort of equivalent to it. He has more capacity for abstraction than Wordsworth: 'The further I ascend from animated Nature . . . the greater becomes in me the intensity of the feeling of life'.[15] But this superiority turns out to be a curse, given the needs and pressures Coleridge labours under. His vulnerability is infinite, and solitude, which confirms Wordsworth's strength, destroys him: 'To become intensely and wholly conscious of (one's) distinctness' is 'to be betrayed into the wretchedness of *division*'.[16] Involved in his relation to nature is his hold upon his own identity. This, as we shall see, is the heart of the problem.

The only form of self-consciousness which does not betray into this state of division is one that is so expansive that it can assert the presence of a power outside itself in the very act of asserting its own power. Coleridge calls that expansiveness 'joy'. But it does not spring, as in Wordsworth, from the interaction of the self and nature. To 'both what we half create/And what perceive', Coleridge replies with a 'We receive but what we give'. Sources of power come wholly from inside:

> Ah! from the soul itself must issue forth
> A light, a glory, a fair luminous cloud
>   Enveloping the Earth – . . .
>
> Joy, virtuous lady! Joy that ne'er was given
> Save to the pure, and in their purest hour,
>   Life, and Life's effluence, cloud at once and shower . . .[17]

Because Joy is thus associated with innocence, darkness, when it comes to Coleridge, far from being a 'visiting' of 'awful promise' 'where greatness makes abode', as in the *Prelude*, destroys the soul. It is perhaps in this that lies the greatest difference between his 'Dejection Ode' and Wordsworth's 'Immortality Ode'. For Wordsworth, it is the very moments of darkness which troubled the joy of childhood which retrospectively, through growth into experience, and encounter with death, become the mainspring of a new joy. Their mystery is recognised, and in this recognition the quality of childhood, the glory, the dream, are recaptured:

> Not for these I raise
> The song of thanks and praise;
> But for those obstinate questionings
> Of sense and outward things,
> Fallings from us, vanishings . . .
>   . . . for those . . .
>   . . . shadowy recollections,
> Which, be they what they may,
> Are yet the fountain-light of all our day,
> Are yet a master-light of all our seeing;[18]

But Wordsworth's 'fountain light', springing, as the image suggests, from the core of things, is for Coleridge something dangerously peripheral, a veil of illusion which once dispelled cannot be again pieced out of the air: 'a fair luminous cloud/Enveloping the Earth', as he describes it. It transfigures a world otherwise 'dark and drear':

> We in ourselves rejoice!
> And thence flows all that charms or ear or sight,
> All melodies the echoes of that voice,
> All colours a suffusion from that light.

Indeed, because Innocence is the state in which this joy blossoms, it is for Coleridge powerfully associated to the moments of blissful reverie which he at times experiences. 'Frost at Midnight' is set in an atmosphere generated by the 'peaceful slumber' of a 'cradled infant'. And felicity, in this beautiful extract from the *Notebooks*, is achieved through a return to the infant state:

> ... and Time drew out his subtle
> Thread so quick, That the long
> Summer's Eve was one whole web,
> A Space on which I lay commensurate –
> For Memory and all undoubting Hope
> Sang the same note and in the selfsame
> Voice, with each sweet *now* of
> My Felicity, and blended momently,
> Like Milk that coming comes and in its
> easy stream Flows ever in, upon the
> mingling milk, in the Babe's murmuring
> Mouth/or mirrors each reflecting each/ –[19]

Time here has become such perfect duration that it is spatialised into a 'web': and 'Memory and Hope' are 'singing' the selfsame note 'as each sweet *now*', as they did in Rousseau's reverie, in which the soul had no need 'de rappeler le passé ni d'enjamber sur l'avenir', and in which the 'present' lasted forever 'sans néamoins marquer sa durée'. And as in Rousseau, it is the internal beat of life, the flowing of milk or the pulsing of blood, which expresses the bliss of the state.

II

Baudelaire in many ways belongs to the 'Romantic' tradition we have just attempted to sketch. His sense that the child's joy is a 'joie de plante' is close to Coleridge's and to Wordsworth's vision of infant joy, as is his belief that in the innocent stages of life man is gifted with an imaginative power which 'reinvents' and 'spiritualises' a fallen world.

But the gap between consciousness and reality which begins to open in Coleridge becomes larger in Baudelaire. For him as for the author of *The Ancient Mariner*, once the 'unity' of joy has fallen into the duality of laughter, once, through a speedy and casual gesture, or simply through growth into awareness, one has killed one's albatross, there is no going back. There is even less going back than in Coleridge: apparently, the only way to regain the childish power of vision is through drugs. Practically all the reveries one finds in Baudelaire take place under the sign of opium, or hashish: when under their spell '. . . . Il arrive . . . que la personnalité disparaît et que l'objectivité, qui est le propre des poëtes panthéistes, se développe en vous si anormalement, que la contemplation des objets extérieurs vous fait oublier votre propre existence, et que vous vous confondez bientôt avec eux . . .;[20]

The fusion that occurs in the hashish state seems to reproduce the in-flowing of reverie. But to Baudelaire this is a degraded state of feeling. There is a distance between the dreamer and 'l'arbre harmonieux courbé par le vent' on which his gaze fastens; a distance which he bridges through a sham: 'Vous prêtez . . . à l'arbre vos passions, vos désirs ou votre mélancolie'. This 'lending' is an exacerbated form of Coleridge's spirit 'interpreting' 'by its own moods'. But in Coleridge, a gentle irony hovered above the reverie, keeping it poised. Here there is no balance, but a see-saw of reciprocal absorption: you project yourself on to the tree; then the tree, in its turn, absorbs you: 'Bientôt vous êtes l'arbre'.

Similarly, if you watch the blue clouds from your pipe,

> L'idée d'une évaporation lente, successive, éternelle, s'emparera de votre esprit, et vous appliquerez bientôt cette idée à vos propres pensées, à votre matière pensante . . . par une espèce de . . . quiproquo intellectuel, vous vous sentirez vous évaporant, et vous attribuerez à votre pipe . . . l'étrange faculté de *vous fumer.*

Having divested the outside world of its power to challenge you by making it an 'image' of your emotions, you then divest yourself of the responsibility of feeling by letting yourself be felt by the outside world. In Rousseau, 'on se souvenait de soi' through awareness of nature; but Baudelaire's dreamer erases the *cogito* altogether: under the influence of hashish, he *forgets* his existence in the contemplation of the object.

Thus what was a reciprocal giving of identity becomes a mutual destruction of identity.

This perception is the source of Baudelaire's deep understanding of the 'atmosphère' which *'trempe'* Poe's *The Fall of the House of Usher*, in which people, things and names forget their existence in the contemplation of their own image. The whole tale could be read as a symbol of the way in which 'internal landscapes' are going to vampirise the consciousness of some Symbolist poets. A perfect example of this might be one of Verlaine's 'Ariettes Oubliées':

> L'ombre des arbres sur la rivière embrumée
> Meurt comme de la fumée
> Tandis que tristes dans les ramures réelles
> Se plaignent les tourterelles.
>
> Combien ô voyageur ce paysage blême
> Te mira blême toi-même
> Lorsque tristes pleuraient dans les hautes feuillées
> Tes espérances noyées.[21]

At this stage all forms of existence melt into one another. Hope is already drowned in the river as are the turtle-doves singing in the trees; the shapes of the trees mirrored by the river are in turn sucked up by the mist. Everything, animals, trees, rivers, feelings, singing voice, vanish up into some new form of impalpable chaos, a damp white tearful mist, which in turn fades into the whiteness of the page, the silence in which nothing but an impression hangs, a scent, a vague sadness, musical notes gently vibrating on the internal ear after the tune has stopped. But the exquisite charm of such poetry must not conceal its lack of blood. One measures it by realising that the solid felicity of Coleridge's each 'sweet *now*' has worn to the melancholy thinness of mist.

Reveries in Baudelaire never carry the metaphysical weight they have in the early Romantics. Indeed, he goes out of his way sometimes to stress the unsubstantiality of the state. There is a poem called 'La Pipe' in *Les Fleurs du Mal* which revolves round the final example of 'objectivité' given in the passage on hashish. It is spoken by the pipe:

> J'enlace et je berce son âme
> Dans le réseau mobile et bleu
> Qui monte de ma bouche en feu,

> Et je roule un puissant dictame
> Qui charme son coeur et guérit
> De ses fatigues son esprit.[22]

Consciousness here has transferred its responsibility to the world. The state is a solace, a vacation: it cures the mind of its cares, not by recalling it to a better sense of its powers, but by inducing oblivion. It relieves man both of his 'I' and of the need to relate himself to the world. It is nearly an inversion of Coleridge's 'I AM'. 'I smoke my pipe' becomes 'my pipe smokes me'. The dream delivers the dreamer from his identity.

The significance of 'La Pipe' is made clear by the situation it occupies in the section 'Spleen et Idéal' – and here for the first time we find that we are able to tally the meaning of the positions of the poems with some chance of success. 'La Pipe' is one of the analogical poems which precede the great autumnal cycle of 'Spleen', through which, little by little, despair prevails. The context shows what a tenuous bulwark its 'reverie' is. Furthermore – and this is crucial – the link between mind and nature which this reverie creates and which abolishes identities, (does away with 'comme',) is set in perspective by other modes of connection. In 'Les Hiboux', the preceding poem, a *mind* is at work, drawing analogies and lessons from the contemplation of the owls. In 'La Musique', which follows 'La Pipe', the poet's surrender to music is a sensitive response to a recognisable reality. It seems to open on the same transference of subject to object as 'La Pipe': 'La Musique souvent me prend comme une mer!' But this does not free the subject from his 'je'. He continues to be the bearer and agent of his own states: 'Je mets à la voile'. And consciousness remains aware that it is its self which is effecting the connections. Coleridge's word occurs to indicate this:

> D'autres fois, calme plat, grand *miroir*
> De mon désespoir![23]

Even the image of a ship sailing *on* the sea to represent the poet sailing on music registers their separateness. There can be no doubt as to the superiority of the state offered in 'La Musique' to that explored in 'La Pipe'. But 'La Musique' involves 'mind', intellect, which Rousseau and Coleridge had found necessary to lull to sleep before reverie could occur.

And indeed when reverie proper occurs in Baudelaire, it excludes intellect. The harmony which it achieves is not, as in Wordsworth, a synthesis, but a blurring. This is striking in 'Harmonie du soir', on which J. P. Richard delicately comments: 'Dans le rythme noyant du *pantoum* toutes les distinctions s'effacent, toutes les qualités s'échangent, les divers mouvements se télescopent, le monde s'égare; mais cet égarement s'achève en cauchemar: l'âme tendre redoute "un néant vaste et noir", et le soleil "se noie dans son sang qui se fige"';[24] and in the opium reverie of 'La Chambre Double':

> Une chambre qui ressemble à une rêverie, une chambre véritablement *spirituelle*, où l'atmosphère stagnante est légèrement teintée de rose et de bleu.
> L'âme y prend un bain de paresse, aromatisé par le regret et le désir. -C'est quelque chose de crépusculaire, de bleuâtre et de rosâtre; un rêve de volupté pendant une éclipse.
> Les meubles ont des formes allongées, prostrées, alanguies. Les meubles ont l'air de rêver; on les dirait doués d'une vie somnambulique, comme le végétal et le minéral . . .
> . . . Ici tout a la suffisante clarté et la délicieuse obscurité de l'harmonie.
>
> Une senteur infinitésimale du choix le plus exquis, à laquelle se mêle une très-légère humidité, nage dans cette atmosphère, où *l'esprit sommeillant est bercé* par des sensations de serre-chaude.[25]

There reigns here a vocabulary of half-shades, half-meanings: 'stagnantes, teintée, aromatisé, crépusculaire, senteur infinitésimale, très-légère humidité . . .' Reverie in Wordsworth was a state of exhilarating vigour, marked by the virile beat of the lines. In 'La Chambre Double' it becomes bloodless, spineless: 'Les meubles ont des formes allongées, prostrées, alanguies . . .' A man in bed is speaking in a hushed voice, with short breath. In Rousseau, in Wordsworth, reverie took place out of doors, in the fresh air; here it is in a closed room, in an atmosphere of 'serre chaude'. 'Spirituelle', which means 'dream-like', 'mind-like', is but a parody of the Wordsworthian equation between 'spirit' and 'life'. Also, for Wordsworth harmony was light, power. In 'La Chambre double' it is defined by its 'délicieuse obscurité'. What it produces is a fainting form of epicureanism: it has a 'suffisante clarté', it is born out of a twilight world in which consciousness has been lulled to sleep. That word 'suffisant', in Rousseau, entailed a confident grasp on the world: 'Un bonheur suffisant, parfait et plein, qui ne laisse dans l'âme aucun vide qu'elle sente le besoin de remplir'. In Baudelaire, 'suffisant' means: not too much. It would hurt my eyes. I could not bear it. This is Des Esseintes's bedroom.

Philosophically speaking, reverie is also degraded. 'Regret' and 'désir' in Rousseau were shown as plaguing a full enjoyment of the present: 'Et comment peut-on appeler bonheur un état fugitif qui nous laisse encore le coeur inquiet et vide, qui nous fait regretter quelque chose avant, ou désirer encore quelque chose après?' One of the merits of reverie, for him, is that it obliterated both regret and desire, that it induced a stable capacity to live here and now and be fulfilled by it. In 'La Chambre double', regret and desire have become ingredients of the delight; as through some highly sophisticated spicing that involves the interplay of all the senses, and regards feelings too as senses – and what a long way we've come from Wordsworth!: 'L'âme y prend un bain de paresse, aromatisé par le regret et le désir . . .'

What catastrophe has shrunk the vast expanses of the Pays de Vaud, of the Lake District and the French Alps, to the cramped hothouse of a crepuscular bedroom? Something happens in the course of the century which turns into a forced and self-conscious activity a state whose moral and philosophical potential seemed infinite in Wordsworth and Rousseau. Following the evolution of the state, one is filled with a sensation of *fall* – which re-enacts, on another level, that which we experienced while tracing Baudelaire's response to politics.

6 'Auras'

What is thus lost may seem negligible, the mere failing of a poetic indulgence in landscape-gazing, until the implications of the state of reverie are seen in full.

For it carries with it, to return to Hegel's words, the possibility of a reconciliation between subject and object. Lived at a highly 'poetic' level, it stands for the possibility of organic wholeness. What the poets experience is the crisis of identity of two generations of men, spread to all levels of society.

The desirability of 'le sentiment de l'existence' is best felt when it is no longer possible to experience the state. Flaubert used to complain of his lack of 'innéité' – by which he meant that he found no consistent and stable centre in his life. Baudelaire too, as Du Bos brilliantly perceived, measuring him by Pascal's claim that true greatness lies in touching both extremities at once and filling at the same time all the in-between space, 'tout l'entredeux', is a man who, while crucified between the two extremities, has no 'entre-deux' no 'innéité'. He is a man devoid of that fullness and confidence of being which makes Wordsworth want to clasp a tree to encounter a solidity equal to that of his own mind, and which alone makes existence a self-justifying process.

What is so important about 'innéité is that in turns it seems to have the power to endow the rest of the world with 'innéité' too. Rousseau's lake, Wordsworth's landscapes, seem to possess it by right, and through some sort of reciprocity, to give it back to the beholder who has perceived it in them. Both kinds of 'innéités' mutually confirm and enrich each other because each radiates towards the outside, because they are, as it were, 'fountain lights'. Walter Benjamin calls this radiating power 'auras': '"Perceptibility", as Novalis puts it, "is a kind of attentiveness" . . . To perceive the aura of an object we look at means to invest it with the ability to look at us in return'.[1] Here is, sharply put, an account of what happens in the Boy of Winander passage which we discussed a little earlier on.

It is important to relate this notion of 'aura', expanding it, perhaps, beyond what Benjamin would have wished, to that of a compact, charged centre: as in the mediaeval mataphysics of light, in which auras emanate from an intense fire, which is essence itself. In such a vision, an aura becomes something like the *meaning* of a thing made manifest. And that meaning is not an interpretation, but what can be seen of the diffused centre – since one cannot penetrate into the strangeness of other centres without losing one's identity or destroying theirs. But if what one perceives of them is the heat or light which they radiate, then it is truly them with which our 'meaning', our perceptions or our language, make contact. Embedded, that is, in the notion of 'auras' is that of the knowability of the world – of its continuity with man's mind.

And poetry which manifests that continuity, which becomes a form of it, is knowledge of the highest kind:

> Visionary power
> Attends upon the motions of the winds
> Embodied in the mystery of words.
> There darkness makes abode . . .
> Even forms and substances are circumfus'd
> By that transparent veil with light divine;
> And through the turnings intricate of Verse,
> Present themselves as objects recognis'd
> In flashes, and with a glory scarce their own.[2]

Through the *Prelude*, Wordsworth develops the most intricate and precise vocabulary of vagueness to make perceptible the aura of things, thus revealing the continuity of man and Nature. He learns to love his 'Fellow-beings' through seeing them appear (one could say, become materialised), through such mists and haloes as these:

> It was a day of exhalations, spread
> Upon the mountains, mists and steam-like fogs
> Rebounding everywhere, not vehement,
> But calm and mild . . .
>   . . . aloft above my head,
> Emerging from the silvery vapours, lo!
> A Shepherd and his Dog! in open day:
> Girt round with mists they stood and look'd about
> From that enclosure small, inhabitants
> Of an aerial Island floating on,
> As seem'd . . .
> By the soft wind breath'd forward.[3]

It is as though the quality of the mist 'calm and mild, gentle and beautiful', as later the quality of the light, the 'liquid gold irradiate' by which the 'setting sun proclaims the love he bears/To mountain regions', dictated to the poet the kind of love he must bear his fellow-men, or rather were the visible embodiment of what it must be – and, as it is recognised (since it is perceived and written), already brought it into existence.

Those auras reveal the immanence of the Eden which each man is naturally born into, and which is most manifest in the early stages of existence:

> Not in entire forgetfulness
> And not in utter nakedness
> But trailing clouds of glory do we come . . .[4]

The infant here is seen as pure soul, pure Godliness – hence his absolute luminosity: as though his complete potentiality made him as receptive and malleable as the uncreated earth at the moment of creation, or as Imagination in the process of being discovered:

> Thou, over whom thy Immortality
> Broods like the Day, A Master o'er a Slave,
> A Presence which is not to be put by . . .[5]

In this perspective, at the start at least, living becomes being gradually shorn of one's aura, losing one's incandescence, like cooling lava:

> Full soon thy Soul shall have her earthly freight,
> And custom lie upon thee with a weight,
> Heavy as frost, and deep almost as life![6]

The frost of custom is neither so heavy nor so numbing as the frozen mound of slain under which the speaker of Baudelaire's 'La Cloche fêlée' is slowly being smothered, but it contains premonitions of the same danger:

> Moi, mon âme est fêlée, et lorsqu'en ses ennuis
> Elle veut de ses chants peupler l'air froid des nuits,
> Il arrive souvent que sa voix affaiblie

> Semble le râle épais d'un blessé qu'on oublie
> Au bord d'un lac de sang, sous un grand tas de morts,
> Et qui meurt, sans bouger, dans d'immense efforts.[7]

By combining a sense of split (the soul *cracked* like a bell, uttering a broken sound) with the image of smothering, Baudelaire makes explicit and carries to its extreme a realisation which in Wordsworth is implied at a complex subterranean level: that the loss of aura is also the loss of oneness, of the continuity between inside and outside. Which is why the rediscovery of that continuity through watchfulness, then Imagination, is so vital.

Like the 'Immortality Ode', *Les Fleurs du Mal*, in their early phase, invoke an Edenic stage of luminosity. The interplay of light and darkness which depth and distance make one in 'Correspondances' is the collective form that the aura assumes:

> Comme de longs échos qui de loin se confondent
> Dans une ténébreuse et profonde unité,
> Vaste comme la nuit et comme la clarté,
> Les parfums, les couleurs et les sons se répondent.[8]

The 'grands piliers, droits et majestueux' which make the 'vastes portiques' of 'La Vie antérieure' similar to caves of basalt, reflect, on the level of an individual subconscious, the 'vivants piliers' of 'Correspondances', with their 'temple' or cathedral suggestion. In the dream of 'La Vie antérieure', the synaesthesia of all the senses is conveyed through a musical aura:

> Les houles, en roulant les images des cieux,
> Mêlaient d'une façon solennelle et mystique
> Les tout-puissants accords de leur riche musique
> Aux couleurs du couchant reflété par mes yeux.[9]

These two poems play a joint role in *Les Fleurs du Mal* in that the atmosphere which bathes them represents an ideally significant world. It represents, that is, a state of perfect continuity between the sensuous and the spiritual, a little in the way in which the 'liquid gold irradiate' in Wordsworth's contemplation of a shepherd, represents the 'love' which the setting sun bears to mountain regions. Walter Benjamin argues that 'the *correspondances* are the data of remembrance – not historical data, but data of prehistory'.[10] 'La Vie antérieure' can definitely be read as this. But Benjamin's interpretation of 'Correspondances' as the working of a Proustian 'mémoire involontaire', although it gives rise to some marvellous ideas,[11] is belied by the strong present tense of the poem. 'La Nature est un temple' is a clean statement of faith, not the exploration of a rediscovered luminosity of perception, nor relish for the depth of a suddenly palpable past. The poem affirms the unity of nature, and its whole movement posits that art is what makes that unity, through correspondences, permanently possible. 'La Vie antérieure' pursues this on the individual level. The private subconscious echoes the collective unconscious at work in the discovery of correspondences, but through a compound past which, though recreating the ideal oneness, ambiguously declares it lost: 'J'ai longtemps habité . . . C'est là que j'ai vécu . . . '. There is an ebbing of ambition and hope from one poem to another.

What Benjamin calls 'aura' would, in our opinion, be more properly applied to the veiled interregnum, the misty or luminous meeting-ground between consciousness and nature, than to the 'power of remembrance', in Baudelaire.[12] One could nearly say that its 'inbetween' quality, half-air, half-light, as a mist is half-air, half-water, implicitly represents the reconciliation of different elements. There is indeed a complex search for edges in the nineteenth century and after, which is one of the forms which the crisis of knowledge assumes. Cézanne could thus be given as an important example. Merleau-Ponty describes him as obsessed with the contours of objects:

> Ne marquer aucun contour, ce serait enlever aux objets leur identité. En marquer un seul, ce serait sacrifier la profondeur,* c'est-à-dire la dimension qui nous donne la chose, non comme étalée devant nous, mais comme pleine de réserves et comme une réalite inépuisable. C'est pourquoi Cézanne suivra dans la modulation colorée le renflement de l'objet et marquera en traits bleus *plusieurs* contours.[13]

Cézanne's quest for what the thing *means* is exactly within the spirit of Wordsworth's pursuit of aura as the 'spirit' or the 'life' of things. Those who refuse to seek it are, for Wordsworth, idolaters who live by the *letter*.

> Call ye these appearances
> Which I beheld of Shepherds in my youth,
> This sanctity of Nature given to Man
> A shadow, a delusion, ye who are fed

> By the dead letter, not the spirit of things,
> Whose truth is not a motion or a shape
> Instinct with vital functions, but a Block
> Or waxen image which yourselves have made,
> And ye adore.[14]

An emphatic illustration of the importance of this interregnum which we are trying to understand is Freud's speculation about the role of the cortex in mental processes, in *Beyond the Pleasure Principle*.[15] The system perception-consciousness, Freud argues, 'must lie in the borderline between outside and inside; it must be turned towards the external world and must envelop the other psychical systems'. The cortex, which is seen as the seat of that system, is shown to be playing a most ambiguous role: for it is both dead and alive. Dying, the outer level protects the deeper ones from a similar fate, shields them against stimuli. But living, it is also what enables stimuli to be received. The cortical layer, that is, is seen as what negotiates between consciousness and nature; what through its complex structure, half organic, half inorganic, as an aura is half air, half light, makes mental life possible. The 'legend' thus offered by Freud bears, even as it were in its geography, a striking analogy to poetic auras. The cortex envelopes the brain like luminosity the object. It is the intermediary space where separateness is transcended.

One could indeed argue that the search for such interregnums is everywhere in the fin de siècle and early part of the twentieth century[16], and that it derives its urgency from the loss of a mediating ground so keenly experienced by Baudelaire, and recorded by the descent into spleen of *Les Fleurs du Mal*. Spleen is the loss of aura, the reduction of things to a naked and single *contour:*

> Je contemple d'en haut le globe en sa rondeur
> Et je n'y cherche plus l'arbri d'une cahute.[17]

In 'Le Goût du néant', the dwarfed earth, seen from a bird's eye perspective, is *stripped* of its aura. But this stripping is everywhere in the society Baudelaire lives in. The development of photography had reduced images to starkness and lack of depth, and the act of being photographed itself represented the lack of reciprocity, since the prolonged gaze into the camera, as Benjamin argues,[18] was a gaze at something which could not return the gaze, which refused to be perceptible in its turn. On a broader level, Marx accused, with some cause it seems, the bourgeoisie of having 'stripped every sacred occupation of its halo'. This is most vividly recorded in *Our Mutual Friend*, in which language becomes reduced to its barest components, loses both verbs and clauses in its frequent approximation to the telegraphic style, and living beings are taken over by their objects, made inanimate by the scrutiny of analytical chemists (the butler serving at table) and impromptu physicist: as when Miss Podsnap is being viewed through the monocle, 'the framed and glazed' eye of an 'ambling stranger', and described as if 'at the bottom of some perpendicular shaft'.[19] The perceived is being orphaned by the perceiver. The link between man and nature which auras – and reveries – stood for has snapped. Baudelaire's spleen poems are largely a record of that stripping, the coming about of an 'entire nakedness', of that 'dead letter' which was so abhorrent to Wordsworth. Spleen is the restless discomfort of the cat vainly seeking where to lie on the clammy bare tiles:

> Mon chat sur le carreau cherchant une litière
> Agite sans repos son corps maigre et galeux . . .[20]

It is the bareness of inert matter:

> Désormais tu n'es plus, ô matière vivante!
> Qu'un granit entouré d'une vague épouvante . . .

That 'vague épouvante' is what becomes substituted for the aura. It is the reverse of it. We return to something like what Baudelaire calls the 'atmosphere' of *The House of Usher*. Atmospheres are the manifestation, not of a compact centre, but of the absence of 'innéité' of 'soul'. The 'life' which they express is so tenuous as to totter into nothingness. In *The Fall of the House of Usher*, the *sameness* of brother and sister, house and family, building and its reflexion in the tarn, is not the fusion of two contending principles, the combination of contour with depth, of protection with receptiveness, of mind with nature, but the flowing into each other of forms of existence that are so weak that their mutual attraction destroys them both: the dead sister kills the brother, the death of the inmates destroys the house, the tarn swallows the buildings which it reflected.

This is also the meaning of the 'brouillard sale et jaune', 'décor semblable à l'âme de l'acteur', of 'Les Sept Vieillards' – of Prufrock's cat-like or soul-like fog. Indeed, one may wonder to what extent Impressionism itself should not be regarded as a manifestation of this process of separation of 'auras' from objects. In Baudelaire's 'Rêve Parisien', the choice is absolute between the sheer radiance of the dream, and the ugly nakedness of the real room, with its brutally ticking clock. It sometimes feels as though the Impressionists were faced with *either* the harshness of daguerreotypes *or* vapourish interplay of light, and chose the latter. As a result, the 'cathédrale de Rouen' ceases to 'exist' as anything else but a noon or twilight atmosphere. Like Flaubert, it has lost its 'innéité', been swallowed up in the infinite divisiveness of time and light. In this perspective, Cézanne's painting could be seen as a magnificent attempt to recreate the union of object and of 'spirit', and through this, the possibility of a common ground between men, of the knowability of the world: 'Le peintre reprend et convertit justement en objet visible ce qui sans lui reste enfermé dans le vie séparée de chaque conscience: la vibration des apparences qui est le berceau des choses . . .'[21] Thus truth, as Wordsworth puts it, becomes 'a motion or a shape/Instinct with vital functions'.

But when auras degenerate into atmospheres, the objects split up. So does consciousness. Only the dream (as in 'La Chambre double' and in 'Rêve parisien') retains the charm which was that of an equipoise between sleep and waking, consciousness and nature, in the reverie of the Romantics. That growing solipsism had been explored by several of them, De Quincey notably,[22] and also Nerval. In this vision from *Aurélia*, the rhythm of the blood flowing through the brain becomes fused with the rhythm of rivers flowing through the earth:

> . . . je crus tomber dans un abîme qui traversait le globe. Je me sentais emporté sans souffrance par un courant de métal fondu, et mille fleuves pareils, dont les teintes indiquaient les différences chimiques, sillonnaient le sein de la terre comme les vaisseaux et les veines qui serpentent parmi les lobes de cerveau . . . Une clarté blanchâtre s'infiltrait peu à peu dans ces conduits, et je vis enfin s'élargir, ainsi qu'une vaste coupole, un horizon nouveau où se traçaient des îles entourées de flots lumineux.[23]

Entrancing as the passage is, one measures how much the state of luminous oneness which it conveys is shrunk by noting that the 'aerial Islands' so blissfully perceived here are a pure mental fabric, unlike those which surrounded Wordsworth's shepherds; and images of milky whiteness, of easy flow, which in Coleridge's verse about the babe sucking are all geared to reality, here are purely internal. It is a comparison one could well carry into Proust. He takes over Romantic images of the subconscious when he descends into the modern netherworld, the world of sleep; into 'la profondeur organique et devenue translucide des viscères mystérieusement éclairés'. Those depths are reminiscent of Baudelaire's 'grottes basaltiques', dyed in the 'mille feux' of the 'soleils marins'. And he sails on the stream of his blood like Nerval through the veins of his brain: '. . . dès que, pour y parcourir les artères de la cité souterraine, nous nous sommes embarqués sur les flots noirs de notre propre sang comme sur un Lethé intérieur aux sextuples replis, de grandes figures solennelles nous apparaissent . . .'[24] Proust tries to square the circle. To recreate, through involuntary memory, the link between sleep and waking, inner and outer world; through his constant quest for the luminosity of things, the aura that had been lost; and through the flow and unbrokenness of his prose, organic continuity.

But Proust only succeeds on an individual level, although he would claim that a 'nous' is implied in his 'je'. Baudelaire, who labours under exactly the same problem, is more ambitious.

He faces the various splits created by the disappearance of 'auras' at their most damaging. He descends into spleen, which is a wakeful and a social state. He also faces the fact that the 'ténébreuse et profonde unité' of light and darkness in 'Correspondances' has been superseded by unsolvable dichotomies:

> Si le ciel et la mer sont noirs comme de l'encre,
> Nos coeurs que tu connais sont remplis de rayons![25]

Only, for him the dream, the 'rays' of the heart, will not do, unless they can affect the inky blackness of sky and sea. He is, that is, both the poet who explores furthest, and most lucidly, the crisis which affects his age, which the loss of 'aura' as it were emblematises. He is also the one who is most ambitious in his attempt to discover ways of recreating possibilities of oneness, and of knowledge. T. S. Eliot, who understood what Baudelaire had been up to through his own experience of it, emphasises this pivotal movement of diagnosis and cure:

> One difference between Baudelaire and the later poets – Laforgue, Verlaine, Corbière, Rimbaud, Mallarmé – is that Baudelaire not only reveals the troubles of his age and predicts those of the age to come, but also foreshadows some issue of these difficulties. When we get to Laforgue, we find a poet who seems to express more clearly even than Baudelaire the difficulties of his own age . . . Only later we conclude

that Laforgue's 'present' is a narrower present than Baudelaire's, and that Baudelaire's present extends to more of the past and more of the future.[26]

Baudelaire finds the remedy at the heart of the evil. It is by a complex inversion of some of the values found in Wordsworth or Coleridge, that he recreates some of their potential. This is not through a perverse choice, but because he finds the values already degraded, in him and around him, and that the only way to salvage their spirit is to live *through* the degradation. There is a lucid realisation of this at the end of 'Mademoiselle Bistouri': 'Seigneur mon Dieu! . . . vous . . . qui avez peut-être mis dans mon esprit le goût de l'horreur pour convertir mon coeur, comme la guérison au bout d'une lame . . .'[27] The scalpel must go to the heart of the infection before it can begin to heal.

7 Cure through the Disease

> Paradise is locked . . . yet to return to the state of innocence we must eat once more of the tree of knowledge.
> Kleist[1]

> The principle of restoration is found in thought, and thought only: the hand that inflicts the wound is also the hand that heals it.
> Hegel[2]

I

Is the state of joy really out of man's reach, in Baudelaire, and can it be recaptured only through opium? Are there no moments of grace, in which creative oneness with nature can be achieved again, as Coleridge longed to do, in the 'Dejection Ode'?

There are, but they are presented in such a way as to set the terms of the problem differently:

> Il est des jours où l'homme s'éveille avec un génie jeune et vigoureux . . . L'homme gratifié de cette béatitude, malheureusement rare et passagère, se sent à la fois plus artiste et plus juste, plus noble, pour tout dire en un mot, . . . je préfère considérer cette condition anormale de l'esprit comme une véritable *grâce*, comme un miroir magique où l'homme est invité à se voir en beau, c'est-à-dire tel qu'il devrait et pourrait être; une espèce d'excitation angélique, un rappel à l'ordre sous une forme complimenteuse.[3]

The irony at the end unravels an aspect of this joy which was not in Coleridge: the rare intimations which we have of joy warn us that it is not only a childhood state gradually destroyed by cares and experience; it also reveals it as ahead of us, a shadow image of what we might be if we could exorcise evil.

So the problem is not how to return to the sources of joy, but how to gain it through and beyond evil. In Baudelaire's experience there hardly exists that connection between joy and creativity asserted by Coleridge. It is very revealing to look at his correspondence during the early months of 1859, one of the most productive periods in his life: the letters are filled with worries about money, harassed attempts to dissociate himself from an attack on Sainte-Beuve, long editorial arguments with publishers. Only, here and there, a 'Nouvelles *fleurs* faites, et passablement singulières. Ici, dans le repos, la faconde m'est revenue', or 'Vous voyez que l'air de la mer me profite', or again 'Tout ceci a été écrit très ardemment et très vite',[4] sound as though he regarded himself as in luck, but are a long way from Hugo's notion of the electrified poet. Baudelaire does not believe in inspiration. And of course, Coleridge's belief was disproved by his own practice: joy led him to passive enjoyment, dejection to writing a beautiful poem.

Dejection is so much the key-note of Baudelaire's life, that, late on, he comes to hate the very word 'joy'. There remains his plan of a letter to Jules Janin, a journalist who had attacked Heine on the ground that he lacked gaiety; the words 'heureux' and 'joie', in that letter, are equated with 'complacent' and 'stupid': 'Faut-il qu'un homme soit tombé bas pour se se croire heureux! . . . Si ma langue pouvait prononcer une telle phrase, elle en resterait paralysée.'

> Byron, Tennyson, Poe et Cie;
> Ciel mélancolique de la poésie moderne. Etoiles de première grandeur.
> . . . Décadence. C'est un mot bien commode à l'usage des pédagogues ignorants, mot vague derrière lequel s'abritent votre paresse et votre incuriosité de la loi.
> Pourquoi donc toujours la joie? Pour vous divertir peut-être? Pourquoi la tristesse n'aurait-elle pas sa beauté? Et l'horreur aussi? Et tout? Et n'importe quoi?[5]

Baudelaire also attacks that term: Decadence, in his defence of Poe. A poet is not decadent because his work registers the evil and sadness of the world; he would be so only if he revelled in it; and he would be shallow and insensitive if he sang his happiness in the midst of misery. The kind of art he must strive for is one that will exactly record the temper of the times. As this one:

> J'ai trouvé la définition du Beau, – de mon Beau. C'est quelque chose d'ardent et de triste, quelque chose d'un peu vague, laissant

carrière à la conjecture . . . Une tête séduisante et belle . . . c'est une tête . . . qui comporte une idée de mélancolie, de lassitude, même de satiété, – soit une idée contraire, c'est-à-dire une ardeur, un désir de vivre, associé avec une amertume refluante, comme venant de privation ou de désespérance . . .

. . . Appuyé sur, – d'autres diraient: obsédé par – ces idées, on conçoit qu'il me serait diffcile de ne pas conclure que le plus parfait type de beauté virile est *Satan*, – à la manière de Milton.[6]

And he adds: 'Je ne prétends pas que la Joie ne puisse pas s'associer avec la Beauté, mais je dis que la Joie (en) est un des ornements les plus vulgaires'. Joy is no longer the mourned-for principle of creativity; its angelism, given the character of 'la vie moderne', is seen as useless. What is central, the tension between the will to live and the oppressive forces of society, is the right source of creation, the keynote.[7]

It is through the artistic expression of experience, however dark that experience may be, that joy can be regained. This belief, fundamental in Baudelaire, pervades his whole poetry:

Nul n'a mieux su (que Gautier) exprimer le bonheur que donne à l'imagination la vue d'un bel objet d'art, fût-il le plus désolé et le plus terrible qu'on puisse supposer. C'est un des privilèges prodigieux de l'Art que l'horrible, artistement exprimé, devienne beauté, et que la *douleur* rythmée et cadencée remplisse l'esprit d'une *joie* calme.[8]

In the famous apothesis of 'Une Charogne', the rhythm of flies buzzing and worms crawling inside the corpse becomes so overwhelming *as* rhythm that it totally transfigures the horror:

Et ce monde rendait une étrange musique,
   Comme l'eau courante et le vent,
Ou le grain qu'un vanneur d'un mouvement rhythmique
   Agite et tourne dans son van.[9]

Proust has analysed some of the rhythmic cycles of Baudelaire's stanzas, shedding light on the quality of this 'joie calme' in terms which exclude plagiarism. But to fully respond to it, one must perhaps accept that such *form* involves one in the contemplation of what is perhaps another world. Form involves some kind of transcendence, which may be why Baudelaire says that 'toute forme créée . . . est immortelle', and which may explain why, however much may be understood by relating 'art' to 'reality', there always remains in it something in *excess* of that understanding.

These moments of 'grace' in which the world appears more luminous and intense are also, Baudelaire claims, moments in which the depth of life seems to reveal itself through the spectacle, however trivial, we have under our eyes. This sounds, in theory at least, very much like Wordsworth. The analogy is strengthened if one confronts the sense of profound recognition which is released by Wordsworth's encounter with a blind beggar, and that which emerges from Baudelaire's meeting with an old showman in comic rags in the midst of a noisy, joyful fair:

> Il ne riait pas, le misérable! Il ne pleurait pas, il ne dansait pas, il ne gesticulait pas, il ne criait pas; . . . Il était muet et immobile. Il avait renoncé, il avait abdiqué. Sa destinée était faite.
> Mais quel regard profond, inoubliable, il promenait sur la foule et les lumières, dont le flot mouvant s'arrêtait à quelques pas de sa répulsive misère!
> . . . m'en retournant, obsédé par cette vision, je cherchai à analyser ma soudaine douleur, et je me dis: Je viens de voir l'image du . . . vieux poète sans amis, sans famille, sans enfants, dégradé par sa misère et par l'ingratitude publique, et dans la baraque de qui le monde oublieux ne veut plus entrer![10]

Baudelaire becomes identified with this *Saltimbanque* more than Wordsworth with the leech-gatherer, or the father of 'Animal Tranquillity and Decay', or the beggar of the *Prelude*:

> . . . Thus have I look'd, nor ceas'd to look, oppress'd
> By thoughts of what, and whither, when and how . . .
> . . . And once . . . lost
> Amid the moving pageant, 'twas my chance
> Abruptly to be smitten with the view
> Of a blind Beggar, who, with upright face,
> Stood propp'd against a Wall, upon his Chest
> Wearing a written paper, to explain
> The story of the Man, and who he was.
> My mind did at this spectacle turn round
> As with the might of waters, and it seem'd
> To me that in this Label was a type,
> Or emblem, of the utmost that we know,
> Both of ourselves and of the universe . . .[11]

The poet here experiences on a mature level what had been revealed to the Boy of Winander, into whose heart 'the voice of mountain torrents' was carried far. It is because he is in the receptive state which bewilderment induces that the 'abrupt' sight of the beggar springs for him into symbolic significance. Imagination presses on him 'as with the might of waters', it is intensely exhilarating, and the power and the weight of the verse carries this exhilaration 'far into' the reader's heart. Baudelaire, on the other hand, feels his throat choking in the grip of hysteria. The encounter does not fill him with a sense of power, it threatens him intimately. When nature whispers to him, it does not bring tidings of strength: it explodes the façade of life and reveals darkness gaping underneath. As in 'Confession' in which a gay young woman, walking with the poet one evening, suddenly utters a plaintive 'immonde' sigh:

> ... Pauvre ange, elle chantait, votre note criarde:
>   'Que rien ici-bas n'est certain,
> Et que toujours, avec quelque soin qu'il se farde,
>   Se trahit l'égoïsme humain;
>
> ...
>
> Que bâtir sur les coeurs est une chose sotte;
>   Que tout craque, amour et beauté,
> Jusqu'à ce que l'oubli les jette dans sa hotte
>   Pour les rendre à l'éternité!'[12]

Here as in *Heart of Darkness*, it is 'the horror', 'cette confidence horrible', which the the whisperings reveal. Moments in which 'the light of sense goes out in flashes' revealed to Wordsworth the 'Soul' of Nature and his own soul, through some marvellous reciprocity. The word 'sublime' so often used about him, is right: his spirit is so 'tranquil', his poise so strong, that all the spaces that challenge him only exhilarate him. It is true that, unlike Blake, he would not be prepared to outstare a Leviathan. But when 'admonished from another world', his own strength is confirmed:

> ... we stood, the mist
> Touching our very feet; and from the shore
> At distance not the third part of a mile
> Was a blue chasm; a fracture in the vapour,
> A deep and gloomy breathing-place through which

> Mounted the roar of waters, torrents, streams
> Innumerable, roaring with one voice . . .
> . . . in that breach
> Through which the homeless voice of the waters rose,
> That dark deep thoroughfare had Nature lodg'd
> The Soul, the Imagination of the whole.[13]

The opposite happens to Baudelaire: in 'Les Sept Vieillards' the procession of old men, seven like the deadly sins, and identical, self-generating, perhaps as an image of the 'spectacle ennuyeux de l'immortel péché', sends his mind *reeling*:

> Exaspéré comme un ivrogne qui voit double,
> Je rentrai, je fermai ma porte, épouvanté,
> Malade et morfondu, l'esprit fiévreux et trouble,
> Blessé par le mystère et par l'absurdité!
>
> Vainement ma raison voulait prendre la barre;
> La tempête en jouant déroutait ses efforts,
> Et mon âme dansait, dansait, vieille gabarre
> Sans mâts, sur une mer monstrueuse et sans bords![14]

The complete opposition between the generative character of Wordsworth's 'mist' and the destructive brood of Baudelaire's 'brouillard' can be understood in terms of what we discovered about 'auras' and 'atmospheres'. The 'vapour' on Mount Snowdon contains at its centre *one* powerful voice, from which all other voices emanate. But Baudelaire's fog is like that of the *House of Usher*, a 'décor semblable à l'âme de l'acteur', and its spineless duplicity breeds endless doubles. This proliferation of selves (which could be related to the proliferation of Mr Golyadkins in Dostoevsky's 'The Double',[15] or the contagion of alter egos among Eugene Wrayburn, Bradley Headstone and Rogue Riderhood in *Our Mutual Friend*) is as it were the result of an initial weakness of selfhood, of a lack of 'innéité'. But this being so, 'seeing into the life of things' for Baudelaire is not exactly uplifting. It amounts to facing madness. What he calls 'le gouffre' has nothing to do with Wordsworth's 'chasm'. It is the discovery of some essential void, in the self as in the world:

> . . . tout est abîme, – action, désir, rêve,
> Parole! . . .

En haut, en bas, partout, la profondeur, la grève,
Le silence, l'espace affreux et captivant . . .

J'ai peur du sommeil comme on a peur d'un grand trou . . .[16]

Wordsworth is always somehow on top of a mountain, mentally, metaphorically, and in the tone and beat of his verse. Baudelaire inhabits the 'cities of the plain'. He has no recourse against a void which is also in him. What Hegel says of the anguish of death, the sovereign master for the bondsman, is strangely similar to what in his exposure he undergoes: 'It [the self-consciousness of the bondsman] has been in that experience melted to its inmost soul, has trembled through its every fibre, and all that was fixed and steadfast has quaked within it.' But, as Hegel goes on, he seems to see in the extremity of the state the seeds of a hope: 'This complete perturbation of its entire substance, this absolute dissolution of all its stability into fluent continuity, is, however, the simple ultimate nature of self-consciousness, absolute negativity, pure self-referrent existence, which consequently is involved in this type of consciousness.'[17]

For Baudelaire, the state fails to turn positive as quickly as in Hegel, but it also insistently points to itself as the only way out of itself.

That way out lies in a sense of imagination in some respects diametrically opposed to Wordsworth's. The horror underlying life is an inescapable evidence, not what imagination discovers. Imagination is not a passive power of insight, it is born through a struggle. It is not the capacity to see the world as it is, but to discover it and make it as it should be for it to become really itself. Mallarmé's phrase is precise, though applied to Poe, not Baudelaire: 'Tel qu'en lui-même enfin l'éternité le change'. The role of imagination is to change the world into itself at last; to control the horror by giving it significance. It is very similar to the secondary imagination in Coleridge, which '. . . dissolves, diffuses, dissipates, in order to re-create; or where this process is rendered impossible, yet still at all events it struggles to idealize and to unify. It is essentially *vital* even as all objects (*as* objects) are essentially fixed and dead.'[18]

In Baudelaire too Imagination gives both life and form:

. . . Elle décompose toute la création, et, avec les matériaux amassés et disposés suivant des règles dont on ne peut trouver l'origine que dans le plus profond de l'âme, elle crée un monde nouveau . . .

... Sans elle, toutes les facultés, si solides ou si aiguisées qu'elles soient, sont comme si elles n'étaient pas . . .[19]

It is true that sometimes Baudelaire seems to regard Imagination as a faculty to perceive intuitively, like Wordsworth: '[L'Imagination] perçoit tout d'abord, en dehors des méthodes philosophiques, les rapports intimes et secrets des choses, les correspondances et les analogies.'[20] Yet this faculty is never separated from the activity of creation; it is part of it. For Baudelaire intuition only becomes a real insight through *work*: he violently attacks Musset for never having learnt to understand what efforts are needed for a reverie to become truly significant. Imagination, through an intense struggle with nature, can recreate the pristine, the luminous ideal of childhood; can effect that return to the lost Eden which is the aim of every lyrical poet, according to Baudelaire; can 'apothéoser' the world. But it does so, not at the cost of adult reason, but through the tension of all grown-up faculties:

... à l'heure où les autres dorment, [le peintre de la vie moderne] est penché sur sa table, dardant sur une feuille de papier le même regard qu'il attachait tout à l'heure sur les choses, s'escrimant avec son crayon, sa plume, son pinceau, faisant jaillir l'eau du verre au plafond, essuyant sa plume sur sa chemise, pressé, violent, actif, comme s'il craignait que les images ne lui échappent, querelleur quoique seul, et se bousculant lui-même. Et les choses renaissent sur le papier, naturelles et plus que naturelles, . . . La fantasmagorie a été extraite de la nature. Tous les matériaux dont la mémoire s'est encombrée se classent, se rangent, s'harmonisent et subissent cette idéalisation forcée qui est le résultat d'une perception *enfantine*, c'est-à-dire d'une perception aigue, magique à force d'ingénuité![21]

It is as though for Baudelaire the only way to find 'nature' was through an initial rejection of it. Tension and disorder conquer harmony; the praxis of art recaptures the ingenuousness of childhood. In his own way, Baudelaire proceeds on the basis of a dialectic that at times bears striking analogy to Hegel's. Thus this belief that it is through an initial accentuation of difference that harmony is reconquered echoes this statement of Hegel's: '. . . the necessary course of evolution is *one* factor of life which advances by opposites: and the totality of life at its most intense is only possible as a new synthesis out of the most absolute separation.'[22] The dynamism at work in Baudelaire is also one that strives for 'the totality of life at its most intense.'

II

'La beauté ne sera plus que *la promesse du bonheur* . . .'

The centre around which all this revolves is happiness. What Rousseau, Wordsworth, Coleridge and Baudelaire are seeking, some of them through nature and others through art, is to achieve a state in which contradictions will be so resolved that a 'joie calme' will prevail.

What is rather surprising, or reassuring, is the extent of their agreement as to what constitutes the tempo of happiness. Thus the combination of regularity and irregularity which was at work in the *Cinquième Promenade* becomes the substance of beauty in *Les Fleurs du Mal*. Beauty is first presented as a stable, aloof, untouchable ideal:

> Je suis belle, ô mortels, comme un rêve de pierre,
> Et mon sein, où chacun s'est meurtri tour à tour,
> Est fait pour inspirer au poète un amour
> Eternel et muet ainsi que la matière . . .[23]

But in 'Hymne à la Beauté' the stress is on passion, ephemerality:

> L'éphémère ébloui vole vers toi, chandelle,
> Crépite, flambe . . .[24]

The union of the stable and the irregular, produces poise, as the mixture of monotony and movement on the surface of the lake did in Rousseau. This stems from a complex theory of aesthetics in Baudelaire, who had found some of his ideas developed by Poe. Poetry, for him, must be equally far from the steadiness of truth and the restlessness of passion. Truth kills poetry, as in Rousseau total stillness killed reverie: 'Un silence absolu porte à la tristesse; il offre une image de la mort'. Baudelaire says: 'Froide, calme, impassible, l'humeur démonstrative repousse les diamants et les fleurs de la Muse; elle est absolument l'inverse de l'humeur poétique.' Agitation, the reverse of stillness, is for Rousseau equally destructive of reverie:

> Si le mouvement est inégal ou trop fort il réveille; en nous rappellant aux objets environnans, il détruit le charme de la rêverie, et nous arrache d'au dedans de nous pour nous remettre à l'instant sous le joug de la fortune et des hommes et nous rendre au sentiment de nos malheurs . . .

Baudelaire refers to similar rhythms of consciousness but applies them to poetry:

> ... la passion est chose *naturelle*, trop naturelle même, pour ne pas introduire un ton blessant, discordant, dans le domaine de la Beauté pure; trop familière et trop violente pour ne pas scandaliser les purs Désirs, les gracieuses Mélancolies, et les nobles Désespoirs qui habitent les régions surnaturelles de la Poésie.[25]

Halfway, like reverie, between violence and rest, beauty, according to Baudelaire, also achieves a balance between time and eternity, as reverie, for Rousseau and Coleridge, mingled in its flow perfect stasis with a serene acceptance of succession – created a perfect duration. The artist

> cherche ce quelque chose qu'on nous permettra d'appeler la *modernité*; car il ne se présente pas de meilleur mot pour exprimer l'idée en question. Il s'agit, pour lui, de dégager de la mode ce qu'elle peut contenir de poétique dans l'historique, de tirer l'éternel du transitoire. ... La modernité, c'est le transitoire, le fugitif, le contingent, la moitié de l'art, dont l'autre moitié est l'éternel et l'immuable.[26]

The great difference is that while reverie achieved salvation from the contradictory strains of time for the individual alone, and only while it lasted, the beauty created by the great artist redeems not only himself, but his fellow-men; and durably so.

Baudelaire, in his description of art, is not so much regaining what was lost after Rousseau, and more, but returning, unconscious as he may be of it, to ideas about poetry developed by Wordsworth and Coleridge. The stress, of course, is different. The word 'pleasure' firmly places within the eighteenth century the claim that 'A poem is that species of composition which is opposed to works of science, by proposing for its *immediate* object pleasure, not truth...'[27] Whereas Baudelaire's notion that 'La Poésie n'a pas la Vérité pour objet, elle n'a qu'elle-même' is already looking to the twentieth century. The difference however is not so great as the similarity: both statements turn away from 'truth' to attend to the actual aim of poetry. Certainly, what Baudelaire says on poetry and passion brings to mind the 'Preface' of the *Lyrical Ballads*:

The end of Poetry is to produce excitement in co-existance with an overbalance of pleasure; but, by the supposition, excitement is an unusual and *irregular* state of the mind; . . . If the words, by which this excitement is produced be in themselves powerful, or the images and feelings have an undue proportion of pain connected with them, there is some danger that the excitement may be carried beyond its proper bounds. Now the co-presence of something *regular*, something to which the mind has been accustomed in various moods and in a less excited state, cannot but have great efficacy in tempering and restraining the passion by an intertexture of ordinary feeling . . .[28]

What matters is not what doubtful filiation may exist between Baudelaire and Coleridge as a theoretician of poetry, but what Baudelaire is making of ideas strikingly similar to Coleridge's and to Wordsworth's in his Coleridgean phase. What seems to be an actual innovation in Baudelaire, in terms of the evolution of feeling, is that, paradoxical as this may seem in a man who feels so much despair, he believes that there can be more union achieved between reality and the creative spirit of the poet, than either Wordsworth or Coleridge.

The point is difficult to make in relation to Wordsworth, because, as Coleridge reflected 'with delight', his theory has little to do with the processes of his own imagination. There still are two remarks one could make about the passage from the 'Preface' which has just been quoted. The first is that Wordsworth talks about the 'tempering' power of metre a little as he talks of the tempering power of Nature; that is, he seems to think of the way the poet 'balances' his material as similar to the way the contemplation of nature moulds and subdues the soul of man.

Yet he argues later that:

. . . from the tendency of metre to divest language, in a certain degree, of its reality, and thus to throw a sort of half-consciousness of unsubstantial existence over the whole composition, there can be little doubt but that more pathetic situations and sentiments, that is, those which have a greater proportion of pain connected with them, may be endured in metrical composition, especially in rhyme, than in prose.

One might take this, at first, to mean what Baudelaire means when he says that pain, in poetry, can fill the mind with calm joy. But further reflection reveals that the two poets stand on very different ground. For Wordsworth, 'real' language is that which is currently spoken, with which men voice their violence and their pain. For it to become 'poetic' it must be divested of its ungainly, dull or brutal reality. The poet must throw 'a sort of half-consciousness of unsubstantial existence' over it. Poetry removes a few degrees from life, helps one stand above it; as Nature curbs and tempers man's evil instincts.

One is reminded at this point of Arthur Hugh Clough's criticisms of the later Wordsworth. Of his sense that in the poet of the 'Ode to the smaller Celandine', outdoor nature becomes the means of divorcing the poet from the nature of 'Life and business, action and fact'; that his 'fine mountain atmosphere of mind', to use Pater's phrase, enables him a little too well as time goes on to temper other people's pains. This is not true of the *Lyrical Ballads* themselves; nor indeed of *The Prelude*. Yet it seems to be quite an admission in a poet to say that he uses metre 'to divest language in a certain degree of its reality'.

Coleridge adopts a different perspective. He is better than Wordsworth at voicing abstract ideas, and he can handle greater complexities in a short space. His discussion of the effect of metre shows great stretch and subtlety of awareness. This passage has direct bearing on the piece which has just been discussed:

> . . . the *origin* of metre. This I would trace to the balance in the mind effected by that spontaneous effort which strives to hold in check the workings of passion. It might be easily explained likewise in what manner this salutary antagonism is assisted by the very state, which it counteracts; and how this balance of antagonists became organised into *metre* . . . by a supervening act of the will and judgement, consciously and for the foreseen purpose of pleasure.[29]

The complexity with which the relation of 'art' to life, of metre to passion, is conceived, is greater than that of the *Preface* to the *Lyrical Ballads*. Here, poetry is seen, not as the means of divesting language from its reality, but of creating a dialectical relationship between will and passion: a 'balance of antagonists'. It should reproduce on the level of language the struggle that goes on in the mind trying to 'hold in check the workings of passion':

> . . . as the *elements* of metre owe their existence to a state of increased excitement, so the metre itself should be accompanied by the natural language of excitement. Secondly, . . . as these elements are formed

into metre *artificially*, by a *voluntary* act, with the design and for the purpose of blending *delight* with emotion, so the traces of present *volition* should throughout the metrical language be proportionally discernible.[30]

Coleridge may be thinking here of the first book of the *Prelude*. But whether he is or not, what stands out from this is the importance which he grants to volition, design, consciousness. Indeed, he does say earlier that without the preliminary workings of intelligence and reflexiveness, language itself is but a barren thing – as the scanty vocabulary of the rustics shows:

The best part of human language, properly so-called, is derived from reflections on the acts of the mind itself. It is formed by a voluntary appropriation of fixed symbols to internal acts, to processes and results of imagination the greater part of which have no place in the consciousness of uneducated man . . .[31]

And summing up the greatness of Shakespeare, he insists – like Schelling– on the part played by deep, voluntary reflexion in the acquirement of poetic power:

. . . Shakespeare, no mere child of nature; no automaton of genius; no passive vehicle of inspiration possessed by the spirit, not possessing it; first studied patiently, meditated deeply, understood minutely, till knowledge, become habitual and intuitive, wedded itself to his habitual feelings, and at length gave birth to that stupendous power, by which he stands alone . . .[32]

Intuition here is shown to be born of its opposite: patient study. It is when Coleridge dares follow the bend of his temperament, as here, that he is perhaps most profound. In his awareness of poetry as an *art* which can be studied in its inward workings by the creator himself, he seems to be heralding, together with the German philosophers who inspired him, the welding of imagination and critical powers which so strongly marks modern poets like Valéry.

But various pressures prevent him from fully accepting this view. His insights remain unorganised; half-hearted, glorious flashes in the dark. He is so committed by his nostalgia, his friendship with Wordsworth perhaps, the sadness of his life, and the strength and freshness of his sensations, to an ideal of pure nature, that he cannot wait to regain it. He lets it blur the sense of volition, which he had at first perceived as an essential element of creativity. Explaining the union which must exist between 'spontaneous impulse' and 'voluntary purpose' in the writing of metre, he uses the *Winter's Tale* to make his point:

> Pol. . . . nature is made better by no mean,
> But nature makes that mean; so, over that art,
> Which you say adds to nature, is an art,
> That nature makes. You see, sweet maid, we marry
> *A gentler scyon to the wildest stock;*
> And make conceive a bark of ruder kind
> By bud of nobler race. This is an art,
> Which does mend nature – change it rather; but
> The art itself is nature.[33]

The speech does make the point beautifully – but in general terms (as general as Burke's 'Art is man's nature'). And these terms obscure rather than elucidate the dialogue between poetic language and life which had been shown at work. Metre may well be, as chanting, dancing, as any form of rhythm, one of the most spontaneous, ancient, 'natural' means of handling life. But asserting this is not going to be much help to a poet writing in the nineteenth century, in the middle of the industrial revolution, except as a reassurance that he is faithful to his origin, to primitive forces which society seems to be stamping out. And Coleridge seems to be turning to Shakespeare precisely for that reason; not only because he is in love with a beautiful passage, but also because that passage upholds a view of life which is sinking under his feet; a view of life according to which nature's failure to give joy means a total loss of power. Deprived of the art that nature makes, there is no recourse.

This is the point where Baudelaire comes in. He is prepared to let nature disappear out of sight altogether in poetic creation, so as to find it again at the end, but *mended, not changed*. Calculation, artificial precision, are for him the means of designing a nature of genius. And that nature is one with which union is possible:

> Il y a dans le style de Théophile Gautier une justesse qui ravit, qui étonne, et qui fait songer à ces miracles produits dans le jeu par une profonde science mathématique. . . . Peu à peu je m'accoutumai à la perfection, et je m'abandonnai au mouvement de ce beau style

onduleux et brillanté, comme un homme monté sur un cheval sûr qui lui permet la rêverie, ou sur un navire assez solide pour défier les temps non prévus par la boussole, et qui peut contempler à loisir les magnifiques décors sans erreur que construit la nature dans ses heures de génie.[34]

'Comme un homme monté sur un cheval sûr qui lui permet la rêverie . . .' The joy of reverie is no longer available to Baudelaire through simple contemplation. But it becomes possible again, once the profound mathematical science of great poetry or great prose restores acces to those 'vehicular motions' that unite one to a rhythmic flux.[35] Thus the business of the artist is to cultivate his awareness, his 'science', as far as he can. Metre is not only a check upon passion, a purpose towards pleasure. It is the means to create passion, to breed ideas. It is a tool whose worth depends entirely upon the skill of the maker:

> pourquoi tout poète qui ne sait pas au juste combien chaque mot comporte de rimes est incapable d'exprimer une idée quelconque;
> que la phrase poëtique peut imiter (et par là elle touche à l'art musical et à la science mathématique) la ligne horizontale, la ligne droite ascendante, la ligne droite descendante; qu'elle peut monter à pic vers le ciel, sans essoufflement, ou descendre perpendiculairement vers l'enfer avec la vélocité de toute pesanteur; qu'elle peut suivre la spirale, décrire la parabole, ou le zigzag figurant une série d'angles superposés; . . .[36]

Baudelaire's originality here does not lie in his description of what poetry can do: all fine poets have known it before him; the phrase 'descendre perpendiculairement vers l'enfer avec la vélocité de toute sa pesanteur' would be a just summary of what Miltonic verse does throughout Satan's fall in *Paradise Lost*. It lies in the stress put upon awareness of workmanship in the writing of poetry as well as in the faith that, the structure of language being fundamentally attuned to the structure of reality, precision in the use of poetic language can capture any experience. Successful language is a new form of *cogito*, since syntax itself spells the intelligibility of the world. This, the hashish-eater perceives through the influence of the drug, as the artist does through the power of imagination:

> La grammaire, l'aride grammaire elle-même devient quelque chose comme une sorcellerie évocatoire; les mots ressuscitent revêtus de

chair et d'os, le substantif, dans sa majesté substantielle, l'adjectif, vêtement transparent qui l'habille et le colore comme un glacis, et le verbe, ange du mouvement, qui donne le branle à la phrase.[37]

It is *language* in Baudelaire, not self-consciousness, which stands as the individual 'I am', as the means towards grasping the great 'I AM': but no longer through intuition; through a striving for precision which calls into play the artist's whole being.

This is even more than an 'optimisme du language', to use J.-P. Richard's expressive terms. It comes close to a religious faith: 'Il y a dans le mot, dans le *verbe*, quelque chose de sacré qui nous défend d'en faire un jeu de hasard. Manier savamment une langue, c'est pratiquer une espèce de sorcellerie évocatoire.'[38] In this perspective, the question for poetry is no longer, how to check passion by means of metre, or how to divest language of its reality by means of metre, but how to create passion and to explore reality by means of language; how to cleanse or improve a reality fallen from what it should be, by means of a language rid of the impurities and perversions that living daily subjects it to.

This is where poetry acquires the rigour of a science: language must be handled 'savamment' for it to probe and heal. Hence the use of etymology, for instance: discovering the original meaning of a word may provide a key to a modern evil which one cannot otherwise penetrate. J. D. Hubert provides a perceptive example of this.[39] It comes from the end of 'Les Aveugles':

> Ils traversent ainsi le noir illimité,
> Ce frère du silence éternel. O cité!
> Pendant qu'autour de nous tu chantes, ris et beugles,
>
> Eprise du plaisir jusqu'à l'atrocité,
> Vois! je me traîne aussi! mais plus qu'eux hébété,
> Je dis: Que cherchent-ils au Ciel, tous ces aveugles?[40]

The word 'atrocité' contains the key to the contrast between physical and spiritual blindness. It comes from the Latin *atrocitas*, built on the adjective *ater*, black, and signifies, not quite an action so dark as to be cruel, as J. D. Hubert thinks, but rather a state of darkness such that it must escalate into infinite cruelty. There is a circle in Dante's Purgatory in which the angry grope their way through impenetrable darkness; it is generated by their own anger, blinding the light of their reason. Baudelaire's city is an infernal version of this. It is so swamped by its insane love of pleasure that it completely blinds and deafens itself, especially to the suffering that its pursuit of gratification causes. And this stands out against the actual darkness encompassing the blind, a darkness which is brother to eternal silence; a darkness which creates that preliminary peace of deprivation in which the pursuit of light – as against 'atrocité' – becomes possible: 'Que cherchent-ils au Ciel, tous ces aveugles?'

Thus the use of a word in its original meaning can expand the moral perspective in which a modern reality is being held, at the same time as the play between the contemporary meaning and the old registers a combination of horror and mercy. The 'science' helps towards a larger humaneness.

Baudelaire was merciless in his pursuit of exactness.[41] Léon Cladel describes him at work:

> Nous, ouvriers littéraires, purement littéraires, nous devons être précis, nous devons *toujours* trouver l'expression absolue... Cherchons, cherchons!... Et les dictionnaires de notre idiome, empoignés, étaient aussitôt compulsés, feuilletés, sondés avec rage, avec amour... s'enfonçant dans les vocabulaires anglais, allemand, italien, espagnol, poursuivant... l'expression rebelle, insaisissable, et qu'il finissait toujours par créer, si elle ne se trouvait point dans notre langue.[42]

There is more to this than passion for precision. Baudelaire is trying to do with language what the landscape artist of *The Domain of Arnheim* was doing with landscape: redeem it. Only, language is a more social commodity than a piece of land. By reclaiming dead or disused meanings of words, the poet is multiplying possibilities of feeling, areas of experience. A good case in point is the use of the word 'gouge' in the address to Death (a female in French) in his 'Danse Macabre': 'Bayadère sans nez, irrésistible gouge!' To A. de Calonne who had suggested another word, he writes:

> *Gouge* est un excellent mot, mot unique, mot de *vieille* langue, applicable à une *danse macabre*, mot contemporain des *danses macabres*. UNITÉ DE STYLE, primitivement, *une belle gouge*, n'est qu'une belle femme; postérieurement, la gouge, c'est la courtisane qui suit l'armée, à l'époque où le soldat, non plus que le prêtre, ne marche pas sans une arrière-garde de courtisanes. Il y avait même des règlements qui autorisaient cette volupté ambulante. Or, la Mort

n'est-elle pas la Gouge qui suit en tous lieux la *Grande Armée universelle*, et n'est-elle pas une courtisane dont les embrassements sont *positivement irrésistibles*? Couleur, antithèse, métaphore, tout est exact. Comment votre sens critique, si net, n'a-t-il pas deviné mon intention?[43]

It is in this scrupulous care to 'donner un sens plus pur aux mots de la tribu', to 'purify the dialect of the tribe', as Eliot will put it, that Baudelaire will be seminal. The pregnant value of his attitude lies in his realisation that language suffering from the same decay and corruptions as the world does, by tightening and enriching its meanings, by exposing its twists and perversions, one makes the world a sharper and cleaner place. The poet, that is, exercises the only praxis which is relevant to his medium and creates the possibility of a future.

III

The secret of his power lies in his acceptance of the elements of the fallen world, in his capacity to make it the material of poetry. The mechanistic debris of the city provide the elements and images for the portraiture of the little old women. They have so completely eschewed their feminity that they are pointed to as 'ils', these monsters. And yet the dingy pathos of the details achieves an overall effect of passionate tenderness:

> Sous des jupons troués et sous de froids tissus
>
> Ils rampent, flagellés par les bises iniques,
> Frémissant au fracas roulant des omnibus,
> Et serrant sur leur flanc, ainsi que des reliques,
> Un petit sac brodé de fleurs ou de rébus;
>
> Ils trottent, tout pareils à des marionettes;
> Se traînent, comme font les animaux blessés,
> Ou dansent, sans vouloir danser, pauvres sonnettes
> Où se pend un Démon sans pitié! Tout cassés
>
> Qu'ils sont, ils ont des yeux perçants comme une vrille,
> Luisants comme ces trous où l'eau dort dans la nuit;
> Ils ont les yeux divins de la petite fille
> Qui s'étonne et qui rit à tout ce qui reluit.[44]

The elements have changed their forms, but their mythical terror remains. The jungle of Paris is as ruthless to those exposed to its rigours as Cooper's American forests. These stanzas are full of primeval mysteries (storms, superstition, animal life, childhood) which spread their contagion to the most contemporary, the most prosaic objects:

> It is not merely in the use of imagery of common life, not merely in the use of imagery of the sordid life of a great metropolis, but in the elevation of such imagery to the *first intensity* – presenting it as it is and yet making it represent something much more than itself - that Baudelaire has created a mode of release and expression for other men.[45]

A wealth of possibilities is thus released by the divorce which Baudelaire effects between nature and imagination. Freed from its links with a declining reality, imagination regains its power, the sublime grows roots in a new soil. It is no longer tied to this vanishing mode of life:

> . . . in his shepherd's calling he was prompt
> And watchful more than ordinary men.
> Hence had he learned the meaning of all winds,
> Of blasts of every tone; and oftentimes
> When others heeded not, He heard the South
> Make subterraneous music, like the noise
> Of bagpipers on distant Highland hills.
> The Shepherd, at such warning, of his flock
> Bethought him, and he to himself would say,
> 'The winds are now devising work for me!'. . .[46]

It can be born of urban dereliction:

> Telles vous cheminez, stoïques et sans plaintes,
> A travers le chaos des vivantes cités,
> Mères au coeur saignant, courtisanes ou saintes,
> Dont autrefois les noms par tous étaient cités.
>
> . . .
>
> Honteuses d'exister, ombres ratatinées,
> Peureuses, le dos bas, vous côtoyez les murs;
> Et nul ne vous salue, étranges destinées!
> Débris d'humanité pour l'éternité mûrs![47]

Wordsworth indeed helps one measure the scope of the change. In the *Prelude*, Bartholomew Fair is shown as the epitome of artifice, laying 'the whole creative powers of man asleep'. The celebrations of the day are in themselves a perversion of its origin – a Martyr's day became the occasion for a pantomime. And the spectacle which it offers is such a threat to the integrity of the ego that the poet's voice becomes contaminated by it. He must become a showman himself, appeal to the 'muse', artificially set himself apart from the crowd in order to survive spiritually:

> For once the Muse's help will we implore,
> And she shall lodge us, wafted on her wings,
> Above the press and danger of the Crowd
> Upon some Showman's platform . . .[48]

The fair is an image of hell on earth:

> . . . what a hell
> For eyes and ears! what anarchy and din
> Barbarian and infernal! 'tis a dream
> Monstrous in colour, motion, shape, sight, sound . . .[49]

The only thing that enables the poet to override this 'blank confusion', the meaninglessness of this 'plain' in which everything is 'melted and reduced/To one identity' is the 'shaping spirit' which Nature, a nature of mountains, through its 'outline and steady form', its 'pure grandeur', has developed in him:

> But though the picture weary out the eye,
> By nature an unmanageable sight,
> It is not so wholly to him who looks
> In steadiness, who hath among least things
> An under-sense of greatness . . .[50]

In Baudelaire, the fair is no longer the acme of artifice, *it has become nature*. Chaos is celebrated as the condition of life. The search is no longer for 'steadiness' or 'majesty', but for swarming energies. The poet, instead of rising above the crowd to deplore its anarchy, mingles with it, sympathises with its joys and sorrows. 'Le Vieux Saltimbanque', in some respects, is the exact counterpoint to Bartholomew Fair:

Partout s'étalait, se répandait, s'ébaudissait le peuple en vacances
. . .
. . .
(Les baraques) se faisaient . . . une concurrence formidable: elles piaillaient, beuglaient, hurlaient. C'etait un mélange de cris, de détonations, de cuivres et d'explosions de fusées. Les queues-rouges et les Jocrisses convulsaient les traits de leurs visages basanés, racornis par le vent, la pluie et le soleil; ils lançaient, avec l'aplomb des comédiens sûrs de leurs effets, des bons mots et des plaisanteries d'un comique solide et lourd, comme celui de Molière . . .
Tout n'était que lumière, poussière, cris, joie, tumulte; les uns dépensaient, les autres gagnaient, les uns et les autres également joyeux. . . . Et partout circulait, dominant tous les parfums, une odeur de friture, qui était comme l'encens de cette fête.[51]

This text is particularly revealing of the change which Baudelaire's writing crystallises. All the discrimination and richness of the prose go into celebrating a reality which Wordsworth could not bear to approach. The text is written from the centre of the crowd. The booths 'piaillaient, beuglaient, hurlaient', instead of making a confused 'din/Barbarian and infernal'. The smell of 'friture' is caught as precisely as the scent of flowers might be in Wordsworth, and it is compared to 'incense' without any sense of desecration. The vitality of the crowd is probed with the kind of scrutiny with which the world of the old Cumberland beggar was analysed, and the puns of the Jocrisses are related to Molière's comedy with the quality of serious enquiry one finds in the 'Idiot Boy'. The focus has moved. Nature is no longer rural. Values are to be found, not in an intercourse with mountains, but in cities.

And nature itself is great only in so far as it speaks of human forms. Chateaubriand felt ecstasy in Gothic cathedrals because they reminded him of tall forests. The reverse is the case for Baudelaire: 'Dans le fond des bois, enfermé sous ces voûtes semblables à celles des sacristies et des cathédrales, je pense à nos étonnantes villes, et la prodigieuse musique qui roule sur les sommets me semble la traduction des lamentations humaines.'[52] It is with cities, not with lakes and mountains, that Baudelaire communes in reverie:

Ivresse religieuse des grandes villes. − Panthéisme. Moi, c'est tous; tous, c'est moi.
Tourbillon.[53]

The individual 'I AM' is an intuition, not of the 'great eternal I AM', but of the great human 'I AM'. And it is instructive to contrast the visceral image at the beginning of 'Les Sept Vieillards' with the image of the babe sucking in Coleridge:

> Fourmillante cité, cité pleine de rêves,
> Où le spectre en plein jour raccroche le passant!
> Les mystères partout coulent comme des sèves
> Dans les canaux étroits du colosse puissant.[54]

The matrix, the mother-earth, the great primitive goddess, is now the industrial world; and its centre: the city.

8 *The Waste Land* and *Les Fleurs du Mal*

I

To appreciate fully Baudelaire's 'modernity', it might not be irrelevant to examine how it stands up to more recent forms of 'contemporaneity' – to ask, for instance, what happens to his 'present' in the poet who thought it extends to much of the past and much of the future – T. S. Eliot. He seems to have had the author of 'Tableaux parisiens' much in mind when he was working on his most extensive poem about the city – *The Waste Land*.

There is a passage in the initial drafts of the 'Fire Sermon', between the Mr Eugenides and the Tiresias sections, which, though discarded for the final version, is worth pondering here in some depth: not only because of the way it illuminates the rest of this third movement of *The Waste Land* and stresses the gloom of Eliot's response to the city, but also because, in some respects, it is a distant echo of some of the preoccupations we found in Wordsworth, Coleridge and Baudelaire and shows one of the ways this particular tradition was continued:

> London, the swarming life you kill and breed,
> Huddled between the concrete and the sky;
> Responsive to the momentary need,
> Vibrates unconscious to its formal destiny, . . .
>
> London, your people is bound upon the wheel!
> Phantasmal gnomes, burrowing in brick and stone and steel![1]

'What a din/Barbarian and infernal!' We are back in Bartholomew Fair, though the decor, still infernal, with Dante lurking in the background, is not so much barbarian as mechanistic. The Wordsworth we have encountered:

> ... The state to which I now allude was one
> In which the *eye* was master of the heart,
> When that which is ...
> The most despotic of our senses gain'd
> Such strength in me as often held my mind
> In absolute dominion ...²

is even more insistently present in:

> ... Knowing neither how to think, nor how to feel,
> But lives in the awareness of the observing eye ...

A kind of industrial minerality threatens to invade and crush the human. Here indeed it is not of Wordsworth one thinks, but of Baudelaire, and one recognises the usefulness of his vocabulary and subject-matter to Eliot. The 'concrete', the 'gnomes burrowing in brick and stone and steel' remind one of the demolition site of 'Le Cygne':

> Je ne vois qu'en esprit tout ce camp de baraques,
> Ce tas de chapiteaux ébauchés et de fûts,
> Les herbes, les gros blocs verdis par l'eau des flaques,
> Et, brillant aux carreaux, le bric-à-brac confus.³

Even more precisely, the 'swarming life you kill and breed/Huddled between the concrete and the sky' brings to mind the Baudelairian vision of the oppressiveness of the urban landscape, in which people 'swarm', not just 'comme un million d'helminthes', but actually 'seethe' in dreadful passiveness to mechanistic cycles:

> Le Ciel! couvercle noir de la grande marmite
> Où bout l'imperceptible et vaste Humanité!⁴

But if, going beyond immediate impressions, in the light of what else one feels and understands about *The Waste Land*, one starts wondering what is Eliot's relation to the Romantic theme we have attempted to delineate, it soon becomes clear that he has worse problems than any of the poets so far considered, without being able to benefit from their solutions. It is self-evident that he has no 'nature' to 'thwart' the 'tyranny' of the eye, no fund of feeling on which to draw (according to many commentators, this is indeed what the poem is about); even less than the Coleridge of the 'Dejection Ode'. It is true that the *memory* of the 'joy' of 'innocent' times – if this is how one must read the hyacinth girl passage – crosses the 'Burial of the Dead' section:

> Yet when we came back, late, from the hyacinth garden,
> Your arms full, and your hair wet, I could not
> Speak, and my eyes failed, I was neither
> Living nor dead, and I knew nothing,
> Looking into the heart of light, the silence.

It is also true that among the many echoes one may find to the passage, one may recognise not only Wordsworth's eye 'made quiet', in the 'my eyes failed', but more importantly the words, dear to Coleridge, in which Nature answers in Plotinus:

> 'Should any one interrogate her, how she works . . . she will reply, it behoves thee not to disquiet me with interrogatories, but to understand in silence, even as I am silent, and work without words' . . . 'we ought . . . to watch in quiet till (knowledge) suddenly shines upon us; preparing ourselves for the blessed spectacle as the eye waits patiently for the rising sun.'[5]

But while Coleridge can use the memory of joy gradually to become elated, in *The Waste Land* such memories have lost all live contact with the present. One may see in Madam Sosostris's pack of cards or in the dead leaves flying about the Sybil something like Coleridge's 'rattling twigs and branches' in which sap has ceased to flow.

Eliot does not either really participate in Baudelaire's solution. Even while reading Baudelaire's image of the sky as a lid over a stewing pot, one cannot help being struck by the grandeur there is in the adjectives applied to mankind: 'L'imperceptible et vaste Humanité'. It creates a bird's eye view, a sudden expanse of landscape which makes the image burst out of all smallness. Not so with Eliot's 'gnomes', 'burrowing', or the 'swarming life' 'Responsive to the momentary need/Vibrates unconscious to its formal destiny.' There is dry contempt in this. It may reflect on, and thus qualify, the speaking voice – but even so, it is revealing that the mood portrayed should be one of desiccation, rather than an attempt to magnify the subject-matter. And if one further compares the

> Some minds . . .
> Record the motions of these pavement toys

> And trace the cryptogram that may be curled
> Within these faint perceptions of the noise . . .

with the 'petites vieilles' who

> . . . dansent sans vouloir danser, pauvres sonnettes
> Où se pend un démon sans pitié!

one feels that the viewing of the human in mechanised terms, in one case has potential viciousness (the 'gnomes' are like the spring of 'Rhapsody on a Windy Night', 'hard and curled and ready to snap'), in the other is redeemed by the passionate sympathy of the voice.

One could go on to explore this in greater detail; and one would probably be confirmed in feeling that in *The Waste Land* Eliot is not interested, as Baudelaire was, in giving grand poetic status to the vocabulary of modern life ('The river bears no empty bottles, sandwich papers,/Silk handkerchiefs, cardboard boxes, cigarette ends . . .'), nor in elevating the dereliction of the metropolis to the 'imagery of first intensity':

> But at my back from time to time I hear
> The sound of horns and motors, which shall bring
> Sweeney to Mrs. Porter in the spring.

When 'first intensity' comes, it is generally in the past:

> (And I Tiresias have foresuffered all . . .
> I who have sat by Thebes below the wall
> And walked among the lowest of the dead.)

Thus it might not be preposterous to argue that in some respects, though he died nearly a century before Eliot, Baudelaire is a more 'modern' poet – in that he takes in more of what the life of industrial, urban civilisation was bringing about.

This would not of course be a limiting judgement on Eliot, but simply an attempt at placing Baudelaire in relation to him. Indeed one might add that perhaps one of the figures one could evoke alongside Baudelaire's when reading 'The Fire Sermon' is that of Coleridge the admirer of Plotinus. An evocation of 'the city whose home is in the ideal', 'whose pattern is laid up in heaven' (in Socrates' words from

Plato's *Republic*) follows the damaging passage on the city of man which we have been discussing:

> Not here, o Ademantus, but in another world.

and it reverberates at the moment of drowning in 'Death by Water', preceding, in the original drafts, the 'Phlebas the Phoenician':

> And if *Another* knows, I know I know not
> Who only know that there is no more noise now.[6]

There is thus conveyed the recognition of a possible mystical dimension of experience – of the longed-for access to 'flowing sap' – and of the necessity, as it were, to 'die' to this world to gain access to it. 'I knew nothing/Looking into the heart of light, the silence.': 'Phlebas ... *forgot* the cry of gulls, and the deep sea-swell/And the profit and loss.' The self at the centre of *The Waste Land* must go through fire and death by water to regain innocence, reverse the desiccating course of experience – 'pass the stages of his age and youth'. Like the Baudelaire of *Mademoiselle Bistouri* it must go to the *end* of the evil, let the scalpel reach the core of the infection, reach a sort of nothingness, of *whiteness*, before it can be healed:

> Something which we knew must be a dawn –
> A different darkness, flowed above the clouds,
> And dead ahead we saw, where sky and sea should meet,
> A line, a white line, a long white line,
> A wall, a barrier, towards which we drove.[7]

One could thus read *The Waste Land* as a striving towards the rebirth of spiritual life, of that 'intuitive knowledge' which Plotinus quoted by Coleridge, says can only be gained through a preliminary darkness of the senses, through death-like surrender. Then, like Thunder – the 'might of waters'? – Nature might vouchsafe to speak.

> If there were water
> And no rock
> If there were rock
> And also water
> And water
> A spring
> A pool among the rock ...

The 'fiat', the surrender of mind and heart to what threatens to destroy them, the 'driving' into the horizon turned wall, turned death, which Baudelaire accomplished in *this* world – the world of guilt and expiation of 'Un Voyage à Cythère':

> Dans ton île, ô Vénus, je n'ai trouvé debout
> Qu'un gibet symbolique où pendait mon image . . .
> – Ah! Seigneur! donnez-moi la force et le courage
> De contempler mon coeur et mon corps sans dégoût![8]

for Eliot can only take place in 'another world'.

II

But we have, several times, come across such 'another world' in Baudelaire's conception of *form*. The 'joie calme' or the 'enlèvement de l'âme' which poetry produces for Baudelaire give access to a world of spirit, which is in excess of, or beyond, the world of actuality.

In this respect too, there is an oblique link between *The Waste Land* and *Les Fleurs du Mal*.

The form of *Les Fleurs du Mal*, we have seen, expresses fragmentation and asserts the primacy of the single life, of individual 'points of view'. It celebrates the energy of a nature that proceeds by opposites, whilst making the reader travel, in an organised way, through a landscape of consciousness. Also, it explores the split of mind and nature while looking for ways of transcending that split, of regaining 'Romantic' modes of communion.

One of the forms which this communing takes, is in the identifying of the self with swarming energies, with crowds, with the city: 'Moi, c'est tous. Tous, c'est moi. Tourbillon.' It is a strange kind of identity which is thus discovered. Is it the identity of the *narrator* of *Les Fleurs du Mal*? It is a problem which, of course, also affects *The Waste Land*, since it is a poem which, even more emphatically than *Les Fleurs du Mal*, parades the refusal of its fragments to cohere, or offers that refusal as the identity of its narrator. The question which is raised here is that which, according to Lukács, nineteenth-century art is most inescapably saddled with: 'The task is to deduce the unity – which is not given – of this disintegrating creation and to prove that it is the product of a creating subject.'[9] Or, as he in other cryptic words puts it, the task is to 'create the subject of the "creator"'. Or again, to use Flaubert's apt term, the task is to regain through art the 'innéité' which is missing in life.

One understands at this stage, not why (such things can only be experienced, not understood), but how there is a need to go under for several writers in this period. A complete consciousness, one that actually encounters reality, must, as Hegel describes it, be subjected to complete dissolution in order to gain formative power. Finding oneself in 'tous' is the only path to a 'moi':

> Should consciousness shape and form the thing without the initial state of absolute fear, then it has a merely vain and futile 'mind of its own'; for its form or negativity is not negativity *per se*, and hence its formative activity cannot furnish the consciousness of itself as essentially real. If it has endured not absolute fear, but merely some slight anxiety, the negative reality has remained external to it, its substance has not been through and through infected thereby. Since the entire content of its natural consciousness has not tottered and shaken, it is still inherently a determinate mode of being.[10]

Baudelaire needs to go through spleen, through the contemplation of his own death, because this is the only place where 'form' – that is, if we believe Hegel, a reborn identity – may be found. Paradise is regained, both in Milton and in Wordsworth, by resistance to temptation. True, the temptation tests the very fibre of the man – or God – subjected to it. But it is resisted. When Wordsworth looks back to his great dejection, he sees that it eclipsed rather than altered him:

> . . . for, though impair'd and chang'd
> Much, as it seem'd, I was no further chang'd
> Than as a clouded, not a waning moon . . .[11]

Though lost in the labyrinth he never let go of his Ariadne thread:

> . . . Nature's self, by human love
> Assisted, through the weary labyrinth
> Conducted me again to open day.[12]

But for those of Baudelaire's age, it seems that Hegel's words hold true, and that Paradise can only be regained through some sort of crucifixion. The three days in the tomb are not only the time in which, by some mysterious chemistry, the forces of life begin to recompose a self, but they expand into a weird limbo. It was not for nothing that one of the early titles to *Les Fleurs du Mal* was to be *Les Limbes*. In 'Un Voyage à Cythère', the contemplation of the corpse on the gibbet –

which turns out to be the poet – is unearthily protracted and intense. It is from that prolonged intensity that the *fiat* is born. It is also worth remembering that both *The Brothers Karamazov* and *Our Mutual Friend* were written within a few years of *Les Fleurs du Mal*. They are both works in which re-birth can only happen through a recomposition of the self by death, or a total surrender to forces of undoing. There is there, if one reverts to Northrop Frye's image of the drunken boat, no longer a 'Romantic' attempt to sail on the forces of life, but a distinctly *post-Romantic* need to sink, and drown: like Baudelaire's 'vieille gabarre' in its monstrous and edgeless sea.

The various deaths by water of *Our Mutual Friend* are very close to Baudelaire's own explorations of identity. One could even speculate on the paradoxical meaning of Dickens' title in the light of Baudelaire's own various 'nous': his 'mon frère' is about as charged with ambiguities as Mr Boffin's designation to Bella of John Harmon supposedly drowned, alias John Rokesmith, alias Julius Handford, as 'our mutual friend'. In that novel, death by water is both horrible (as in the battering in of Wrayburn's face) and the only place where love can be found. When Rogue Riderhood, whom everyone hates, gets drowned everyone tries to revive him. It is only in that limbo that through the impersonality thus conferred him he can shed his distasteful identity. From the moment he revives, everyone loses interest in him.

And of course, it is through 'Death by Water' that there is created the peace which permits the thunder to speak, in *The Waste Land*. The initial draft not only included a longish parodic section which played on notions of loss of identity, with clear reference to *Our Mutual Friend* ('He do the police in different voices'). What survives of the section 'Death by Water', in which identity is thrown to the winds ('He passed the stages of his age and youth/Entering the whirlpool'), concluded a long Ulysses-like voyage, itself ending with drowning and the surrender of *will* which we have already noted: 'And if Another knows, I know I know not . . .'. It is only through death that the fragments can cease to proliferate their lack of aura, their starkness, their randomness, and begin to recompose themselves around a self to come.

And in *Les Fleurs du Mal* the consciousness at work is a consciousness in search of its own creativity, of its selfhood, through its gradual fragmentation, stripping and failure. It seems that, in the light of all the readings we have unearthed, we are at last in the position to look at that formidable stumbling-block of Baudelairian criticism, the 'architecture' of *Les Fleurs du Mal*.

PART TWO

Form as Transcendence

9 *Les Fleurs du Mal*

> Ce qu'il a décrit... ce n'est pas un mal qui lui fut propre, c'est le mal, c'est les angoisses du temps où il a vécu. Ce qu'il porte dans un cadre... ce n'est pas, comme vous l'avez cru, son portrait; c'est un miroir, où se reflètent les visages douloureux, ahuris et convulsés des passants.
> Théodore de Banville[1]

> Quant à la moralité du livre, elle en jaillit naturellement comme la chaleur de certains mélanges chimiques.
> Baudelaire[2]

I

Baudelaire himself and his early commentators insist on the value of the form given to *Les Fleurs du Mal*. The passages stating this have been used many times before, but they make a case in themselves, and are worth quoting once more rather than paraphrasing.

The notion that the order in which his poems occur is a significant part of their meaning is there from the start in Baudelaire, as Professor M. A. Ruff has shown, discussing the initial volumes he planned to publish, *Les Lesbiennes* and *Les Limbes*. The preoccupation is still strongly there when Baudelaire writes to Victor Mars, the secretary of the *Revue des Deux Mondes*, who had accepted some of the 'fleurs': 'Je tiens très vivement, quels que soient les morceaux que vous choisirez, à les mettre en ordre *avec vous*, de manière qu'ils se fassent, pour ainsi dire, suite.'[3] And he pursued Poulet-Malassis, the publisher of *Les Fleurs du Mal*, with the same aim in mind: I reserve for myself, he said, the right to arrange with you 'l'ordre des matières des *Fleurs du Mal*, – *ensemble*, entendez-vous, car la question est importante.'[4] Even after the condemnation of the book and its poor success, Baudelaire went on working on new poems which could fit in the frame chosen. He claimed to Vigny that the value of the *Fleurs* as an *ensemble* was what he most wished to be recognised: 'Le seul éloge que je sollicite pour ce livre est qu'on reconnaisse qu'il n'est pas un pur album et qu'il a un commencement et une fin. Tous les poëmes nouveaux ont été faits pour être adaptés à un cadre singulier que j'avais choisi.'[5]

The warmest contemporary critics of Baudelaire, Swinburne and Barbey d'Aurevilly, both recognised the validity of this claim. Barbey in particular stated the case with striking clarity:

> Chaque poésie a, de plus que la réussite des détails ou de la fortune de la pensée, une valeur très importante d'ensemble et de situation, qu'il ne faut pas lui faire perdre, en la détachant; les artistes qui voient les lignes sous le luxe et l'efflorescence de la couleur percevront très bien qu'il y a ici une architecture secrète, un plan calculé par le poète méditatif et volontaire. Les *Fleurs du Mal* ne sont pas à la suite les unes des autres comme autant de morceaux lyriques dispersés par l'inspiration et ramassés dans un recueil, sans d'autre raison que de les réunir. Elles sont moins des poésies qu'une oeuvre de la plus forte unité. Au point de vue de l'art et de la sensation esthétique elles perdraient beaucoup à n'être pas lues dans l'ordre . . . Mais elles perdraient bien davantage au point de vue de l'effet moral.[6]

The words 'architecture secrète' have had an amazing critical fortune – something like Blake's remark on Milton being of the devil's party without knowing it – and the question has been probed with such impeccable scholarly thoroughness, such sensitivity and intelligence, that there is little need to re-open it – as a question.[7] However, though it is now generally agreed that the book must be read as a volume, and as a volume with a number of recognisable cycles (the cycle of beauty, the cycle of the black Venus, of the white Venus, of the *Belle aux cheveux d'or*, of Spleen, etc.) and a definite 'downward' direction, what its overall meaning is remains highly debatable. What ultimately leaves one dissatisfied with all the fine studies written on this question is that none of them tries to work together all the elements which Barbey d'Aurevilly mentions. They offer partial truths where Baudelaire strove for wholeness.

One position is to regard the *Fleurs du Mal* as a critical autobiography with large human significance. This is Robert Vivier's reading: '. . . Les *Fleurs du Mal*, tout en n'étant – si l'on veut – que la confession poétique d'un homme, nous apportent l'expression de l'une des manières dont tout homme peut considérer le problème de la vie . . .'[8] A. Feuillerat supports this, with a shift of emphasis. For him, Baudelaire, faced with poems conceived at different times and in different moods, but all expressing *one* sensibility, must have thought that a connection existed between them which would explain their origin and the character of that sensibility. He then distributed the poems into groups in order to represent faces of his experience. Also, considering that he was presenting a particularly interesting human case, he tried to extract by a significant arrangement the reasons accounting for the state of suffering of this human case.[9] The main idea behind the *Fleurs du Mal* is that Satan holds Baudelaire under his sway and renders useless his efforts to regain original purity and to soar towards beauty.

Perhaps simply the vocabulary used – I have been translating straightforwardly – may warn the reader that however good a scholar Feuillerat is, there is a coarseness in his apprehension of the workings of a poet's mind which casts a doubt on the judgement he offers. It is difficult to imagine Baudelaire thinking: 'I am a particularly interesting human case'! But this is not so much what one might quarrel with as the autobiographical perspective which Feuillerat adopts. According to him, the 1857 edition – the one condemned at court, from which six pieces had to be suppressed – is more virile, more dynamic, clearer, and therefore better than the 1861 edition, which includes thirty-five new poems, is less unified, and faces us with a less attractive personality. The lines of its architecture are less pure, Feuillerat adds.

This objection only holds in so far as one takes the metaphor of 'architecture' literally – which is nonsense. It would be more apposite to talk about those 'lines' in terms of painting, with which Baudelaire was much more preoccupied. For instance, the remarks on 'colour' in the 1846 *Salon* have some bearing on Baudelaire's own poetical practice. Even the opening of a passage which should be read in full makes one feel that it was mobility and contrast, not purity, which Baudelaire looked for in reality:

> Supposons un bel espace de nature où tout verdoie, rougeoie, poudroie et châtoie en pleine liberté, où toutes choses, diversement colorées suivant leur constitution moléculaire, changées de seconde en seconde par le déplacement de l'ombre et de la lumière, et agitées par le travail intérieur du calorique, se trouvent en perpétuelle vibration, laquelle fait trembler les lignes et complète la loi du mouvement éternel et universel . . .[10]

Colour in nature is an 'hymne compliqué', a 'succession de mélodies', the 'accord' of two contrasting tones in nature. And for Baudelaire, the great 'coloriste' painter is he who, through a native sense and also acquired skill, is capable of creating a melody out of multiplicity and potential discord. Great 'coloristes' are 'epic poets', Baudelaire adds in this chapter which leads straight on to a meditation on Delacroix, presented, through the famous parallel with Hugo, as more of a true poet than many poets. This seems to suggest that for Baudelaire the reality which confronts a painter and that which a poet deals with are not dissimilar; that the description of outdoor nature as infinitely mobile and in a state of perpetual antagonism would be relevant to human nature too. In fact, what Baudelaire says of Delacroix' internal world would be true of himself:

> Pour un pareil homme, doué d'un tel courage et d'une telle passion, les luttes les plus intéressantes sont celles qu'il a à soutenir contre lui-même; les horizons n'ont pas besoin d'être grands pour que les batailles soient importantes; les révolutions et les événements les plus curieux se passent sous le ciel du crâne, dans le laboratoire étroit et mystérieux du cerveau.[11]

This suggests not only that it would be misleading to evaluate the *Fleurs du Mal* in architectural terms, because the reality Baudelaire sees himself as dealing with is essentially mutable, but also that his understanding of painting, especially Delacroix's use of colours, springs from his own experience in dealing with language, and therefore is informative about his own practice.

For instance one should beware of placing too much emphasis on the neat division of 'Spleen et Idéal' into cycles – initiated by Benedetto and followed by Feuillerat.[12] It is useful as a working tool, because the eighty-odd poems of that section are too complex a unit to be handled as a whole. But one should remember that Baudelaire, who could give a whole section to the three poems of 'Révolte', introduced no formal separations between those of 'Spleen et Idéal' because he meant them to work together – perhaps like the figures of Delacroix's 'Dante et Virgile aux Enfers'. While there would be sense in talking isolatedly for a while of the expression on Virgil's face, there would not be sense in treating it like a separate portrait: it is the working part of a complex outside which it would change significance. Thus one should talk of the 'cycles' of 'Spleen et Idéal' with the sense that what separates them from each other is as little clear-cut as the separations between coloured masses in nature or in the paintings of 'coloristes': 'Les coloristes dessinent comme la nature; leurs figures sont naturellement délimitées par la lutte harmonieuse des masses colorées.'[13]

What Baudelaire says of Delacroix, is here again true of himself:

> Delacroix est le seul aujourd'hui dont l'originalité n'ait pas été envahie par le système des lignes droites; ses personnages sont toujours agités, et ses draperies voltigeantes. Au point de vue de Delacroix, la ligne n'est pas; car, si ténue qu'elle soit, un géomètre taquin peut toujours la supposer assez épaisse pour en contenir mille autres; et pour les coloristes, qui veulent imiter les palpitations éternelles de la nature, les lignes ne sont jamais, comme dans l'arc-en-ciel, que la fusion intime de deux couleurs.[14]

You would think that he had foreseen the 'purity of outline' argument when he attacked precisely that in Hugo:

> M. Victor Hugo laisse voir dans tous ses tableaux, lyriques et dramatiques, un système d'alignement et de contrastes uniformes. L'excentricité elle-même prend chez lui des formes symétriques. Il possède à fond et emploie froidement tous les tons de la rime, toutes les ressources de l'antithèse, toutes les tricheries de l'apposition...[15]

There is a manifold significance in this rejection of 'ligne' in favour of movement and colour. It emerges when seen in the perspective of the kind of 'Romanticism' which was defined in the preceding section as essentially Baudelairian. The refusal to draw straight lines is a denial of fragmentation, a search for continuity in the midst of discontinuity. The striving towards a plastic form which would express the 'eternal palpitations' of nature is an attempt to overcome determinism as well as to find a meeting-ground in which the mobile energy of the mind can be seen as reflecting the dynamism of nature. It would take a great deal of space and delicacy of touch to show how the *Fleurs du Mal* are, structurally, the work of a coloriste.[16] One instance might at least suggest that they are so, while supporting a claim that the current edition, the 1861 edition, is not inferior to the 1857 one – is in fact superior to it.

Let us choose the moment of 'Spleen et Idéal' whose revision for the later version makes Feuillerat most unhappy.

The major movement of 'Spleen et Idéal', the pursuit, as Feuillerat and Professor Ruff call it, of beauty through love, proceeds through three cycles, the first of poems occasioned by Jeanne Duval, Baudelaire's mulatto mistress, the second of poems written for Mme

Sabatier, the third centred around Marie Daubrun, the 'Belle aux cheveux d'or', an actress. The Marie Daubrun cycle was ended, in the 1857 edition, by 'l'Héautontimorouménos', which Baudelaire, planning it to be the epilogue to an earlier series of poems, had described in these terms:

> L'Epilogue (adressé à une dame) dit à peu près ceci: 'Laissez-moi me reposer dans l'amour, – mais non, – l'amour ne me reposera pas. – La candeur et la naïveté sont dégoûtantes. – Si vous voulez me plaire et rajeunir les désirs, soyez cruelle, menteuse, libertine, crapuleuse et voleuse: et si vous ne voulez pas être cela, je vous assommerai sans colère. Car je suis le vrai représentant de l'ironie et ma maladie est absolument incurable.[17]

In fact, as the poem turned out, Feuillerat notices, it centres around the second part of this plan:

> Je te frapperai sans colère
> Et sans haine, comme un boucher, . . .[18]

The first part is represented by the end of the cycle to Marie Daubrun – poems like 'Chant d'automne':

> Ah! laissez-moi, mon front posé sur vos genoux,
> Goûter, en regrettant l'été blanc et torride,
> De l'arrière-saison le rayon jaune et doux![19]

And 'l'Héautontimorouménos', still in the 1857 edition, was followed by three 'antithetical' poems, written for women Baudelaire had known or loved in his youth, 'purifying youth memories', Feuillerat says, which neatly repeat the serene note on which each love cycle ends.

In the 1861 edition, 'L'Héautontimorouménos' is translated to the end of 'Spleen et Idéal'; it becomes the last poem but two, reinforcing the darkness of the final mood. But it is the 'cycle des femmes diverses' which Feuillerat is dissatisfied with. Baudelaire has added four poems to it, which distort the initial serenity:

> Le joli bouquet 'd'amours printanières' de la première édition a été défait par l'arrangement nouveau, et a été remplacé par un défilé confus dont la variété frappe seule. Baudelaire a sans doute voulu

rendre un compte complet de ses expériences amoureuses; mais son premier groupement était plus heureux: il s'harmonisait mieux du moins avec le sens général du chapitre – la recherche de l'idéal.[20]

This is where the autobiographical explanation is misleading: the suggestion that Baudelaire made these changes in order to represent more women he might have had connections with seems preposterous in the light of his sense that, for a 'romantic' artist 'les révolutions et les événements les plus curieux se passent sous le ciel du crâne'. And the issue is further obscured by the 'architectual' assumption that, by complicating his pattern, Baudelaire messed it up. If one is but willing to stop attributing poems to this or that woman, as though this were important, and is prepared to read them as modulations of feeling, then a series which starts from 'Causerie' (LV) and ends with 'Sonnet d'Automne' (LXIV), that is a series which includes some of the so-called 'Marie Daubrun poems' as well as the 'Femmes diverses' poems emerges, through which there occurs precisely what Baudelaire, in his initial draft, meant 'l'Héautontimorouménos' to do, as a fitting epilogue to the love poems. Only the oscillations between the movement 'Laissez-moi me reposer dans l'amour', the 'Mais non: soyez menteuse, libertine, crapuleuse et voleuse' and the 'Je vous assommerai sans colère', do not take place in a simple sequence or inside a particular poem, but as a restless movement. The various 'dames' to whom the poems refer are there only to emphasize the fretful misery to which love has reduced the unique speaker. They are a better means (than the simple 1857 confrontation of the Marie Daubrun terminal poems and 'L'Héautontimorouménos') of effecting what Baudelaire had called 'un joli feu d'artifice de monstruosités': the multiplicity of directions intensify and dramatize the fireworks: the self-contradictory élans of an ailing soul, 'l'agitation de l'esprit dans le mal', as Baudelaire himself called it.[21]

Thus moments of gentleness are to be found in the opening of 'Causerie' (LV):

> Vous êtes un beau ciel d'automne, clair et rose!

and in the second part of 'Chant d'automne':

> Et pourtant aimez-moi, tendre coeur! soyez mère,
> Même pour un ingrat, même pour un méchant;
> Amante ou soeur, soyez la douceur éphémère
> D'un glorieux automne ou d'un soleil couchant.

in the remote, nostalgic experiences of 'Sisina' (LIX), 'Franciscae' (LX), 'A une dame créole' (LXI) and 'Moesta et errabunda' (LXII). The demand that she be 'menteuse, libertine, crapuleuse et voleuse' is presented through 'Chanson d'après-midi' (LVIII):

> Quoique tes sourcils méchants
> Te donnent un air étrange
> Qui n'est pas celui d'un ange,
> Sorcière aux yeux alléchants,
>
> Je t'adore, ô ma frivole,
> Ma terrible passion!
> Avec la dévotion
> D'un prêtre pour son idole . . .

in the mildly blasphemous tone of 'Franciscae', in moments of 'Sonnet d'automne'. And the desecration and sadism, the 'je vous assommerai sans colère', in 'A une Madone' (LVII):

> Enfin, pour compléter ton rôle de Marie,
> Et pour mêler l'amour avec la barbarie,
> Volupté noire! des sept Péchés capitaux,
> Bourreau plein de remords, je ferai sept Couteaux
> Bien affilés, et comme un jongleur insensible,
> Prenant le plus profond de ton amour pour cible,
> Je les planterai tous dans ton Coeur pantelant, –
> Dans ton Coeur sanglotant, dans ton Coeur ruisselant!

and in 'Le Revenant' (LXIII):

> Comme d'autres par la tendresse,
> Sur ta vie et sur ta jeunesse,
> Moi, je veux régner par l'effroi.

Thus what separates the cycles of love from each other and from the ensuing collapse into spleen are not neat changes of tone and subject-matter but, as with Delacroix, the harmonious struggle of coloured masses. There is something profoundly 'Romantic', in the sense which Baudelaire gives to the word – intimacy, spirituality, depth – about the framework of the *Fleurs du Mal*. What is particularly interesting about that 'Romanticism' is that it is asserted through the plastic interplay of the poems, while on other planes its failure is being exhibited. While the poems oscillate between a nostalgic lust for, and a savage destruction of, intimacy, their formal interweaving speaks of a deep underlying intimacy. In other words, the 'Romantic' possibilities which are shown as fading on one level are dynamically recreated at another. The form both contains and transcends the contradiction.

The unpredictability and violence of contrasts in the *Fleurs du Mal* not only holds a faithful mirror up to a divided and uncertain era, as Théodore de Banville saw so well, but reflects the struggles which go on beneath the heaven of the skull. Also, the combined effects of these contrasts strike immediate chords of feeling, for Baudelaire, as do violently contrasting colours side by side: 'J'ai eu longtemps devant ma fenêtre un cabaret mi-parti de vert et de rouge crus, qui étaient pour mes yeux une douleur délicieuse.'[22] On a more complex level, there emerges, from the quality and interplay of contrasts, an overall mood which is really the temperamental effect of the melody. Baudelaire often spoke of the 'terrible tristesse' exuding from his book, and he is again talking perhaps as much about the *Fleurs du Mal* as about Delacroix when he says:

> C'est non-seulement la douleur qu'il sait le mieux exprimer, mais surtout, – prodigieux mystère de sa peinture, – la douleur morale! Cette haute et sérieuse mélancolie brille d'une éclat morne, même dans sa couleur, large, simple, abondante, en masses harmoniques, comme celle de tous les grands coloristes, mais plaintive et profonde comme une mélodie de Weber.[23]

Thus, if one should re-read the section (LV-LXIV) which has just been discussed, one might be struck by the truly mysterious autumnal atmosphere that pervades it. One must use Baudelaire's word 'mysterious', for the effect occurs at such a deep level of creation that analysis 'cannot note its many chords'.[24] It is also a profoundly 'natural' level, in which the cyclical sway of seasons secretly pervades the psyche. From the opening of 'Causerie' ('Vous êtes un beau ciel d'automne, clair et rose . . .') to the end of 'Sonnet d'automne':

> Comme moi n'es-tu pas un soleil automnal,
> O ma si blanche, ô ma si froide Marguerite?

there is a sense of chill only alleviated by the memory or illusion of warmth, a taste of bitterness, impending doom in the sounds which people the lines and landscape of poems like 'Chant d'automne', blasé refinement too, a strange sense of *age* in the erotic tastes and the memories of childhood. Autumn is there as a complex sensory and emotional presence, as a season in the year, in man's life and in the descent into evil. And the cycle of 'Spleen', which opens straight afterwards with 'Tristesses de la lune' (LXV), beautifully prolongs the transitional effect of this autumnal series. Poems LXV to LXIX ('La musique') are gentle, shaded, they really do what 'Chant d'automne' sets out to effect: '. . . goûter, en regrettant l'été blanc et torride/De l'arrière-saison le rayon jaune et doux'. The hushed, unambitious thoughts of 'Les Chats' and 'Les Hiboux', the private sentimentality or voluptuousness of 'Tristesses de la lune' or 'La pipe', cast a last illusory glow upon the sky of the brain, masking the arrival of night, winter and spleen: so that the breaking in of 'Spleen' with 'Sépulture' is both as surprising and expected as the abrupt presence of night while we were watching a sunset.

Analogies between poetry and painting are notably dangerous. Yet Baudelaire himself was tantalised by them. And so one may feel tempted to think of the poems which open 'Spleen' in terms of Baudelaire's own description of Delacroix's *Pietà*, where the contrast between colour and texture of background and front figures emphasises the drama of the scene:

> . . . Des deux saintes femmes, la première rampe convulsivement à terre, encore revêtue des bijoux et des insignes du luxe; l'autre, blonde et dorée, s'affaisse plus mollement sous le poids énorme de son désespoir.
>
> Le groupe est échelonné et disposé tout entier sur un fonds d'un vert sombre et uniforme, qui ressemble autant à des amas de rochers qu'à une mer bouleversée par l'orage. Ce fonds est d'une simplicité fantastique . . . Ce chef-d'oeuvre laisse dans l'esprit un sillon profond de mélancolie.[25]

The combination of ominous animality, dry lucidity and voluptuous dreaminess of LXV to LXIX, unified by the tone of quietness and privacy, acts towards the ensuing outburst of 'Spleen' like Delacroix's green, neither rocks nor sea, to the actors of the drama: not in similarity of effects, but of means employed. There is, in Baudelaire as in Delacroix, a complicated dialectic at work between foreground and background, between what is proffered as a failing of energy and continuity, and a formal texture which recreates both energy and continuity at a deeply organic level.

II

Professor Mossop has adopted an attitude which is at the antipodes of Feuillerat's. For him, it is futile to try and read autobiographical details into *Les Fleurs du Mal*. One should, on the contrary, think of Baudelaire as dramatising a contemporary plight: hence the title of the work: *Baudelaire's Tragic Hero*. There are great demystifying advantages to such an approach. But it leaves doubts in the mind. And one of these is that by seeing Baudelaire as portraying a 'tragic hero', distanced from himself, you diminish the notion of evil which is at the real heart of *Fleurs du Mal*, and you ignore Baudelaire's declared aesthetic intention of extracting beauty from evil. To concentrate on the first point for a while: be it 'character' or 'fate', 'tragedy' summons a concept of inevitability. And that is at odds with Baudelaire's own insistence upon lucidity – and upon responsibility. Not that *Les Fleurs du Mal* lack a 'tragic' dimension, or that they fail to raise the question of 'fate'. But privileging these at the expense of the rest ignores the poet's commitment to *ethics*.

This commitment is perhaps not sufficiently stressed in otherwise admirable works like those of Martin Turnell and Professor L.-J. Austin. Martin Turnell, in his laudable insistence on the modernity of Baudelaire as a poet, tends to by-pass the word 'péché' in his poetry. Baudelaire's 'mal' becomes equated with the destructive pressures which the modern world brings to bear not only on the individual's life but on his consciousness and subconsciousness. Nowhere is it suggested that evil, for Baudelaire, could involve moral responsibility; that it lies in a *wilful*, self-destructive failure to act, a conscious indulgence in sadism, escapism, aestheticism, with the knowledge that these ultimately shrink and wither life. Here is Mr Turnell:

> The *Fleurs du Mal* is . . . a record not merely of a circular tour of the modern world, but of the progressive loss of spiritual unity. The world described by the poet is continually growing smaller and the sense of stifling oppression greater. He had seen at the outset that this problem was the resolution of the conflict between man and his environment, between the inner and the outer life, and the recovery of unity. He had tried to achieve it through art and love, but all his attempts had failed. He found himself driven further and further into himself, into the desolating inner solitude . . .
> . . . The drama is twofold. It lies in the impact of a hostile environment on his consciousness which continually cheats his dream of reaching a unity outside him, and in the sudden eruption of destruc-

tive impulses from the depths of the unconscious which destroys internal unity.[26]

Much of this is true. But it ignores the possibility that the speaker's attempts at reaching unity might fail, in the poet's opinion and as the ordering of the book reveals, *through his own fault*, at least as much as through that of the modern world. In fact Martin Turnell, through avoidance of the moral issue, may be making Baudelaire into a worse pessimist about the possibilities of modern life than he actually is.

L.-J. Austin, however, is convinced that the 'moral' line of enquiry is wrong. For him, in Baudelaire, ethics and aesthetics pull in different directions, and aesthetics wins:

> ... Dans la pensée de Baudelaire ... il y a un conflit irréductible entre l'art et la morale, conflit qui résulte peut-être dans sa tentative pour accorder la primauté à l'esthétique, après avoir pris comme point de départ une idée toute morale: celle d'illustrer 'la beauté du Mal'.[27]

The real focus of *Les Fleurs du Mal*, L.-J. Austin argues on lines similar to J. Pommier's, [28] is the sixth poem, 'Correspondances'. Belief that earth and the events which occur on earth, are correspondences of heaven, a belief held around 1845 or 1846, confirmed by the opening poems of 'Spleen et Idéal', constitutes an ideal from which a terrible fall occurs through the volume. Loss of faith in the value of correspondences is 'une des causes majeures de cette chute qui nous mène des hauteurs de l'*Idéal* jusque dans le gouffre du *Spleen*'.[29]

With remarkable perceptiveness, L.-J. Austin underlines the numerous contradictions between the opening and the closing poems of 'Spleen et Idéal', which bear witness to the slackening of the initial *élan* and the defeat of 'correspondances'. And it is true that there are counterpoints throughout this cyclical fall, of a complexity which can only be felt and not described, and which is due, as we have seen the complexity of Baudelaire's vocabulary to be, to the number of levels at which the poetry works. The movement is from birth – 'Bénédiction' – to death – 'l'Horloge'; from fertility to the devastation of 'l'Irrémédiable'; from the height and superb mobility, both bodily and spiritual, of 'Elévation' to the prostrate paralysis of 'La Cloche fêlée'; from dawn to the darkest night, going through all the shades of daylight and twilight; from solar influences – the second poem of 'Spleen et Idéal' in the 1857 edition was 'Le Soleil', and the whole opening is steeped in sunlight – to lunar ones, starting with 'Tristesses de la lune'; from spring to winter, as Mr Turnell shows so well in his study; from the open future and fresh possibilities of the six initial poems to the 'irrémédiable' and the 'trop tard' of the closing ones. L.-J. Austin's special merit lies in his pointing out the echoes which show the decline of the ideal of correspondences: for instance, in 'Obsession' a black pessimism denies the reciprocity of man and nature which was stated in 'Correspondances', 'L'Homme et la mer' and 'Moesta et errabunda'; so do, in an even more claustrophobic way, 'Alchimie de la douleur' and 'Horreur sympathique'. To the prayer of 'Phares':

> Ces malédictions, ces blasphèmes, ces plaintes,
> Ces extases, ces cris, ces pleurs, ces *Te Deum*, ...
> C'est pour les coeurs mortels un divin opium!

replies the cynical misery of 'La Muse vénale':

> Il te faut pour gagner ton pain de chaque soir,
> Comme un enfant de choeur, jouer de l'encensoir,
> Chanter des *Te Deum* auxquels tu ne crois guère, ...

For L.-J. Austin, the growing pessimism and impiety of *Les Fleurs du Mal* reflect Baudelaire's own evolution. The direction of the book is that of his thought. Baudelaire cast his lot with Satan:

> ... Tournant le dos résolument à la symbolique traditionelle, Baudelaire a tenté la gageure de fonder une symbolique nouvelle, fortement influencée par l'occultisme, et qui évoquerait l'idéal immatériel par son reflet grossièrement déformé dans la matière. Gageure sans doute intenable, dans laquelle Baudelaire finira par discerner un piège tendu par le Diable lui-même.[30]

As often with Professor Austin, the analysis of individual poems convinces by its admirable delicacy. But one must be allowed to disagree with the general thesis. It rests on a questionable chronological view of the writing of the *Fleurs du Mal*: in fact, several of the depressed poems were written at the same time as the hopeful ones, and as Professor Ruff has shown beyond dispute, the movement from hope to depression repeated itself several times in Baudelaire's life and was not a simple movement. Furthermore, why give so much emphasis to the sixth poem rather than to the first, or indeed to the first six, which in themselves constitute a distinct opening? Baudelaire's sense of correspondences is ambiguous – as Georges Blin described so well[31] – and changeable: why make the bulk of his work rest on what is but an element, important, one grants, but part of a larger whole? Also, to return to a point we briefly touched on in the Introduction, why grant more weight to the 'Muse vénale' than to 'Phares'? Because it occurs afterwards? But why see growing truth in the downward movement of 'Spleen et Idéal' rather than a diagnosis of failure? Professor Ruff seems much closer to the truth when he describes the movement of the book in these terms: 'Le cas du poète est en effet le cas examplaire entre tous: la grandeur aussi bien que la misère de l'homme s'y rencontrent l'une et l'autre au plus haut degré. C'est bien la misère qui est le *sujet* du livre. Mais pour mesurer la chute, il fallait d'abord lever les yeux vers la crime.'[32]

In this perspective, poems I–VI constitute a 'cime' which Baudelaire does not go on to doubt, but which the speaker of the *Fleurs du Mal* becomes gradually incapable of reaching. Professor Ruff lays strong emphasis on the hopeful aspect of the book: '(Le thème des *Fleurs du Mal*) . . . pourrait donc être défini comme l'action de Satan sur le destin et la condition terrestres du poète, dans la perspective entrevue du salut éternel, grâce au prix rédempteur de la souffrance, à la réversibilité ou communion des saints, grâce aussi à la justice et à la miséricorde divines.'[33]

Perhaps this stress is a little too strong, and Professor Ruff gives so much space to Baudelaire's ethics in the *Fleurs du Mal* that he does not leave himself enough to talk about them 'du point de vue de l'esthétique'.

Having thus passed Olympian judgment on our predecessors, we can now proceed to make our own blunders.

III

In *Les Fleurs du Mal*, Baudelaire takes his reader through an interacting series of 'points of view', as Ellison does the visitor of the Domain of Arnheim, with as thorough a knowledge of the emotional impact of rhythms and metaphors as Delacroix has of that of colours. The 'point of view' of each poem is absolutely commanding and seductive within the space of that particular poem. But the gradation of the differing points of view of surrounding poems, and its place in the volume, reflect upon it, and qualify it. Moreover, as the book is a descent into hell, into the maelstrom, the record of a fall, whether it be from unity, from *correspondances*, from belief in the redemptive power of suffering, or, as we attempted to establish in the first part of our study, from 'Romantic' values, each new poem, or new series of poems, must be read as a step downwards, or a pause in a downwards process.

The shuttle goes back and forth: '. . . à un blasphème j'opposerai des élancements vers le Ciel, à une obscénité, des fleurs platoniques. . . . il était impossible de faire autrement un livre destiné à représenter (. . .) L'AGITATION DE L'ESPRIT DANS LE MAL';[34] but the fall proceeds all the same, so that each new 'blasphème' is worse, each new 'fleur platonique' less effective. While each poem is a study, conducted with passionate insight and magnifying capacity, but also with admirable impartiality – 'Le poète n'est d'aucun parti' – of states of feeling which contradict and complete each other, yet each also gets its meaning from the ensemble. L.–J. Austin recalls Mallarmé's description of the significant silence, the intellectual framework which the words of a poem create, beside and through themselves: '. . . L'armature intellectuelle du poème se dissimule et tient – a lieu – dans l'espace qui isole les strophes et parmi le blanc du papier: significatif silence qu'il n'est pas moins beau de composer, que les vers . . .'[35]

One could similarly speak of the 'significatif silence', a moral as well as an aesthetic one, which the 'composition' of the *Fleurs du Mal* create, outside but also through the series of individual poems. In this perspective, it is futile to ask whether Baudelaire's 'je' is a self-confessing 'je' or a dramatised persona. What matters is what results from the interaction of total endorsement and total control.

Unless one sees that a strong moral perspective emerges from the *Fleurs du Mal* without any moral judgment being offered at any stage, one is left with a subjective and atomistic vision of experience which Baudelaire was precisely trying to transcend.

For instance, Professor L.–J. Austin supports his theory that in his search for *correspondances*, having found Satan a more useful ally than God, Baudelaire, like the Nietzschean Superman, finally rejects both good and evil, with the 'qu'importe' which rings in 'L'Hymne à la Beauté':

> De Satan ou de Dieu, qu'importe? Ange ou Sirène,
> Qu'importe si tu rends, . . .
> . . . L'univers moins hideux et les instants moins lourds?[36]

and is echoed by the cry of the 'voyageurs' in the last poem of the *Fleurs du Mal*:

> Nous voulons, tant ce feu nous brûle le cerveau,
> Plonger au fond du gouffre, Enfer ou Ciel, qu'importe?
> Au fond de l'Inconnu pour trouver du *nouveau*![37]

Why think that this 'qu'importe' represents Baudelaire's own choice rather than qualifies the quest which is being pursued? The very recklessness of this 'qu'importe' is precisely what stands between the seekers and the ideal. It is the state of indifference to values which, on a lower but related level, characterises the drunkard who has killed his wife:

> Me voilà libre et solitaire!
> Je serai ce soir ivre mort;
> Alors, sans peur et sans remord,
> Je me coucherai sur la terre,
>
> Et je dormirai comme un chien!
> Le chariot aux lourdes roues . . .
> . . . peut bien . . .
>
> Ecraser ma tête coupable
> Ou me couper par le milieu,
> Je m'en moque comme de Dieu,
> Du Diable ou de la Sainte Table![38]

That the blasphemy here should so clearly portray the state of mind of the speaker, that evasion through brutal drunkenness should make him indifferent to death and salvation, ought to alert us to similar possibilities in the pursuit of beauty and of 'du nouveau'. Admittedly such a pursuit is nobler. But the carelessness of the main speaker as to human or moral consequences in the quest for an ideal state is, in pattern at least, the same. And why should Baudelaire have placed the section 'Le Vin' where he did if not to make this felt?

It is indeed difficult to read the strain of revolt which runs through the book and bursts out in 'Révolte', as Professor Austin would have us do, as Baudelaire's own brand of Nietzschean rebellion. In the first place, one cannot but agree with Pierre Jean Jouve that the three poems which make it up are among Baudelaire's worst, and this because he probably invested little of his imagination in them. In the second, as Professor Ruff has shown, the poems are written solidly within the 'satanic' tradition of French Romanticism. R. Vivier and J. Pommier would probably regard them as plagiarism, but one could wonder whether a poet as aware of what he was doing as Baudelaire was 'plagiarising' by accident, or rather whether he was not trying to represent, in its mood and vocabulary, that particular trend of Romanticism – but diagnosing it as one of the diseases of the times just as much as entering into its spirit. What we came to see as Baudelaire's particular relation to Romanticism earlier on strongly supports this interpretation. In the third place, again as Professor Ruff suggests, we have Gautier's assurance that Baudelaire had very little of himself at stake in these poems – and we have found that Gautier knew what Baudelaire was talking about:

> Les 'Litanies de Satan', dieu du mal et prince de ce monde, sont une de ces froides ironies familières à l'auteur où l'on aurait tort de voir une impiété. L'impiété n'est pas dans la nature de Baudelaire, qui croit à une mathématique supérieure, établie par Dieu de toute éternité et dont la moindre infraction est punie par les plus rudes châtiments, non seulement dans ce monde, mais encore dans l'autre.[39]

Finally, and this weighs more than all the rest, the placing of 'Révolte' profoundly limits its bearing. It is the ultimate attempt to break from the bonds of reality, in a search for some ecstatic infinite, left after the waning of substance brought about by the section 'Fleurs du Mal'. And it evidently turns out to be futile, since what follows it is the section 'La Mort'. Furthermore, the self-destructive nature of revolt against God's 'mathématique supérieure', against what is close to 'nature' in a Burkean sense, is announced, on a smaller level and in a gentler key, in one of the opening moments of 'Spleen et Idéal': it summarises the quest which is going to take place throughout the ampler movement of *Les Fleurs du Mal*. To the Romantic peak of the first six poems has succeeded the barren plain of VII–XI. There then begins a movement of escape from actual life, modern life, with 'La Vie antérieure' (XII) and 'Bohémiens en voyage'; the titles speak for themselves. The search for an infinite *away* from the here and now is continued with 'L'Homme et la mer':

> Homme libre, toujours tu chériras la mer!
> La mer est ton miroir; tu contemples ton âme
> Dans le déroulement infini de sa lame...[40]

There happens in these few poems, what happens repeatedly on a larger scale in 'Spleen et Idéal', in 'Tableaux Parisiens' and in 'Le Vin': an attempt to make room for the infinite longing of the soul through, or in despite of, reality. But 'L'Homme et la mer' (in premonition of where the pursuit of the ideal through beauty, love, wine, is going to take the speaker) leads, as does the section 'Fleurs du Mal', later on, to merciless struggle:

> Vous êtes tous les deux ténébreux et discrets:
> Homme, nul n'a sondé le fond de tes abîmes,
> O mer, nul ne connaît tes richesses intimes...
>
> Et cependant voilà des siècles innombrables
> Que vous vous combattez sans pitié ni remord,
> Tellement vous aimez le carnage et la mort,
> O lutteurs éternels, ô frères implacables![41]

The mood then changes: just as 'Révolte' follows 'Fleurs du Mal'. In 'Don Juan aux Enfers' and 'Châtiment de l'orgueil' we have two types of revolt against the conditions of life, in one case splendid, in the other blasphemous and demented. And 'Châtiment de l'orgueil' leads to spiritual death, as 'Révolte' will lead to 'La Mort'. It does so very clearly, one could argue, too crudely, with the evident purpose of setting the terms of the great quest for the ideal which begins with the following poem, 'La Beauté', as unambiguously as possible:

> ... On raconte qu'un jour un docteur des plus grands, ...
> Comme un homme monté trop haut, pris de panique,
> S'écria, transporté d'un orgueil satanique:
> 'Jésus, petit Jésus! je t'ai poussé bien haut!
> Mais, si j'avais voulu t'attaquer au défaut
> De l'armure, ta honte égalerait ta gloire,
> Et tu ne serais plus qu'un foetus dérisoire!'
>
> Immédiatement sa raison s'en alla.
> L'éclat de ce soleil d'un crêpe se voila;
> Tout le chaos roula dans cette intelligence,

Temple autrefois vivant, plein d'ordre et d'opulence . . .
Le silence et la nuit s'installèrent en lui . . .[42]

It is with a wide-eyed knowledge of the moral dangers of his quest that Baudelaire's seeker after the infinite is going to set out. 'Against his better knowledge, not deceived'. There will be a self-destructive 'orgueil satanique' in his 'qu'importe'. The words 'mathématique supérieure' are apt indeed.

At the same time it is a 'mathématique' which the patterns of poems draw upon silence, which no explicit statements support. Indeed, the poems which make up the section just described have a peculiar neutrality and impersonality in their themes, as though their cool distance from the main speaker of *Fleurs du Mal* was somehow needed to balance the directness with which they draw a moral lesson on the wall for him, and the several directions into which they radiate universalised the predicament which is going to come into being.

The central movement of 'Spleen et Idéal', which the following sections enlarge and bring to a close, starts with 'La Beauté'. Much has been written about how much more Baudelaire meant 'Hymne à la Beauté' than the 'Parnassian' 'La Beauté', which has been put right by Professor Mossop, reminding us that in his definition of 'beauté' Baudelaire speaks of an 'ephemeral', 'modern' element as well as an 'eternal' one, and that poems XVII to XXI make up between themselves a statement of this: 'La Géante' and 'La Beauté' lay the stress on the 'eternal', uninvolved aspect of beauty, 'L'Idéal', 'Le Masque' and 'Hymne à la Beauté, on the 'ardent' and 'melancholy' Romantic traits which characterise what was for Baudelaire 'modern' beauty.

This is important on the aesthetic level of that particular cycle. What must be added, on the plane of the overall structure, is that the choice made through these poems is the first major step in the fall announced by the two preceding movements. Both the beauty of 'La Beauté' and that of 'Hymne à la Beauté' are distinguished by a coldness, an indifference to ordinary humanity which is recognised as potentially destructive but still chosen as the only access to infinite scope. A frigid impregnability characterises the first beauty:

Je suis belle, ô mortels! comme un rêve de pierre,
Et mon sein, où chacun s'est meurtri tour à tour,
Est fait pour inspirer au poëte un amour
Éternel et muet ainsi que la matière . . .[43]

the ruthless crushing of human emotions the second:

> Tu marches sur des morts, Beauté, dont tu te moques;
> De tes bijoux l'Horreur n'est pas le moins charmant,
> Et le Meurtre, parmi tes plus chères breloques,
> Sur ton ventre orgueilleux danse amoureusement...[44]

Yes, there is a contradiction at the centre of the *Fleurs du Mal*, and inherent in the title. The 'fleurs du mal' are the diseased aestheticism, the treading on the dead which the passage on the *Ecole païenne* denounced as soul-killing. But they are also the capacity to extract beauty from evil in disregard of moral notions. And in a moral sense, they are the offspring of evil, what Baudelaire called these 'fleurs maladives' in the dedication to Gautier. In this sense, the poems to Beauty are central, and the complex beauty portrayed between XVII and XXI contains all these senses, all pulling against each other, as we saw Baudelaire's vocabulary doing, and yet made to work towards a coherent view of life. But we can perceive this only by following one strain at a time. We need not stress at this point the 'extracting beauty from evil' element, obvious in 'Hymne à la Beauté'. What must be underlined is the 'fleurs maladives' side, the fact that the ideal presented in these poems is a diminution of that which shines in 'Phares' and in 'Bénédiction'. A sense of the fullness of life, and of the companionship of artists, a 'boundless' Romantic faith, pervades 'Phares':

> Car c'est vraiment, Seigneur, le meilleur témoignage
> Que nous puissions donner de notre dignité
> Que cet ardent sanglot qui roule d'âge en âge
> Et vient mourir au bord de votre éternité![45]

The redemptive acceptance of suffering, through which the highest form of beauty is reached in 'Bénédiction', points quite unequivocally towards God:

> Je sais que la douleur est la noblesse unique
> Où ne mordront jamais la terre et les enfers,
> Et qu'il faut pour tresser ma couronne mystique
> Imposer tous les temps et tous les univers.[46]

Perhaps because the discouraged sense of waste of VII–XI, the rebellious urge of XV–XVII have already paralysed the *élan*, all that seems to remain of the opening ideal, when we get to 'La Beauté', is splendour. But the humility and companionship have dwindled into a reckless quest for the immediate satisfaction of the taste for the infinite. In 'Bénédiction, the source of ultimate beauty was reached through a Platonic hierarchy emblematised by the word 'miroirs':

> '. . . ce beau diadème . . .
> . . . ne sera fait que de pure lumière,
> Puisée au foyer saint des rayons primitifs,
> Et dont les yeux mortels, dans leur splendeur entière,
> Ne sont que des miroirs obscurcis et plaintifs!'[47]

In 'La Beauté' beauty has become the thing itself. It is still prognostic of eternity, but is to be reached for its own sake. The mirrors are there to magnify reality, not to point to finer realms of perception:

> Car j'ai, pour fasciner ces dociles amants,
> De purs miroirs qui font toutes choses plus belles:
> Mes yeux, mes larges yeux aux clartés éternelles![48]

The Platonician ordering of the universe has disappeared. And in 'Hymne à la Beauté' there is a further degradation. Far from initiating to higher things, the 'regard' of Beauty becomes a philtre, an enchantment, escape from reality. Since the *sensation* of infinity is treasured in itself, what does it matter whether it comes from heaven or hell:

> Viens-tu du ciel profond ou sors-tu de l'abîme,
> O Beauté? ton regard, infernal et divin,
> Verse confusément le bienfait et le crime,
> Et l'on peut en cela *te comparer au vin* . . .[49]

Reading this, the existence of 'Le Vin' becomes justified.[50] From the moment when Beauty becomes sought purely for the immediate access which it gives to infinite ecstasy:

> . . . ton oeil, ton souris, ton pied, m'ouvrent la porte
> D'un Infini que j'aime et n'ai jamais connu . . .[51]

it follows, in the logic of passions, that the pursuit of beauty through love having failed in 'Spleen et Idéal', and the more complex quest of 'Tableaux parisiens' having turned sour, the appetite for ecstasy, novelty, escape from the self, will have to continue through the coarser means of alcohol. That all these quests should be, each in its way magnificent, must not blind us to the fundamental degradation which the order in which they take place traces. One could nearly argue that the heavenward hierarchy of 'Bénédiction' is negatively confirmed by the hell-bound hierarchy which emerges from disregarding it.

The appropriateness of moving from the cycle of Beauty to that of love will be evident if the reader remembers Samuel Cramer's attitude to love: '. . . l'amour était chez lui . . . surtout l'admiration et l'appétit du beau . . . Il aimait un corps humain comme une harmonie matérielle . . .' There is a striking similarity of mood between Samuel's love scene with La Fanfarlo and 'Les Bijoux', which brilliantly and irreplaceably (it was one of the 'Pièces Condamnées') opened the cycle of love in the 1857 edition.

However damaging withdrawing 'Les Bijoux' from the Jeanne Duval cycle was, the rhythm remains. It is one of splendid inebriation followed by deep despair – a sense of shrinking – and only relieved by impulses of magnanimous mercy which briefly recapture the closing mood of 'Bénédiction'.

It is true that in 'Parfum exotique' (XXII), 'La Chevelure' (XXIII), and 'Le Serpent qui danse' (XXVII), all inhabited by images of ships sailing away, heaven is conquered:

> Cheveux bleus, pavillon de ténèbres tendues,
> Vous me rendez l'azur du ciel immense et rond . . .[52]

> Je crois boire un vin de Bohême,
> Amer et vainqueur,
> Un ciel liquide qui parsème
> D'étoiles mon coeur![53]

and it is also true that a poem like 'La Chevelure' is, as Martin Turnell claims, among Baudelaire's finest. But that 'beauty' should have been so successfully extracted from evil must not make us forget that it *is* evil Baudelaire is dealing with. What he says of Samuel Cramer – that his was a depraved imagination – and that in his attempt to sail towards heaven the woman was left behind, so that he suffered from the 'mélancolie du bleu' – is also true of the speaker of these poems. For such high moments as that of 'La Chevelure' to happen, the 'love' must remain below love. It must be a non-relationship. The woman who is the occasion for such ecstasies has all the attributes of Beauty – its coldness and rapacity too. These are what create the sense of infinity: while, animal-like ('Les Chats' – 'Le Serpent qui danse' – 'O *toison, moutonnant* jusque sur *l'encolure*') she is a perfect erotic and aesthetic object, she remains emotionally and sensually unreachable, thus creating air and space, leaving the man free to pursue his own sensations:

> Je t'adore à l'égal de la voûte nocturne,
> O vase de tristesse, ô grande taciturne,
> Et t'aime d'autant plus, belle, que tu me fuis,
> Et que tu me parais, ornement de mes nuits,
> Plus ironiquement accumuler les lieues
> Qui séparent mes bras des immensités bleues.[54]

> Ses yeux polis sont faits de minéraux charmants,
> Et dans cette nature étrange et symbolique
> Où l'ange inviolé se mêle au sphinx antique,

> Où tout n'est qu'or, acier, lumière et diamants,
> Resplendit à jamais, comme un astre inutile,
> La froide majesté de la femme stérile.[55]

But these very traits which make the woman so precious are also those which make her hateful – and the relationship inhuman. The worship of 'Je t'adore . . .' is broken by a vicious impulse:

> Je m'avance à l'attaque, et je grimpe aux assauts,
> Comme après un cadavre un choeur de vermisseaux . . .[56]

There are cries of anguish begging the woman to become capable of involvement, in 'Une nuit que j'étais près d'une affreuse Juive':

> Car j'eusse avec ferveur baisé ton noble corps . . .

> Si, quelque soir, d'un pleur obtenu sans effort
> Tu pouvais seulement, ô reine des cruelles!
> Obscurcir la splendeur de tes froides prunelles.[57]

The 'Remords posthume' which will gnaw her is not that predicted for the 'Coy Mistress' or Ronsard's 'Mignonne', but remorse not to have *felt*.

And alternately with the sailing away, the celebration of, or mourning for, her coldness, there ring accents of growing despair. Experience of the 'azur immense et rond' is paid for by this:

> J'implore ta pitié, Toi, l'unique que j'aime,
> Du fond du gouffre obscur où mon coeur est tombé.
> C'est un univers morne à l'horizon plombé . . .[58]

As the depression becomes more intense, as the call to 'her' becomes more urgent and remains answered only by what the speaker first sought her for and, as an addict, can no longer give up:

> Toi qui, comme un coup de couteau
> Dans mon coeur plaintif es entrée;
>
> –Infâme à qui je suis lié
> Comme le forçat à la chaîne,
>
> Comme au jeu le joueur têtu,
> Comme à la bouteille l'ivrogne . . .[59]

he becomes the victim of possession ('Le Vampire'; 'Le Possédé'); his own passion turns vengeful and destructive, like the end of 'l'Homme et la mer':

> Les glaives sont brisés! comme notre jeunesse,
> Ma chère! Mais les dents, les ongles acérés,
> Vengent bientôt l'épée et la dague traîtresse.
> – O fureur des coeurs mûrs par l'amour ulcérés![60]

Immensely true of this relationship is Baudelaire's statement that 'La volupté unique et suprême de l'amour gît dans la certitude de faire le mal'. But the lucidity with which what is evil in it is diagnosed leaves room for countless other possibilities of relationship. The moral structure creates space beyond the passionate utterances.

The only redemptive moments in a cycle which records the degradation of the hope to find infinity through eroticism are those which come to grips with reality instead of using it to sail away. This is paradoxically true of 'Tu mettrais l'univers entier dans ta ruelle', which critics have been keen to show was not written for Jeanne but for the 'affreuse Juive', seeing jarring, vicious accents in it. This is not what matters about this poem, but what emerges from the aggressive viciousness:

> La grandeur de ce mal où tu te crois savante
> Ne t'a donc jamais fait reculer d'épouvante,
> Quand la nature, grande en ses desseins cachés,
> De toi se sert, ô femme, ô reine des péchés,
> – De toi, vil animal, – pour pétrir un génie?
>
> O fangeuse grandeur! sublime ignominie![61]

The mood of 'Bénédiction' is, for the first time since the fall, recaptured. In 'Bénédiction' the poet's wife, idol-like, boasted of her usurping in the poet's heart 'les hommages divins' – as we have seen that Beauty does, that the woman of 'Je t'adore à l'égal de la voûte nocturne' does – and of her savaging his heart – as the woman of 'Le Vampire' does. The answer was the blessing:

> –'Soyez béni, mon Dieu, qui donnez la souffrance
> Comme un divin remède à nos impuretés . . .

Similarly, in 'Tu mettrais l'univers entier dans ta ruelle', the sublimity of the tone, the serene sadness of the mood, translate both the man and the woman to a grand meditative level, Pascalian in accent, in which pain rocks itself and becomes contemplative. And it is the attention paid to the woman herself, however degraded, rather than to the 'harmonie matérielle' of her body, which gains this.

Similarly, 'Une Charogne', 'Le Balcon' and the closing poems of the Jeanne cycle, 'Un fantôme' and 'Je te donne ces vers', are moments of gentle or passionate tenderness gained through the fire. 'Le Balcon' follows the savage 'Duellum', as though confrontation with one extreme released a capacity for the other. In 'La Charogne' the contemplation of the corpse is so intense that it frees the gazer from the horror. 'Form' becomes pre-eminent, and the spirituality of that form expands the possibilities of the 'matière' to such an extent that it is imaginatively transmuted. From the vision of the decaying corpse we do not 'sail' but soar to that of Du Bellay's 'D'un vanneur de blé aux vents':

> Les mouches bourdonnaient sur ce ventre putride,
>   D'où sortaient de noirs bataillons
> De larves, qui coulaient comme un épais liquide
>   Le long de ces vivants haillons.

> Tout cela descendait, montait comme une vague,
>   Ou s'élançait en pétillant,
> On eût dit que le corps, enflé d'un souffle vague,
>   Vivait en se multipliant.
>
> Et ce monde rendait une étrange musique,
>   Comme l'eau courante et le vent,
> Ou le grain qu'un vanneur d'un mouvement rhythmique
>   Agite et tourne dans son van.
>
> Les formes s'effaçaient et n'étaient plus qu'un rêve
>   Une ébauche lente à venir,
> Sur la toile oubliée, et que l'artiste achève
>   Seulement par le souvenir.[62]

This metamorphosis, gained through art, but also quietness of endurance, courage in the exploration of horror, becomes a warrant that out of a relationship which promised exotic ecstasies but has bred preying impulses, as the potential eroticism of the corpse reveals corruption,[63] a 'form' will also survive the wreck, the final decomposition:

> Alors, ô ma beauté! dites à la vermine
>   Oui vous mangera de baisers,
> Que j'ai gardé la forme et l'essence divine
>   De mes amours décomposés![64]

What must be acknowledged, however, is that the hope gained through such poems is speedily drowned by moods whose darkness seems insuperable. 'La Charogne' is followed by 'De Profundis clamavi'; to this in 'Le Balcon':

> Ces serments, ces parfums, ces baisers infinis,
> Renaîtront-ils d'un gouffre interdit à nos sondes,
> Comme montent au ciel les soleils rajeunis
> Apres s'être lavés au fond des mers profondes?
> — O serments! ô parfums! ô baisers infinis![65]

answers 'Le Possédé':

> Le soleil s'est couvert d'un crêpe. Comme lui,
> O Lune de ma vie! emmitoufle-toi d'ombre . . .
> Et plonge tout entière au gouffre de l'Ennui . . .[66]

Yet the spirit in which the Jeanne cycle closes is one of belief in the Ronsardian promise which ended 'Une Charogne'. As the form of the carrion suggested a sketch, on a forgotten canvas, which the artist completes 'seulement par le souvenir', all that remains of the love for Jeanne, in 'Un fantôme', is a 'dessin fort pâle, aux trois crayons', which Time rubs with his 'aile rude', but which the poet completes with his memory:

> Noir assassin de la Vie et de l'art,
> Tu ne tueras jamais dans ma mémoire
> Celle qui fut mon plaisir et ma gloire.[67]

That is, as happens with Ronsard's 'Sonnet à Hélène', the poet is he who saves from the wreck of time the 'forme et essence divines' of the aged or 'décomposé' love. The first two stanzas of XXXIX have the sustained magnificence of the best Pléiade sonnets, and continue the theme of salvation of life through art:

> Je te donne ces vers afin que si mon nom
> Aborde heureusement aux époques lointaines,
> Et fait rêver un soir les cervelles humaines,
> Vaisseau favorisé par un grand aquilon,
>
> Ta mémoire, pareille aux fables incertaines,
> Fatigue le lecteur ainsi qu'un tympanon,
> Et par un fraternel et mystique chaînon
> Reste comme pendue à mes rimes hautaines . . .[68]

Yet that sonnet is of a strangely dual nature. For the tercets return to the ideal of beauty from which the love cycle started, and the woman loses the strong individuality which was hers in 'Un fantôme' and regains the impersonality, or rather perhaps allegorical stature, of Beauty:

> – O toi qui, comme une ombre à la trace éphémère,
>
> Foules d'un pied léger et d'un regard serein
> Les stupides mortels qui t'ont jugée amère,
> Statue aux yeux de jais . . .

echoes the first 'La Beauté':

> Je suis belle, ô mortels! comme un rêve de pierre,
> Et mon sein, où chacun s'est meurtri tour à tour . . .[69]

The

> Être maudit, à qui, de l'abîme profond
> Jusqu'au plus haut du ciel, rien, hors moi, ne répond!

answers:

> Ce ne seront jamais ces beautés de vignettes,
> Produits avariés, nés d'un siècle vaurien . . .
> Qui sauront satisfaire un coeur comme le mien.
> . . .
>
> Ce qu'il faut à ce coeur profond comme un abîme,
> C'est vous, Lady Macbeth, âme puissante au crime . . .[70]

and the closing lines correspond to the 'Ange ou Sirène' of 'Hymne à la Beauté'. At the same time, the ring of these tercets, the way the lines soar and fall, the defiant exaltation, are definitely 'Romantic' in opposition to the more 'Renaissance' quality of the quatrains.

This has two effects, as though, for a 'bilan' of a first failure and in an attempt to rescue it, the speaker restated the dichotomy in 'fleurs du mal'. One impact of this confrontation of a traditional view of poetry with modern, Romantic, feelings, is to place the effort to save life through art, to make gold out of mud, lasting forms out of the waste of time, to grow flowers out of evil, within a large and durable framework. To the 'cri' of the 'Renaissance' 'sentinelle' answers the cry of the nineteenth-century Baudelaire. But the other effect is on opposite lines, and it is to suggest the inescapability of the moral dimension. The indifference to good and evil, happiness and suffering which there is in the quatrains, breaks down with the passionate address: 'Être maudit . . .'. It is the grandeur of the speaker that he responds as he does to the damnation and solitude of this 'être', be it real or allegorical; but whereas in Ronsard the salvation of its 'mémoire' through verse would have been the end itself, in Baudelaire life remains to be lived, and responding to a damned being means damning oneself. The continuity from cycle to cycle, the lapse into despair after poems of superb artistic fulfilment, means, among other things, that one may salvage life through art, but not living. Which is why 'Le Masque', where a beautiful, Renaissance-style statue hides a real face of despair behind a smiling face, is placed at the centre of the cycle of beauty:

> – Mais pourquoi pleure-t-elle? Elle, beauté parfaite
> Qui mettrait à ses pieds le genre humain vaincu,
> Quel mal mystérieux ronge son flanc d'athlète?
> – Elle pleure, insensé, parcequ'elle a vécu!
> Et parcequ'elle vit! Mais ce qu'elle déplore
> Surtout, ce qui la fait frémir jusqu'aux genoux,
> C'est que demain, hélas! il faudra vivre encore!
> Demain, après-demain et toujours! – comme nous![71]

There is another structural aspect in which the closing poems of the Jeanne cycle are a 'bilan' of failure. One of the problems most strongly at the heart of the *Fleurs du Mal* is that of time, – of the quality of confidence with which one inhabits one's present and faces one's future, and how this is imperilled by efforts to expand the present or take refuge in the past. 'Bénédiction' is written under the sign of an active present, of an open future – of a 'Romantic' optimism:

> Je *sais* que la douleur *est* la noblesse unique
> Où ne *mordront* jamais la terre et les enfers . . .

and so are 'Elévation', 'Correspondances' and 'Phares'. A degradation of these tenses accompanies that of 'La Muse malade' onwards. There seems to be no energy to stretch beyond the present:

> Ma pauvre Muse, hélas! qu'as-tu donc ce matin? . . .[72]
> O moine fainéant! quand saurai-je donc faire . . .[73]

As expanse is gained through moments made boundless in 'Parfum exotique' and 'La chevelure', time shrinks and stops moving. Speeding it up has slowed it down:

> Je jalouse le sort des plus vils animaux
> Qui peuvent se plonger dans un sommeil stupide,
> Tant l'écheveau du temps lentement se dévide![74]

And as spleen strengthens its hold upon the soul, that soul becomes capable of mercy or tenderness *only in retrospect*. The gentleness of 'Un fantôme', the magnanimity of 'Je te donne ces vers' are gained through the knowledge that the relationship is *over*.

This is why the love cycles which follow are not, as is usually agreed, higher, or more complete human experiences than the Jeanne Duval one. It is only in the most visible dimension that to 'black' poems there succeed 'white' ones, those to Madame Sabatier. The deeper dimension is that Baudelaire had invested more of his faith in beauty as well as life in the initial series, and that the series that follows is embarked on as a fundamentally illusory and half-hearted commitment. And also with the awareness that carrying on with what has once turned out to be a delusion is only going to destroy you further:

> – Quand notre coeur a fait une fois sa vendange,
> Vivre est un mal.[75]

It is of much significance that the poem which opens the Sabatier cycle should be called 'Semper eadem'. The title is not meant simply to characterise the sunny evenness of mood of the woman, 'âme toujours ravie', but to underline the continuity between the women – between what is being sought through them. The quest is still under the sign of the 'Beauty' cycle. In 'La Géante' there was this:

> J'eusse aimé vivre auprès d'une jeune géante,
> Comme aux pieds d'une reine un chat voluptueux . . .
>
> Et parfois en été. . . .
>
> Dormir nonchalamment à l'ombre de ses seins,
> Comme un hameau paisible au pied d'une montagne.[76]

The same dream is pursued now through the bodily pretext of Madame Sabatier, as it will be later through that of Marie Daubrun. The woman offers some statuesque, maternal haven from the security of which warmth, peace, summer are briefly recaptured[77]:

> Laissez, laissez mon coeur . . .
> . . . sommeiller longtemps à l'ombre de vos cils![78]

Only much of the hope has gone out of the attempt. The incantation cannot conceal the awareness of self-deceit:

> Laissez, laissez mon coeur *s'enivrer* d'un *mensonge,* . . .

Inebriation has lost substance. What with Jeanne was thought to give access to a superior reality is now recognised to rest on a lie. And by nonetheless opting for it the speaker further diminishes his possibilities of life.

It is true that the new 'she' holds promise of a return to the unified world of 'Correspondances':

> Et l'harmonie est trop exquise,
> Qui gouverne tout son beau corps,
> Pour que l'impuissante analyse
> En note les nombreux accords.
>
> O métamorphose mystique
> De tous mes sens fondus en un!
> Son haleine fait la musique,
> Comme sa voix fait le parfum![79]

true also that she seems to be pulling him towards the heavenly beauty:

> Son fantôme dans l'air danse . . .
>
> Parfois il parle et dit: 'Je suis belle, et j'ordonne
> Que pour l'amour de moi vous n'aimiez que le Beau;
> Je suis l'Ange gardien, la Muse et la Madone.'[80]

Her presence marks a return to strong present tenses, and a bright pause in a dark progress. At the same time, the attempt to create a new sort of distance between the self and the woman – with Jeanne her coldness and animality did it; with Mme Sabatier it is angelism which is used – with the knowledge that this distance is indispensible to the survival of the ideal, will be made vain by the smallest true contact. Du Bos was right indeed to refer to Petrarch in relation to this. In life, as is well known, Baudelaire's Laura turned out to be a fleshy proposition indeed, thus destroying the relationship. In 'Spleen et Idéal' it is 'Confession' which acts as an agent of rupture. Just a sigh, a bitter sigh, uttered by the gay angel, reveals worlds of dark experience which destroy the fabric the poet had been trying to erect around her.

From the start of the cycle, the effort to make the woman into Beauty itself – a further desecration of the 'Bénédiction' ideal – had rendered her shadowy, insubstantial. The word 'fantôme' which applied to Jeanne when *memorised* characterises the *present* Mme Sabatier as much as words like angel, muse, Madonna. And after 'Confession'. which has gutted the relationship, 'She' becomes even more ghost-like, the dream of a débauché at dawn – worse than this, a dream which, as the capacity to idealise and soar wanes, can only be achieved *through* debauchery:

> Quand chez les débauchés l'aube blanche et vermeille
> Entre en société de l'Idéal rongeur,
> Par l'opération d'un mystère vengeur,
> Dans la brute assoupie un ange se réveille.
>
> . . .
>
> Ainsi, chère Déesse, Être lucide et pur,
> Sur les débris fumeux des stupides orgies
> Ton souvenir plus clair, plus rose, plus charmant,
> A mes yeux agrandis voltige incessamment.
>
> Le soleil a noirci la flamme des bougies;
> Ainsi, toujours vainqueur, ton fantôme est pareil,
> Ame resplendissante, à l'immortel soleil![81]

A Balzacian dawn indeed, and which is as much used to characterise the fallen voice of the speaker as Raphaël de Valentin's or Lucien de Rubempré noble aspirations in the cold light of sunrise after a night of orgy. No wonder that, after the sad, *retrospective* gentleness of 'Harmonie du soir', and the mixture of shimmering sensuality, necrophilia and irony of 'Le Balcon', a more 'debauched' cycle should follow. One in which, that is, the two quests which have been pursued separately through the Jeanne and the Sabatier cycles, for ecstasy through eroticism, then through idealisation, become the condition for one another. There is a speeding up of the 'agitation de l'esprit dans le mal' as well as a corruption, not simply of hierarchy but of boundaries of experience. As in 'L'Aube spirituelle' purity of *élan* was achieved through a 'stupide orgie', in the Marie Daubrun series of poems the most refined and potentially vicious eroticism leads to voyeur aestheticism, this to a hushed tenderness, which in its turn releases forces of violence.

At the same time, the relative unreality of the Sabatier cycle has worsened the time disease. In 'Harmonie du soir' there are premonitions of the growing paralysis which finally grips the speaker of 'La Cloche fêlée'. Despite the gentleness of the voice the harmony is born, not out of unified complexity, as in 'Tout entière', even less as the deep-lying correspondences of reality, but as a trance which makes reality outside expressive of the mood. The 'mensonge' of the relationship has subjectivised the world to such an extent that its otherness disappears. And with the capacity to relate to people, to things, as separate from oneself, there disappears the capacity to inhabit a moving time:

> Un coeur tendre, qui hait le néant vaste et noir,
> Du passé lumineux recueille tout vestige!
> Le soleil s'est noyé dans son sang qui se fige . . .
> Ton souvenir en moi luit comme un ostensoir![82]

The memory is luminous, here, but we are on the way to 'L'Irrémédiable'. That is to a state where the present has become stilled by the past, where time has clotted like blood, where life is imprisoned as by ice. The image of the sun, drowning in 'son sang qui se fige', is premonitory of 'Chant d'automne':

> Et comme le soleil dans son enfer polaire,
> Mon coeur ne sera plus qu'un bloc rouge et glacé . . .[83]

itself a prediction of this, in 'L'Irrémédiable':

> Un navire pris dans le pôle,
> Comme en un piège de cristal,
> Cherchant par quel détroit fatal
> Il est tombé dans cette geôle . . .[84]

In other words, the corruption of the ideal of 'correspondances' does not so much register a waning trust in man's capacity to penetrate nature (as Professor Austin would have it) as it is brought about by evil human relationships. As Poe saw it, when man fell, nature fell. And what several critics regard as the gentle, reconciled mood on which the love cycles end, are fundamentally steps towards a realisation of the unredeemable quality life has assumed. Satan does know his man. Every way out he seems to offer closes another door. The immediate lyrical impact that the poems have puts one in the exact frame of mind of the tempted. Only where he gets to, and how, reveal where and how he went wrong. 'Ce livre doit être jugé *dans son ensemble*, et alors il en ressort une terrible moralité.'[85]

It is the degradation of images and themes which point to this 'terrible moralité'. Thus 'Le Flacon', which ends the Sabatier cycle, repeats the hope of 'Une Charogne'. But the tenderness and faith in the immortality of art of the latter have been replaced by vicious, addicted irony and self-indulgent relish of decrepitude:

> Ainsi, quand je serai perdu dans la mémoire
> Des hommes, dans le coin d'une sinistre armoire
> Quand on m'aura jeté, vieux flacon désolé,
> Décrépit, poudreux, sale, abject, visqueux, fêlé,
>
> Je serai ton cercueil, aimable pestilence!
> Le témoin de ta force et de ta virulence,
> Cher poison préparé par les anges! liqueur
> Qui me ronge, ô la vie et la mort de mon coeur![86]

How easily the Sabatier cycle glides into the Marie Daubrun cycle can be felt when one notices that to the 'Cher poison préparé par les anges' answers 'Le Poison'. The weary commitment to the woman, with the knowledge that the relationship is going to be destructive, which we found in the 'Laissez mon coeur s'enivrer d'un mensonge' to Mme Sabatier, becomes savage recklessness in 'Causerie' – a title of truly Laforguian irony:

> Mon coeur est un palais flétri par la cohue;
> On s'y soûle, on s'y tue, on s'y prend aux cheveux!
> – Un parfum nage autour de votre gorge nue! . . .
>
> O Beauté, dur fléau des âmes, tu le veux!
> Avec tes yeux de feu, brillants comme des fêtes,
> Calcine ces lambeaux qu'ont épargnés les bêtes![87]

To the noble urge of this question in 'L'Ennemi':

> Et qui sait si les fleurs nouvelles dont je rêve
> Trouveront dans ce sol lavé comme une grève
> Le mystique aliment qui ferait leur vigueur?[88]

replies the self-regarding, desperate eroticism of 'Ciel brouillé':

> O femme dangereuse, ô séduisants climats!
> Adorerai-je aussi ta neige et vos frimas,
> Et saurai-je tirer de l'implacable hiver
> Des plaisirs plus aigus que la glace et le fer?[89]

Eroticism had once given access to heaven:

> Comme un flot grossi par la fonte
>   Des glaciers grondants,
> Quand l'eau de ta bouche remonte
>   Au bord de tes dents,
>
> Je crois boire un vin de Bohême,
>   Amer et vainqueur,
> Un ciel liquide qui parsème
>   D'étoiles mon coeur![90]

Now, all that is asked from it is to carry the poet towards death. The final section, 'La Mort', has its seed in 'Le Poison':

> Tout cela ne vaut pas le terrible prodige
>   De ta salive qui mord,
> Qui plonge dans l'oubli mon âme sans remord,
>   Et, charriant le vertige,
> La roule défaillante aux rives de la mort![91]

Instances of this could be multiplied, as each image, each theme, has its history through the book. Several of the most important come to their 'conclusion', as Baudelaire said, that is, really reach the bottom in the closing poems of 'Spleen et Idéal'. For instance, the 'flambeau', the torch illumining darkness, once in 'Phares' and then in 'Hymne à Beauté', stood for ideal beauty:

> L'éphémère ébloui vole vers toi, chandelle,
> Crépite, flambe et dit: Bénissons ce flambeau![92]

In 'Le Flambeau vivant', to Mme Sabatier, the torch is no longer Beauty itself, but a single woman. We have gone down in the neo-Platonic ladder:

> Ils marchent devant moi, ces Yeux pleins de lumières,
> Qu'un Ange très-savant a sans doute aimantés . . .
>
> Me sauvant de tout piège et de tout péché grave,
> Ils conduisent mes pas dans la route du Beau;
> Ils sont mes serviteurs et je suis leur esclave;
> Tout mon être obéit à ce vivant flambeau.[93]

When we reach 'L'Irrémédiable', both 'flambeau' and 'phares' have lost all sense of guidance, of something pointing heavenwards, or forwards. They have become images of sterile, self-consuming lucidity. There is no longer any breaking away from the self. Even the voice, redeeming on another plane up to now, has lost all *élan*, all lyricism. The last four poems of 'Spleen et Idéal', with the exception of 'l'Horloge', which reopens the hope necessary for the following section, 'Tableaux parisiens', to take place, are written in dry, ironic eight-syllable lines:

> Tête-à-tête sombre et limpide
> Qu'un coeur devenu son miroir!
> Puits de Vérité, clair et noir,
> Où tremble une étoile livide,
>
> Un phare ironique, infernal,
> Flambeau des grâces sataniques,
> Soulagement et gloire uniques,
> – La conscience dans le Mal![94]

The same thing happens to the image of a ship sailing away, which we saw powerfully inhabiting the poems to Jeanne, and which again glides through those to Marie Daubrun – 'Le Beau navire', 'L'Invitation au voyage' – and later ones – 'Moesta et errabunda', 'La Musique'. The sensuality and longing which informed this image were part of a fine aesthetic sense, a noble aspiration. But in 'L'Héautontimorouménos', the only experience that can still provoke this sailing away is sadism. (And the speaker soon turns his cruelty against himself, so that even that *élan* is deadened):

> Je te frapperai sans colère
> Et sans haine, comme un boucher,
> Comme Moïse le rocher!
> Et je ferai de ta paupière
>
> Pour abreuver mon Saharah,
> Jaillir les eaux de la souffrance.
> Mon désir gonflé d'espérance
> Sur tes pleurs salés nagera
>
> Comme un vaisseau qui prend le large . . .[95]

The reprieve which 'Tableaux parisiens' at first offer fails. From the opening a choice appears, fundamentally similar to that of 'Spleen et Idéal'. It lies between confronting, (and through an enlargement of sympathies, or acceptance of suffering, expanding the possibilities of) reality, and evading that reality for a better, artificial world. It is presented through the first two poems. 'Paysage', similar to the mood of Keats's 'Fancy', and reminiscent of Gautier's *Emaux et camées*, ignores what is going on in the world outside for the sake of hothouse sensations:

> L'Emeute, tempêtant vainement à ma vitre,
> Ne fera pas lever mon front de mon pupitre;
> Car je serai plongé dans cette volupté
> D'évoquer le Printemps avec ma volonté,
> De tirer un soleil de mon coeur, et de faire
> De mes pensers brûlants une tiède atmosphère.[96]

In 'Le Soleil' on the contrary, the sun stands as an emblem of the poet's penetrative imagination, as well as of his capacity to transfigure reality through language:

> Quand, ainsi qu'un poëte, il descend dans les villes,
> Il ennoblit le sort des choses les plus viles
> Et s'introduit en roi, sans bruit et sans valets,
> Dans tous les hôpitaux et dans tous les palais.[97]

Once again, that is, the alternative is between using the world for one's purposes at the risk of not being able to get away from those purposes, as happened in 'Spleen et Idéal', where all things started mirroring the poet's moods:

> Cieux déchirés comme des grèves,
> En vous se mire mon orgueil . . .[98]

and gaining insights into reality. In the first part of 'Tableaux parisiens' insights prevail – in 'Le Cygne', 'Les Petites vieilles', 'A une passante', 'Les Aveugles'. Yet even there, in 'Les Sept vieillards' and 'Le Squelette laboureur', horror threatens. And though the deep seriousness of the involvement universalises and thus controls the despair, the confidence slackens. The nocturnal cycle which follows, despite moments of gentle or courageous awareness, and the largesse of its opening and end – 'Le Crépuscule du soir' and 'Le Crépuscule du matin' – finds little resting-place between savage probing and illusion. The mood of 'Paysage' wins, with 'Brumes et pluies' and 'Rêve parisien'. Escape becomes imperative. The section leads up to 'Le Vin'. And, as the opium trance of 'Rêve parisien' ended on brutal awakening,[80] the dream state of 'Le Vin' is superseded by the lucid horror of 'Fleurs du Mal' – starting with 'La Destruction'. From then on the fall is relentless, as we saw when discussing the place of 'Révolte' in the volume. It leads straight to 'La Mort'. But, as happened with beauty, love, wine, embarking on death as a door to the infinite is a self-damning delusion. The closing poem, 'Le Voyage', falls under the shadow of 'Rêve d'un curieux', where the death the speaker is dreaming of is like the opening of a theatre curtain on an *empty* stage. That Baudelaire feels close to the 'étonnants voyageurs', his seekers after the infinite, does not mean that he approves of the short-cuts they take towards it. Dante faints with sympathetic anguish when meeting Francesca da Rimini. But he has put her in hell. And that is where Baudelaire's travellers are going.

So on a structural level, the *Fleurs du Mal* are a fall into sin, the self-induced damnation of a soul. One could argue that 'Au lecteur', among other things, acts in the framework of the book as original sin: a seed in all humans – 'Hypocrite lecteur, mon semblable, mon frère!' – whose sprouting and growth and blossoming is studied in a particular soul. One could also regard the *Fleurs du Mal* as a 'constat' (as Du Bos said of Constant's *Adolphe*) of Romanticism. The solitude and paralysis of conquering Ennui, the speaker's gradual loss of power to reach outwards, to transmute experience, are the result of a noble, but sensation-craving egotism which is in the grain of French Romanticism[99] – as descended from Byron, Sade and Sainte-Beuve. The imprudent traveller of 'L'Irrémédiable', the angel tempted by love of deformity,

> Au fond d'un cauchemar énorme
> Se débattant comme un nageur,
>
> Et luttant, angoisses funèbres!
> Contre un gigantesque remous
> Qui va chantant comme les fous
> Et pirouettant dans les ténèbres . . . [100]

is descended from Lamartine's *La Chute d'un ange*, Vigny's *Eloa*, Nerval's *Aurélia*. Only, in Baudelaire the image becomes psychologically more precise, and rooted in contemporary experience. We can recognise the sin of angelism which crosses the Sabatier poems in a way in which it is difficult to do with Lamartine or Vigny.

It must be added that the various meanings which emerge on the level of the composition of the book, cross, but do not interfere with, the 'poetic' impact of each poem. And also, that the evil which is the subject-matter of the book remains evil while being made beautiful without becoming corrupting. The quest for beauty which damns is contradicted, while it happens, by a redemptive achievement of beauty, without its becoming seductive. This is difficult to explain: but if we read 'Une Martyre' of 'Femmes damnées' aloud, are we not converted to a level at which vision is too magnanimous for distinct or separate impulses to be felt? This is a question which is best understood within a larger framework.

10 *Le Spleen de Paris*

The 'aesthetic' of *Le Spleen de Paris* is looser, more sociable, less pessimistic than that of the *Fleurs du Mal*. But, as several of the prose poems which make it up grew from 'Tableaux parisiens', it might be useful to see what is the continuity between the two works.

In the nocturnal series of 'Tableaux parisiens', 'L'Amour du mensonge' advocates a Samuel Cramer-type of aesthetic choice and echoes the mood of 'Semper eadem':

> Je sais qu'il est des yeux, des plus mélancoliques,
> Qui ne recèlent point de secrets précieux;
> Beaux écrins sans joyaux, médaillons sans reliques,
> Plus vides, plus profonds que vous-mêmes, ô Cieux!
>
> Mais ne suffit-il pas que tu sois l'apparence
> Pour réjouir un coeur qui fuit la vérité?
> Qu'importe ta bêtise ou ton indifférence?
> Masque ou décor, salut! J'adore ta beauté.[1]

The impact of this poem is qualified by the main preoccupation of the section, which is the coming to terms with modern life, the life of the city. The interplay of this poem with surrounding ones sets its meaning in perspective. It follows a 'Danse macabre' in which Death is shown as hideously there under the surface of life. The apostrophe is to the skeleton who has joined the ball:

> Bayadère sans nez . . .
> Dis donc à ces danseurs qui font les offusqués:
> 'Fiers mignons, malgré l'art des poudres et du rouge,
> Vous sentez tous la mort! O squelettes musqués,
>
> Antinoüs flétris, dandys à face glabre,
> Cadavres vernissés, lovelaces chenus,

Le branle universel de la danse macabre
Vous entraîne en des lieux qui ne sont pas connus!

. . .

En tout climat, sous tout soleil, la Mort t'admire
En tes contorsions, risible Humanité,
Et souvent, comme toi, se parfumant de myrrhe,
Mêle son ironie à ton insanité![2]

By contrast, 'L'Amour du mensonge' rings shallow; though the elegance of the tone remains seductive. Also, the two poems which follow it make it sound gaudy and perverse, though again they do not destroy its magic. The quiet, delicate intimacy of 'Je n'ai pas oublié, voisine de la ville', the urgent piety of 'La servante au grand coeur dont vous étiez jalouse' expose its narrowness and fallacy. In a way, Baudelaire's poems in 'Tableaux parisiens' are like people: with complete, diverse but definite individualities, and yet living in a world of relations, exchanges, pressures, interaction with each other. Their internal world is indisputable, but questioned by the existence of adverse internal worlds.

It is this confrontation of contradictory self-contained attitudes which Baudelaire adopts for *Le Spleen de Paris*. 'Les Fenêtres', like 'L'Amour du mensonge', commends illusions, artifice:

Celui qui regarde du dehors à travers une fenêtre ouverte ne voit jamais autant de choses que celui qui regarde une fenêtre fermée. Il n'est pas d'objet plus profond, plus mystérieux, plus fécond, plus ténébreux, plus éblouissant qu'une fenêtre éclairée d'une chandelle . . . Dans ce trou noir ou lumineux vit la vie, rêve la vie, souffre la vie.

Peut-être me direz-vous: 'Es-tu sûr que cette légende soit la vraie?' Qu'importe ce que peut être la réalité placée hors de moi, si elle m'a aidé à vivre, à sentir que je suis et ce que je suis?[3]

The 'qu'importe' echoes the other 'qu'importe', those of 'le Vin de l'assassin', the 'Hymne à la Beauté' and 'Le Voyage'.

It quietly undermines the option for total subjectivism, the deforming prism of fancy, which seems seductive in the circumscribed world of the poem. But the privacy advocated by 'Les Fenêtres' clashes with the intellectual curiosity of the narrator of 'Mademoiselle Bistouri' and that of 'La Corde:

> Les illusions, – me disait mon ami, – sont aussi innombrables peut-être que les rapports des hommes entre eux, ou des hommes avec les choses. Et quand l'illusion disparaît, c'est-à-dire quand nous voyons l'être ou le fait tel qu'il existe en-dehors de nous, nous éprouvons un bizarre sentiment, compliqué moitié de regret pour le fantôme disparu, moitié de surprise agréable devant la nouveauté, le fait réel.[4]

Edouard Manet, the presumed narrator of 'La Corde', is thus taken through a formative reading of facts. A little in the way in which, in 'Point-Rash-Judgement', different readings of the same object pass comment on the narrator's values and educate him into a less hasty, deeper understanding of reality. In *Le Spleen de Paris* the open-mindedness of 'La Corde' highlights the reductiveness of 'Les Fenêtres'. But 'Les Fenêtres' loses none of its weight, and no explicit judgement inside or outside the poem corrupts the atmosphere of the dreamer's world.

Baudelaire often shows the paradoxical nature of a value by confronting its contradictory aspects in a context which forces them to reflect on each other, like people meeting in a street made to talk by a traffic jam. The encounter will be brief, never repeated in the same terms, but striking while it happens. A good instance of this might be the light thrown on artifice by two successive poems, 'Une Mort héroïque' and 'La Fausse monnaie'.

In 'Une Mort héroïque' artifice is presented as a moral ideal. The Prince's Fool, Fancioulle, has been sentenced to death by his master for having conspired against him. The Prince, a would-be Nero, makes him act for the last time, to see how he will perform a comical part in his real tragic role of 'condamné à mort'. Fancioulle shows magnificent exuberance. His involvement in his 'artificial' part is so total that it makes him forget he is nearing death. He masters circumstances: 'Fancioulle me prouvait, d'une manière péremptoire, irréfutable, que l'ivresse de l'Art est plus apte que toute autre à voiler les terreurs du gouffre; que le génie peut jouer la comédie au bord de la tombe avec une joie qui l'empêche de voir la tombe, perdu, comme il est, dans un paradis excluant toute idée de tombe et de destruction.'[5]

The reverse occurs in 'La Fausse monnaie'. There, a recourse to artifice in a real situation is presented as a degradation, not a triumph. The narrator's friend gives a false gold coin to a poor man. The narrator imagines that his friend is acting so out of intellectual curiosity, that he is perversely speculating on the turmoil that his gesture might create in the beggar's life. But his friend soon undeceives him saying, Tartuffe-

like: 'Oui, vous avez raison; il n'est pas de plaisir plus doux que de surprendre un homme en lui donnant plus qu'il n'espère.'
The narrator comments:

> Je vis alors clairement qu'il avait voulu faire à la fois la charité et une bonne affaire; gagner quarante sols et le coeur de Dieu; emporter le paradis économiquement; je lui aurais presque pardonné le désir de la criminelle jouissance dont je le supposais tout à l'heure capable; j'aurais trouvé curieux, singulier, qu'il s'amusât à compromettre les pauvres; mais je ne lui pardonnerai jamais l'ineptie de son calcul. On n'est jamais excusable d'être méchant, mais il y a quelque mérite à savoir qu'on l'est; et le plus irréparable des vices est de faire le mal par bêtise.[6]

The friend is demeaned by his inability to face what he is doing, very much in the way in which several of Balzac's characters are. For instance, Rastignac is horrified by Vautrin's lucid cynicism; he does not have the strength to resist him - he lets him commit a murder for his sake - and he does not have that to follow him either; he is conscience-stricken when he hears that the murder has taken place. He does not have the courage to succeed by 'honest' means, like Bianchon. But he clings to the conviction that he is truly honourable, sensitive and proud, while he lets himself be kept by Delphine, while he participates, through her and despite his humanitarian feelings, in the protracted murder of Goriot. The greatness of *Le Père Goriot* lies in Balzac's ability to show that a man can morally destroy himself, be twice a murderer, simply through his failure to see with courageous lucidity what each of his acts entails, and to choose himself accordingly. Vautrin is morally superior to Rastignac because he is without self-deceit (which is also the virtue of Baudelaire's seeker after the infinite), and able to adjust his acts to his moral views - even though these views are ruthless, and his acts, criminal. 'Je lui aurais presque pardonné le désir de la criminelle jouissance dont je le supposais tout à l'heure capable'. What is unforgiveable however is 'l'ineptie (du) calcul'. By attempting to 'gagner quarante sols et le coeur de Dieu', to make one's fortune by dishonourable means while trying to remain honourable, one sins against *intelligence*, against the fundamental laws of the moral world.

What is striking, in Baudelaire as in Balzac, is the rigour of the laws that thus emerge. The fact that we are *born* sinful, that we live under the shadow of the deadly sins of 'Au lecteur', makes each slip terrible. Even postponing or avoiding choice is still a manner of choice, a corrosive one. That might even reduce you to the contemptible state of the 'vigliacchi', the cowards of Dante's Inferno, who were able to opt for neither good nor for evil, and are cast away by both heaven and hell. The world that imposes such drastic options forces you to live on a knife's edge. This what Delphine and Hippolyte, the 'femmes damnées', know. At least they have the greatness to choose themselves 'damned':

> Maudit soit à jamais le rêveur inutile
> Qui voulut le premier, dans sa stupidité,
> S'éprenant d'un problème insoluble et stérile,
> Aux choses de l'amour mêler l'honnêteté!
>
> Celui qui veut unir dans un accord mystique
> L'ombre avec la chaleur, la nuit avec le jour,
> Ne chauffera jamais son corps paralytique
> A ce rouge soleil que l'on nomme l'amour!
> . . .
> On ne peut ici-bas contenter qu'un seul maître![7]

Their voice is echoed by Satan's ironical address to the ditherers of 'L'Imprévu':

> Avez-vous donc pu croire, hypocrites surpris,
> Qu'on se moque du maître, et qu'avec lui l'on triche,
> Et qu'il soit naturel de recevoir deux prix,
>   D'aller au Ciel et d'être riche?[8]

'La Fausse monnaie' follows 'Une Mort héroïque', and their closeness is calculated to release meaning. There is a contradiction between them: in 'Une Mort héroïque', concealing the truth from oneself, creating a joy which prevents one from 'voir la tombe' is shown as a feat; in 'La Fausse monnaie', it is called 'le plus irréparable des vices'. Artifice as a mode of self-deceit is in one text a saving grace and in the next a crime. The contradiction itself, however, suggests a coherent pattern: in the first case the self-deceit is deliberate, it entails an awareness of the situation. In the other it is a form of blindness. Fancioulle knows full well that he is going to die. And by the power of his will, the drive of his talent, by his elation in performing finely, he makes death negligible. His 'paradis' may be artificial, but he has constructed it without cheating. The friend of 'La Fausse monnaie' wants to win paradise 'économiquement'. That is, to enjoy the pleasure of doing a good deed without its costing him anything – as Rastignac would be quite pleased to get the Taillefer millions through a crime, provided he knew nothing about it – in fact, while doing a bad deed – swindling a poor man, perhaps sending him to prison if he is caught peddling a false coin. He is trying to unite 'l'ombre avec la chaleur', to satisfy two masters at once. So doing, he only satifies the devil.

But – and this is crucial – reading *Le Père Goriot* involves one in Rastignac's fate. The reader does not feel sorry for him, but he feels in his shoes. He lives out his predicament. He wants him to win, to become rich, to succeed at the cheapest cost. He is contaminated by Rastignac's disease, and no judgment inside the book is going to help him out, because all characters, the moral (Bianchon) and immoral ones alike, weigh the same. This is true also of *Le Spleen de Paris*. Each poem in it asserts with passionate force the presence of a particular reality, or form of sensibility. But it is the 'recoupements' of these presences that eventually create perspectives, as in *Les Fleurs du Mal* it is the direction into which the poems are going which set the values within which the book operates. This respect for the felt weight of experience at the same time as for the totality of reality is a central aesthetic principle for Baudelaire – and one, incidentally, that sets him, and Balzac, miles away from the 'Great Tradition'. Judgement must be left to emerge as it does in life, by profound and integral knowledge, not injected nor dictated: 'La poésie est essentiellement philosophique; mais comme elle est avant tout *fatale*, elle doit être involontairement philosophique.'[9] And again: '. . . la grande poésie est essentiellement *bête*, elle *croit*, et c'est ce qui fait sa gloire et sa force.'[10] Which helps one to understand how 'La chevelure' can be both so *fatally* spell-binding and an enquiry into love as evil.

Such 'bêtise' and 'sens de la fatalité' imply, at the same time as a capacity to refrain from pre-constructed meanings, that of adhering to reality with emotional power, freshness, innocence. Allowing ratiocinative or moralising faculties to intervene is to endanger poetry itself:

> 'Je ne veux pas dire que la poésie n'ennoblisse pas les moeurs . . . Je dis que si le poète a poursuivi un but moral, il a diminué sa force poétique; . . . La poésie ne peut pas, sous peine de mort ou de déchéance, s'assimiler à la science ou à la morale; elle n'a pas la Vérité pour objet, elle n'a qu'Elle-même . . .

And Baudelaire adds these Platonic remarks:

'L'Intellect pur vise à la Vérité, le Goût nous montre la Beauté, et le Sens Moral nous enseigne le Devoir. Il est vrai que ie sens du milieu a d'intimes connexions avec les deux extrémes, et il n'est séparé du Sens Moral que par une si légère différence, qu'Aristote n'a pas hésité à ranger parmi les vertus quelques-unes de ses délicates opérations . . . comme outrage à l'harmonie, comme dissonance, le vice blessera plus particulièrement de certains esprits poétiques; et je ne crois pas qu'il soit scandalisant de considérer toute infraction à la morale, au beau moral, comme une espèce de faute contre le rhythme et la prosodie universels.'[11]

Absolute respect for the *lived* quality of experience, not only allows poetry to remain faithful to its nature and powers, but it also entails trust in man's capacity to relate himself meaningfully to the world he inhabits. Manipulating experience in order to make it release reassuring meanings may only reveal pessimism and insecurity. If things were left alone they might not fall into the required patterns. By contrast, 'impartiality' in the portrayal of experience may be the mark of a profound optimism. For you can only afford to leave things alone if you believe that a large enough, deep enough study of them will ultimately open onto values, though not containing them. Values to which 'significatifs silences', not your words, will directly point:

L'art est-il utile? Oui. Pourquoi? Parcequ'il est l'art. Y a-t-il un art pernicieux? Oui. C'est celui qui dérange les conditions de la vie. Le vice est séduisant, il faut le peindre séduisant; mais il traîne avec lui des maladies et des douleurs morales singulières; il faut les décrire. . . . La première condition nécessaire pour faire un art sain est la croyance à l'unité intégrale.[12]

It is because the art of 'La chevelure' respects both the conditions of life and of beauty that it is redemptive of a lived attempt to derange the 'conditions de la vie'.

Baudelaire then quotes Balzac answering those who acused the *Comédie humaine* of immorality: 'Malheur à vous, messieurs, si le sort des Lousteau et des Lucien vous inspire de l'envie!' And he comments: 'En effet, il faut peindre les vices tels qu'ils sont, ou ne pas les voir. Et si le lecteur ne porte pas en lui un guide philosophique et religieux qui l'accompagne dans la lecture du livre, tant pis pour lui.'[13]

This supports the sense that Baudelaire's poems, the prose poems especially, are to be encountered as people: with the guidance of one's own sense of values. Similarly, the reader lives through the *Comédie humaine* as he does through life, confronting corruptions and weaknesses raw. One could even argue that Balzac's propensity to share the foibles of his characters – for instance their snobbery, a trait brilliantly analysed by Proust – contributes to the strange rawness of his world. This lack of moral guidance and loftiness, is one of the difficulties which English critics encounter when trying to 'appraise' Balzac. In a way he cannot be appraised any more than a city.

There is one sense in which the *Fleurs du Mal* read like a nineteenth century novel – or rather Balzac's whole *Comédie humaine*, in which a dimension of depth is created through the spatial recurrence, in several novels of the opus, of the same characters, seen from different angles, becoming aged or established, or brutally crashing down. One could follow the history of Baudelaire's images and themes bearing in mind the sobering evolution of Félix de Vandenesse from *Le Lys dans la vallée* to *Une Fille d'Ève* or of Lucien de Rubempré through *Les Illusions perdues* and *Splendeurs et misères des courtisanes*. The impartiality of the level of happenings, in the *Fleurs du Mal* as in the *Comédie humaine*, is the condition of the 'terrible moralité' which emerges from them at the level of 'l'unité intégrale'.

Le Spleen de Paris is more modern, if one dares use the word. That is, the casualness and short-lived quality of the encounters, like the speed of consciousness which is created by the swift changes of moods and focus from poem to poem and the lack of a 'story', are much more acutely attuned to contemporary relations in an urban milieu. But it is out of the same sense of art as having to stay close to reality that the prose poems are born:

> Quel est celui de nous qui n'a pas, dans ses jours d'ambition, rêvé le miracle d'une prose poétique, musicale sans rhythme et sans rime, assez souple et assez heurtée pour s'adapter aux mouvements lyriques de l'âme, aux ondulations de la rêverie, aux soubresauts de la conscience?
> C'est surtout de la fréquentation des villes énormes, c'est du croisement de leurs innombrables rapports, que naît cet idéal obsédant.[14]

The metropolis provides the images of modern consciousness, but it is in and by the metropolis, that this consciousness is shaped. And the experience which the metropolis offers is one of 'innombrables rapports' *crossing* one another. Thus the self-contained worlds of 'Les Fenêtres', 'La Corde' and 'Mademoiselle Bistouri' confront each other, and there are as many levels and possibilities of relations as there are, in the volume, poems which connect or contrast: as in a city in which people meet, impenetrable to each other, in which disjointed spectacles or characters – the 'vitrier', the beggar, the prostitutes – cross, relations are infinitely varied, yet inconclusive, soon assuming the sealed-off impermanence of things which have once sprung to intense meaning but are no longer there. And so, the initial poems are half-forgotten when you get to the later ones, like that man you met on a bench in the underground, like that street-singer who cowed you into giving him ten francs. The form of the book is wide open, and Baudelaire was right indeed to say that, like the rings of the worm, individual poems could be taken out or added without destroying the life of the whole. One can indeed continue the book in one's experience, or it can live as part of one's experience in one's imagination.

True, it is the poet's consciousness which serves as a focus – for change, for instance, as in 'La Belle Dorothée', 'Vocations' and 'Portraits de maîtresses', which juxtapose experiences or degrees of reality and mutually enlarge them – and which endows reality with meaning. But this meaning is an 'approfondissement', not an arbitrary injection. This admirable balance is well expressed by the ideal of the style, 'une prose poétique, musicale sans rhythme et sans rime'. Prose, whose course is closer to *durée* than verse, is the means of adhering to reality; rhythm and rhymes would pull language too much towards *internal* harmony. They do, as Baudelaire himself, remarked, 'répondent dans l'homme aux immortels besoins de monotonie, de symétrie et de surprise . . .', and the words 'monotonie' and 'symétrie' are those which he applies to 'l'artificiel pur'. The openness and irregularity of prose on the contrary let experience exist 'naturally'. At the same time, harmony must be there, 'poétique', 'musicale', in the *temperament* of the voice itself.

Le Spleen de Paris: Paris, the metropolis, feels spleen, like Baudelaire. But Baudelaire feels spleen because the Paris he apprehends *is* splenetic. The poet does not feel a subjective mood, he experiences it as the atmosphere of reality itself, one might say, remembering his thoughts on colour, as the melody of reality. The state of mind of modern man is created by the milieu in which he lives. The more deeply he perceives it, the more 'typical' his personal feelings will be. And he can triumph over what depresses both him and it, the disconnectedness, the isolation, the randomness, by expressing it as it is, but also as his mind wants it. The formal schemes by means of which the artist creates a meeting-place between mind and nature, the 'croisements' and the 'prose poétique', here create an actual meeting-place between mind and nature. For they make nature exist more truly as itself, and the mind discover itself through discovering it. This is the highest reach of artifice: 'Qu'est-ce que l'art pur suivant la conception moderne? C'est créer une magie suggestive contenant à la fois l'objet et le sujet, le monde extérieur à l'artiste et l'artiste lui-même.'[15]

The 'Romantic' ideal which Coleridge and Hegel defined as 'the making the internal external, and the external internal', or the 'transcendence' of the antitheses between 'absolute subjectivity' and 'absolute objectivity', is reached by Baudelaire through a complete endorsement of all that in the 'modern' world seemed to threaten Romantic values. The 'transcendence is attained, as we have tried to show, both on the aesthetic and on the moral plane, through 'silent' workings: the undulating, many-coloured 'lignes' which harmonise the separate poems, and the 'sens' (as meanings) which either the 'sens' (as direction) or the interplay (the crossings) of poems draw upon the space surrounding the poems.

And this transcendence is not an escape. For it emerges from a close adherence to the individual and collective realities of the world Baudelaire was living in, as we discovered in the previous section. A truly dialectical process is at work in *Les Fleurs du Mal* and *Le Spleen de Paris*, through which values, thanks to the magic of form, phoenix-like, rise from their own ashes.

PART THREE

The Moral World: Baudelaire and De Quincey

Introduction

Baudelaire takes art as far as it will go. But it will not hide forever the 'terreur du gouffre'. By a dichotomy which is ingrained in 'Le Masque', the salvation of art, the 'beauté parfaite' of the mask, never delivers the real face behind it from the agony of living. Personal values must be constructed to grapple with that.

Les Paradis artificiels is the work where this dichotomy is most visible. The study of drugs becomes, magnified as everything Baudelaire touches, a search for a way out of a splenetic world, and an enquiry into the validity of such escapes. It is also another kind of dialogue with Romanticism, much of the work being concerned with De Quincey's *Confessions of an English Opium-Eater*. The title is as loaded as the inscription on the gate of Dante's Hell: there is an awing contradiction between the sublime justice which created Hell:

> Fecemi la Divina Potestate,
> La Somma Sapienza e il Primo Amore . . .

and the shattering injunction which soon follows: 'Lasciate ogni speranza, voi ch'entrate . . .' You cannot reconcile them, but they co-exist. So of the two antagonistic meanings which the word 'artifice' gives to *Les Paradis artificiels*. It involves both sublimity and contempt. And the work is written in that antithetical spirit.

11 Baudelaire and Translation

I

Two-thirds of *Les Paradis artificiels* consist of a translation from De Quincey's *Confessions*.[1] It is the degree of freedom which Baudelaire manifests towards the original which, combined with the more open and decisive attitudes of the section on hashish, gives us insights into his moral values.

But there are other reasons why it is essential to think about Baudelaire as a translator. Two-fifths of Baudelaire's not very extensive work consists in translations. Why is it that so much of his energy was dedicated to the service of foreign writers? One immediate reason may be found in a fairly neglected side of his character; that amazing generosity which made him campaign all his life for men whose work he admired: Delacroix, Constantin Guys, Wagner, Poe, Gautier, Balzac, Flaubert, De Quincey . . . But it is not simply a question of temperament. Openness to what is irreducibly 'other' is a virtue which Baudelaire admires in a man like Gautier:

> Quand il me vit un volume de poésies à la main, sa noble figure s'illumina d'un joli sourire; il tendit le bras avec une sorte d'avidité enfantine; car c'est chose curieuse combien cet homme, qui sait tout exprimer et qui a plus que tout autre le droit d'être blasé, a la curiosité facile et darde vivement son regard sur le *non-moi*.[2]

And he himself is eminently capable of that lively, magnanimous curiosity about the 'non-moi'. Translation is part of a whole complex of relations he establishes between his 'inner' self and the moment of history he inhabits.

Thus one could argue that translating from one language into another calls into play attitudes not altogether different from translating paint into words, or life into art. When Baudelaire uses the image of 'croisements' in *Le Spleen de Paris*, he does so because it provides him with the form most characteristic of the city, and of man's relations to the city. He translates, that is, life into the form that changes it, most revealingly, into itself. When he attempts to put one of Daumier's caricature into prose, he mimics, in his temporal (successive) medium, the qualities which he regards as essential in Daumier:

> Comme artiste, ce qui distingue Daumier, c'est la certitude . . . Toutes ses figures sont bien d'aplomb, toujours dans un mouvement vrai . . . Quant au moral, Daumier a quelques rapports avec Molière. Comme lui, il va droit au but. L'idée se dégage d'emblée. On regarde, on a compris . . . Son comique est, pour ainsi dire, involontaire. L'artiste ne cherche pas, on dirait plutôt que l'idée lui échappe. Sa caricature reste formidable d'ampleur, mais sans rancune et sans fiel . . .[3]

The directness and naturalness are re-embodied in the prose. As the medium makes it impossible for him to express the caricature 'at a glance', he renders the movement of the eye travelling over it, mimicking with verbal gestures those of a sharp, accurate, confident pencil: as in his account of 'Le Dernier Bain', in which the moral idea is made beautifully clear by the graphic details, and the order in which they are given:

> *Le Dernier Bain*, caricature sérieuse et lamentable. – Sur le parapet d'un quai, debout et déjà penché, faisant un angle aigu avec la base d'où il se détache comme une statue qui perd son équilibre, un homme se laisse tomber roide dans la rivière. Il faut qu'il soit bien décidé; ses bras sont tranquillement croisés; un fort gros pavé est attaché à son cou avec une corde. Il a bien juré de n'en pas réchapper. Ce n'est pas un suicide de poëte qui veut être repêché et faire parler de lui. C'est la redingote chétive et grimaçante qu'il faut voir, sous laquelle tous les os font saillie! Et la cravate maladive et tortillée comme un serpent, et la pomme d'Adam, osseuse et pointue! Décidément, on n'a pas le courage d'en vouloir à ce pauvre diable d'aller fuir sous l'eau le spectacle de le civilisation. Dans le fond, de l'autre côté de la rivière, un bourgeois contemplatif, au ventre rondelet, se livre aux délices innocentes de la pêche.[4]

Translating from one language into another seems to be less of a jump than translating from one form of art into another, or from reality into art, and yet the problems are similar. There are in each case decisions to make which can be successful only if a certain balance is achieved between the 'moi' and the 'non-moi'. When Baudelaire is trying to say what Paris is like, he must first be able to experience and discover it, and then find a form that will express what Paris is as experienced by him. When he renders Daumier's caricature into words, he must understand what the plastic effects of that caricature are, be capable of expressing it in moral terms, and of reproducing, in words, the effects of the caricature: and the account of the caricature, or the form given to Paris, are successful, for Baudelaire, not merely to the extent that the new reality is expressive of the original one, but so far as it is lit by an individual sensibility. He makes his position very clear when he states his preference for the 'imaginatif' painter as against the 'positiviste':

> ... l'immense classe des artistes ... peut se diviser en deux camps bien distincts: celui-ci, qui s'appelle *réaliste,* mot à double entente et dont le sens n'est pas bien déterminé, et que nous appellerons, pour mieux caractériser son erreur, un *positiviste,* dit: 'Je veux représenter les choses telles qu'elles sont, ou bien qu'elles seraient, en supposant que je n'existe pas. L'univers sans l'homme. Et celui-là, l'imaginatif, dit: 'Je veux illuminer les choses avec mon esprit, et en projeter le reflet sur les autres esprits'.[5]

In this perspective, for Baudelaire, the 'imaginitif' translator would be preferable to the 'positiviste' translator. The task of a writer who translates is to render the 'non-moi', foreign thoughts and words, into the 'moi', his own created language. He must at all costs preserve the 'feel' of the original, and yet he cannot but give his tone to the foreign text. The 'positiviste' translator would, like Eliot dealing with St John Perse's *Anabasis,* attempt to make abstraction of himself in order to cling to the original. The 'imaginatif' would, on the contrary, like Pound, 'illumine' the foreign text with his own sensibility, believing that he must be as forceful, not as effaced as possible, in order to give life to the strange reality.

II

One cannot write on Baudelaire as a translator without at least taking into account the fact that the bulk of his translations is from Poe. Much has been written on the topic. The 'truth' probably lies somewhere between Valéry and Eliot, with a bias towards Eliot.[6] But Baudelaire's translations from Poe are not so 'imaginitive' as his translations from De Quincey, and therefore much less relevant to the purpose of this study. Dealing with Poe, Baudelaire relaxes that struggle between the 'moi' and the 'non-moi' which makes translation such a rich activity. For he identifies himself with Poe to such an extent that he lends him his words and values and rhythms without, probably, even realising how much he improves him by doing so. There is a total naturalness about his assumption that Poe's language is as loaded as his own, a generous deafness in his failure to hear how often Poe's rhythms are defective. One instance can show this, from the first paragraph of *The Fall of the House of Usher*. The narrator is depicting the profound depression he fell into when catching sight of the house. He calls it

> an utter depression of soul which I can compare to no earthly sensation more properly than the after-dream of the reveller upon opium – the bitter lapse into everyday life – the hideous dropping of the veil. There was an iciness, a sinking, a sickening of the heart – an unredeemed dreariness of thought which no goading of the imagination could torture into aught of the sublime.

Here is Baudelaire:

> ... J'éprouvais cet entier affaissement d'âme qui, parmi les sensations terrestres, ne peut se mieux comparer qu'à l'arrière-rêverie du mangeur d'opium, – à son navrant retour à la vie journalière, – à l'horrible et lente retraite du voile. C'était une glace au coeur, un abattement, un malaise, – une irrémédiable tristesse de pensée qu'aucun aiguillon de l'imagination ne pouvait raviver ni pousser au grand.[7]

If one reads both passages aloud, one feels how much the breathing has been improved in Baudelaire. In Poe, the long-winded last sentence, which is meant to create the dreariness it is about, exhausts the lungs so that one fails to take the point. In Baudelaire, because a slight breathing pause is managed after 'tristesse de pensée', one runs out of breath, but not to the point of pain: the state of depression grips you, but within the knowing limits of your body. It is the idea made flesh.[8] More importantly, words which are affected or pompous, and images which are inconsequent, in Poe, are delicately pulled into tangible sense in Baudelaire. The 'goading' which 'tortures' 'into aught of the sublime' becomes an 'aiguillon' which could not 'raviver ni pousser au grand': the image is made perceptible by being carried through by the verbs, and the irrelevant magniloquence is discreetly removed. Also, vapid words are loaded with Baudelairian meaning: 'unredeemed', a mere trimming, undergoes a metamorphosis when it becomes 'irrémédiable', one of the states of Spleen explored in *Les Fleurs du Mal*; 'bitter' assumes tragic stature by becoming 'navrant'; and the banal 'utter depression of soul' is magnified by the physical expressiveness of 'cet entier affaissement d'âme'.

We do not get here at all what is so exciting in Pound: a sense that the translator's strong reaction to the text is making it alive. True, like Pound, translating, for instance, *Donna mi priegha*, Baudelaire lends his words, his rhythms to Poe. But in Pound's translation we feel that we are being offered a judgment of Cavalcanti's work; it says, 'this is what that poem is like to me', but it also gives us a sense of the separation between Pound and Cavalcanti. Thus he makes us feel how removed we are from people who believed in the metaphysics of light. And despite archaisms meant to remind us of where this stands in time, the diction clearly springs from a twentieth-century ear:

> . . . He, caught, falleth
> Plumb on to the spirit of the targe . . .
> . . . In the midst of darkness light light giveth forth
> Beyond all falsity . . .[9]

But we are sometimes sorry that Baudelaire should have read himself so thoroughly into Poe: his powers of sympathy seem at times to have run away with his intelligence. The opposite is the case when Baudelaire translates De Quincey. He is fully involved there.

III

Baudelaire stands to De Quincey somewhat in the relation he stands to Constantin Guys. This is not surprising, for *Le Peintre de la vie moderne* and *Les Paradis artificiels* were written within months of each other,[10] and Baudelaire's unifying turn of mind makes him pursue the same concerns through different media, without however doing them violence. This power to synthetise experience without distorting it is the most compelling aspect of his mind, and the translations reveal it well.

Baudelaire admires the work of 'le peintre de la vie moderne' in a less ambiguous way than he does that of the author of the *Confessions*, but he is equally interested in the two men for providing him with data on contemporary life. He himself is most interested in some of the areas of consciousness, or the modes of behaviour, they have explored. Guys was fascinated by the figure of the Dandy: and it is in his account of Guys's dandies that Baudelaire presents his own enthusiastic version of the moral character of the dandy. Similarly, he feels that his love for outcasts: 'Je le dis sans honte, parceque cela part d'un profound sentiment de pitié et de tendresse, Edgar Poe, ivrogne, pauvre, persécuté, paria, me plaît plus que calme et *vertueux*, un Goethe ou un W. Scott'[11] is echoed by De Quincey:

. . . il laisse cyniquement s'envoler cet aveu, qui a pour moi, je le confesse avec la même candeur, un charme presque fraternel: 'Généralement, les rares individus qui ont excité mon dégoût en ce monde étaient des gens florissants et de bonne renommée. Quant aux coquins que j'ai connus, et ils ne sont pas en petit nombre, je pense à eux, à tous sans exception, avec plaisir et bienveillance.'[12]

Baudelaire pursues his own preoccupations through his studies of Guys and De Quincey. Once or twice the two texts actually touch. For instance, in *Le Peintre de la vie moderne* he celebrates Guys's perpetual 'convalescent' state, a state in which vision is always fresh, as an image of the child-like eye of real artists. In 'Un Mangeur d'opium' he endorses De Quincey's claim that childhood is the source of all our powers and emotions. He says of Guys: '. . . le génie n'est que *l'enfance retrouvée* à volonté, l'enfance douée maintenant, pour s'exprimer, d'organes virils et de l'esprit analytique qui lui permet d'ordonner la somme de matériaux involontairement amassée'[13] and as a sequel to his meditation on De Quincey's remarks, he asks whether one couldn't say that: '. . . le génie n'est que l'enfance nettement formulée, douée maintenant, pour s'exprimer, d'organes virils et puissants?'[14] Starting from different directions, that is, he ends on a statement that is wholly his.

The fifth section of *Le Peintre de la vie moderne* is called 'L'Art Mnémonique'. Baudelaire is speaking of Guys's capacity to 'synthetise' when he paints. He calls it 'barbarie': it is a way of magnifying reality.

Je veux parler d'une barbarie inévitable, synthétique, enfantine, qui reste souvent visible dans un art parfait (mexicaine, égyptienne, ou ninivite), et qui dérive du besoin de voir les choses grandement, de les considérer surtout dans l'effet de leur ensemble. Il n'est pas superflu d'observer ici que beaucoup de gens ont accusé de barbarie tous les peintres dont le regard est synthétique et abbréviateur . . .[15]

This 'synthetic' power of vision is attained by trusting to memory instead of trusting to the eye. Memory is not only accumulated experience, gestures patiently learnt, but also a capacity, developed through time, to create meanings, emphases, and to use already acquired meanings to integrate the present. When memory is thus used, the translation from reality acquires legendary, that is both great and memorable, proportions:

> Il est une condition qui ajoute beaucoup à la force vitale de cette traduction *légendaire* de la vie extérieure. Je veux parler de la méthode de dessiner de M.G. Il dessine de mémoire, et non d'après le modèle. . . . En fait, tous les bons et vrais dessinateurs dessinent d'après l'image écrite dans leur cerveau, et non d'après la nature.[16]

In fact, Baudelaire argues, when the artist is too much assailed by reality, when his memory cannot help him read nature, he is struck by paralysis:

> Il arrive même que des hommes tels que Daumier et M.G., accoutumés dès longtemps à exercer leur mémoire et à la remplir d'images, trouvent devant le modèle et la multiplicité de détails qu'il comporte, leur faculté principale troublée et comme paralysée.
> . . . Un artiste ayant le sentiment parfait de la forme, mais accoutumé à exercer surtout sa mémoire et son imagination, se trouve alors comme assailli par une émeute de détails, qui tous demandent justice avec la furie d'une foule amoureuse d'égalité absolue. Toute justice se trouve forcément violée; toute harmonie détruite, sacrifiée; mainte trivialité devient énorme; mainte petitesse, usurpatrice. Plus l'artiste se penche avec impartialité vers le détail, plus l'anarchie augmente.[17]

Mnemonic art, on the contrary, is that which, instead of falling a victim to such democratic search from impartiality, doomed to end in chaos and injustice, aristocratically *orders* it. (The same impulses dictate the politics and the aesthetics.) It introduces a *hierarchy* of importance. And, in its turn, it becomes memorable. It is made salient by the memory of the creator and remains salient in that of the spectator.

What Baudelaire admires in Constantin Guys as a translator of modern life, he himself applies. Or perhaps he discovers it in Guys because it is so strong in himself. It is fascinating to watch him interpret Guys's drawings as he says that Guys's drawings interpret reality: for instance, he celebrates the ship as a perfect form of Beauty, which gathers in itself two aspects of the ideal, 'regularity and symmetry' on the one hand, the multiplication of curves and imaginary figures on the other. He reads his own meditation upon ships into Guys's water-colour of carriages:

> Dans quelque attitude qu'elle soit jetée, avec quelque allure qu'elle soit lancée, une voiture, comme un vaisseau, emprunte au mouvement une grâce mystérieuse et complexe très-difficile à sténographier. Le plaisir que l'oeil de l'artiste en reçoit est tiré, ce semble, de la série de figures géometriques que cet objet, déjà si compliqué, navire ou carrosse, engendre successivement et rapidement dans l'espace.[18]

De Quincey being the digressive and disorderly writer that he is, it is imperative that a translator meaning to present the best of his experience in his own perspective, should not be foolishly 'impartial', but should be capable of those choices, and despotic emphases, that a poetic memory dictates.

In 'The Pleasures of Opium', De Quincey tells how, a young man in London, he would take opium on Saturday nights and go to Covent Garden to hear Grassini sing. The combined pleasures of opium and music were of a sublime quality and had the effect of resurrecting his past at will. Baudelaire translates this at the beginning of 'Un Mangeur d'opium'.

De Quincey is describing the combined effects of opium and music upon his sensibility:

> ... a chorus, &c., of elaborate harmony displayed before me, as in a piece of arras-work, the whole of my past life – not as if recalled by an act of memory, but as if present and incarnated in the music; no longer painful to dwell upon, but the details of its incidents removed, or blended in some hazy abstraction, and its passions exalted, spiritualised, and sublimed.[19]

This is the Baudelaire:

Toute sa vie passée vivait, dit-il, en lui, non pas par un effort de la mémoire, mais comme présente et incarnée dans la musique; elle n'était plus douloureuse à contempler; toute la trivialité et la crudité inhérentes aux choses humaines étaient exclues de cette mystérieuse résurrection, ou fondues et noyées dans une brume idéale, et ses anciennes passions se trouvaient exaltées, ennoblies, spiritualisées. Combien de fois dut-il revoir sur ce second théâtre, allumé dans son esprit par l'opium et la musique, les routes et les montagnes, qu'il avait parcourues, écolier émancipé, et ses aimables hôtes du pays de Galles, et les ténèbres coupées d'éclairs des immenses rues de Londres, et ses mélancoliques amitiés, et ses longues misères consolées par Ann et par l'espoir d'un meilleur avenir.[20]

Baudelaire is reading his own view of life into De Quincey's. The word '*noyées* dans une brume idéale' is that of 'Harmonie du soir' ('Le soleil s'est noyé dans son sang qui se fige'), and the added phrase 'toute la trivialité et la crudité inhérentes aux choses humaines étaient exclues de cette mystérieuse résurrection' associates De Quincey's reverie to 'La Chambre double' and 'L'Invitation au voyage'.[21] But doing so, Baudelaire is being intellectually more precise than when he lends his 'irrémédiable', so bitterly experienced, to Poe. Poe's 'unredeemed' means little, but De Quincey's attempt to relive his past in a 'sublimed' form is a search for salvation from spleen, and Baudelaire knows exactly what De Quincey is talking about.

The reasons for which Baudelaire alters De Quincey's expressions are as pregnant as when he was reading his own meditations on the appeal of a ship into Guys's pictures of carriages. He is trying to make prominent, in the light of his own experience, meanings or simply features which otherwise would remain unnoticed, or would be swamped in the bulk of material. De Quincey, for instance, says in the passage just quoted, that he could see his whole past life 'as on a piece of arras-work'. Baudelaire changes the image into a 'theatre'. There are complicated reasons for this *mnemonic* reading.

The image of the theatre is a familiar one in *Les Fleurs du Mal*. In 'L'Irréparable' it stands for the vacant space of the heart, waiting for the appearance of 'l'Idéal':

> – J'ai vu parfois, au fond d'un théâtre banal
> Qu'enflammait l'orchestre sonore,
> Une fée allumer dans un ciel infernal
> Une miraculeuse aurore;

> J'ai vu parfois au fond d'un théâtre banal
> Un être qui n'était que lumière, or et gaze,
> Terrasser l'énorme Satan;
> Mais mon coeur, que jamais ne visite l'extase,
> Est un théâtre où l'on attend
> Toujours, toujours en vain, l'Être aux ailes de gaze![22]

Here, as in 'Le Rêve d'un Curieux', one of the poems in the section 'La Mort', the theatre is a black space where remorse, 'l'énorme Satan', one of the figures of Spleen, reigns. But the theatre is also a place waiting to be lit, a place whose function is that a sudden illumination should briefly change its reality. That illumination is *artificial*: she who lights up a 'miraculous dawn' in 'L'Irréparable' is a *fairy* dressed in gauze as well as gold and light. These two aspects of theatre, lights, sudden, magic splendour and artifice, are contained in Baudelaire's fascination for the chandelier as the main actor at the theatre:

> Mes opinions sur le théâtre. Ce que j'ai toujours trouvé de plus beau dans un théâtre, dans mon enfance et encore maintenant, c'est *le lustre* – un bel objet lumineux, cristallin, compliqué, circulaire et symétrique.
> . . . Après tout, le lustre m'a toujours paru l'acteur principal, vu à travers le gros bout ou le petit bout de la lorgnette. [23]

Celebrating Guys's sense of the 'pomp' of life, Baudelaire describes a water-colour which he says is endowed with a sense of *magic*. It is a theatre scene which culminates on a vision of the chandelier, in his account. The light, radiating from the chandelier, and the lime-lights constitute the unity and reality of the picture: the space, the uniforms, are created by that light just as the theatre of 'L'Irréparable' is made from a banal into a miraculous place by the illumination of a fairy:

> . . . Une surtout de ces aquarelles m'a ébloui par son caractère magique. Sur le bord d'une loge d'une richesse lourde et princière, l'Impératrice apparaît dans une attitude tranquille et reposée. l'Empereur se penche légèrement comme pour mieux voir le théâtre; au-dessous, deux-cent gardes, debout, dans une immobilité militaire et presque hiératique, reçoivent sur leur brillant uniforme les éclaboussures de la rampe. Derrière la bande de feu, dans l'atmosphère idéale de la scène, les comédiens chantent, déclament, gesticulent harmonieusement; de l'autre côté s'étend un abîme de lumière

vague, un espace circulaire encombré de figures humaines à tous les étages: c'est le lustre et le public.[24]

Baudelaire thus despotically imposes his image of the theatre upon De Quincey's reverie because it is to him a very apt description of it. First, because opium suddenly illumines De Quincey's mind ('ce second théâtre, *allumé* dans son esprit par l'opium et la musique'), bringing with it the miraculous pageant of his past. And this power to enhance, colour, brighten up reality is to Baudelaire most characteristic of drugs.[25]

But the other aspect of the theatre is equally present in drugs: the chandelier will be put out, the play will end, the feasts of the Second Empire will be brutally interrupted by the *Débâcle*: and the opium-eater will wake up, as in 'La Chambre Double', aware of Time again. The radiant objects of his reverie will turn out to be as paltry as the gauze of the fairy might look in the light of the morning. This is why in *Le Poëme du haschisch*, the section which describes the effects of the drug is called 'Le Théâtre de Séraphin'. The title epitomises the two aspects of drugs: Séraphin, running then in Paris, was a theatre of Chinese shadows and puppets, and 'Séraphin' was simply the name of the director. But *séraphin* also means 'seraph', it suggests perfect angelism, pure light.

The substitution of 'théâtre' for 'piece of arras-work' is even more complex than this. Speaking of 'a piece of arras-work', De Quincey claims that his whole past suddenly stood before him all at once. He was freed from succession. He held it all at his bidding. And he was completely dissociated from his surroundings. But Baudelaire says: 'Combien de fois dut-il revoir sur ce second théâtre ... les routes et les montagnes qu'il avait parcourues, écolier émancipé, et ses aimables hôtes du pays de Galles ... et ... et ...' He is implicitly denying, that is, both by the image he uses and the syntax of his sentence, which sums up in chronological order the main events of childhood and youth De Quincey has been recounting in the early part of the *Confessions*, that the reverie was taking place *sub specie aeternitatis*. He is insisting that experience, even memorised experience, is lived in time. He is also suggesting that the reverie was much more closely attuned to the real theatre, the opera De Quincey was watching, than De Quincey is prepared to admit. He is casting doubt on De Quincey's interpretation of his own experience, though not on the experience itself. This is not only mnemonic translation. It becomes a problem of judgement.

IV

It does not take much reading of *Les Paradis artificiels*, in fact, to realise that Baudelaire stands apart from De Quincey. He translates his 'I' by 'il', 'un auteur', and when he lets him have 'je', puts it between inverted commas. De Quincey was asking for love and forgiveness from his reader, like Rousseau, simply by calling his work 'Confessions'. Baudelaire in the final version, replies with a plain 'Un Mangeur d'opium'. He gets rid of personalities. De Quincey wants to present his case on an impartial plane, to discuss the medical and psychological advantages and disadvantages of opium. Baudelaire is mainly concerned with the moral dimensions he finds to drugs: 'Dans tout cela il y a beaucoup de choses qui regardent les médecins. Or je veux faire un livre non pas de pure physiologie, mais surtout de morale.'[26] It is true that he claims not to know with how much criticism his translation from De Quincey is pervaded:

> . . . J'y ai joint, par-ci par-là, mes réflexions personnelles; mais jusqu'à quelle dose ai-je introduit ma personnalité dans l'auteur original, c'est ce que je serais actuellement bien empêché de dire. J'ai fait un tel amalgame que je ne saurais reconnaître la part qui vient de moi, laquelle, d'ailleurs, ne peut être que fort petite.[27]

But before we accept this statement, we should remember how much weight he can put into a word like 'théâtre'. If he means to translate De Quincey into a moral perspective, his critical attitude is going to be a passionate one:

> Je crois sincèrement que la meilleure critique est celle qui est amusante et poétique; non pas celle-ci, froide et algébrique, qui sous prétexte de tout expliquer, n'a ni haine ni amour, et se dépouille volontairement de toute espèce de tempérament . . . pour être juste, c'est-à-dire pour avoir sa raison d'être, la critique doit être, partiale, passionnée, politique, c'est-à-dire faite à un point de vue exclusif, mais au point de vue qui ouvre le plus d'horizons.[28]

Baudelaire uses the word 'juste' here exactly in the same way as he does in 'L'Art Mnémonique'. The painter who is trying to be impartial, to let in all the details, violates all justice. *Justice* in art, in life, in criticism, in translation, is creative, passionate bias. At the same time

Baudelaire is a scrupulous translator. How do these elements, judgement of the text, respect for the text, balance?

One very good example of their struggle is in the passage which immediately precedes the one just discussed. De Quincey, talking of his Saturday nights at Covent Garden, argues that musical pleasure depends entirely on the sensibility of the hearer: as opium increases mental powers, it heightens musical pleasure. It is therefore an agent of intellectual refinement. Baudelaire in the main disagrees, but his disagreement has to make itself felt through a faithful account of what De Quincey says. It is entertaining to watch the gymnastics by means of which he succeeds in both translating and expressing his own opinion. But also the issue, though slight in itself, has important consequences.

A friend of De Quincey's is complaining that music means nothing to him, because sounds suggest no ideas to him: they are 'like a collection of Arabic characters'. De Quincey replies: 'Ideas! my dear friend! there is no occasion for them; all that class of ideas, which can be available in such a case has a language of representative feelings.' Baudelaire translates:

> Beaucoup de gens demandent quelles sont les idées positives contenues dans les sons; ils oublient, ou plutôt ils ignorent que la musique, de ce côté-là parente de la poésie, représente des sentiments plutôt que des idées; suggérant des idées, il est vrai, mais ne les contenant pas par elle-même.

When De Quincey says that ideas have a language of 'representative feelings', he means that the feelings represent the ideas; the ideas are in the listener's head, 'available'; and anything, music included, especially when it is seconded by opium, might get them moving. Feelings provoked by music, that is, are representative of the sensibility of the listener, not of the piece heard. Baudelaire easily endorses the notion that music does not contain ideas. He even adds 'la musique, de ce côté-là parente de la poésie', thus assimilating De Quincey's reflexion to his own sense, confirmed by Gautier and Poe, that poetry has nothing to do with truth. But, by a sly reversal, his 'représente' does not refer to the listener's sensibility, but to the music. He further adds that though music does not 'contain' ideas, it suggests them. By keeping De Quincey's word 'représente', he pretends to be faithful to the original. Yet he is making his text claim just about the opposite of De Quincey's. His reasons for doing so are deeply rooted.

De Quincey has been arguing that the impact of any musical piece depends on who is hearing it. He has quoted Sir Thomas Browne: 'And even that tavern music, which makes one man merry, another mad, in me strikes a deep fit of devotion . . .', as a good instance of this. He wants to suggest that his delight in the opera came from the exquisiteness of his own mind, and not from the fineness of the performance, the quality of the music, etc. But Baudelaire (who carefully omits any mention of Sir Thomas Browne) is in radical disagreement with this view of musical pleasure, and one can read the waverings and tensions of his translation at this point as signs of the unease he must have felt in having to render a reasoning he disapproved of. In his *Richard Wagner et Tannhäuser à Paris*, he precisely contradicts the author of *Religio Medici*:

> J'ai souvent entendu dire que la musique ne pouvait pas se vanter de traduire quoi que ce soit avec certitude, comme fait la parole ou la peinture. Cela est vrai dans une certaine proportion, mais n'est pas tout à fait vrai. Elle traduit à sa manière, et par les moyens qui lui sont propres.[29]

He then argues that '. . . plus la musique est éloquente, plus la suggestion est rapide et juste, et plus il y a de chances pour que les hommes sensibles conçoivent des idées en rapport avec celles qui inspiraient l'artiste.'[30] This he shows by comparing the nearly identical texts of Berlioz's, Liszt's and his own reactions to the overture of *Lohengrin*.[31] And he adds: 'Le lecteur sait quel but nous poursuivons: démontrer que la véritable musique suggère des idées[32] analogues dans des cerveau différents.'[33] But De Quincey says: 'Therefore it is that people of equally good ear differ so much in this point from one another.' To translate him without betraying his own sense of truth, he has to have recourse to his best veering skill, like Ulysses trying to sail between Charybdis and Scylla.

One of the things he does is to reduce reasoning to a minimum and instead insist on the magic, the splendour, of the reverie which De Quincey induced by the combined means of opium and music: '. . . une série de *memoranda*, . . . les accents d'une sorcellerie qui évoquait devant l'oeil de son esprit . . . dont tout esprit un peu raffiné peut aisément concevoir la grandeur et l'intensité . . .'. It is indeed for this that drugs interest him: because the visionary powers which they produce in men like De Quincey resemble those produced by imagination in men of genius. We must look into this and move away from the comparison of texts for a while. For only an informed sense of Baudelaire's interest in drugs will allow us to understand his attitude to De Quincey at this point.

The parallel between drugs and imagination is a conscious one in Baudelaire:

> Mais d'où vient (que Delacroix) produit la sensation de nouveauté? Que nous donne-t-il de plus que le passé? . . . On pourrait dire que, doué d'une plus riche imagination, il exprime surtout l'intime du cerveau, . . . C'est l'infini dans le fini. C'est le rêve! et je n'entends pas par ce mot les capharnaüms de la nuit, mais la *vision produite par une intense méditation, ou, dans les cerveaux moins fertiles, par un excitant artificiel*.[34]

To produce 'l'infini dans le fini', to transcend 'Spleen', is what we long for, and a sign of our divine nature: 'La soif insatiable de tout ce qui est au-delà, et que révèle la vie, est la preuve la plus vivante de notre immortalité'.[35] Art is eminently fitted to do this, as Delacroix's painting show. But drugs provide an obvious analogue for art: Baudelaire speaks of a vision which, in the less fertile minds, may be produced by 'un excitant artificiel'. The equation often recurs:

> 'Edgar Poe dit, je ne sais plus où, que le résultat de l'opium pour les sens est de revêtir la nature entière d'un intérêt surnaturel qui donne à chaque objet un sens plus profond, plus volontaire, plus despotique. Sans avoir recours à l'opium, qui n'a connu ces admirables heures, véritables fêtes du cerveau, où les sens plus attentifs perçoivent des sensations plus retentissantes, où le ciel d'un azur plus transparent s'enfonce comme un abîme plus infini, . . . Eh bien, la peinture de Delacroix me paraît la traduction de ces beaux jours de l'esprit. Elle est revêtue d'intensité et sa splendeur est privilégiée. Comme la nature perçue par des nerfs ultra-sensibles, elle révèle le surnaturalisme.[36]

Man's vision then is god-like. And 'excitants' make this divine state perpetually available: wine and hashish are described as 'ces moyens artificiels, par lesquels l'homme, exaspérant sa personnalité crée, pour ainsi dire, en lui une sorte de divinité.' The word 'divinité' is literally meant, or if this sounds absurd, employed with a precise and cogent meaning. As in this text on the effects of alcohol:

... certaines boissons contiennent la faculté d'augmenter outre mesure la personnalité de l'être pensant, et de créer, pour ainsi dire, une troisième personne, opération mystique où l'homme naturel et le vin, le dieu animal et le dieu végétal, jouent le rôle du Père et du Fils dans la Trinité; ils engendrent un Saint-Esprit, qui est l'homme supérieur, lequel procède également des deux.[37]

And, just as a superman, a 'Holy Ghost', proceeds from the addition, or rather multiplication of man by wine, the work of art, which proceeds from the conjunction of imagination with reality, is of all human endeavours that which comes closest to God: it is the 'ardent sob', the 'divine opium' of 'Phares' which, like a wave, comes to die on the edge of eternity.

This analogy between imagination and drugs is so strong that the same images are used to describe their creative effects: that is, their ability to give life, order and meaning to reality. Here is painting:

'La nature n'est qu'un dictionnaire', répétait (Delacroix) fréquemment. Pour bien connaitre l'étendue du sens impliqué dans cette phrase, il faut se figurer les usages nombreux et ordinaires du dictionnaire ... mais personne n'a jamais considéré le dictionnaire comme une composition dans le sens poétique do mot ...

... Tout l'univers visible n'est qu'un magasin d'images et de signes auxquels l'imagination donnera une place et une valeur relative; c'est une espèce de pâture que l'imagination doit digérer et transformer. Toutes les facultés de l'âme humaine doivent être subordonnées à l'imagination, qui les met en réquisition toutes à la fois.[38]

and here is what happens to you when you are under the spell of hashish:

La musique ... vous parle de vous-même et vous raconte le poème de votre vie: elle s'incorpore à vous, et vous vous fondez en elle. Elle parle votre passion, non pas d'une manière vague et indéfinie, comme elle fait ... un jour d'opéra, mais d'une manière circonstanciée, positive, chaque note se transformant en mot, et le poème entier entrant dans votre cerveau comme un dictionnaire doué de vie.

... L'oeil intérieur transforme tout et donne à chaque chose le complément de beauté qui lui manque pour qu'elle soit vraiment digne de plaire.[39]

The external world is a 'dictionary' which hashish endows with life, just as nature is regarded by the artist as a 'dictionary' which imagination makes into meaningful sentences. And the inner eye of the drugged man gives each thing 'le *complément* de beauté qui lui manque pour qu'elle soit vraiment digne de plaire', as the creative imagination has 'la permission de *suppléer*. To give, that is, human meanings to the world: 'C'est l'imagination qui a enseigné à l'homme le sens moral de la couleur, du contour, du son et du parfum. Elle a créé, au commencement du monde, l'analogie et la métaphore . . .'[40]

Also, there is a lovely unreflexive ease, 'the obvious force of a feeling', in the vision of the hashish-eater. And this 'obviousness' is precisely what the landscape-gardeners of *Landor's Cottage* and *The Domain of Arnheim* were seeking to create through calculated effort. In Poe's two artificial landscapes the various points of view are continually perceived in moral terms, as suggestive of oppression, mystery, voluptuousness. Heart of Darkness, for him, should not be a metaphorical quality transferred to a landscape by establishing analogies between its successive features and the emotions of the characters who journey through it. But the landscape itself should be metaphorical: the emotions it generates should be 'objective', 'positive'. As they are in Delacroix's paintings. As Baudelaire wishes music to be. And it seems that drugs induce that privileged state of perception-feeling that Poe was striving for.

How valuable that state is to Baudelaire can be shown by placing side by side this crucial remark from the *Journaux intimes*: 'Dans certains états de l'âme presque surnaturels, la profondeur de la vie se révèle tout entière dans le spectacle, si ordinaire qu'il soit, qu'on a sous les yeux. Il en devient le symbole,'[41] and this description of the effects of hashish:

> . . . Cependant se développe cet état mystérieux et temporaire de l'esprit, où la profondeur de la vie, hérissée de ses problèmes multiples, se révèle tout entière dans le spectacle, si naturel et si trivial qu'il soit, qu'on a sous les yeux, – où le premier objet venu devient symbole parlant. . . . L'intelligence de l'allégorie prend en vous des proportions à vous-même inconnues . . .[42]

Yet, despite the similarities of the two states, there is an immense difference, for Baudelaire, between the metaphorical perceptions created by an artist – the landscapes fashioned by Delacroix's or Ellison's 'imagination suppléante' – and the allegorical perceptions of the drugged man. The artist, or the listener to music, are responding to a reality existing outside themselves, describable in universal human terms: the overture of *Lohengrin*, for instance. But also, for Delacroix, for Poe as Baudelaire sees him, for Baudelaire himself, the object becomes the 'symbol' of our emotion because, through the 'operation' of imagination, it becomes more profoundly himself.

V

This could be shown by *Tableaux parisiens* 88–97, and 'Le Cygne' is perhaps the most striking of all these expansions into symbolic significance of a spectacle of the city: 'tout pour moi devient allégorie . . .'. The poem is dedicated to Victor Hugo, who went into self-imposed exile in Jersey to protest against the establishment of the Second Empire. It is about exile, understood as a clash between the aspirations of the heart and the world we are forced to inhabit. What gives this feeling presence and force is a sudden coincidence between the state of mind of the poet walking through Paris which is being 'rebuilt' by Haussmann (a reconstruction which entails the destruction of Balzac's Paris, the Paris which Baudelaire loves), and his encounter with a swan on the dry pavement; in other words, a *correspondence* between the inner and the outer world.

Disjunction is built into the poem. On the level of the spectacle: we are made to feel physical and plastic misery through watching an animal which could glide, awkwardly dragging itself on dust. Dryness is conveyed so acutely that the lines make you, like the swan, pant for water:

> . . . Un cygne, qui s'était évadé de sa cage,
> Et, de ses pieds palmés frottant le pavé sec,
> Sur le sol raboteux traînait son blanc plumage.
> Près d'un ruisseau sans eau la bête ouvrant le bec
>
> Baignait nerveusement ses ailes dans la poudre . . .[43]

We also feel an emotional, a cultural sadness, faced in metre with an animal which symbolised the purity, the *élan* of the soul in an agricultural, if not pastoral world, trapped in an ugly urban milieu which denies it existence and makes its nostalgia tragically helpless:

> . . . Et disait, le coeur plein de son beau lac natal:
> 'Eau, quand donc pleuvras-tu? quand tonneras-tu, foudre?'.

This disjunction torments the poet too, who finds, by an ironic reversal of Ronsard's world, a world in which swans retained their mythical stature and in which the changeability of man was contrasted with the stability of nature, that

> Le vieux Paris n'est plus (la forme d'une ville
> Change plus vite, hélas! que le coeur d'un mortel);

The *sympathy* which the poet feels for the swan's exile from its natural milieu is informed by his own experience of exile, environmental and cultural. But because he thus encounters an image of his own predicament outside himself, a movement of expansive generosity is created: 'Dans certains états de l'âme presque surnaturels, la profondeur de la vie se révèle tout entière dans le spectacle . . . qu'on a sous les yeux. Il en devient le symbole'. Through the perfection of his identification with the spectacle outside himself, he goes beyond himself, in ever-expanding sympathy. And out of that generosity, of the largesse of that state of mind, there emerges some principle of reconciliation of the old and the new, of the land of heart's desire and the new conditions. The tension which best renders the agonised writhing of the swan's neck is also that which enables the swan to regain that mythic stature he seemed to have lost. The more expressive of reality the verse, the more it triumphs over it:

> Je vois ce malheureux, mythe étrange et fatal,
>
> Vers le ciel quelquefois, comme l'homme d'Ovide,
> Vers le ciel ironique et cruellement bleu,
> Sur son cou convulsif tendant sa tête avide,
> Comme s'il adressait des reproches à Dieu!

Baudelaire's verse, here, has the power to override the very divorce which it is exploring and mourning: that between the old splendour and the trivial new milieu. The same stanza-form[44] integrates the debris of modern cities:

> . . . tout ce camp de baraques,
> Ces tas de chapiteaux ébauchés et de fûts,
> Les herbes, les gros blocs verdis par l'eau des flaques,
> ·Et, brillant aux carreaux, le bric-à-brac confus.

with Virgil and Racine:

> Andromaque, des bras d'un grand époux tombée,
> Vil bétail, sous la main du superbe Pyrrhus,
> Auprès d'un tombeau vide en extase courbée;
> Veuve d'Hector, hélas! et femme d'Hélénus!

It elevates the new dereliction, what in Laforgue will be 'la phtisie pulmonaire attrisant les grands centres', to the old splendour. The consumptive negress can be sympathised with in the same rhythm as Andromache. The Gaulois of *Salammbô* has been translated to the nineteenth century:

> Je pense à la négresse, amaigrie et phtisique,
> Piétinant dans la boue, et cherchant, l'oeil hagard,
> Les cocotiers absents de la superbe Afrique
> Derrière la muraille immense du brouillard . . .

And the sublimation of modern experience, modern vocabulary, is so complete, that the 'trivial' ending: '[Je pense . . .] à bien d'autres encor!', instead of reading like a platitude, becomes a grandiose gesture towards ever-enlarging areas of human misery. And this, partly because 'Je pense', through the last five stanzas, has gathered tremendous impetus, partly because the exclamation mark which closes the poem is the same as that which has registered despair, then bitter shame in the Virgilian line:

> Veuve d'Hector, hélas! et femme d'Hélénus!

The expansion of human sympathies and scope which occurs through this poem is due to the realisation that, if you understand your here and now, you understand similar theres and thens. That is, your capacity to feel kinship with a stranded swan encountered on a building-site is identical with your capacity to feel kinship with Ovid or Virgil. It is what one can admire in Pound and in a way the Montaigne creed: what I find out about myself makes me capable of finding it out about you. But this implies that your looking inwards should be the natural correlative of your looking outwards.

Here is the gap. The sense of perception artificially exalted by 'excitants nerveux', if its rhythms and phenomena are similar to those of the artistic imagination, revolves in the vicious circle of the ego. Drugs do, to use Baudelaire's expression, 'multiply individuality' in a superb way. But they never achieve any truthful (in the Thomist sense) or durable contact between the self and the world.

This perhaps explains why Baudelaire in the passage on music, to which we must now return, omits to translate any of De Quincey's insistence on the activity of his *mind* in his opium pleasure: 'It is by the reaction of the mind upon the notices of the ear . . . that the pleasure is *constructed* . . . we are able to *construct* out of the raw material of organic sound an *elaborate* intellectual pleasure . . .'[45] In fact, Baudelaire suggests just about the opposite: that De Quincey was the passive subject of a reverie whose matter was his own life but which took place without any control of his: '. . . Toute sa vie passée vivait . . . non par un effort de mémoire, mais comme présente et incarnée dans la musique . . . sorcellerie qui évoquait . . . la musique interprétée et illuminée par l'opium . . .' So, where one man claims to be a philosophical 'constructor', the other shows him to be a prey to witchcraft. The centre of the disagreement is that word 'construct', and Baudelaire may have been so annoyed to see it used by De Quincey in a sense which seemed sacrilegious to him that he punished him accordingly by making him seem even less in control than he was. For Baudelaire translates 'construct' as 'créer', when quoting the Coleridge-inspired Mme Crowe on Imagination:

> 'By imagination, I do not simply mean to convey the common notion implied by that much abused word, which is only *fancy*, but the *constructive* imagination, which is a much higher function, and which, in as much as man is made in the likeness of God, bears a distant relation to that sublime power by which the Creator projects, creates, and upholds his universe.'

> 'Par imagination, je ne veux pas seulement exprimer l'idée commune impliquée dans ce mot dont on fait si grand abus, laquelle est simplement *fantaisie*, mais bien l'imagination *créatrice*, qui est une fonction beaucoup plus élevée, et qui, en tant que l'homme est fait à la ressemblance de Dieu, garde un rapport éloigné avec cette puissance sublime par laquelle le Créateur conçoit, crée et entretient son univers.'[46]

'Créer', for Baudelaire, implies a recognition of the reality internal or external, from which one starts. When we create, we do not separate ourselves from a 'raw material', but grapple with it. When De Quincey says, speaking of his 'constructed' musical pleasure, that the 'matter' comes from the senses, and the 'form' from the mind, he is treating music as a heap of clay which his *fancy* is free to model whichever way it pleases, for his individual enjoyment. Baudelaire's creator has to deal with a rich and difficult reality, and his imagination must have insight into it if it is to make anything valid out of it: the struggle exists when the reality you are trying to render is another art form; when Baudelaire is trying to translate De Quincey, or Constantin Guys's paintings of *filles*:

> Ce qui fait la beauté particulière de ces images, c'est leur fécondité morale. Elles sont grosses de suggestions, mais de suggestions cruelles, âpres, que ma plume, bien qu'accoutumée à *lutter* contre les représentations plastiques, n'a peut-être traduites qu'insuffisamment.[47]

The struggle also exists between the artist and 'nature': 'Le dessin est une *lutte* entre la nature et l'artiste, où l'artiste triomphera d'autant plus facilement qu'il comprendra mieux les intentions de la nature . . .'[48]

Talking about the power of wine, Baudelaire had used that same word 'lutte':

> . . . le vin joue un rôle intime dans la vie de l'humanité, si intime, que je ne serais pas étonné que, séduits par une idée panthéistique, quelques esprits raisonnables lui attribuassent une espèce de personnalité. Le vin et l'homme me font l'effet de deux lutteurs amis sans cesse combattant, sans cesse réconciliés. Le vaincu embrasse toujours le vainqueur.[49]

But in this struggle between wine and man, which is to understand the intentions of which?

Thus Baudelaire would regard as justified the form given by De Quincey's mind to music only if that form were a recognition of the qualities of that music. But it is a *rêverie-souvenir*. There is not the slightest hint of creativity in reliving oneself 'exalted, spiritualised, sublimed', thanks to the music. If anything, it is a misreading, both of oneself and of the music. Why then should Baudelaire lie to himself by accepting De Quincey's valuation of his experience?

His disapproval is most startling when he uses the words 'débauche intellectuelle' to render poor De Quincey's 'elaborate intellectual pleasure', even though he softens the blow by a few flattering additions: 'La musique interprétée et illuminée par l'opium, telle était cette débauche intellectuelle dont tout esprit un peu raffiné peut aisément concevoir la grandeur et l'intensité.' For the word 'débauche', in Baudelaire's vocabulary, is suggestive of sterility. It is to be contrasted with the fertility of truly symbolic states like that which led to the writing of 'Le Cygne':

> . . . ce petit fleuve . . .
> A *fécondé* soudain me mémoire *fertile* . . .

Contrast this with 'Les Deux bonnes soeurs':

> La Débauche et la Mort sont deux aimables filles,
> Prodigues de baisers et riches de santé,
> Dont le flanc toujours vierge et drapé de guenilles
> Sous l'éternel labeur n'a jamais enfanté.[50]

They have never 'enfanté' because they achieve neither contact nor fruitful knowledge. 'Autrui', the 'non-moi', remains a pretext, a shadow: a theatre of Chinese puppets. 'Après une débauche, on se sent toujours plus seul, plus abandonné'.[51] De Quincey's pleasure is a 'débauche' because it 'confirms a prison'.

Thus a cursory confrontation, first of the relation between Baudelaire's way of translating Guys's plastic world into his own, and De Quincey's English experience into his French sense of reality, then of the discrepancies between De Quincey's text and his own, reveal many things about Baudelaire's own preoccupations. In the first place, the need to translate from other art forms, or another language, is part of a belief in the fundamental unity of reality, and the possibility of communication between all forms of human expression, so strongly asserted in the essay on Wagner:

> . . . ce qui serait vraiment surprenant, c'est que le son *ne pût pas* suggérer la couleur, que les couleurs *ne pussent pas* donner l'idée d'une mélodie, et que le son et la couleur fussent impropres à traduire des idées; les choses s'étant toujours exprimées par une analogie réciproque, depuis le jour où Dieu a proféré le monde comme une complexe et indivisible totalité.[52]

Then, translation for Baudelaire as for Pound is fundamentally an activity of the same nature as creating. The same values, the same choices operate in both. And the description which Baudelaire gives of Constantin Guys as the translator of the 'modernité' of the world could

serve as an epigraph to his own critical translation from De Quincey
(and it does remind one of his definition of the true kind of criticism):

> ... M.G., traduisant fidèlement ses propres impressions, marque
> avec une énergie instinctive les points culminants ou lumineux d'un
> objet ... ou ses principales caractéristiques, quelquefois même avec
> une exagération utile pour la mémoire humaine; et l'imagination du
> spectateur, subissant à son tour cette mnémonique si despotique,
> voit avec netteté l'impression produite par les choses sur l'esprit de
> M.G. Le spectateur est ici le traducteur d'une traduction toujours
> claire et enivrante.[53]

A third horizon is opened by Baudelaire's disagreement with De
Quincey on the creative powers of opium. Dealing with a subject,
drugs, which fascinates him as a remedy for spleen and a shortcut to
genius, and with a man for whom he feels deep sympathy, Baudelaire is
yet using De Quincey's text as a means of establishing his own values,
and these are often harsh on his material. It is this mixture of sympathy
and severity which we must now examine in *Les Paradis artificiels*,
taking it as representative of Baudelaire's morality.[54]

12 Solitude and Communication

I

It was necessary to exaggerate Baudelaire's disapproval of De Quincey in order to point to the reasons underlying it. In fact, Baudelaire's tone is warm and generous. In a note on De Quincey's death, he lashes out at the 'envious and goutty spirit' of 'moralising' critics who have meanly denounced De Quincey's unimportant failings. He likes the aristocracy of De Quincey's tone. Remark, he says at one point, 'que l'homme qui parle ainsi est un homme grave, aussi recommandable par la spiritualité de ses moeurs que par la hauteur de ses écrits.' One reason for this sympathy may be the great temperamental similarities between himself and De Quincey. There is a strong correspondence between their childhood experiences. Both lost their fathers young, both felt, though with different emphases and for different reasons, cast out by their mothers, both were wretched at school. When we read this remark from the *Journaux intimes*: 'Sentiment de *solitude*, dès mon enfance. Malgré la famille, – et au milieu des camarades, surtout, – sentiment de destinée éternellement solitaire'[1] we can well imagine how Baudelaire responded to De Quincey's conclusion to *The Affliction of Childhood*: 'Oh, burden of solitude, that cleavest to man through every stage of his being! in his birth, which *has* been, – in his life, which *is*, in his death, which *shall* be, – mighty and essential solitude!'[2]

De Quincey's sense of being the prisoner of his own internal world must also have found an echo in Baudelaire's deeply pessimistic view of relations between man and woman. The same word, 'incommunicable', presides over De Quincey's failure to explain to his mother why he ran away from school:

And, if another Sphinx should arise to propose another enigma to man – saying, What burden is that which only is insupportable by human fortitude? I should answer at once – *It is the burden of the Incommunicable*. At this moment, sitting in the same room of the Priory with my mother, knowing how reasonable she was – how patient of explanations – how candid – how open to pity – not the less I sank away in a hopelessness that was immeasurable from all the effort at explanation. She and I were contemplating the very same act; but she from one centre, I from another . . .[3]

and over Baudelaire's sarcastic account of love:

Dans l'amour comme presque dans toutes les affaires humaines, l'entente cordiale est le résultat d'un malentendu. Ce malentendu, c'est le plaisir. L'homme crie: 'Oh! mon ange!' La femme roucoule: 'Maman! Maman!' Et ces deux imbéciles sont persuadés qu'ils pensent de concert. – Le gouffre infranchissable, qui fait l'incommunicabilité, reste infranchi.[4]

The prose poem 'les Yeux des Pauvres' both illustrates this and provides a striking equivalent to De Quincey's verbal paralysis. Having sworn to each other that all their thoughts would be in common and their souls 'désormais n'en feraient plus qu'une', the narrator and his mistress sit at the terrace of a café. Three poor people, a father and his young children, come and gape at the lit splendour of the café. The narrator reads their feelings with poignant clarity. And the mistress says: 'Ces gens-là me sont vraiment insupportables avec leurs yeux ouverts comme des portes cochères! Ne pourriez-vous pas prier le maître du café de les éloigner d'ici?' The narrator concludes, with an ironic mundaneness which shows the gap open between himself and his mistress: 'Tant il est difficile de s'entendre, mon cher ange, et tant la pensée est incommunicable, même entre gens qui s'aiment!'[5] 'We were contemplating the very same act; but she from one centre, I from another.'

So both men know solitude in its romantic sense: as a disease, or curse, which seals consciousnesses off from each other. But here opium enters and the likeness ends. De Quincey eats opium as a means of reinforcing that solitude of which he has been the victim through his childhood. But also, one must immediately add, even in his early childhood, he had a passion for solitude: to him it was a means of preserving himself from exertion, from engagement. He is disturbingly lucid about this, when he talks of his brother's contempt for him:

... I had a perfect craze for being despised. I doted on it; and considered contempt a sort of luxury that I was in continual fear of losing. Why not? Wherefore should any rational person shrink from contempt, if it happen to form the tenure by which he holds his repose in life? ... to me, at that era of life, it formed the main guarantee of an unmolested repose.... The slightest approach to any favourable construction of my intellectual pretensions alarmed me beyond measure; because it pledged me in a manner with the hearer to support this first attempt by a second, by a third, by a fourth – O heavens! there is no saying how far the horrid man might go in his unreasonable demands upon me.... Professing the most absolute bankruptcy from the very beginning ... I never could be made miserable by unknown responsibilities.[6]

One can easily sympathise with De Quincey's position then: he had, at the age of six, been deeply wounded by the death of his sister Elizabeth, to whom he was very close. And no doubt he was trying to preserve himself from ever being hurt in this way again by bluntly refusing to become involved with anybody. But when he says that he was looking for 'unmolested repose' 'at that era of life', the lack of present self-knowledge contrasts strangely with the precision with which he interprets his past. For one could argue, on the basis of the opera passage which we discussed in the previous chapter, and of the passages which surround it, that he was taking opium for the very same reason he was encouraging his brother to believe that he was effeminate and stupid; in order to be preserved from 'unknown responsibilities'. He was taking opium so that he could enjoy reliving his past without feeling any moral responsibility towards it, so that he could let the music evoke his past for him without actually listening to that music. He was, he also recounts, taking extreme pleasure in the conversation of Italian women around him, because, not knowing the language, he could respond in purely aesthetic terms to the sound of their words. And he goes on to say that some Saturday nights, instead of going to the opera, he would stroll around the streets of London, mixing with the crowds of poor people out, for once, for enjoyment. He says of the London poor: '... I, at that time, was disposed to express [my interest] by sympathising with their pleasures.'[7] Baudelaire carefully preserves the strained syntax of De Quincey's sentence: it is for him a means of underlining the forced quality of De Quincey's feelings: '... j'étais porté à cette époque à exprimer mon intérêt pour eux en sympathisant avec leurs plaisirs.'[8] He had already passed comment on what he thought of such a pleasure: 'La jouissance en question, assez alléchante pour rivaliser avec la musique, pourrait s'appeler le dilettantisme dans la charité.'[9] The, it would seem, laudatory terms 'alléchante', 'dilettantisme dans la charité' subtly point to the condescending, perverse bent which he finds to De Quincey's relish. De Quincey himself confesses that there was something artificial about his excursions, and that he was going for therapeutic reasons:

> Thus I have shown, or tried to show, that opium does not of necessity produce inactivity or torpor; but that, on the contrary, it often led me into markets and theatres. Yet, in candour, I will admit that markets and theatres are not the appropriate haunts of the opium-eater, when in the divinest state incident to his enjoyment. In that state, crowds become an oppression to him; music even, too sensual and gross. He naturally seeks solitude and silence, as indispensible conditions of those trances, or profoundest reveries, which are the crown and consummation of what opium can do for human nature. I, whose disease it was to meditate too much and to observe too little, . . . was sufficiently aware of these tendencies in my own thoughts to do all I could to counteract them.[10]

But it is revealing that it should be precisely through the artifice of opium, which, as he himself acknowledges, transfigures and internalises reality,[11] that De Quincey should be trying to counteract his tendencies to solitude. That is, that he should attempt contact with others only when he has engineered in himself a state that will make contact impossible. And this makes one wonder, was it because communication between himself and his mother was actually impossible through the disparity of their characters, as De Quincey claims, or because he preferred known contempt to 'unknown responsibilities', that he 'sank away from all effort at explanation'? How far was he himself the creator of the incommunicable? One feels all the more entitled to ask the question as the only intimate relations we see him enter into as a grown man, with Ann or his wife, involve him with beings socially and intellectually his inferiors: they are 'soeurs de charité', and up to a point, part of the paraphernalia of his life. The 'Paint me' passage, in which he describes his surroundings at the peak of his bliss, place the wife sitting at the table on the same plane as the tea-pot and the 'little golden receptacle of the pernicious drug'.[12]

This is suggesting that by deciding to take opium, De Quincey has chosen to cultivate both his refined sensibility and his inability to communicate. He has chosen to be overwhelmed by what he could acutely feel, perhaps because this was the recurrent pattern of his childhood, and he had become *addicted* to it. His childhood, lived as both poignant and paralysing, in the episodes of his sister's death, of the encounter with the hearse-like carriage bringing home his dying father, of the suffering and death of the little idiot girls persecuted by their mother for their idiocy, of the appearance of a mad dog on a fine June morning, has made exertion again and again seem futile. And by contrast, it has taught him that deep, private feeling is our only mode of relation to reality. Opium, by reinforcing this divorce between action and feeling, imprisons him inside a private agony: not only can he do nothing to break away from it, but that other mode of communication with reality, understanding, eludes him. In this nightmare, all the circumstances are vague; only the feelings are precise; and the feelings destroy the possibility of acting:

> Somewhere, but I knew not where – somehow, but I knew not how – by some beings, but I knew not by whom – a battle, a strife, an agony, was travelling through all its stages – was evolving itself, like the catastrophe of some mighty drama, with which my sympathy was the more insupportable from deepening confusion as to its local scene, its cause, its nature, and its undecipherable issue. I (as is usual in dreams where, of necessity, we make ourselves central to every movement) had the power, and yet had not the power, to decide it. I had the power, if I could raise myself to will it; and yet again had not the power, for the weight of twenty Atlantics was upon me, or the oppression of inexpiable guilt.[13]

What a revealing parenthesis! Is not the necessity by which in dreams 'we make ourselves central to every movement' a chosen, a cherished one in a man who has opted for dream-states to cultivate his sensibility at the expense of human relations? But the vagueness which pervades this passage also tells us a great deal about what opium is doing for De Quincey, and why he has chosen it as a mode of life.

The agony of this nightmare is caused, De Quincey tells us, by the 'deepening confusion' in which he is as to the 'local scene, [the] cause, [the] nature' of the dream taking place. But this anguished confusion is only the evil face of the 'dreamy', vague states which he has been cultivating all his life. It is very instructive to watch the way in which he twists Wordsworth's 'wise passiveness', in the *Autobiography*, when he is claiming that childhood, being an age of deep feeling, is an age in which our contact with truth is more authentic than at later times in life. Wordsworth's 'wise passiveness' leads to detailed knowledge; it is part of a dialogue. De Quincey presents it as a 'narrow' intensity in which we are rescued from the frittering perception of details:

> The heart in this season of life is apprehensive; and, where its sensibilities are profound, is endowed with a special power of listening for the tones of truth – hidden, struggling, or remote: for, the knowledge being then narrow, the interest is narrow in the objects of knowledge: consequently the sensibilities are not scattered, are not multiplied, are not crushed and confounded (as afterwards they are) under the burden of that distraction which lurks in the infinite littleness of details.[14]

Truth here is presented as 'hidden' and 'remote'; a thing which we can only perceive by listening passively, forgetful of the 'infinite littleness' of what some other man might have called 'reality'. And of course opium promotes that forgetfulness: when Beatrice Webb crossed the district in which the 'London poor' lived, the shock she felt led her to change her whole life. Opium blurs all the ugly 'details' for De Quincey; it helps him concentrate on the rosy side of life:

> The pains of poverty I had lately seen too much of – more than I wished to remember; but the pleasures of the poor, their hopes, their consolations of spirit, and their restings from toil, can never become oppressive to contemplate. . . . If wages were a little higher, or were expected to be so – if the quartern loaf were a little lower, or it was reported that onions and butter were falling – I was glad; yet, if the contrary were true, I drew from opium some means of consolation.[15]

Would he have called that 'wise passiveness' a communion with 'truth'? He tells how once he was so horrified by the way Lamb attacked *The Ancient Mariner* that he stopped his ears with his hands in order not to hear the sacrilegious words. It does seem here that opium is an even better way of stopping his ears and blinding his eyes. Baudelaire's 'dilettantisme dans le charité', loaded with his denunciation of the cult of 'la plastique', seems well deserved.

For Baudelaire, you cannot feel sympathy if you are vague or confused as to what you are sympathising with. Sympathy is equalitarian. It involves risk, exertion. 'Assommons les pauvres', written against all customary good feelings, shows this strikingly. The narrator has just met a plaintive beggar: urged by his 'Démon de combat' who whispers that 'he alone is worthy of liberty who can conquer it', he jumps on the beggar and starts beating him up:

> ... Tout à coup – ô miracle! ô jouissance du philosophe qui vérifie l'excellence de sa théorie! – je vis cette antique carcasse se retourner, se redresser avec une énergie que je n'aurais jamais soupçonnée dans une machine si singulièrement détraquée, et avec un regard de haine qui me parut *de bon augure*, le malandrin décrépit se jeta sur moi, me pocha les deux yeux, me cassa quatre dents, et avec la même branche d'arbre, me battit dru comme plâtre. – Par mon énergique médication, je lui avais donc rendu l'orgueil et la vie.
>
> Alors je lui fis force signes pour lui faire comprendre que je considérais la discussion comme finie, et me relevant avec la satisfaction d'un sophiste du Portique, je lui dis: 'Monsieur, *vous êtes mon égal*! veuillez me faire l'honneur de partager avec moi ma bourse.[16]

For Baudelaire, to communicate is not to co-exist with people in a cloud of benevolent feelings, but to create and offer oneself to contacts which entail mutual exposure, a recognition of otherness, and with it, the recognition of a common humanity: '*Vous êtes mon égal*'.

And it is because he believes in the importance of such contacts that the parallel between wine and hashish celebrates the virtues of wine and denounces hashish as isolating. The section on wine is a prose double of 'L'Ame du vin' and 'Le Vin des chiffoniers' in *Les Fleurs du Mal*. Baudelaire celebrates the magnificent generosity of wine, which translates harassed rag-pickers into Napoleons:

> Les bannières, les fleurs et les arcs triomphaux
>
> Se dressent devant eux, solennelle magie!
> Et dans l'étourdissante et lumineuse orgie
> Des clairons, du soleil, des cris et du tambour,
> Ils apportent la gloire au peuple ivre d'amour!
> ...
> Pour noyer la rancoeur et bercer l'indolence
> De tous ces vieux maudits qui meurent en silence,
> Dieu, touché de remords, avait fait le sommeil;
> L'Homme ajouta le Vin, fils sacré du Soleil![17]

'Fils sacré du Soleil'. Through an amazing, splendid rhetoric, which mimics that of a drunk man, wine is made into a new Saviour of mankind, loving the wretched and the derelict, warm, expansive: wine becomes an allegory for largesse, mercifulness:

> Voilà ce que chante le vin dans son langage mystérieux. Malheur à celui dont le coeur égoïste et fermé aux douleurs de ses frères n'a jamais entendu cette chanson!
> J'ai souvent pensé que si Jésus-Christ paraissait aujourd'hui sur le banc des accusés, il se trouverait quelque procureur qui démontrerait que son cas est aggravé par la récidive. Quant au vin, il récidive tous les jours. . . . C'est sans doute ce qui explique l'acharnement des moralistes contre lui.[18]

By contrast with wine, here is how Baudelaire judges hashish:

> Je montrerai les inconvénients du haschisch, dont le moindre, malgré les trésors de bienveillance inconnus qu'il fait germer en apparence dans le coeur, ou plutôt dans le cerveau de l'homme, dont le moindre défaut, dis-je, est d'être antisocial, tandis que le vin est profondément humain, et j'oserais presque dire homme d'action.[19]

And although he recognises that hashish, like wine, helps to the 'développement poétique excessif de l'homme', he adds at the end of the section on hashish: 'Le vin rend bon et sociable. Le haschisch est isolant . . . le vin est pour le peuple qui travaille et qui mérite d'en boire. Le haschisch appartient à la classe des joies solitaires; il est fait pour les misérables oisifs.'[20]

True, this apotheosis of wine, written in 1851, breathes a 'socialistic', '1848' love of 'mankind' which is no longer Baudelaire's in 1859, when he is translating De Quincey. But the priorities, the choices, remain the same. The condemnation of the isolating effect of hashish, in 'Le Poëme du haschisch', prolongs, with different emphases and different arguments, the condemnation of hashish in the earlier essay. The question in any case is not whether Baudelaire is 'right' abour hashish- and opium-eaters. Nor do his own motives for condemning drug-takers really matter, as some would argue (it seems that he himself was one, and his severity may be directed at himself, with all that this can imply). According to his own sense of 'justice', however, what does matter is what can illumine the issue at stake: beyond personalities, beyond self-interest. So the point is, why should he, who in so much of his work praises the virtues of solitude, so severely condemn the isolating effect of drugs?

II

For if one reads 'La Solitude', a prose poem revised under the influence of Poe's *The Man of the Crowd,* one is struck by Baudelaire's detestation of the democratic spirit. Against sociability, fraternisation, he upholds an ideal of proud isolation. The man of the crowd, in Poe's story, behaves like a frantic whore, perpetually offering to sell his individuality to the thickest crowd. He becomes neurotic whenever the crowd diminishes and he is threatened with being on his own. To the narrator watching him, this refusal to be alone makes him into 'the type and the genius of deep crime'. Baudelaire calls it 'prostitution':

> 'Ce grand malheur de ne pouvoir être seul! . . .' dit quelque part La Bruyère . . .
> 'Presque tous nos malheurs nous viennent de n'avoir pas su rester dans notre chambre', dit un autre sage, Pascal, je crois, rappelant ainsi dans la cellule du recueillement tous ces affolés qui cherchent le bonheur dans le mouvement et dans une prostitution que je pourrais appeler *fraternitaire*, si je voulais parler la belle langue de notre siècle.[21]

'S'oublier dans la foule' is abhorrent to Baudelaire. When Satan-Eros offers him the ever-renascent pleasure of forgetting himself in others, and of fusing his soul with others, he contemptuously replies: '. . . Grand merci! je n'ai que faire de cette pacotille d'êtres qui sans doute, ne valent pas mieux que mon pauvre moi. Bien que j'aie quelque honte à me souvenir, je ne veux rien oublier . . .'[22]

Baudelaire shrinks from endangering his identity, wasting his power, bleeding his substance away, as in the nightmare of 'La Fontaine de sang' through so-called states of fusion. Hence his sense that an artist can never fully make love: 'Foutre, c'est aspirer à entrer dans un autre, et l'artiste ne sort jamais de lui-même.' Hence his contempt for 'love', which for him is also a form of prostitution:

> Goût invincible de la prostitution dans le coeur de l'homme, d'où naît son horreur de la solitude. – Il veut être *deux*. L'homme de génie veut être *un*, donc solitaire.
> . . . C'est cette horreur de la solitude, le besoin d'oublier son *moi* dans la chair extérieure, que l'homme appelle noblement *besoin* d'aimer.[23]

To an admirer of D. H. Lawrence, such reading of love relations will appear a heresy and a disease. A heresy, because Lawrence, one may argue, believes that people achieve a true sense of identity only through a continuous encounter, or clash, with otherness: as do Birkin and Ursula in *Women in Love*. A disease, because the total separation which Baudelaire seems to be establishing between the instinctual life and consciousness reminds one of the divorce between 'mind' and 'body' which makes Hermione so deadly. When such separation exists, again in what one may take to be Lawrence's view, we are unable to give or achieve fulfilment. Baudelaire's views are only the upshot of a failed love life, of a sick sensibility.

There is truth in this.[24] One could answer that nobody but a lunatic would recommend Baudelaire's life as a pattern to be imitated, that what matters is what he does with that life, but it leaves open the question of whether his insights, his 'art' are not made eccentric by his neurosis. One could then add that Baudelaire is not concerned with 'normality'. At the start he is beyond, or beneath it, as one pleases. Inhabited as he is by spleen, greatness is the only way out left to him. And for him it is to be attained, not through mad and private quests, but through a growing insight into central states of consciousness. Like the desire to fraternise. And the desire not to. But the real plea one would make is that, conditioned as he was by private and public history, he could still create such a space of freedom in and through the forcefulness of his utterances.

The merit of such a statement on love is the cleanness of its bias. There is at times something unmanning, unclean in the way in which Lawrence forces you to get involved in one way of looking at things, or be damned. If you try to think that Hermione or Sir Clifford Chatterley are more interesting characters than Ursula or the gamekeeper, you are perverse (you are not if you become more concerned with Alexei Karenin's predicament than with Vronski's; and you certainly are not if you disagree with Baudelaire's view of love). Baudelaire's refusal to fuse his soul with yours has the merit that he offers himself to you with full force, but at the same time leaves you free. The ground is cut between you and him. He is not going to save your soul, but to tell you, with full passion, what he learnt through trying to save his. His sense of an art beyond personalities, beyond truths, is not a form of diseased aestheticism, but an attempt to communicate on a level which frees both you and him from predatoriness: like attacking the beggar. He gives him back both dignity and life by trying to destroy him, not by telling him what is good for his soul.

This is where the contrast with De Quincey is instructive. Both men are neurotic, but they draw very different insights from their neuroses. Yet their starting-point is, again and again, very similar. They both see solitude as a source of power which it is urgent to preserve and develop in a world of speed and dissipation of substance. Baudelaire, in his account of *Suspiria*, quickly summarises this passage, in full agreement with his own views, where De Quincey describes the revolution which political upheavals and technical changes are bringing about:

> . . . it becomes too evident that, unless this colossal pace of advance can be retarded (a thing not to be expected), or, which is happily more probable, can be met by counter-forces, of corresponding magnitude, – forces in the direction of religion or profound philosophy that shall radiate centrifugally against this storm of life so perilously centripetal towards the vortex of the merely human, – left to itself, the natural tendency of so chaotic a tumult must be to evil; for some minds to lunacy, for others a reagency of fleshly torpor . . . the action of thought and feeling is consciously dissipated and squandered. To reconcentrate them into meditative habits, a necessity is felt by all observing persons for sometimes retiring from crowds. No man ever will unfold the capacities of his own intellect who does not at least checker his life with solitude. How much solitude, so much power.[25]

This exactly echoes 'La Solitude' and *The Man of the Crowd*. But De Quincey and Baudelaire mean very different things by the 'power' of solitude. In De Quincey, it leads inward, towards dreaming. In Baudelaire, outwards, in a very strange form of sympathy, or insight.

For De Quincey, the world inside, Coleridge might say, the world of fancy, is more substantial than the world outside.[26] The true way for him to counter the dissolving, dissipating impetus of reality is to harmonise it to an internal key. Recounting how, after his sister's death, he used the music at church to soar imaginatively above grief, he hits upon a phrase 'gathering by strong coercion the total storm into unity' which cannot but remind one of that which he used in the *Suspiria* passage: 'forces . . . that shall radiate centrifugally against this storm of life so perilously centripetal towards the vortex of the merely human . . .' So that one cannot help but wonder whether, by 'the merely human' he does not mean the harmonious aerial fabrics which our minds can weave in solitude:

> These visions were self-sustained. These visions needed not that any

sound should speak to me, or music mould my feelings. The hint from the litany, the fragment from the clouds – those and the storied windows were sufficient. But not the less the blare of the tumultuous organ, wrought its own separate creations. And oftentimes in anthems, when the mighty instrument threw its vast columns of sound, fierce yet melodious, over the voices of the choir – high in arches, where it seemed to rise, surmounting and overriding the strife of the vocal parts, and gathering by strong coercion the total storm into unity – sometimes I seemed to rise and walk triumphantly upon those clouds which, but a moment before I had looked up to as mementos of prostrate sorrow . . .[27]

No wonder that, with such early training, opium, which can 'overrule all feelings into a compliance with the master-key', should be sufficient to console him for the drop in wages which was going to make the 'poor' starve. The only solid, 'human' reality being his feelings, all that mattered was to straighten them out. The power of solitude works solely for the individual entrenched in the private world of his sensibility.

For Baudelaire, one of the powers of solitude which works against 'dissipation' is work. Talking about Delacroix, he says:

Qui a plus aimé sa *tour d'ivoire*, c'est-à-dire le secret? . . . Qui a plus aimé le *home*, santuaire et tanière? Comme d'autres cherchent le secret pour la débauche, il cherche le secret pour l'inspiration, et il s'y livrait à de véritables ribotes de travail. '*The one prudence in life is concentration; the one evil is dissipation*', dit [Emerson] . . .[28]

Baudelaire, here again, is concerned with what is possible for an artist, not an 'ordinary man'. But then, in his view, an artist is a 'concentré' of an ordinary man, he is only, like Balzac's characters, 'chargé d'énergie jusqu'à la gueule'. His powers all work in a normative direction. But Baudelaire insists on the high tension of these powers.

So one of the justifications of solitude is the amount of creative energy which it enables one to accumulate. Its other aspect is more provocative. The ability to be alone is for Baudelaire the necessary condition for insight and generosity. You are only capable of entering into valid relations with reality, with people, if you are first able to do without the relations which the structure of society seems to force on to you.

The key to this paradoxical view is in the antithetical use of the word 'prostitution'. The man of the crowd indulged in a 'prostitution fraternitaire' which damaged his identity. But having said that 'l'homme de génie veut être *un*, donc solitaire', Baudelaire adds: 'La gloire, c'est rester *un*, et se prostituer d'une manière particulière'. The word accrues significance in these two passages:

> L'amour peut dériver d'un sentiment généreux: le goût de la prostitution; mais il est bientôt corrompu par le goût de la propriété.
>
> L'être le plus prostitué, c'est l'être par excellence, c'est Dieu, puisqu'il est l'ami suprême pour chaque individu, puisqu'il est le réservoir commun, inépuisable de l'amour.[30]

One sees why the words 'être' and 'prostitution' are thus coupled in this sense of God. Generosity can only come from strength. It is the being who, in men's imaginations, most strongly *is*, who can most continuously and most completely give himself. The man who surrenders his conscience, his identity, to a notion of public opinion, a form of prejudice, or a 'romantic' passion, deprives himself of the ability to give. His opposite, the man, in Baudelaire's view, most like God, is the poet. He is intensely alive, and in this, as the poet-narrator of Poe's story makes him able to perceive, he is the antithesis to the absent-minded man of the crowd:

> ... je me trouvais dans une de ces heureuses dispositions qui sont précisément le contraire de l'ennui, – dispositions où l'appétence morale est merveilleusement aiguisée, quand la taie qui recouvrait la vision spirituelle est arrachée, ... où l'esprit électrisé dépasse aussi prodigieusement sa puissance journalière que la raison ardente et naïve de Leibnitz l'emporte sur la folle et molle rhétorique de Gorgias.... Chaque chose m'inspirait un intérêt calme, mais plein de curiosité...[31]

Because of the power which solitude has given him, because he is not searching for 'fusion', the poet's personality can multiply itself into insights. The nature of imagination is double:

> Multitude, solitude: termes égaux et convertibles par le poète actif et fécond...
> Le poète jouit de cet incomparable privilège, qu'il peut à la guise être lui-même et autrui. Comme ces âmes errantes qui cherchent un corps, il entre, quand il veut, dans le personnage de chacun. Pour lui

seul, tout est vacant; . . . Ce que les hommes nomment amour est bien petit, bien restreint et bien faible, comparé à cette ineffable orgie, à cette sainte prostitution de l'âme qui se donne tout entière, poésie et charité, à l'imprévu qui se montre, à l'inconnu qui passe.[32]

There is a marvellous passage in which the painter of modern life is presented as the epitome of such poetic prostitution. There is a strong contrast between what is thus released and De Quincey's outings in the London crowd:

La foule, est son domaine, comme l'air est celui de l'oiseau, comme l'eau celui du poisson. Sa passion et sa profession, c'est d'*épouser la foule*. Pour le parfait flâneur, pour l'observateur passionné, c'est une immense jouissance que d'élire domicile dans le nombre, dans l'ondoyant, dans le mouvement, dans le fugitif et l'infini . . . l'amoureux de la vie universelle entre dans la foule comme dans un immense réservoir d'électricité. On peut aussi le comparer, lui, . . . à un kaléidoscope doué de conscience, qui, à chacun de ses mouvements, représente la vie multiple et la grâce mouvante de tous les éléments de la vie. C'est un *moi* insatiable du *non-moi*, qui, à chaque instant, le rend et l'exprime en images plus vivantes que la vie elle-même, toujours instable et fugitive . . .[33]

By being thus open to life outside, the artist becomes multiplied. 'Il élit domicile dans le nombre'. 'Il représente la vie multiple'. Baudelaire uses this word 'multiple' when he calls wine and hashish means to multiply the individuality. But they only multiply the self by itself. And De Quincey, who hoped to achieve unity through dreaming, finds that his personality is more terribly than ever at the mercy of the centripetal forces of life, when the Malay, who only once called at his house, nightly haunts his dreams. 'Comme l'espace, comme le temps, le Malais s'était multiplié', Baudelaire says. Such solitary, sterile multiplication of the individuality is at the opposite of the 'multiplication du coeur', of the imaginative love which pervades 'Les Petites vieilles':

. . . Telles vous cheminez, stoïques et sans plaintes,
. . .
Mères au coeur saignant, courtisanes ou saintes, . . .
. . .
Mais moi, moi qui de loin tendrement vous surveille,
. . .
Tout comme si j'étais votre père, ô merveille!
Je goûte à votre insu des plaisirs clandestins:

> Je vois s'épanouir vos passions novices;
> Sombres ou lumineux, je vis vos jours perdus;
> *Mon coeur multiplié* jouit de tous vos vices!
> Mon âme resplendit de toutes vos vertus!....[34]

III

There is a 'philosophical' (in Baudelaire's very special use of the word) dimension to this understanding and cult of multiplication. It is difficult to grasp otherwise than by imaginative experience, for Baudelaire is concise to the point of elusiveness; and the ideas are worth having for their body more than their logical rigour.

The dimension appears in the passage on crowds from the *Peintre de la vie moderne* quoted a little while ago: '... pour l'observateur passionné, c'est une immense jouissance que d'élire domicile dans le nombre, dans le mouvement, dans le fugitif et l'infini ...' *Fusées* repeats and develops this (that is, as generally with Baudelaire, makes it more compact, not elucidates it):

> Le plaisir d'être dans les foules est une expression mystérieuse de la jouissance de la multiplication du nombre.
> *Tout* est nombre. Le nombre est dans *tout*. Le nombre est dans l'individu. L'ivresse est nombre.[35]

Here again, Joseph de Maistre turns out to be necessary to an understanding of Baudelaire. The following text illuminates 'Fusées' if reading it one remembers how much like a God, or rather like a Christ in the host, the artist 'communing' with the crowd is to Baudelaire:

> Le *nombre* est la barrière évidente entre la brute et nous. ... Dieu nous a donné le nombre, et c'est par le nombre qu'il se prouve à nous, comme c'est par le nombre que l'homme se prouve à son semblable. Otez le nombre, vous ôtez les arts, les sciences, et par conséquent l'intelligence. Ramenez-le: avec lui reparaissent ses deux filles célestes, l'harmonie et la beauté; le *cri* devient *chant*, le bruit reçoit le *rhythme*, le saut est *danse*, la force s'appelle *dynamique*, et les traces sont des *figures*. Une preuve sensible de cette vérité, c'est que dans les langues ... les mêmes mots expriment le nombre et la pensée: on dit, par exemple, que la *raison* d'un grand homme a découvert la *raison* d'une telle progression: on dit *raison sage* et *raison inverse*,

> *mécomptes* dans la politique et *mécomptes* dans les calculs . . .
> L'intelligence comme la beauté se plaît à se contempler: or, le miroir
> de l'intelligence, c'est le nombre . . .

Perhaps we should remember here that the painter of modern life can be compared to 'un miroir aussi immense que cette foule'.

> De là vient le goût que nous avons pour la symétrie; car tout être intelligent aime à placer et à reconnaître de tout côté son signe qui est l'*ordre*. . . . Pourquoi la rime, les pieds, les ritournelles, la mesure, le rythme, nous plaisent-ils dans la musique et dans la poésie? . . . parce que l'intelligence se plaît dans tout ce qui prouve l'intelligence, et que son signe principal est le nombre . . .[36]

There can be no doubt that Maistre is in Baudelaire's memory when he analyses what makes a ship aesthetically so appealing (and a carriage for that matter). Even the vocabulary echoes Maistre's:

> . . . le charme infini et mystérieux qui gît dans la contemplation d'un navire . . . tient, . . . à la *régularité* et à la *symétrie* qui sont un des besoins primordiaux de l'esprit humain au même degré que la complication et l'*harmonie*, – et, à la *multiplication* successive et à la génération de toutes les courbes et figures imaginaires opérées dans l'espace par les éléments réels de l'objet . . .

The point is that what seems to be pure mathematical and geometrical analysis instantly resolves itself into *human* (emotional) significance:

> l'idée poétique qui se *dégage* de cette opération du mouvement dans les lignes est l'hypothèse d'un être vaste, immense, compliqué, mais eurythmique, d'un animal plein de génie, souffrant et soupirant tous les soupirs et toutes les ambitions humaines.[37]

This is one of the most striking lessons Baudelaire has learnt from Maistre: a conviction that what is most abstract is not cut away from 'life', but is an essential form of it, a way into it. 'L'entousiasme qui s'attache à autre chose que les abstractions est un signe de faiblesse et de maladie'.[38] It is a sign of weakness, because one has not had the energy to penetrate deep enough; of disease, because one fails to perceive the fundamental correspondence of mind at its most abstract, with reality at its most complex.

Just as Baudelaire believes that the geometrical analysis of a ship will lead to respond to its human suggestiveness, that abstract forms can express emotional, instinctive realities, Maistre goes on from what he has said about number to posit that the 'order' of the universe which appeals to the intelligence, is the manifestation, not only of a divine intelligence, but of a divine *presence*. Perhaps this is philosophically indefensible: but there is something moving about the dynamic optimism of such trust, and its value for a writer like Baudelaire lies in the connection, asserted with such confidence, between language and reality:

> Comme ces mots que je prononce dans ce moment vous prouvent l'existence de celui qui les prononce, et que s'ils étaient écrits, il la prouveraient de même à tous ceux qui liraient ces mots arrangés suivant les lois de la syntaxe, de même tous les êtres créés prouvent par leur *syntaxe* l'existence d'un suprême écrivain qui nous parle par ces signes; en effet, tous ces êtres sont des lettres dont la réunion prouve Dieu, c'est-à-dire l'intelligence qui la prononce . . .[39]

By multiplying himself into number, by sympathy with and insight into the crowd, the artist is not only opening himself to the 'non-moi', which he then reflects and expresses. Choosing to inhabit number, he is participating in a very instinctual form of understanding. Because number is in him (in the many ways Maistre states: 'Le nombre est dans l'individu'), he can communicate with the number outside him: '*Tout* est nombre. Le nombre est dans *tout*.' The artist is reading the syntax of reality because there is in him the ability to understand that syntax, to be it imaginatively: 'Mon coeur multiplié jouit de tous vos vices . . .' It is then his task, by his syntax, to make it perceptible to others. Doing so, he creates the '*subject* of the creator'.

13 The Voyage

'Le Voyage', the crowning poem in *Les Fleurs du Mal*, that which closes the section 'La Mort', is an allegory of the modern forms of the 'metaphysical' journey: an image of the course of public or private life; of the quest for knowledge and satisfaction; of the exploration of space, external and internal. Ulysses and Dante are vaguely present in its background. There is a terrible compulsion to run, to fly even, in Baudelaire's travellers:

> . . . Mais les vrais voyageurs sont ceux-là seuls qui partent
> Pour partir; coeurs légers, semblables aux ballons,
> De leur fatalité jamais ils ne s'écartent,
> Et sans savoir pourquoi disent toujours: Allons!
>
> Ceux-là dont les désirs ont la forme des nues,
> Et qui rêvent, ainsi qu'un conscrit le canon,
> De vastes voluptés, changeantes, inconnues,
> Et dont l'esprit humain n'a jamais su le nom![1]

Among those travellers who dream, not only of 'voluptés inconnues', but of unknown insights, are drug-takers like De Quincey. In fact, his claim that opium is a means of accomplishing spiritual voyages is the most valid, the most interesting he makes in its support. What if the cultivation of dreams, instead of being a means towards solipsism, were the way to a deeper understanding of reality?

This is what De Quincey asserts at the opening of *Suspiria*:

> Among the powers in man which suffer by this too intense life of the *social* instincts, none suffers more than the power of dreaming. . . . That faculty, in alliance with the mystery of darkness, is the one great tube through which man communicates with the shadowy. And the dreaming organ, in connexion with the heart, the eye, and the ear, composes the magnificent apparatus which forces the infinite

into the chambers of a human brain, and throws dark reflections from eternities below all life upon the horrors of that mysterious *camera obscura* – the sleeping mind.

But, if this faculty suffers from the decay of solitude, ... some merely physical agencies can and do assist the faculty of dreaming preternaturally ... beyond all others is opium: which indeed seems to possess a *specific* power in that direction; not merely for exalting the colours of dream-scenery, but for deepening its shadows, and, above all, for strengthening the sense of its fearful *realities*.[2]

I

This is the crucial question as regards 'excitants nerveux': because Rimbaud's cry 'Le poète se fait voyant par un long, immense et raisonné dérèglement de tous les sens' was to show the way to many of his generation and the next two; because several of De Quincey's most significant contemporaries shared in his view of the importance of man's 'communication with the shadowy'. And one may well wonder why it should have been at that particular period in History that faith in dreams revived so.

The opening of Poe's *Eleonora* clearly sets the terms of the problem:

... Men have called me mad; but the question is not yet settled, whether madness is or is not the loftiest intelligence – whether much that is glorious – whether all that is profound – does not spring from disease of thought – from *moods* of mind exalted at the expense of general intellect. They who dream by day are cognisant of many things which escape those who dream only by night ... They penetrate, however rudderless or compassless, into the vast ocean of the 'light ineffable' and again, like the adventurers of the Nubian geographers, '*Aggressi sunt mare tenebrarum, quid in eo esset exploraturi*'.[3]

The last image heralds the 'Nous nous embarquerons sur la mer des Ténèbres' of Baudelaire's 'voyageurs'. So does Nerval's 'séjour des limbes', placed in the tradition of the *Divine Comedy*, Swedenborg's *Memorabilia*, Apuleius's *Golden Ass*:

Le Rêve est une seconde vie. Je n'ai pu percer sans frémir ces portes d'ivoire ou de corne qui nous séparent du monde invisible. Les premiers instants du sommeil sont l'image de la mort; un engourdissement nébuleux saisit notre pensée, et nous ne pouvons déterminer l'instant précis où le *moi*, sous une autre forme, continue l'oeuvre de l'existence. C'est un souterrain vague qui s'éclaire peu à peu, et où se dégagent de l'ombre et de la nuit les pâles figures gravement immobiles qui habitent le séjour des limbes . . .

. . . Je vais essayer . . . de transcrire les impressions d'une longue maladie qui s'est passée tout entière dans les mystères de mon esprit; et je ne sais pourquoi je me sers de ce terme maladie, car jamais, quant à ce qui est de moi-même, je ne me suis senti mieux portant . . . l'imagination m'apportait des délices infinies. En recouvrant ce que les hommes appellent raison, faudra-t-il regretter de les avoir perdues?[4]

The question asked by De Quincey, Poe and Nerval – whether 'abnormal' states carry with them more insights than normal ones – can perhaps only be answered by personal exploration. But one can attempt to understand what kind of insights they are talking about, and to weigh their respective experience of 'darkness' by assessing the value of their *record* of it.

Baudelaire's response to De Quincey's claim for dreams is a good point of departure. As with everything that can expand life, he evinces both sympathy and suspicion. He too is exploring 'les limbes'; but his search is hedged round with fallacy and failure. His 'voyageurs' go a long way to find that they have not escaped from the essential dreariness of living:

> Amer savoir, celui qu'on tire du voyage!
> Le monde, monotone et petit, aujourd'hui,
> Hier, demain, toujours, nous fait voir notre image:
> Une oasis d'horreur dans un désert d'ennui![5]

This view of the ultimate circularity of escape permeates even ecstatic dream-poems like the prose 'L'Invitation au voyage':

> Fleur incomparable, tulipe retrouvée, allégorique dahlia, c'est là, n'est-ce pas, dans ce beau pays si calme et si rêveur, qu'il faudrait aller vivre et fleurir? Ne serais-tu pas encadrée dans ton analogie, et ne pourrais-tu pas te mirer, pour parler comme les mystiques, dans ta propre *correspondance*?[6]

'Encadrée' and 'te mirer' are a give-away. The ideal world is once more attained through framing a space from reality, but what it reveals is our own image. Baudelaire in fact doubts that the 'great tube' De Quincey speaks of should communicate with the infinite.

De Quincey's case is most strongly and ingenuously put in *The Affliction of Childhood*. The passage occurs when the little child has come to see the body of his beloved sister, who is dead:

> ... instantly a trance fell upon me. A vault seemed to open in the zenith of the far blue sky, a shaft which ran up forever. I, in spirit, rose as on billows that also ran up the shaft forever; and the billows seemed to pursue the throne of God; but *that* also ran before us and fled away continually. The flight and the pursuit seemed to go on for ever and ever. Frost, gathering frost, some Sarsar wind of death, seemed to repel me; I slept – for how long I cannot say: slowly I recovered my self-possession, and found myself standing, as before, close to my sister's bed.[7]

One could say, armed with Baudelaire's suspicions, that what in a way matters most is that the child, at the end of the trance, finds himself standing near his sister's bed. The 'passion of grief' may have been mercifully relieved for a while, but when the trance is over, it is still there, and still to be borne. Yet De Quincey claims that the trance led to the understanding of 'truths' that were to modify the whole of his future life: '... even by the grief of a child, as I will show you, reader, hereafter, were confounded the falsehoods of the philosophers'. But these 'truths' were never written down, as *Suspiria* was left unfinished. Perhaps one should regard this omission as significant in the same way as the 'bains de multitude'. Just as De Quincey chose to commune with the crowd precisely in the state which forbade contact, he never wrote down the 'truths' that were supposed to have changed his whole life because they had not. And this, because while he was capable of deep sensations and feelings, he did not have the integrity of personality that might make these into active principles. All we have to rely on is *Suspiria*: and the insights revealed by the trance seem to have ended, not in release from the deadlock of grief, but in narcissistic relish of the condition, and ultimately a fainting of consciousness. De Quincey himself is lucid about this:

> ... grief may wax and wane; ... and grief again may rise, as in impassioned minds it often does, even to the heaven of heavens; but

there is a necessity that, if too much left to itself in solitude, finally it will descend into a depth from which there is no reascent; . . . Now . . . you are passionately delighted in your condition . . . when we stretch out our arms in darkness, vainly striving to draw back the sweet faces that have vanished, slowly arises a new strategem of grief, and we say, – 'Be it that they no more come back to us, yet what hinders but we should go to *them*?'[8]

The attempt to 'communicate' with the 'shadowy' fails, and the afflicted child alights on the same desperate way out as Baudelaire's 'voyageurs':

> O Mort, vieux capitaine, il est temps! levons l'ancre!
> . . .
> . . . Nous nous embarquerons sur la mer des Ténèbres
> Avec le coeur joyeux d'un jeune passager.
> Entendez-vous ces voix, charmantes et funèbres,
> Qui chantent:
> . . . 'Venez vous enivrer de la douceur étrange
> De cette après-midi qui n'a jamais de fin!'[9]

Baudelaire's magnificent endorsement of this longing for death must not blind us to its tragic fallacy, which he sees even more clearly than De Quincey. Consciousness deludes itself by believing that it wants to die in order to reach a lost being, or 'du nouveau'. It wants to obliterate itself, to escape from despair or 'ennui'. True, its desire to die, for De Quincey, manifests its sense of a vaster reality, for Baudelaire, its 'godlike' dimension, But De Quincey, even while talking of this childish longing as a 'disease', is fundamentally committed to it; whereas for Baudelaire, the desire for death is the ultimate form of the circularity of flight. Consciousness makes its maximum effort at getting away from itself, and thus destroys itself. The gesture whereby you smash the window to fly out kills you:

> Est-il moyen, ô Moi qui connais l'amertume,
> D'enfoncer le cristal par le monstre insulté
> Et de m'enfuir, avec mes deux ailes sans plumes
> – Au risque de tomber pendant l'éternité?[10]

And Baudelaire's falling Icarus feels his wings melting 'sous je ne sais quel oeil de feu'.

It is also significant, from Baudelaire's perspective, that in the child's trance, the throne of God should, like the land of bliss of the 'voyageurs', forever flee in front of him. There stands, between the child and the infinite, the window not only of his wakeful consciousness (finding himself still by his sister's bed), but of the very fact that he is alive.

And for Baudelaire, all the 'fenêtres' that 'excitants nerveux' or states of madness seemed to open turn into mirrors. It is an image which keeps recurring in *Les Paradis artificiels*: when for instance he describes wine as 'semblable à l'homme', or more explicitly in this on hashish:

> Le cerveau et l'organisme sur lesquels opère le haschisch ne donneront que leurs phénomènes ordinaires, individuels, augmentés, il est vrai, quant au nombre et à l'énergie, mais toujours fidèles à leur origine. L'homme n'échappera pas à la fatalité de son tempérament physique et moral: le haschisch sera, pour les impressions et les pensées familières de l'homme, un miroir grossissant, mais un pur miroir.[11]

This image later on assumes moral dimensions:

> Ajouterai-je que le haschisch, comme toutes les joies solitaires, rend l'individu inutile aux hommes et la société superflue pour l'individu, le poussant à s'admirer sans cesse lui-même et le précipitant jour à jour vers le gouffre lumineux où il admire sa face de Narcisse?[12]

The strength of Baudelaire's moral preoccupation is evident if we contrast his use of the Narcissus myth with Valéry's. Valéry is concerned with the mind in the mirror; Baudelaire, envisaging a notion of *wholeness* which might remind one of Ficino, however little he may have been aware of him. For Ficino, Narcissus is a man who clings to a limited order of reality (the element of water), thus maiming his human potential, which urges him to soar through the various orders of reality, corresponding to the 'ladder' of the elements – air, then fire. Instead of soaring, he leans. Towards himself. As in Baudelaire's sarcastic remark on Hugo: 'Hugo-Sacerdoce a toujours le front penché; – trop penché pour rien voir, excepté son nombril.'[13] Narcissus's crime is against the integrity of his own being, against the totality of life. Which implies that you should believe that there is such a thing. Baudelaire does, not of course in a constructed metaphysical way, but with the implicit coherence which we discovered when discussing the form of the *Fleurs du Mal*. For him, searchers after the infinite, like De Quincey, maim their human potential. They choose to perceive themselves through a 'reflective' mirror – in the etymological sense: bent towards itself, and bent backwards, towards the past.[14]

De Quincey is acutely aware of the reflective quality of his opium-dreams, so much so that one wonders how he manages to avoid moral issues. He says of the Dark Interpreter: 'You are now satisfied that the apparition is but a reflex of yourself; and, in uttering your secret feelings to *him*, you make this phantom the dark symbolic mirror for reflection to the daylight what else must be hidden forever.' He immediately adds, however, that the phantom only reveals what 'would or might have occurred to your own meditative heart, had only time been allowed for its motions'. So it seems that dreams are only a short cut to what you would have known anyway. True, De Quincey also says that 'in dreams always there is a power not contented with reproduction, but which absolutely creates or transforms'. But he provides no illustration for this; and ends announcing that he was going to become a prey to the 'dark being' – that the mirror was to close in upon him. Dreams never seem, on the evidence of his writing, to have led De Quincey further into knowledge of the 'shadowy' than his childhood dream, in which he was forever sailing after what was forever fleeing from him. It is difficult not to feel sympathy with Baudelaire's suspicion of such knowledge.

II

Yet, when Baudelaire applies the word 'rêve' to Delacroix, he means insight: 'Et je n'entends pas par là les capharnaüms de la nuit, mais la vision produite par une intense méditation . . .'. And this imaginative insight is of a 'scientific' nature, since it reveals the analogical nature of reality.

Dante might help clarify this apparent contradiction, and very relevantly too, since we saw how nineteenth-century 'voyageurs' like Nerval regarded him as a patron.

Indeed, his Ulysses could be seen as a predecessor of De Quincey and of Poe's protagonist, as well as of Nerval. He is a man who commits himself to the high sea, trusting that his breaking beyond the boundaries of 'normal' human experience will release valuable knowledge. Even the 'straits' 'dov'Ercole segnò gli suoi confini' correspond to De

Quincey's image of the tube or Baudelaire's image of the 'cadre', or more clearly Nerval's 'portes d'ivoire ou de corne'; and the open sea which he starts exploring at random, westwards – with their *backs* to the rising sun – 'E volta la nostra *poppa* nel mattino' – resembles Poe's ocean into which one penetrates, 'however rudderless or compassless', and Baudelaire's 'mer des Ténèbres'. Ulysses's ship becomes a bird winged with oars, 'madly' flying: flight is also central to De Quincey's dreams, to Nerval's visions, [15] to Baudelaire's escape poems. It is sunk by a whirlwind born of a mountain which rises out of the sea; similarly, Poe's characters go mad, the dreams of the opium-eater turn into nightmares that imprison him in his past, and Nerval, at the end of the first part of *Aurélia*, feels a blight descend upon his soul: 'J'étais maudit peut-être pour avoir voulu percer un mystère redoutable en offensant la loi divine; je ne devais plus attendre que la colère et le mépris! Les ombres irritées fuyaient en jetant des cris et en traçant dans l'air des cercles fatals, comme les oiseaux à l'approche d'un orage.'[16] What seemed to be a new way out turns into a more terrible form of enclosure.

Dante's attitude to Ulysses is similar to Baudelaire's attitude to De Quincey – and all 'voyageurs'. Both feel admiration for their hero, and zest, Dante for Ulysses's superb spirit of enterprise, Baudelaire for De Quincey's sensibility, for the modernity and exemplariness of his plight, for the 'arabesque' grace of his style. But Dante *places* Ulysses in hell, in the circle of the 'seminatori di fraudi', of those who played havoc with *truth*. 'E volta la nostra poppa nel mattino . . .' The light of the morning is Christ, the Way, the Truth, Life. Ulysses's grandiose enterprise bears the mark of his whole character: 'seminatore di fraudi'. There is an obvious parallel between Dante's exploration of the Underworld, and Ulysses's attempt at exploring it. In Ulysses, the pilgrim encounters an aspect of himself, as he does when he meets Francesca or Farinata. And when Baudelaire is writing about 'les voyageurs', he is also writing about himself. Ulysses foundered because he embarked on his exploration unguided by 'reason' (unlike Dante who is led by Virgil), itself undirected by Grace (Beatrice who sent Virgil to Dante). That is, Ulysses undertook his journey an incomplete man. A man who, like Narcissus, chooses to regard reality with only part of himself. The man who electrifies his companions by telling them that it is our highest dignity to get to *know* the universe is a man who is potentially damned for his disregard of truth, and of the consequences of such disregard. A man therefore eminently unsuited for getting to know anything; who, while speaking such splendid words, is once more disseminating fraud. In other terms, for Dante, you can only explore the Underworld, or the inner world – call it what you will – without endangering yourself and others, if you undertake the journey *whole* – that is, with the full exercise of your intelligence, even though the insights themselves do not come *through* it, and with a full sense of the moral implications of your act.

The way in which Baudelaire places his discussion of, and translations from, De Quincey, somehow resembles Dante's placing of Ulysses. The *Mangeur d'opium* is preceded by the shorter span of *Le Poëme du haschisch*, which sets up the moral terms within which De Quincey's experience is to be examined. The very succession of the titles announce the rise and fall of 'Voluptés de l'opium' and 'Tortures de l'opium': Is there not, as Balzac would say a 'monde' of comment in this series: 'Le Goût de l'infini'; 'Qu'est-ce que le haschisch?'; 'Le Théâtre de Séraphin'; 'L'Homme-Dieu'; and the brutal drop of 'Morale' which begins: 'Mais le lendemain! le terrible lendemain!'? Furthermore, the clarity with which Baudelaire criticises the use of drugs in this first section, while contrasting with his complex treatment of De Quincey's material, both places it and builds strong meanings into his veiled disagreements, his very omissions. Words like 'débauche' or 'miroir' become as loaded in their way as 'E volta la nostra poppa nel mattino' is. Loaded because of the continual reference to the moral world as whole. The partiality of De Quincey's exploration is measured by a sense of the close interrelation of all the elements of our personality, and the necessity to make or find ourselves whole, and parts of a whole whose workings we cannot comprehend, but whose laws we must obey – or else be destroyed.[17]

Could one not derive a standard of judgment from Dante's and Baudelaire's attitudes to their respective Ulysses? Could one not say that the more 'wholly' a writer is involved in his exploration of the shadowy, the more chances he has to attain universally valid insights?

III

Nerval's tragic experience, contrasted with De Quincey's self-indulgence, might illustrate this more effectively than all reasonings. Nerval integrates his experience of madness to a sense of moral issues, and to a trust in the power of reason: this makes his experience ultimately more fruitful than De Quincey's. Could one infer that it also makes him a better writer?

Unlike De Quincey, Nerval has time for the 'non-moi'. He is capable of detaching himself from his experience and of questioning it:

> Si je ne pensais que la mission d'un écrivain est d'analyser sincèrement ce qu'il éprouve dans les graves circonstances de la vie, et si je ne me proposais un but que je crois utile, je m'arrêterais ici, et je n'essayerais pas de décrire ce que j'éprouvai ensuite dans une série de visions insensées peut-être, ou vulgairement maladives . . .[18]

How strong this directness is by contrast with De Quincey's oblique coquetry: he hopes, he says, that the record of his life will be 'useful and instructive':

> . . .*that* must be my apology for breaking through that delicate and honourable reserve which, for the most part, restrains us from the public exposure of our own errors and infirmities. Nothing, indeed, is more revolting to English feelings than the spectacle of a human being obtruding on our notice his moral ulcers . . . for any such acts of gratuitous self-humiliation from those who can be supposed in sympathy with the decent and self-respecting part of society, we must look to French literature, or to that part of the German which is tainted with the spurious and defective sensibility of the French . . .
> . . . For my own part, without breach of truth or modesty, I may affirm, that my life has been, on the whole, the life of a philosopher . . .[19]

And the self-praise goes on, for a whole paragraph. How much De Quincey here resembles Hogg's Justified Sinner! He flatters his English reader with a little self-righteous chauvinism so that, from a position of warm approval on the part of his audience, he can be ruthless to others – foreign writers here, and later on Coleridge: he is quite scornful of Coleridge's subjection to opium: 'A slave he was to this potent drug not less abject than Caliban to Prospero – his detested and yet despotic master.'[20] And in the next breath he evinces murderous pity: 'Am I the man to reproach Coleridge with this vassalage to opium? Heaven forbid! having groaned myself under the yoke, I pity, and blame him not.'[21] But, still like the Justified Sinner, the whole energy of his prose goes towards showing how impeccable he himself is. Yes, Coleridge was grossly 'guilty', but 'in my case the self-conquest was unquestionable, but the self-indulgence open to doubts of casuistry'. And what brilliant casuistry it is! De Quincey makes you want to ask, as Rousseau, one of these French writers gifted with 'spurious and defective sensibilities', did, 'Who dare say, "I was better than that man?"'. The difference is that Rousseau does have the courage to show himself as odious where he thought he was – as in the episode of the stolen ribbon – whereas De Quincey is never free from the need to be both loved and admired.

Nerval's strength comes from the intense seriousness with which he faces himself - 'Il voyait sa folie face à face' in Dr Blanche's impressive words[22] – and from his ceaseless attempt to come out of 'le cercle étroit ... des impressions personnelles'.[23] But one could argue that De Quincey's weaknesses as a man to a certain extent jeopardise him as a writer. His enquiry into the Underworld is made limp by the various ties which still connect him with social aspirations: respectability, official ethics. He wants to succeed in both worlds, and the tortuous nature of his style is produced by his acrobatics between them. He performs 'spirales', in Baudelaire's word to describe De Quincey's thought. But Nerval's self-forgetfulness enables him to establish connections between dreams and conscious life: 'Le Rêve est une seconde Vie'. There are quietness and open power in this first sentence of *Aurélia*.

And one is disturbed by the 'épanchement du songe dans la vie réelle' in Nerval's account, while in De Quincey one feels quite convinced that his dream-life is simply echoing his waking life:

> ... whatsoever I happened to call up and to trace by a voluntary act upon the darkness was very apt to transfer itself to my dreams ... As Midas turned all things to gold that yet baffled his hopes and defrauded his human desires, so whatsoever things were capable of being visually represented I did but think of in the darkness, immediately shaped themselves into phantoms for the eye ... .[24]

This may be because 'le songe' in Nerval continues waking life and is continued by it, and is the means of exploring something which the writer feels to be greater than himself; whereas there is a total gap between what dreams do for De Quincey and what his own life is. Emamples of Nerval's continuity could be multiplied, but none is more striking than the way in which the waking activity of the beginning of Chapter VII of *Aurélia* tries to prolong what the dream at the end of Chapter VI has revealed; or his success in redeeming himself from evil dreams by the kindness of his behaviour to another 'madman'. But the lack of 'connection' in De Quincey is well shown by this:

> ... All the feet of the tables, sofas, &c, soon became instinct with life: the abominable head of the crocodile, and his leering eyes,

looked out at me, multiplied into ten thousand repetitions . . . So often did this hideous reptile haunt my dreams that many times the very same dream was broken up in the very same way: I heard gentle voices speaking to me . . . and instantly I awoke; it was broad noon, and my children were standing, hand in hand, at my bedside . . .[25]

This is where the notion of 'wholeness' seems to be apt. Despite De Quincey's moving delicacy, despite admirable passages, the *Confessions* half fail, for the intelligence and sensibility at work are undermined by the shirking of moral issues – and *Suspiria* is a better work, because there is more urgency, more integrity in De Quincey's handling of his experience. But Nerval's conviction that nothing in his life is morally indifferent, that even his dreams set at stake his growth or decay as a conscious being, both expand the significance of the episodes of *Aurélia*, and also give the book the impact and depth of a great parable of fall and redemption.

14 Time

I

The title *Les Paradis artificiels* contains the ugly dimension of artifice which we discovered in 'La Fausse monnaie': 'On n'est jamais excusable d'être méchant, mais il y a quelque mérite à savoir qu'on l'est; et le plus irréparable des vices est de faire le mal par bêtise.' Baudelaire accuses drugs of creating a moral state of 'bêtise'. Their artifice brings about a loss of *conscience* – meaning both consciousness and conscience. What is wrong about opium consoling De Quincey for the wretchedness of the London poor is not only the solipsistic aestheticism of the attitude. It is the moral degradation of the blindness thus created. Satan once confesses to Baudelaire that the only time he feared for his power on earth was when he heard a preacher exclaim that the finest piece of deceit of the devil was to persuade people that he does not exist.[1] Drugs are an effective agency to this.

Lucidity in *Les Fleurs du Mal* to a point redeems the gambler who:

> . . . préférerait, en somme,
> La douleur à la mort, et l'enfer au néant![2]

and endows with moral dignity states like those of 'L'Irrémédiable'. 'La conscience dans le mal' may be, in its agony, close to damnation. But at least it is truthful. The benevolence and conceit generated by hashish are abhorrent pieces of self-deceit to Baudelaire:

Avais-je tort de dire que le haschisch apparaissait, à un esprit vraiment philosophique, comme un parfait instrument satanique? Le remords, singulier ingrédient du plaisir, est bientôt noyé dans une délicieuse contemplation du remords, . . .

Voilà donc mon homme supposé, . . . (qui) . . . confond complètement le rêve avec l'action, . . . il finit par décréter son apothéose en ces

termes nets et simples, qui contiennent pour lui tout un monde d'abominables jouissances: '*Je suis le plus vertueux de tous les hommes!*'
Cela ne vous fait-il pas souvenir de Jean-Jacques, qui, lui aussi, après s'être confessé à l'univers, non sans une certaine volupté, a osé pousser le même cri de triomphe ... Jean-Jacques s'était enivré sans haschisch.[3]

Drug-taking, according to Baudelaire's analysis of De Quincey's condition, asserts the supremacy of the very society from which the drug-taker meant to escape. The cycle through which he goes in his addiction reproduces that of the society of 'Progress': because of the needs which the addiction creates, and of the increasing limits it imposes on the freedom of the addict. It is with loaded intention that Baudelaire emphasises the word 'contraint' when, describing the state of mind of the hashish-eater, he says: 'Il est *contraint* de s'admirer lui-même'. Hashish is described as not only destroying freedom, but as confusing conscience with satanic casuistry. And this is very similar to the indictment of Progress which we encountered earlier. Progress acts, in Baudelaire's sense of the word opium, as an opium for the people: it blinds them to their real interests, freeing them from their responsibilities. But that freedom turns into a tyranny worse than that which one was attempting to flee. The endless escalation of Progress turns into an ever-renewed suicide. The same is true of opium. De Quincey had gone into the London crowds of poor in order to be sociable, he had taken exquisite delight in his excursions under the influence of opium. But

> For all this ... I paid a heavy price in distant years, when the human face *tyrannised* over my dreams and the perplexities of my steps in London, came back and haunted my sleep, with the feeling of perplexities, moral or intellectual, that brought confusion to the reason, that brought anguish and remorse to the conscience.[4]

And talking of the anguish of a hashish-eater among his friends, Baudelaire expresses the very idea he had formulated about progress: that the sensibility can be refined again and again in the escalation of new enjoyments to the point of having to destroy itself: 'Au fond de l'inconnu pour trouver du nouveau', 'Le Voyage' says. The word 'délicat' which was used about progress ('délicatisant l'humanité...') reappears here about hashish:

... Il s'était demandé ce que deviendraient son intelligence et ses organes, si cet état, qu'il prenait pour un état surnaturel, allait toujours s'aggravant, si ses nerfs devenaient toujours de plus en plus délicats ... '... c'était un galop effroyable, et ma pensée, *esclave* de la circonstance, du milieu, de l'accident et de tout ce qui peut être impliqué dans le mot *hasard* avait pris un tour purement et absolument rapsodique. Il est trop tard! me répétais-je sans cesse avec désespoir'...[5]

II

Being a prey to 'le hasard' is a nightmare to a poet who thinks that the greatest achievement is to accomplish 'juste', exactly, what he has planned to do. This is perhaps why Baudelaire insists so much on the tyranny of opium on De Quincey:

Le lecteur a déjà remarqué que depuis longtemps l'homme n'évoque plus les images, mais que les images s'offrent à lui, spontanément, despotiquement. Il ne peut pas les congédier; car la volonté n'a plus de force et ne gouverne plus les facultés.[6]

This is obviously much worse for him than for De Quincey, who acknowledges with serene defeatism that: 'the Dream knows best; and the Dream, I say it again, is the responsible party.'[7]

The contrast between the two men's responses is very striking. When De Quincey states that he was unable to write the dedication to Ricardo, he concludes with weird, half-satisfied resignation: 'The arrangements were countermanded, the compositor dismissed, and my "Prolegomena" rested peacefully by the side of its elder and more dignified brother.'[8] Baudelaire not only passes harsh comment on this by translating 'peacefully' by 'honteux'; he reads into De Quincey's impotency that terrible 'impuissance' which dogged him all his life. He introduces his own image of 'L'Irrémédiable' into De Quincey's quiet account:

> Un navire pris dans le pôle
> Comme en un piège de cristal, ...[9]

O humiliation d'un auteur nerveux, tyrannisé par l'atmosphère intérieure! L'impuissance se dressa, terrible, infranchissable, *comme les glaces du pôle*; tous les arrangements furent contremandés, le compositeur congédié, et les *Prolégomènes, honteux*, se couchèrent, pour longtemps, à côté de leur frère aîné, le fameux livre suggéré par Spinosa.[10]

And Baudelaire goes on to comment with passion:

> Horrible situation! avoir l'esprit fourmillant d'idées, et ne plus pouvoir franchir le pont qui sépare les campagnes imaginaires de la rêverie des moissons positives de l'action! Si celui qui me lit maintenant a connu les nécessités de la production, je n'ai pas besoin de lui décrire le désespoir d'un noble esprit, clairvoyant, habile, luttant contre cette damnation d'un genre si particulier.[11]

Le Poëme du haschisch had already described that state of damnation for an artist: 'Celui qui aura recours à un poison *pour* penser ne pourra bientôt plus penser *sans* poison. Se figure-t-on le sort affreux d'un homme dont l'imagination paralysée ne saurait plus fonctionner sans le secours du haschisch ou de l'opium?'[12]

This is another respect in which drugs, like progress, increase, instead of diminishing, the difficulty of living. By lessening the sense that each individual must exert himself fully if he is to achieve real growth, by committing that growth to external, physical agencies, progress undermines our wills. So do drugs, as the Jean-Jacques passage tells us, by making us forget what radical distinction exists between 'dream' and 'action'. That gap between dream and action is for Baudelaire one of the main problems of living. The Polish sculptor of Balzac's *La Cousine Bette* had failed to become a great artist because of the split in him between 'conception' and 'execution'. So does Samuel Cramer: 'Le soleil de la paresse qui resplendit sans cesse au-dedans de lui, lui vaporise et lui mange cette moitié de génie dont le ciel l'a doué.'[13] Baudelaire knew this through his own defeat: 'How hard it is, not to think a book out, but to write it!'[14] But by yielding to laziness, by letting it 'vaporise' our energies, we are playing into the hands of Time, the destroyer of 'L'Horloge', which wins 'every time, without cheating'. We are letting Satanic forces win, allowing life to be but a fruitless 'progress' towards death:

> . . . Et le riche métal de notre volonté
> Est tout vaporisé par ce savant chimiste.[15]

The only way to counter the destructive impact of living, to make living through time a progressive gain instead of a progressive loss, is to exert one's will *against* the forces of reality: laziness, moral blindness, comfort, ageing, prejudice. And this is where drugs are seen as destructive. They reinforce the dissolving, wasteful impetus of life. They *vaporise* the will even more, they make exertion impossible. Hashish makes you, Baudelaire says:

> incapable de travail et d'énergie dans l'action.
> C'est la punition méritée de la prodigalité impie avec laquelle vous avez fait une si grande dépense du fluide nerveux. Vous avez jeté votre personnalité aux quatre vents du ciel, et maintenant vous avez de la peine à la rassembler et à la concentrer.[16]

Against this 'impious prodigality', Baudelaire holds up Balzac's *thrift*. The word is right if one remembers how Gobseck's miserliness is built into an image of spiritual and social energy. Balzac himself shared in it. Baudelaire describes him refusing to take hashish:

> On lui présenta du dawamesk; il l'examina, le flaira, et le rendit sans y toucher. La lutte entre sa curiosité presque enfantine et sa répugnance pour l'abdication se trahissait sur son visage expressif d'une manière frappant. L'amour de la dignité l'emporta. En effet, il est difficile de se figurer le théoricien de la volonté, ce jumeau spirituel de Louis Lambert, consentant à perdre une parcelle de cette précieuse substance.[17]

Balzac's material existence was so similar to his own that Baudelaire is continuously identifying himself with him: 'I have neither Balzac's courage nor his genius', he remarks to his mother,[18] 'and I have all the troubles which made him so wretched'. He must have had Balzac strongly in mind when he wrote in 'Hygiène': 'Tout recul de la volonté est une parcelle de substance perdue. Combien donc l'hésitation est prodigue! Et qu'on juge de l'immensité de l'effort final pour réparer tant de pertes.'[19] No doubt his ideal of style was devised as the means to counter best all possibilities of loss, of dissolution: 'La faculté de répondre à la nécessité de chaque minute, l'exactitude, en un mot, doit trouver infailliblement sa récompense.'[20] Only *will* applied continuously and lucidly can achieve this exactitude.

This ideal of work, and of style, as means or media through which will can exert itself with full force is fulfilled by another artist whom Baudelaire passionately admires too: Delacroix. Delacroix, like Balzac, epitomises some of the virtues which Baudelaire most desperately wishes to acquire: 'Ce qui marque le plus visiblement le style de Delacroix, c'est la concision et une espèce d'intensité sans ostentation, résultat habituel de la concentration de toutes les forces spirituelles vers un point donné.' Baudelaire must have thought of Louis Lambert, writing these words. He goes on: 'On pourrait dire . . .: "Le héros littéraire, c'est-à-dire le véritable écrivain, est celui qui est immuablement concentré."'[21] Delacroix struggled successfully against the 'vaporisation' of reality: '. . . la préoccupation de toute sa vie . . . était . . . d'exécuter assez vite et avec assez de certitude pour ne rien laisser s'évaporer de l'intensité de l'action ou de l'idée.[22] He was responding victoriously to the challenge of Time:

> Les minutes, mortel folâtre, sont des gangues
> Qu'il ne faut pas lâcher sans en extraire l'or . . .[23]

And Baudelaire is looking for ways of answering that challenge too.

III

Drugs exalt and unify your personality. They deepen and sublime your sensations. But, for Baudelaire, as a necessary corollary, they diminish both 'conscience' and 'will'. And it is too expensive a price to pay. For one must pay. History, individual and public, has taught him and others that. As Nerval writes in one of his last letters to his father: 'Napoléon a dit: "tout se paie". C'est Balzac qui m'a appris ce mot'.[24]

If what is gained on one hand is lost on the other, then you have to learn an economy of the self. Baudelaire as we saw believes that we are part of an organic nature which he calls 'la vie', to whose laws we are ineluctably subjected, and which we cannot cheat, because it far exceeds not only our control, but our understanding, of the world outside as well as within us. Drugs are seen, through the image of Balzac's Wild Ass's Skin, as creating a fatal state of imbalance which endangers our moral economy:

> Les proportions du temps et de l'être sont dérangées par la multitude innombrable et par l'intensité des sensations et des idées. On vit plusieurs vies d'hommes en l'espace d'une heure. C'est bien là le sujet de la *Peau de Chagrin*. Il n'y a plus équation entre les organes et les jouissances.[25]

There are indeed two terrible drawbacks to the infallible power which the skin gives to Raphaël. His multiplied capacity to feel and so get whatever he wishes wears his organism out (and organism implies the vitality of the will); hence the shrinking of the skin. Also, the infallibility that the skin gives him destroys the mainspring of active desire, of desire that would lead to exertion: and only the exertion would be creative and fulfilling. A Valéry who could write 'Cimetière Marin' just by wishing it would never wish another line of poetry into being. The shorthand of infallible fulfilment destroys all capacity for involvement, for Raphaël. Just as, for the opium-eater, the opium taken destroyed all possibility of relation between himself and the music, himself and the London poor. This is also the curse upon Melmoth:

> En puisant à pleines mains dans le trésor des voluptés humaines dont la clé lui avait été remise par le démon, il en atteignit promptement le fond. Cette énorme puissance, en un instant appréhendée, fut en un instant exercée, jugée, usée. Ce qui était tout, ne fut rien . . . Son plaisir ressemblait au coup de hache du despotisme, qui abat l'arbre pour en avoir les fruits. Les transitions, les alternatives qui mesurent la joie, la souffrance, et varient toutes les jouissances humaines, n'existaient plus pour lui.[26]

Baudelaire uses Melmoth to illustrate his theory of laughter as a *rupture* expressing, in an extreme form, the duality of our nature: 'Melmoth est une contradiction vivante. Il est sorti des conditions fondamentales de la vie; ses organes ne supportent plus sa pensée.'[27] And in *Le Poëme du haschisch*, Melmoth becomes an emblem of the hashish-eater, the man who, trying to fulfil his divine aspirations, has in fact increased the rupture in him, has 'fallen' further:

> Souvenons-nous de Melmoth, cet admirable emblème. Son épouvantable souffrance gît dans la disproportion entre ses merveilleuses facultés, acquises instantanément par un pacte satanique, et le milieu où, comme créature de Dieu, il est condamné à vivre. . . . Il est facile de saisir le rapport qui existe entre les créations sataniques des poètes et les créatures vivantes qui se sont vouées aux excitants. L'homme a voulu être Dieu, et bientôt le voilà, en vertu d'une loi morale incontrôlable, tombé plus bas que sa nature réelle. C'est une âme qui se vend en détail.[28]

'Tout homme qui n'accepte pas les conditions de la vie vend son âme'. He who believes that there is a 'great secret' which, once discovered, will radically transform his existence; that one gesture is going to change life; renews Eve's sin. The small teaspoon of jam of hashish, the 'happiness to be carried in the waistcoat-pocket' are tests and traps like Eve's apple: you believe that your nature will change magnificently, that one bite will make you like Gods. For that is what you want to be:

> Personne ne s'étonnera qu'une pensée finale, suprême, jaillisse du cerveau du rêveur: *'Je suis devenu Dieu!'* qu'un cri sauvage, ardent, s'élance de sa poitrine avec une énergie telle, une telle puissance de projection, que, si les volontés et les croyances d'un homme ivre avaient une vertu efficace, ce cri culbuterait les anges disséminés dans les chemins du ciel: 'Je suis un Dieu!'[29]

The sin of the drug-taker, who wants to 'gagner le paradis d'un seul coup', not knowing that, by some strange irony, the privilege of winning 'à tout coup' is that of Time, the destroyer, is similar to that of the friend of 'La Fausse Monnaie' who is trying to win 'cent sous et le coeur de Dieu'. He wants to win without cost, without exertion, without 'engaging' himself. He, unlike Time, cheats. In his sense of reality, and in his sense of sin, Baudelaire is strongly beholden, like Balzac, to a Catholic mode of thinking.

The 'à tout coup' is crucial in Baudelaire's condemnation of drug-taking. For it is the desire to create a necessary causality that will save one the pains of active engagement, the desire to discover truths without having made oneself morally worthy of their discovery (as Ulysses did), that seem to him to be criminal, as witchcraft seemed criminal to the church:

> Si l'Eglise condamne la magie et la sorcellerie, c'est qu'elles militent contre les intentions de Dieu, qu'elles suppriment le travail du temps et veulent rendre superflues les conditions de pureté et de moralité; ... Nous appelons escroc le joueur qui a trouvé le moyen de jouer à coup sûr; comment nommerons-nous l'homme qui veut acheter, avec un peu de monnaie, le bonheur et le génie? C'est l'infaillibilité même du moyen qui en constitue l'immoralité, comme l'infaillibilité supposée de la magie lui impose son stigmate infernal.[30]

So, for Baudelaire, 'les conditions de la vie' imply risk, continuous risk, as is asserted by the current image of the 'joueur'. (And one cannot but be reminded of Pascal's view of moral life, of the 'pari'. 'Vous êtes embarqués'.) Also, the forces which rule us live in us, are not under our control: they are forces of 'durée', the slow gradation of time, not sublimed, not multiplied, not made up into perfect moments or meaningful episodes. And this in a way is hateful. The substance of time, marked by the clock, is the very substance of 'Spleen', which twists the secret face of 'Le Masque', and which galls the speaker of 'La Chambre double' when he wakes up: 'Oui! le Temps règne: il a repris sa brutale dictature. Et il me pousse, comme si j'étais un boeuf, avec son double aiguillon. – "Et hue donc! bourrique! Sue donc! esclave! Vis donc! damné!"'[31] And yet this rhythm of slow gradation, this dreariness, is what we have to accept. Because it is also the rhythm of *growth*. The moment when the molecule becomes a cell is precisely not the moment but part of millions of years of imperceptible change. The apparently gratuitous and stunning illuminations of saints, mystics, what is called 'conversion' (Pascal's night, Claudel in Notre-Dame) have afterwards to be 'bought' by years of strenuous straining. No 'moment' that is not integrated in the fullness of life can be a conversion. There is need of 'le travail du temps':

> Etudier dans tous ses modes, dans les oeuvres de la nature et dans les oeuvres de l'homme, l'universelle et éternelle loi de la gradation, du peu à peu, du *petit à petit*, avec les forces progressivement croissantes, comme les intérêts composés, en matière de finance.
> Il en est de même dans *l'habileté artistique et littéraire,* il en est de même dans le trésor variable de la volonté.[32]

Hence the importance of Balzac's refusal to 'perdre une parcelle de cette précieuse substance'. Through this use of capital and interest, one turns to a positive moral use one of the economic laws of the new industrial society. That is, one integrates it, but makes absolutely valid what may be, in economic and social terms, either good or bad.

The term 'Hygiène' which stands as an ideal in the *Journaux intimes* is remarkably apt. It implies a series of small efforts, daily renewed, whose accumulation will eventually give health to the sick man, preserve and increase that of the sound man. A moral 'hygiène' for an artist like Baudelaire, means a daily struggle against 'laisser-aller', laziness, despair, and the complicated apparatus of casuistical resistance which rises in most people who are actually 'trying' when they are faced with a white sheet of paper. All one's energies have to be summoned up to 'execute' instead of just, delightfully 'conceive'. There is such a thing as 'la dynamique intellectuelle':

> Il y dans la prière une opération magique. La prière est une des grandes forces de la dynamique intellectuelle. Il y a là comme une récurrence électrique.
>
> . . .
>
> Le travail, force progressive et accumulative, portant intérêts comme le capital, dans les facultés comme dans les résultats.
>
> Le jeu, même dirigé par la science, force intermittente, sera vaincu, si fructueux qu'il soit, par le travail, si petit qu'il soit, mais continu.[33]

And this is confirmed by 'Du Travail journalier et de l'inspiration':

> L'orgie n'est plus la soeur de l'inspiration: nous avons cassé cette parenté adultère . . .
>
> . . . L'inspiration est décidément la soeur du travail journalier. Ces deux contraires ne s'excluent pas plus que tous les contraires qui constituent la nature. L'inspiration obéit, comme la faim, comme la digestion, comme le sommeil. Il y a sans doute dans l'esprit une espèce de mécanique céleste, dont il ne faut pas être honteux, mais titer le parti le plus glorieux, comme les médecins, de la mécanique du corps . . .[34]

There, in this daily renewed tension of energies, lies the key, the only key, according to Baudelaire, to the 'miracle' that the drug-eaters were trying to accomplish. *Le Poëme du haschisch* ends with a crucial distinction between what is merely 'opium' and the '*divin* opium' which 'Phares' claims artists create:

> . . . le poète attristé se dit: 'La magie (. . .) dupe ces infortunés et elle allume pour eux un faux bonheur et une fausse lumière; tandis que nous, poètes et philosophes, nous avons régénéré notre âme par le travail successif et la contemplation; par l'exercice assidu de la volonté et la noblesse permanente de l'intention, nous avons créé à notre usage un jardin de vraie beauté . . . . . . nous avons accompli le seul miracle dont Dieu nous ait octroyé la licence!'[35]

This miracle truly effaces the traces of original sin. It restitutes 'L'éclatante vérité de [l'] harmonie native' of the world. And this, Baudelaire believes, can only be accomplished by the individual working with, in the direction of, the forces of life:

> Théorie de la vraie civilisation.

Elle n'est pas dans le gaz, ni dans la vapeur, ni dans les tables tournantes, elle est dans la diminution des traces du péché originel.[36]

By attempting to create 'le rêve' (that is, perhaps, a world free from the traces of original sin), by finding out relations between the mind and the world that will bridge the gap which some 'fall' brought about, the artist transfigures reality in a way that is exactly the opposite of Satan's. The line 'Tu m'as Donné ta boue et j'en ai fait de l'or'[37] and the desire to work 'comme un parfait chimiste et comme une âme sainte', pitch themselves against the Satan of 'Au Lecteur' who, a 'savant chimiste', 'vaporise' 'le riche métal de notre volonté'. The artist's chemistry redeems the world.

IV

Baudelaire's attempt to turn the tables on what has become destructive; to employ the laws of capitalist accumulation to build himself up instead of being frittered away, is so reminiscent of Marxist attitudes to time that one is bound to confront the two.

The 'impotency' which becomes De Quincey's lot under the sway of opium, and which Baudelaire translates into images of frozen stillness, the polar ice of the 'irrémédiable', would probably be interpreted in a Marxist analysis as one of the forms which the domination of the past over the present, of a blind dynamic over consciousness, takes in a capitalist society. It is, as Lukács puts it, 'the image of a frozen reality that nevertheless is caught up in an unremitting, ghostly movement'.[38] This being so, the task of a Marxist dialectic is to transform once again what has become a thing back into human relations, what now looks like 'quantity' back into 'quality', 'being' back into 'becoming'.[39]

This immediately reopens a question which we had faced earlier on. For, still in the Marxist perspective which we are evoking, bourgeois thought (and this would include Baudelaire) is unable to 'produce an interpretation of the present in all its radical novelty. The inner perfection of the work of art can hide [the] gaping abyss [between subject and object] because', and this is the important reservation, 'in its perfected immediacy it does not allow any further questions to arise about a mediation no longer available to the point of view of contemplation'. But, Lukács adds, 'the present is a problem of history, a problem that refuses to be ignored and one which imperiously demands such mediation'.[40]

What we have so far discovered about Baudelaire's attitude to time already suggests that far from wishing to gloss over the need to confront the present as a problem of history, this is the task he regards as most important. He instals at the centre of his poetry, as we have seen, the dichotomy between art's power to 'redeem' life, to 'hide the gaping abyss', and art's inability to save man from living. He is crucified by the impossibility to adjust to each other the two faces of 'Le Masque', and through the torment this causes him, he confronts a real, a historical present. Furthermore, the pains of creation in time and against time involve a form of praxis, of 'becoming', of live 'durée', which is analogous to, though not identical with, that of political commitment which Lukács, rather narrowly, seems to regard as the only valid form of praxis in the world of advanced capitalism. The artist's chemistry, which makes gold out of mud, creates spirit out of numbers, is effectively a *transformation of quantity back into quality*. What we wish to suggest, thus closing the circle we opened when considering the value of *form* in art, is that Baudelaire, in his moral vision as in his verse, creates a dialectic which courageously and authentically confronts the problems of his age.

This can be shown by, once again, contrasting his attitude to time with De Quincey's. We must be forgiven for thus making a foil of De Quincey, and seemingly ignoring the seduction and fineness of much of his prose. But we are dealing with fundamental questions. Our injustice is for the sake of a higher kind of *justice*.

The urgency with which Baudelaire experiences his being in time continuously translates itself into moral perspectives. De Quincey's equally acute sense of time leads him to neutrality, withdrawal from life. In both men there is a deep knowledge of 'le gouffre'. They both long for redemption. But heaven and hell are at strife in one man's writings; deep happiness and misery in the other's. In De Quincey, opium deals out 'pains' and 'pleasures'. For Baudelaire, it entails 'voluptés', *then* 'tortures'. This is not a matter of British understatement as against French magniloquence. It is the problem of deciding whether what happens to you is your own responsibility, whether you believe that it is in your making, or whether you are in the hands of forces which you cannot control.

The splitting up of time into drops rushing through a Roman clepsydra, in *Savannah-la-Mar*, illuminates De Quincey's impulse to create stasis: the drop which *is* passing is an infinitesimal fraction between past and future:

... again divide that solitary drop ... into a lower series of ... fractions, and the actual present which you arrest measures but the thirty-sixth-millionth of an hour; ... Therefore the present, which only man possesses, offers less capacity for his footing than the slenderest film that ever spider twisted from her womb. Therefore, also, even this incalculable shadow from the narrowest pencil of moonlight is more transitory than geometry can measure, or thought of angel can overtake. The time which *is* contracts into a mathematic point; and even that point perishes a thousand times before we can utter its birth. All is finite in the present; and even that finite is infinite in its velocity of flight towards death.[41]

De Quincey deploys the most eloquent energy to make himself and make you dizzy. But his language gives him away: he is landed with Achilles[42] and the tortoise because of his temperamental needs: because for him the 'actual present' is that which you can 'arrest' which 'offers capacity for man's footing'; that which can be 'possessed'. In other words, he posits that the only time that would 'exist' is at the antipodes of the time that does exist; ergo, time does not exist. But it is a tautological argument: which springs from his equating 'is' with 'stays'; and 'stays' with 'stays forever'. And what he expresses there is what he confesses directly when meditating on the resurrection of the flesh after his sister's death: 'For here lay the sting of it, namely, in the fatal words – "We shall be *changed*". How was the unity of my interest in her to be preserved, if she were to be altered, and no longer to reflect in her sweet countenance the traces that were sculptured on my heart?' In other words: I am loath to have the '*involutes*' whereby my sister has become entangled with my feelings disturbed. Let the palimpsest rest in peace. Let my heart be a tombstone, with 'traces sculptured' on it.

> Old yew, that clutchest at the stones
> Which hide the under-lying dead,
> Thy fibres net the dreamless head
> Thy roots are wrapt about the bones ... .[43]

The image of the clepsydra only leads to a sense of an evanescent present slowly gnawed by 'before' and 'after', because De Quincey imaginatively instals himself at the centre of that present that would exist, and watches it, in a twice repeated movement, shrink from both ends; for the same image, through the different action of verbs and rhythm, becomes, in Baudelaire's *L'Horloge*, a successive one: it makes time feel like a thick, tangible reality, though a perpetually flying one – flying, as in De Quincey, towards death:

> Trois mille six cent fois par heure, la Seconde
> Chuchote: *Souviens-toi*! – Rapide, avec sa voix
> D'insecte, Maintenant dit: Je suis Autrefois,
> Et j'ai pompé ta vie avec ma trompe immonde!
>
> *Remember! Souviens-toi!* prodigue! *Esto memor!*
> (Mon gosier de métal parle toutes les langues)...
>
> ...
>
> Le jour décroît; la nuit augmente; *souviens-toi*!
> Le gouffre a toujours soif; la clepsydre se vide.[44]

In order to establish the infinite divisibility of time, De Quincey has to place himself in a linguistic situation in which he has plenty of time: 'Put into a Roman clepsydra... every drop measuring... Now, count the drops as they race along...' Nothing in the prose does give you the sense that the drops are 'racing along'. A similar use of numbers, but inserted in a fast-moving rhythm, produces the opposite effect in Baudelaire: the dog-time is at your heels, he even bounds over the line and catches you up at the beginning of the next:

> Trois mille six cent fois par heure, la Seconde
> Chuchote: *Souviens-toi*!

The movement whereby the present is shown to be forever evanescent, in De Quincey, puts you in the middle of a dwindling, still space: 'when the fiftieth of the hundred *is* passing, behold! forty-nine are not, because they have perished; and fifty are not, because they are yet to come.' In 'L'Horloge', the gliding motion: 'Maintenant dit: Je suis Autrefois' is, through each word, a solid passing: 'Now' becomes 'Once' in the time of the verse as in 'real' time. The verb 'dit' is an act, and action implies passage. De Quincey stills that possibility with a protracted present: 'Is passing'. But all the verbs in Baudelaire's poem register movement: 'Le jour décroît; la nuit augmente; la clepsydre se vide.' This is 'no vacuous *durée réelle* but', as in the Marxian dialectical process, 'the unbroken production and reproduction of those relations that, when torn from their context and distorted by abstract categories, can appear to bourgeois thinkers as things'.[45]

If however the only present is that which you can arrest, then the longer you can hold it, with present participles, with opium, the better. De Quincey cherishes opium because it saves him from the tenuity of time:

> ... time it is upon which the exalting and multiplying power of opium chiefly spends its operation. Time becomes infinitely elastic, stretching out to such immeasurable and vanishing termini that it seems ridiculous to compute the sense of it, on waking, by expressions commensurate to human life . . .[46]

De Quincey's energies are so much directed towards mummifying any movement in which, by some unlucky chance, he might be caught, or to which he might have to respond, that in the section of *The English Mail-Coach* called, of all things, 'The Glory of Motion', he celebrates the mail-coach not as a means to go speedily from one place to another, but as a unifying agent in the land. Through his neurotic chemistry, the mail-coach becomes assimilated to those 'centripetal' agents (like dreams!) he says are needed, at the beginning of *Suspiria*. He writes about it as he does of the 'mighty' organ which enables him to soar above grief, as a child; as he does of opium which 'overrules all feelings into a compliance with the master-key'. His language is extraordinary:

> These mail-coaches . . . [have] had [a large] share in developing the anarchies of my subsequent dreams: an agency which they accomplished . . . through the conscious presence of a central intellect, that, in the midst of vast distances – of storms, of darkness, of danger – *overruled all* obstacles into one steady co-operation to a national result. For my own feelings, this post-office service spoke as by some *mighty orchestra*, where a thousand instruments, all disregarded each other, and so far in danger of discord, yet all obedient as slaves to the supreme *baton* of some great leader, terminate in a perfection of harmony like that of heart, brain, and lungs in a healthy animal organisation . . .[47]

For Baudelaire, on the contrary, clinging to the present, expanding it in order to relish it, is a form of suicide: because time for him is a motion independent of one's will: 'Celui qui s'attache au plaisir, c'est-à-dire au présent, me fait l'effet d'un homme roulant sur une pente, et qui voulant se raccrocher aux arbustes, les arracherait et les emporterait dans sa chute.'[48] The only solution is to adapt one's motion with *exactitude* to the motion of time; to extract gold from its ore. The moving compactness of time lends itself to the action of our wills. Of our verbs:

> Que de pressentiments et de signes envoyés déjà par Dieu qu'il est *grandement temps* d'agir, de considérer la minute présente comme la plus importante des minutes, et de faire ma *perpétuelle volupté* de mon tourment ordinaire, c'est-à-dire du Travail![49]

> A chaque minute nous sommes écrasés par l'idée et la sensation du temps. Et il n'y a que deux moyens pour échapper à ce cauchemar, – pour l'oublier: le plaisir et le travail. Le plaisir nous use. Le travail nous fortifie. Choisissons.
> . . .
> Tout ne se fait que peu à peu.[50]

'Peu à peu' expresses both the rhythm of the slowly but ineluctably passing minutes and the law of our moral accomplishment. The same sense of the ineluctable advance of time, in De Quincey, leads to the opposite attitude. And his paralysed helplessness demonstrates in itself the truth, but also the moral viability, of Baudelaire's maxim: 'On ne peut oublier le temps qu'en s'en servant'. De Quincey has felt for so long that 'using' time would entail destroying the precious past inscribed in his sensibility; he has cultivated, through fear of commitment and initiative, such a disproportion between his capacity to expand time internally, imaginatively, and his capacity to act, to be responsible, in other people's time, outside time, real time; that he remains trapped inside his own present participle. Nothing shows this better than the *Vision of Sudden Death*, in which he is a helpless spectator, as always. His time there is that of suspense; and the word is expressive. It means that people are passionately *hanging on* to what is happening, because they know or apprehend the climax towards which things are moving, but that they are suspended from acting upon the course of events; their internal time never touches 'real' time; upon that they have no 'footing'. It is worth quoting large sections of the passage, for the lucidity of the self-analysis is impressive, and the division of time, the numbering of seconds, repeats the framework of *Savannah-la-Mar*: the future is already there, and what separates one from it is a dwindling space:

> The palsy of doubt and distraction hangs like some guilty weight of dark unfathomed remembrances upon my energies, when the signal

is flying for *action*. But, on the other hand, this accursed gift I have, as regards *thought*, that in the first step towards the possibility of a misfortune I see its total evolution; in the radix of the series I see too certainly and too instantly its entire expansion; in the first syllable of the dreadful sentence I read already the last . . .[51]

. . . All was apparently finished. The court was sitting; the case was heard; the judge had finished; and only the verdict was yet in arrear . . .[52]

To the time of *praxis*, De Quincey stands in the same position as God, the eternal observer, in Bergson's parable, to the successive motion of life. And he is aware of what he is doing: 'From my elevated station I looked down, and looked back upon the scene, which in a moment told its own tale, and wrote all its records on my heart for ever.' Through his inability to influence events, people, to direct the course of his own life, De Quincey has withdrawn into such privacy that the future is to him deducible from the past: one grows out of the other through an entirely predictable pattern: 'the radix of the *series*'. Time splits up into a series of points; it belongs to the realm of *quantity* which Bergson defines[53] as implying space (in the example of numbers). Being in the world means that one is caught in a spacialised, determined series gradually diminishing towards its own extinction. Let us therefore translate ourselves to the immovable and all-knowing realm of duration, and from high up there, God-like, watch the desperate struggle of the poor mortals still caught in the series, Time: like the young man in the gig who realises that the mail-coach, on top which the narrator sits, will run into him in seventy seconds:

> For seven seconds, it might be, of his seventy, the stranger settled his countenance steadfastly upon us . . . For five seconds more of his seventy he sat immovable, like one that mused on some great purpose. For five more, perhaps, he sat with eyes upraised like one that prayed in sorrow, . . . Then suddenly he rose; stood upright; and by a powerful strain upon the reins, raising his horse's fore-feet from the ground, he slewed him round on the pivot of his hind-legs, . . . Thus far his condition was not improved; . . . Yet even now it may not be too late; fifteen of the seventy seconds may still be unexhausted; and one almighty bound may avail to clear the ground. Hurry, then, hurry! for the flying moments – *they* hurry. Oh, hurry, hurry, my brave young man! for the cruel hoofs of our horses – *they* also hurry!

... The rear part of the carriage – was that certainly beyond the line of absolute ruin? What power could answer the question? Glance of eye, thought of man, wing of angel, which of these had speed enough to sweep between the question and the answer, and divide the one from the other?[54]

The speed of the horses, here, is an image of time's 'velocity of flight towards death'. At this ultimate moment, the chances for and against catastrophe are so 'entangled' (as are the 'involutes' of De Quincey's heart) that both the observer and the actor are a prey to fatality: they are helpless and apprehending the worst. It is no more possible for man's knowledge or praxis to overtake the speed of approaching disaster than, in *Savannah-la-Mar*, to get a footing on the present. The words of the *Postscript* 'this duel between life and death narrowing itself to such a point of such exquisite evanescence as the collision neared',[55] exactly echo those of *Savannah-la-Mar*: 'by infinite declensions the true and very present, in which only we live and enjoy, will vanish into a mote of a mote, distinguishable only by heavenly vision'. Of course, the helplessness of watcher and sufferer, in the *Vision of Sudden Death*, is for De Quincey the expression of what his own experience has been (the sudden death of his sister): it typifies his view of life; it is no indulgence in exceptional drama. But precisely because it is so, one must underline that the helplessness is created by the narrator's attitude to time: the duel between life and death narrows to a point of exquisite evanescence in which man's powers are dazed, the present vanishes into a mote of a mote, because the future is already there. And the observer is able to feel the dwindling of the space separating past and future, of the space in which it is possible to 'live and enjoy', because the time in which he has installed himself is different from the time of the actors of the drama: for instance he can create an effective sense of the terrible suspense of the speed of the horses, devouring the 'fifteen seconds' left, because his sentences have more than fifteen seconds to create and expound that anguish. And they relish it too. And one cannot argue that, thought being faster than language, he has chosen to combine an artificial sense of speed with the full exposition of the thoughts. What he has chosen is to pay attention to his thoughts and his feelings at the expense of trying to live in the time and world of other men.

Thus his account of these seventy seconds is like the slow-motion repeat of a race. Not quite: it is better in that he combines this with a successful suggestion of speed. The time of the recounting is ampler than the time of happening, in order to allow the feelings of the observer their full development: he responds to 'the scene' both aesthetically ('like one that mused on some great purpose'): morally ('faithful was he that drove to his terrific duty') and emotionally. And he can do that because he towers above the scene; because his writing is not subject to the same pace as the actors of the event are; because he has, through a deliberate choice (perhaps so as never to expose himself to the Affliction of Childhood) translated himself outside the time of 'living'.

His inability to affect the temporal series, once bitterly experienced in the shock of his sister's death, then cultivated and repeated, puts him entirely at the mercy of the patterns of the past: once things have happened, they are forever inscribed in his sensibility; partly because he will not have anything change, at least inside himself, so as to maintain some stable grip on life; and partly because, having thus trained his sensibility fixedly to memorise the past, he can no longer stop it from doing so: The 'traces that were sculptured on [his] heart', when he speaks of his sister, were sculptured through passionate, wilful love. The scene of the *Vision* which writes 'all its records on [his] heart for ever', which is 'swept . . . into [his] dreams for ever' is a curse that, in the *Dream Fugue*, repeats its terrible pattern again and again. He is now subject to what once he chose. Time after time, in every dream, the hand of a girl reappears:

. . . one hand clutched amongst the tackling – rising, sinking, fluttering, trembling, praying –[56]
. . . [I] saw this marble arm, as it rose above her head and her treacherous grave, tossing, faltering, rising, clutching, as at some false deceiving hand stretched out from the clouds. . .[57]
. . . Clinging to the horns of the altar, voiceless she stood – sinking, rising, raving, despairing . . .[58]

reproducing the gesture of the girl in the gig, who 'threw up her arms wildly to heaven, clutched at some visionary object, in the air, fainting, praying, raving, despairing.'[59]

Here, De Quincey is providing a striking illustration of Hegel's account of the state of self-consciousness which follows the collapse of mediation:

Therefore consciousness has become an enigma to itself as a result of the very experience which was to reveal its truth to itself; it does not regard the effects of its deeds as its own deeds . . . *Abstract neces-*

sity, therefore, passes for the merely negative, uncomprehended *power of the universal* by which individuality is destroyed.[60]

The dream can thus reproduce the scene endlessly because the scene was experienced in the present participle. That is, the activity of mind through which the event was apprehended was one which protracted the present, made it endless even while it occurred? or was occurring? certainly, was occurring, since that tense registers detachment of the main subject from the verb. This might be clearer if one compares De Quincey's impotence in this dream-scene with Nerval's in one of the dreams of *Aurélia*:

> Je me perdis plusieurs fois dans les longs corridors, et en traversant une des galeries centrales, je fus frappé d'un spectacle étrange. Un être d'une grandeur démesurée, – homme ou femme, je ne sais, – voltigeait péniblement au-dessus de l'espace et semblait se débattre parmi des nuages épais. Manquant d'haleine et de force, il tomba enfin au milieu de la cour obscure, accrochant et froissant ses ailes le long des toits et des balustres. Je pus le contempler un instant. Il était coloré de teintes vermeilles; et ses ailes brillaient de mille reflets changeants. Vêtu d'une longue robe à plis antiques, il ressemblait à l'Ange de la Mélancolie, d'Albrecht Dürer. – Je ne pus m'empêcher de pousser des cris d'effroi, qui me réveillèrent en sursaut.
> Le jour suivant, je me hâtai d'aller voir tous mes amis . . .[61]

Nerval's anguish at sympathetically experiencing the fall and bruising of the angel, and at being unable to do anything but watch, is similar to De Quincey's emotional situation in the *Vision*. But Nerval's dream and his life, are caught in a successive movement (marked by the *passé simple*: 'je me perdis, je fus frappé, il tomba, je me hâtai'), and whatever pauses occur (through a use of the *imparfait*, an equivalent of the past continuous: 'voltigeait, brillaient') are 'natural' pauses: that is, they are dictated by a slowing down or a repetition of movement, not by the mental attitude of the watcher and that of the watched: the watcher is not manipulating what he sees in order to make it his own, to digest it, even while he is living through it. Which means that once the dream is over, the experience is over, and leaves way for another one: for acting in accordance with what has happened. Nerval in a way is delivered from the burden of his anguish by accepting to live through it with full committal. De Quincey hangs an albatross round his neck by not living experience fully: by projecting a pattern onto it even while it happens; by remaining isolated in his own duration without committing himself to other people's time – the theme of Yeats's *Crazy Jane and Jack the Journeyman*:

> A lonely ghost the ghost is
> That to God shall come;
> I – love's skein upon the ground,
> My body in the tomb –
> Shall leap into the light lost
> In my mother's womb.
>
> But were I left to lie alone
> In an empty bed,
> The skein so bound us ghost to ghost
> When he turned his head
> Passing on the road that night,
> Mine must walk when dead.[62]

De Quincey's past haunts his dream because he never unwinds the skein that binds him to life. He has put opium as a door between himself and Jack the Journeyman.

V

Like Nietzsche, but in a different sense, De Quincey is preoccupied with *recurrence*. The recurring rhythms which opium has introduced into his life become, in his imagination, connected with the recurring rhythms of nature: he is helpless in the face of them. They are part of the cosmic order of things:

> Too generally the very attainment of any deep repose seemed as if mechanically linked to some fatal necessity of self-interruption. It was as though a cup were gradually filled by the sleepy overflow of some natural fountain, the fulness of the cup expressing symbolically the completeness of the rest: but then in the next stage of the process, it seemed as though the rush and torrent-like babbling of the redundant waters, when running over from every part of the cup, interrupted the slumber which in their earlier stage of silent gathering they had so naturally produced. Such and so regular in its swell and collapse – in its tardy growth and its violent dispersion – did this

endless alternation of stealthy sleep and stormy awakening, travel through stages as natural as the increments of twilight, or the kindlings of the dawn.[63]

Hans Pfaall, in Poe's story, is also landed with an overflowing cup which periodically wakes him up. But it is neither 'natural' nor 'symbolical'. It is a mechanical device put together to help him survive in his balloon. There is, one might argue, a moral casuistry at work, not only in De Quincey's interpretation of his experience, in the polemical intentions of his prose, but also in the state of feeling through which he lives, or engineers, his experience.

The only freedom De Quincey was interested in was private: not a freedom to act, nor even to will, but to feel himself, and for others according to his own passive lights. Opium at first had increased that freedom he wanted. But when De Quincey gets to the point of having his sleep made again and again impossible by nightmares of multiplied Malays, even that freedom turns into slavery. What is interesting though is that, in the above passage, prophetic of the opium pains, he persists in calling the mechanism which interrupts his sleep 'natural' (whereas Poe's character, who is using it to control his situation, treats it as a harmless little piece of *artificiality*). What has De Quincey at stake that should make him invest that recurrence with the status of twilights and dawns?

His purpose is double. He is still trying to establish his lack of responsibility in the face of the ordeal: what can he be expected to do about a repetitiveness which is that of nature? and that passiveness justifies in advance that which he will evince when under opium. But also, he is trying to make clear to himself that his life unravels itself according to repetitive patterns. If even a nightmarish rhythm recurs with the predictability of sunsets and sunrises, then what has happened to him, which he wants to retain forever, will happen again. He has a hold on his future. Recurrence is the curse of the opium dreams. But, as Hillis Miller has shown, it announces the return of the paradise of childhood:

Man is doubtless *one* by some subtle *nexus*, some system of links, that we cannot perceive, extending from the new-born infant to the superannuated dotard: . . . love, which is *altogether* holy, like that between two children, is privileged to revisit by glimpses the silence and the darkness of declining years; and, possibly, this final experience in my sister's bedroom, or some other in which her innocence was concerned, may rise again for me to illuminate the clouds of death.[64]

For Hillis Miller, who writes very much under the influence of Georges Poulet, what matters is that De Quincey's wish was fulfilled. He did regain some vivid sense of his sister on his deathbed. But by taking such an attitude, by saying that the satisfaction of feeling is the important thing, one may lock De Quincey even more tightly within his own sense of himself. The question to ask is rather: what sort of a man, what sort of a writer did he make himself into through deciding that the aim of his life was to play up to the poignant sense of nostalgia which inhabited him? Is it not sad that De Quincey, because he mourns for the 'vert paradis des amours enfantines' should be prepared to sacrifice much of his manhood to regain it? The unity, the 'nexus' which he wants to find in himself, is engineered at the expense of engagement in life, with people. To it, De Quincey sacrifices his real originality: an eccentric gift for noticing and penetrating details of human behaviour, based on great sympathy, which had he allowed it to take him where it wanted, might have made of him a very creative writer. One sees evidence of this in the *Memorials of Grasmere*: the little episode of the Green children is worthy of Dickens, in its inventive, detailed pathos.

Instead of giving it rope, De Quincey makes his eccentricity futile by forcing it to *play* around a stem, that of his 'unity'. He makes of it a 'parasite' – his own word! – instead of treating it like a serious form of sensibility. Examining closely his idea of the *caduceus*, one thinks it is a pity he should have needed to wind his talent round the pole of opium. Baudelaire says that De Quincey's thought is 'naturellement spirale'. He certainly made it so by forcing it to display itself in musical 'motives', recurrently. But doing so, he was draining his actual experience (which would be 'nothing', he claims, without all the pretty decorations he has put round it). He was also destroying the inventiveness of his sensibility: it could lead him nowhere, since he only wanted it to meander gracefully around his nostalgically induced unity: the whole passage is – coquettish:

> ... The true object of my *Opium Confessions* is not the naked physiological theme, – on the contrary, *that* is the ugly pole, the murderous spear, the halbert, – but those wandering musical variations upon the theme, – those parasitical thoughts, feelings, digressions, which climb up with bells and blossoms round the arid stock; ramble away from it at times with perhaps too rank a luxuriance; but

at the same time, . . . spread a glory over incidents that for themselves would be – less than nothing.[65]

But the really negative aspect of De Quincey's need to believe in the unity of his being is the doubtful determinism it leads him to. As a piece of reasoning, whether of the intellect or the sensibility, it is dishonest: it springs from the desire to be exonerated all along the line of ever having done anything wrong: everything that happened to him was ineluctable, fated. The causality he discovers at work in his life is the product of various faults of logic which the reader can ponder for himself: 'Thomas s'était enivré . . . avec de l'opium', Baudelaire might have said:

> Here is the briefest possible abstract of the total case: The final object of the whole record lay in the dreams. For the sake of the dreams the entire narrative arose. But what caused the dreams? Opium used in unexampled excess. But what caused this excess in the use of opium? Simply the early sufferings; these, and these only, through the derangement which they left behind in the animal economy. On this mode of viewing the case, moving regressively from the end to the beginning, it will be seen that there is one uninterrupted bond of unity running through the entire succession of experiences – first and last: the dreams were an inheritance from the opium; the opium was an inheritance from the boyish follies.[66]

There is here an extraordinary assumption that, since the present followed the past, it was *caused* by it, and nothing could have changed the series. And further, that since you can move *regressively* when you trace the line of events which led you to a state, you can equally move progressively: decide to consider the first episodes of your life as the 'radix of the series'. The conclusion this establishes, and which De Quincey is keen to establish in order to whiten his record and be exonerated from 'unknown responsibilities', is that all you can do with such a radix is *watch* it grow its trunk and branches. The metaphor is fully deterministic: 'Whatsoever in a man's mind blossoms and expands to his own consciousness in mature life, must have preened in germ during his infancy.' The growth is so unavoidable that you can play the prophet with human life: 'As "in to-day walks tomorrow", so in the past experience of a youthful life may be seen dimly the future.'[67]

But if one decided instead that the feelings with which one takes life are a matter of moral choice; then De Quincey's sense that he is the helpless spectator of the relentless sports of fate will be seen as a shrinking from engagement. Could one not say, about the *Vision of Sudden Death*, that: it is because De Quincey feels that the catastrophe is already there, in the space ahead of him, that he cannot do anything about it? But it is also because he cannot do anything about it, because he is paralysed by opium, that the catastrophe is sure to happen. Opium is an insurance against active time.

The strength with which De Quincey manipulates the account of his life to preserve his sense of its unity comes out when, reading Baudelaire's interpretation of the 'germ' passage, one sees him introduce *will* where De Quincey saw a necessary development:

> C'est dans les notes relatives à enfance que nous trouverons le germe des étranges rêveries de l'homme adulte, et, disons mieux, de son génie.... Souvent, en contemplant des ouvrages d'art, non pas dans leur *matérialité* facilement saisissable, ... mais dans l'âme dont ils sont doués, dans l'impression atmosphérique qu'ils comportent, dans la lumière ou dans les ténèbres spirituelles qu'ils déversent sur nos âmes, j'ai senti entrer en moi comme une vision de l'enfance de leurs auteurs. Tel petit chagrin, telle petite jouissance de l'enfant, démesurément grossis par une exquise sensibilité, deviennent plus tard, dans l'homme adulte, même à son insu, le principe d'une oeuvre d'art.

This sentence might have been written for Proust.

> Enfin, pour m'exprimer d'une manière plus concise, ne serait-il pas facile de prouver, par une comparaison philosophique entre les ouvrages d'un artiste mûr et l'état de son âme quand il était enfant, que le génie n'est que l'enfance nettement formulée, douée maintenant, pour s'exprimer, d'organes virils et puissants?[68]

The only crucial difference which De Quincey acknowledges between himself as a child and himself as an adult is consciousness: 'I, the child, had the feelings; I, the man, decipher them.' In Baudelaire, the feelings have to be transformed by the 'organes virils et puissants' of the artist: they are but the 'principe' of the work of art. The 'germ' would come to nothing without the active exertion of the adult: and that image of the germ, suggestive of 'natural' growth, is soon superseded by that of the 'atmosphere' which makes the relation between childhood and the adult stage much more diffuse, less definable than De Quincey would have it. Through it, Baudelaire retains De Quincey's claim for the unity of being. But he makes that unity a much less logical, more open one.

This suppleness, as against De Quincey's more rigid view of personality, stands out again in his response to the theme of the palimpsest.

Through such privileged moments as impending death, De Quincey states, the effect of opium is naturally produced: man becomes a God who views the expanse of his life as 'on a piece of arras-work', as on a 'map', or a still theatre. This happened to his mother when she nearly drowned as a child. Her vision was a truly mystic insight. Eternity was here and now, transmuting time:

> At a certain stage of this descent [into the abyss of death], – a blow seemed to strike her; phosphoric radiance sprang forth from her eyeballs; and immediately a mighty theatre expanded within her brain. In a moment, in the twinkling of an eye, every act, every design of her past life, lived again, arraying themselves not as a succession, but as parts of a coexistence. Such a light fell upon the whole path of her life backwards into the shades of infancy, as the light, perhaps, which wrapt the destined Apostle on his road to Damascus. Yet that light blinded for a season; but hers poured celestial vision upon the brain, so that her consciousness became omnipresent at one moment to every feature in the infinite review.[69']

By recounting such an experience, De Quincey implicitly justifies his attitude to Time. When he reads past and future into the scene of the torn letter; when he regressively retraces the chain of causality in his life; when he re-lives his past 'exalted, spiritualized, sublimed' through opium; he is translating himself *sub specie aeternitatis*, viewing reality as it ought to be viewed. From such experiences as his mother's, De Quincey deduces that the brain preserves all that impresses it, layer *upon* (not *after*) layer. He thus asserts his faith not only in the unity of human life (one, because various experiences inscribe themselves on a sensibility which is one, and which, like music, harmonises the disparate elements), but in its recurring nature. What is there is bound to emerge to consciousness again:

> What else than a natural and mighty palimpsest is the human brain? . . . Everlasting layers of ideas, images, feelings, have fallen upon your brain softly as light. Each succession has seemed to bury all that went before. And yet, in reality, not one has been extinguished . . . in our own heaven-created palimpsest, the deep memorial palimpsest of the brain . . . The fleeting accidents of man's life,

and its external shows, may indeed be irrelate and incongruous; but the organising principles which fuse into harmony, and gather about fixed pre-determined centres, whatever heterogeneous elements life may have accumulated from without, will not permit the grandeur of human unity greatly to be violated, or its ultimate repose to be troubled, in the retrospect from dying moments, or from other great convulsions.[70]

Who has established these 'fixed predetermined centres'? Who made De Quincey's mother 'destined' like the Apostle on his road to Damascus? To De Quincey's rigid, passive view of personality, Baudelaire, in his translation, responds with open suppleness: 'dans le (palimpseste du cerveau) . . . la fatalité du tempérament human met forcément une harmonie parmi les éléments les plus disparates'. 'Fatalité du tempérament' acts like 'atmosphère'; it recognises unity without making it as binding as a logic; the vagueness of the word leaves the problem unsolved, the options free.

Thus, for De Quincey the question is closed. We are the subjects of mechanisms in whose functioning we can hope, but which we cannot control. And in a way it is a pity that new layers should be adding themselves to the old ones, which were best. Let us make our lives as much of a repetition as possible, so as to make unity easy. But Baudelaire is led by the image of the palimpsest to meditate about responsibility. If there is a palimpsest of each individual brain, is there a palimpsest of action? And is there a collective palimpsest? He quotes the answer of a 'man of genius' who burned all his manuscript works:

'Qu'importe? ce qui était important, c'était que ces choses fussent *créées*; elles ont été créées, donc elles *sont*.' Il prêtait à toute chose créée un caractère indestructible. Combien cette idée s'applique plus évidemment encore à toutes nos pensées, à toutes nos actions, bonnes ou mauvaises! . . . Dans le spirituel non plus que dans le matériel, rien ne se perd. De même que toute action, lancée dans le tourbillon de l'action universelle, est en soi irrévocable et irréparable, abstraction faite de ses résultats possibles, de même toute pensée est ineffaçable. Le palimpseste de la mémoire est indestructible.[71]

By merging the image of the palimpsest which 'draws to itself' all experiences, which acts, that is, centripetally, into the image of the 'tourbillon de l'action universelle', which suggests a centrifugal movement, Baudelaire radically alters the meaning of De Quincey's theory. It is a crucial transformation.

In his remarkable article on Gautier,[72] Georges Poulet shows how the author of *Mademoiselle de Maupin*, tormented by his longing for some 'eternal' form of beauty, and his realisation of the evanescence of all things, first looked for solutions to De Quincey. The expansion of Time, the revival of the past through opium, was the means of fixing the flow of life, of resurrecting what seemed dead. But he then found, in the symbol of the 'Mothers' of Goethe's *Second Faust*, (translated and interpreted by Nerval in 1840) an idea which eventually altered his whole attitude to the problem of time (and of poetry). An idea which changed his desire to grasp the past into a preoccupation to make the present expand into the future. The idea (which he developed)[73] is this:

> Goethe, dans son *Second Faust*, suppose que les choses qui se sont passées autrefois se passent encore dans quelque coin de l'univers. Le fait est, selon lui, le point de départ d'une foule de *cercles excentriques* qui vont agrandissant leurs orbes dans l'éternité et dans l'infini: dès qu'une action est tombée dans le temps, comme une pierre dans un lac sans bornes, l'ébranlement causé par elle ne s'éteint jamais, et se *propage en ondulations* plus ou moins sensibles jusqu'aux limites des espaces. Ainsi, dans son étrange poème, la guerre de Troie étend ses rayonnements jusque'à l'époque chevaleresque; la belle Hélène monte dans le donjon en poivrière du moyen age . . .
> Ce que fait le passé, le présent ne peut-il le produire, lui aussi, et *prolonger ses vibrations* dans les siècles qui ne sont pas encore? . . .[74]

> En effet, *rien ne meurt, tout existe toujours*; nulle force ne peut anéantir ce qui fut une fois. Toute action, toute parole, toute forme, toute pensée tombée dans l'océan universel des choses y produit *des cercles qui vont s'élargissant* jusqu'aux confins de l'éternité . . .[75]

Poulet goes on to mention Gautier's influence on Baudelaire's poetics, and then to say that Baudelaire gave back to Gautier what he owed him by acquainting him, through his translation of *The Power of Words*, with Poe's striking echo of Goethe's idea:

> . . . as no thought can perish, so no act is without infinite result. We moved our hands, for example, when we were dwellers on the earth, and, in so doing, we gave vibration to the atmosphere which engirdled it. This vibration was indefinitely extended, till it gave impulse to every particle on the earth's air, which thenceforward,

and for ever, was actuated by the one movement of the hand . . . !
. . . It is indeed demonstrable that every such impulse *given the air*, must, *in the end*, impress every individual thing that exists *within the universe* . . .[76]

Whether Baudelaire adopted the image of the eccentric circles from Gautier or from Poe, he is clearly referring to it, in his meditation of the palimpsest. 'De même que toute action, lancée dans le tourbillon de l'action universelle, est en soi irrévocable et irréparable, . . . de même toute pensée est ineffaçable.' And this image, for him as for Gautier, implies that the relation between past and present, present and future, is not, as in De Quincey, a static but a dynamic one: the propagation of impulses replaces the accumulation of layer upon layer, or the linear deduction. 'It is no vacuous *durée réelle* but the unbroken production and reproduction of . . . relations', as Lukács would say. It also means that the crucial problem is not to recover the lost layers of the past, but so to live one's present as not to prejudice one's future. For if each action (like each thought and each feeling) lives for ever, and we do not know and cannot control its repercussions, we may, by irresponsible or even casual deeds, store up a future hell for ourselves or for others. Hence Baudelaire's remark about the episode of the Malay who was to haunt De Quincey's dreams:

Notez bien ce Malais; nous le reverrons plus tard; il reparaîtra, multiplié d'une manière terrible. Car qui peut calculer la force de reflet et de répercussion d'un incident quelconque dans la vie d'un rêveur? Qui peut penser, sans frémir, à l'infini élargissement des cercles dans les ondes spirituelles agitées par une pierre de hasard?[77]

Furthermore, if all we think, feel, do is an action upon the air; and our language too: '. . . did there not cross your mind some thought of the *physical power of words*? Is not every word an impulse on the air?' then what we are, the way we live, what we write, affects everybody else. There is a collective palimpsest, a complex and uncontrollable interaction of man upon man. The way we feel our time, and think it, and act it, involves all mankind. Time is not a matter of subjective apprehension, but a moral choice. Where De Quincey found an excuse for 'se replier sur lui-même', for believing that his past would dramatically resurrect in his last moments and living in that hope, Baudelaire was urged to realise that he was in and of the world.

VI

How does Baudelaire justify his belief that individual existence is so bound up with collective existence?

De Quincey had to adopt a deterministic attitude to his own life to establish its unity. His sense of fatality destroyed his freedom. For Baudelaire, fatality on the contrary is the condition of freedom. And freedom creates fatality. The paradox is offered in one of the last segments of 'Mon Coeur mis à nu':

> Pour que la loi du progrès existat (sic), il faudrait que chacun voulut (sic) la créer; c'est-à-dire que quand tous les individus s'appliqueront à progresser, alors, et seulement alors, l'humanité sera en progrès.
> Cette hypothèse peut servir à expliquer l'identité des deux idées contradictoires, liberté et fatalité. – Non seulement il y aura, dans le cas de progrès, identité entre la liberté et la fatalité, mais cette identité a toujours existé. Cette identité, c'est *l'histoire*, histoire des nations et des individus.[78]

Progress is the collective product of the state of moral worth of mankind. One remembers the phrase: 'La vraie civilisation . . . est dans la disparition des traces du péché originel'. In the balance of good and evil, or 'backwardness and forwardness', to employ words more congruent with the notion of progress, only the action of our *wills* is going to make a difference. Progress cannot be committed to the discoveries of others, to the state, to private enterprise. Each individual must work to make it good in his own life: 'Pour que la loi du progrès existat, il faudrait que chacun *voulut* la créer.'

Baudelaire goes on to say that if such progress were brought about, there would then exist an identity between the two contraries, liberty and fatality. This is very difficult. Maybe one can understand it by thinking of 'Le Voyage': progress, as a movement forward brought about by the modern pace of advance, is 'fatal' in that it is outside the control of any individual. But if all individuals were, through their own free wills, to try and make that movement into a real progress, a moral progress, liberty and fatality would run along the same channel. But what does Baudelaire precisely mean by 'liberté'? And the remark which follows in the same breath, that the identity between liberty and fatality has always existed, that it constitutes history, private and individual, remains an enigma. Only Maistre and Baudelaire himself can clarify this.

Maistre hits upon freedom in the discussion on prayer in the sixth *Entretien*. The Count is arguing against Nicole's proposition that 'le fond de la prière est le désir'. He maintains that if this were so one could just about never pray, because aridity and boredom are more current emotions towards God than desire. He equally resists Locke's assertion that we could elevate or cultivate desire in us in proportion to the dignity of the good offered to us, saying that desire is a spontaneous, instinctive motion which no rational consideration is going, on its own, to modify:

> *Le désir . . . n'est qu'un mouvement de l'âme vers un objet l'attire.* Ce mouvement est un fait du monde moral, c'est certain, aussi palpable que le magnétisme et de plus aussi général que la gravitation universelle dans le monde physique. Mais l'homme étant continuellement agité par deux forces contraires, l'examen de cette loi terrible doit être le commencement de toute étude de l'homme . . . si un objet n'agit pas de sa nature sur l'homme, il ne dépend pas de nous de faire naître le désir, puisque nous ne pouvons faire naître dans l'objet la force qu'il n'a pas; et . . . si, au contraire, cette force existe dans l'objet, il ne dépend pas de nous de le détruire, l'homme n'ayant aucun pouvoir sur l'essence des choses extérieures qui sont ce qu'elles sont, sans lui et indépendamment de lui. A quoi donc se réduit le pouvoir de l'homme? A travailler autour de lui et sur lui, pour affaiblir, pour détuire, ou au contraire pour mettre en liberté ou rendre victorieuse l'action dont il éprouve l'influence . . .[79]

Maistre places man's freedom in his power to act upon himself and around himself. Our freedom is in our wills. We cannot change the conditions of life, but we can change the relation to them.

This Baudelaire believes too. Claiming that 'guignon', bad luck, does not exist, or rather that it is the product of the feebleness of our wills, he develops the dynamism latent in Maistre's image of magnetism: there is already present in it the image of 'les tourbillons de l'action universelle' with which he will answer to De Quincey's image of the palimpsest:

> Je fais la part des mille circonstances qui enveloppent la volonté humaine et qui ont elles-mêmes leurs causes légitimes; elles sont une circonférence dans laquelle est enfermée la volonté: mais cette circonférence est mouvante, vivante, tournoyante, et change tous les jours,

toutes les minutes, toutes les secondes son cercle et son centre. Ainsi, entrainées par elle, toutes les volontés humaines qui y sont cloîtrées varient à chaque instant leur jeu réciproque, et c'est ce qui constitue la liberté.

Liberté et fatalité sont deux contraires; vues de près et de loin, c'est une seule volonté.

C'est pourquoi il n'y a pas de guignon. Si vous avez du guignon, c'est qu'il vous manque quelque chose: ce quelque chose, connaissez-le, et étudiez le jeu des volontés voisines pour déplacer plus facilement la circonférence . . .[80]

This throws a light on why, in Baudelaire's perspective, the identity of liberty and fatality constitutes history: history is the result, forever in the making, of the combination of the circumstances surrounding human wills, and of the exertion of these wills.

And 'guignon' is produced by our failure to summon up the high concentration of will that would displace the forces of defeat. The strange poem 'Le Guignon'[81] is an exploration of the defeat of will which buries forever, in sterile solitude and silence, treasures that should have been communicated, brought to light. In the

> Maint joyau dort enseveli
> Dans les ténèbres et l'oubli . . .

we have the prophetic outline of Mallarmé's

> Ce lac dur oublié que hante sous le givre
> Le transparent glacier des vols qui n'ont pas fui![82]

But in Mallarmé the irredeemable accumulation of past failures, of frozen flights, is seen as a tragic condition: one that is inherent in human life, that nothing can change. *Guignon* is a state of things, no longer a moral condition. This perhaps is a loss. A loss continued through Proust, at least through Proust seen by Beckett:

> Here, as always, Proust is completely detached from all moral considerations . . . There is no right and wrong in Proust's world.
> . . . Tragedy is not concerned with human justice. Tragedy is the statement of an expiation, but not the miserable expiation of a codified breach of a local arrangement, organised by the knaves for the fools. The tragic figure represents the expiation of original sin, of the original and eternal sin of him and all his 'soci malorum', the sin of having been born.[83]

For Baudelaire too, having been born is a sin. 'Bénédiction', the first of 'Spleen et Idéal', is sufficient evidence of that: as soon at the poet is born, his mother curses the night in which her womb 'conceived her expiation'. But that poem precisely ends with the famous prayer:

> – 'Soyez béni, mon Dieu, qui donnez la souffrance
> Comme un divin remède à nos impuretés . . .'[84]

And *guignon* in Baudelaire is not tragic in Beckett's sense of the word. The opposite: by yielding to a sense of bad luck, we are wasting precious energies, precious time. Like good writers who complain about the inflated reputations of Eugène Sue and Paul Féval, instead of working to develop the energy that could overthrow such reputations. Like the speaking voice of 'Le Guignon', feeding with its substance the 'Enemy' of the preceding poem:

> – O douleur! o douleur! Le Temps mange la vie,
> Et l'obscur Ennemi qui nous ronge le coeur
> Du sang que nous perdons croît et se fortifie![85]

Through *guignon*, fate is fed with the weakness of our freedom. But it is entirely in our power to turn the identity of fate and freedom to profit. 'Vae victis! car rien n'est vrai que la force, qui est la justice suprême.' It is a tense and arduous dialectic. But its dynamism is thrilling, and much ahead, in the solutions which it outlines, of much literature to come.

Conclusion
A Fire to Conquer Darkness

>   ... un foco, ch'emisperio di tenebre vincìa ...
>   Dante, *Divine Comedy*

We have come to a stage when it is finally possible to view Baudelaire's contradictions in their 'ensemble' – as part of a wholeness of vision which finds its equivalent only perhaps in Dante. The antagonistic meanings which swarm in Baudelaire's work are not inconsistencies, capricious changes of mood, the systematic cultivation of unpredictability, nervous clutching at freedom of utterance. They spring from a deeply-felt belief in the self-contradictory nature of reality, which can only be understood and dealt with through, not in avoidance of, paradox. Antagonisms, aggression, self-exposure, are the only means, however taxing, to attain 'l'unité intégrale'.

It is this capacity for risk and challenge which gives Baudelaire's work its centrality: not only in a historical sense, in that he concentrated in his work so much 'Romantic' experience, transforming it so that its values could survive, and led to so very much: each interpreter of Baudelaire sees his inheritance in some line or other, Martin Turnell in Laforgue and Eliot, Marcel Ruff in Rimbaud, Lautréamont and Surrealism, L.-J. Austin in Mallarmé and Valéry – and each of them is right. But this centrality is not only a matter of tradition. It has a moral dimension, it is born of a faith in dialectics.

Time and time again in the chapters contrasting De Quincey and Baudelaire, we have encountered this: on solitude and communication, on spleen and ideal, on liberty and fatality, De Quincey makes a self-destructive choice between two opposites which to him are incompatible. Baudelaire reconciles the opposites into a synthesis which retains their antagonism, but makes each one appear as the necessary condition for the existence of the other.

And before this, the same dialectical pattern had appeared, at work in Baudelaire's language, in his view of contemporary civilisation and of the artists's response to it (in the form of *Les Fleurs du Mal* and of *La Spleen de Paris*): artifice and nature exclude each other, but also compensate for each other, complete each other, become each other. Beauty can redeem the horror of life, and fails to save you from the horror of living. And the city, which is destroying the instinctual forces of the earth, is also the place where they are being reborn.

The energies which inform Baudelaire's dialectics have, as must have become clear in the course of this study, nothing much to do with historical materialism, and yet they are amazingly close in pattern to it. They are called forth by the same reality, they attempt to solve the same problems, they operate on the same lines. And, as we have tried to argue, they offer a valid alternative to it.

What they have most strikingly in common with it is the urge to go *forward* – *through* the thing, rather than resist it, or deny it. Baudelaire's urge, in relation to 'Romantic' hopes of unity, to language, to changed social and economic realities, to human relations, to the 'shadowy' world, or to 'responsibilities', is always to explore the predicament, the fall, to its bitter end *in order to* find an opening on the other side of it – to make things worse before they can be made better. The reversal process, the rebirth, can only occur once the bottom has been reached.

These energies, if they can be labelled at all, have a strongly Catholic bias. *Catholic* by contrast with *Protestant*: in that the Protestant 'ego' tends to discover or assert itself by remaining whole through darkness and temptation, to regain Paradise through *resistance*, while in the Catholic ethos redemption cannot come without Calvary. This is one of the major sources of the difference from Wordsworth, perhaps also the reason for Baudelaire's appeal to Eliot. In all respects, as we have tried to show, Baudelaire seeks for the cure at the end of the scalpel; through a dialectic of negation, fall and suffering. If contradictions are part and parcel of his sensibility, it is also because, implicitly and explicitly, he sees them as ingrained in the very fibre of reality; and believes in the need to produce, in poetry as in life, values that are concomitant with it. To one system of contradictions there must answer an equal, if not similar, system of contradictions. To a reversed reality there must respond a reversed system of values. In this conviction that man needs to pitch his mind against the *actual* energies of life, Baudelaire again, strangely, meets with historical materialism. The analyses differ, the 'materialism' too: but, strangely again, the basic *optimism* is not so dissimilar as one might think. The optimism is not, of course, in the vision, which is dark enough; nor in the state of feeling, so often attuned to despair. But in the dynamism which makes the continued exploration of living, however painful and because it is painful, preferable to the avoidance of life, the cessation of pain. The nobility of the gambler who would prefer 'la douleur à la mort et l'enfer au néant'; even the final plunge into death, 'au fond de l'Inconnu pour trouver du nouveau', rather than a statement of recklessness, nihilism or pride, are the vibrant assertion of the spirit's need to go on perpetuating itself and tending towards a future.

Baudelaire says that great poetry is essentially stupid, *bête*: it *believes*, and that is its strength. One could add that through sheer power of existence, of projection, it also *hopes*, and that too is part of its strength.

'De Maistre et Poe m'ont appris à raisonner': they are not, those two black masters, by Baudelaire's own admission, his initiators into pessimism, but into *reasoning*. And a kind of reasoning that leads him to permanently re-insert himself into life. With Poe, Baudelaire shared a vital concern for artifice and lucidity which led him to construct aesthetics that *grappled* with reality, *fought* 'nature'; were *actively because exactly* engaged, despite all that Sartre and Lukács may have to say.

The devising of embattled ethics in Baudelaire has much to do with Maistre's peculiar theory of Nature.

Indeed, it is *through* an apocalyptic vision of lethal, swarming energies, that Maistre arrives at the possibility of salvation. The *movement* of Baudelaire's own vision of life, if not its terms, is germane to Maistre's.

Baudelaire was as embattled as Maistre. He was engaged in a life-long battle with spleen like Jacob with his angel. He believed in the terrifying actuality of the artist's 'struggle' with nature. 'Ce monde est une milice, un combat éternel', Maistre had said. Wars for Maistre echo, on the human scale, the violence which rules all creation. But that violence is also the necessary principle of creation, as for Baudelaire Time the destroyer is also Time the edifier:

> ... cette loi déjà si terrible de la guerre n'est cependant qu'un chapitre de la loi générale qui pèse sur l'univers.
>
> Dans le vaste domaine de la nature vivante, il règne une violence manifeste, une espèce de rage prescrite qui anime tous les êtres *in mutua funera*: dès que vous sortez du règne insensible, vous trouvez

le décret de la mort violente écrit sur les frontières mêmes de la vie. Déjà, dans le règne végétal, on commence à sentir la loi: depuis l'immense catalpa jusqu'à la plus humble graminée, combien de plantes *meurent*, et combien sont *tuées*! mais dès que vous entrez dans le règne animal, la loi prend tout à coup une épouvantable évidence. Und force, à la fois cachée et palpable, se montre continuellement occupée à mettre à découvert le principe de la vie par des moyens violents . . .
 . . . la guerre s'allume. L'homme, saisi tout à coup d'une fureur *divine*, étrangère à la haine et à la colère, s'avance sur le champ de bataille sans savoir ce qu'il veut ni même ce qu'il fait. Qu'est-ce donc que cette horrible énigme? Rien n'est plus contraire à sa nature, et rien ne lui répugne moins: il fait avec enthousiasme ce qu'il à en horreur . . .[1]

It is because war is a blind, resistless force, and a living contradiction ('il fait avec enthousiasme ce qu'il a en horreur'), that Maistre regards it as so revealing of our nature. It is fundamental because it exists everywhere, in all races and civilisations, because it has always existed and will always exist where there are men. It is fundamental also because it completely baffles reason. For Maistre, this is a sign of truth. Truth is a scandal. It is disturbing, unnerving, blinding. Anything crucial in this world offers itself as beyond our grasp. The vocabulary operating here is most revealing of this:

> Plus on examine l'univers, et plus on se sent porté à croire que le mal vient d'une certaine division qu'on ne sait expliquer, et que le retour au bien dépend d'une force contraire qui nous pousse sans cesse vers une certaine unité tout aussi inconcevable. . . . En réfléchissant sur la croyance générale et sur l'instinct naturel des hommes, on est frappé par cette tendance qu'ils ont à unir des choses que la nature semble avoir totalement séparées . . .[2]

'Une certaine division qu'on ne sait expliquer . . . une certaine unité tout aussi inconcevable . . . l'instinct naturel des hommes . . .' For Maistre the pedestrian pace of reason is unable to deal with the essential realities of life. One has to by-pass it from the bottom and from the top. From the bottom, by discovering man's fundamental *instincts*, and by treating them as unexplainable *facts*. From the top, through a trust in revelation, in dogma, in prayer, which can only be sensed by what Maistre, following Pascal, calls 'l'esprit du coeur'.[3] But the study of instincts releases a capacity to penetrate mystery. The study of war, for instance, reveals the great complex of crime and expiation which for Maistre is at the core of the human reality. *Because* war is instinctive, because in all its respects it 'absolutely evades the speculations of human reason', it is *divine*.

Maistre believes that the most subterraneous forces in us could touch our highest energies, were it not that our spirits have been made sterile by the cult of reason. Only the extraordinary, the 'superfluous', will enable man to assume his full stature (hence Baudelaire's sense that strength is supreme justice). And when he does, contraries, the highest and the lowest, will touch. An authentic unity will be discovered beyond, through the rupture of, the glib unity which rationalism establishes. The great man must be a 'seer' (as Baudelaire thought that Maistre was), since his glance must penetrate beneath and beyond what 'the lights of reason' are supposed to show. And through the depth and height of his vision, he revivifies reality:

> Il est donc très certain, mon digne ami, qu'on ne peut arriver que par *ces routes extraordinaires* que vous craignez tant.... Tous les inventeurs, tous les hommes originaux ont été des hommes religieux et même exaltés. L'esprit humain, dénaturé par le scepticisme irréligieux, ressemble à une friche qui ne produit rien, ou qui se couvre de plantes spontanées, inutiles à l'homme. Alors même sa fécondité naturelle est un mal: car ces plantes, en mêlant et entrelaçant leurs racines, durcissent le sol, et forment une barrière de plus entre le ciel et la terre. Brisez, brisez cette croûte maudite; détruisez ces plantes mortellement vivaces; appelez toutes les forces de l'homme; enfoncez le soc; cherchez profondément les puissances de la terre pour les mettre en contact avec les puissances du ciel.
>
> ... Le génie ne se traîne guère appuyé sur des syllogismes. Son allure est libre; sa manière tient de l'inspiration: on le voit arriver, et personne ne l'a vu marcher...[4]

What better definition of the prose of the *Journaux intimes* could one find than this? And what better justification? There are no transitions there – they would savour of syllogisms, pare life away: the roots, and the sky, are in the words themselves, and in their combinations into sentences: words like 'prostitution'.

'Enfoncez le soc; cherchez profondément les puissances de la terre pour les mettre en contact avec les puissances du ciel.' Baudelaire is searching for that 'ténébreuse et profonde unité' of life: his 'Correspondances' are informed by Maistre's ambitious summons:

> La Nature est un temple où de vivants piliers
> Laissent parfois sortir de confuses paroles;
> L'homme y passe à travers des forêts de symboles
> Qui l'observent avec des regards familiers . . .

Pierre Jean Jouve has some marvellous things to say about these lines.[5] But his claim that: 'Le secret de Baudelaire, dont il ne connaît pas lui-même l'étendue est la recherche de l'inconscient comme moteur de la Poésie, sous l'impulsion d'une curiosité intense et quelque peu perverse, avec le guide qu'il nomme "spiritualité"'[6] should be *reversed* as well in order to be true. Baudelaire is also exploring 'spirituality' with the tools of the subconscious – the instinctive. It is not through some whimsical taste for scope that things always expand to such grandiose dimensions in him: that the love of crowds becomes the enjoyment of 'number', the drunkenness of the ragpicker a dream of heroism, drug-taking a new form of magic, or that the encounter with Mademoiselle Bistouri poses so ardently the mystery of madness. It is because unexplainable human facts, through a correspondence which it is the poet's task to bring to light, only achieve their true dimension when they reach towards 'les puissances du ciel'.

But, for Baudelaire, the infinite dimension of life is known negatively: he knows darkness infinitely better than light:[7] 'Au moral comme au physique, j'ai toujours eu la sensation du gouffre, non seulement du goffre du sommeil, mais du gouffre de l'action, du rêve, du souvenir, du désir, du regret, du remords, du beau, du nombre, etc.'[8] The sensation is sickeningly embodied in the instinct of the poem 'Le Gouffre'. But 'La Fontaine de sang' is perhaps the most horrifying example of this subconscious sense of uncontrollable abyss:

> Il me semble parfois que mon sang coule à flots,
> Ainsi qu'une fontaine aux rhythmiques sanglots.
> Je l'entends bien qui coule avec un long murmure,
> Mais je me tâte en vain pour trouver la blessure.
>
> A travers la cité, comme dans un champ clos,
> Il s'en va, transformant les pavés en îlots,
> Désaltérant la soif de chaque créature,
> Et partout colorant en rouge la nature.[9]

But Baudelaire can both explore his neurosis and strive for ways of control over it. That is, his knowledge of darkness is a knowledge of light, his blasphemies a reversed form of love. And this, because Maistre has taught him (or he has found, and Maistre has confirmed it) that all deep realities generate their own contradiction. The remedy to the horror lies in the horror itself.

War, for Maistre, is man perpetuating upon himself that death which he brought about. Wars are the instrument of divine punishment. God is the God of armies. The earth thirsts for blood:

> La terre entière, continuellement imbibée de sang, n'est qu'un autel immense où tout ce qui vit doit être immolé sans fin, sans mesure, sans relâche, jusqu'à la consommation des choses, jusqu'à la mort de la mort.[10]

> ... La terre avide de sang, ... ouvre la bouche pour le recevoir et le retenir dans son sein jusqu'au moment où elle devra le rendre ...[11]

But as blood is the sign of our scourge, it is also the instrument of our redemption. Maistre celebrates the notion of sacrifice, which he calls *réversibilité* (the principle of blood reversed into its opposite; the suffering of innocence reversed to the profit of the guilty); and on grounds very similar to those he applies to war: sacrifices are of all times and all religions; they cannot be explained rationally; they are a revelation through instinct, confirmed by Christ's revelation. Through reversibility, sin and blood become their opposites:

> ... l'idée du *péché* et celle du *sacrifice pour le péché* s'étaient si bien amalgamées dans l'esprit des hommes de l'antiquité que la langue sainte exprimait l'un et l'autre par le même mot. De là cet hèbraïsme si connu, employé par Saint Paul *que le Sauveur a été fait péché pour nous.*

The use of circumcision too manifests this sense of salvation by blood:

> ... toujours on retrouve *une opération douloureuse et sanglante faite sur les organes de la reproduction.* C'est-à-dire: *Anathème sur les générations humaines,* et SALUT PAR LE SANG.
> Le genre humain professait ces dogmes depuis sa chute, lorsque la grande victime, *élevée pour attirer à elle,* cria sur le Calvaire:
> TOUT EST CONSOMMÉ

Alors le voile du temple étant déchiré, le grand secret du sanctuaire fut connu, autant qu'il pouvait l'être dans cet ordre de choses dont nous faisons partie. Nous comprimes pourquoi l'homme avait toujours cru qu'une âme pouvait être sauvée par une autre et pourquoi il avait cherché sa régénération dans le sang.[12]

Thanks to the principle of reversibility, suffering can be made redemptive. It is a 'divine remedy' for our own 'impuretés', but also for those of others. When Baudelaire says of Poe 'Il a beaucoup souffert pour nous', he means fully what he says. The torments of Poe's life can serve to atone for Baudelaire's dalliance with neurosis. Baudelaire has his own communion of saints, very similar to Maistre's in which spirits can enjoy their own forces and those of the others.[13] But for one to benefit from the others, he must *will* it:

> Non seulement (l'homme) jouit de ses propres mérites, mais les satisfactions étrangères lui sont imputées par la justice éternelle, pourvu qu'il ait voulu, et qu'il se soit rendu digne de cette *réversibilité* . . . il faut que, par une humble et courageuse coopération, l'homme s'approprie cette satisfaction, autrement elle lui demeurera étrangère . . .[14]

And De Maistre answers the guilty who, questioning God's justice, ask why innocence should suffer in the world: 'Elle souffre pour vous, si vous le voulez'. The existence of suffering radically demands that one should do something about it, but above all in one's own life. We are very close to Pascal: 'Le Christ est en agonie jusqu'à la fin du monde. Il ne faut pas dormir pendant ce temps-là.'

Baudelaire does not go so far. But he does write, late on in his life: 'Je crois qu'il est bon que les innocents souffrent'.[15] In his resolution to pray for strength, using Mariette, his father and Poe as intercessors; in the prayer of the poem 'Réversibilité'; and also, in his sense that in the gain or loss of substance of each minute, more is at stake than himself, he moves towards it. But had we not overtaken him at this point, we would not have done him justice.

In the name of this same sense of *justice* we must proceed.

It would not be absurd to stand towards Baudelaire in the relation he stands to Poe. The call which closes the 'Epigraphe pour un livre condamné':

> Lecteur . . .
> Mais si, sans se laisser charmer,

> Ton oeil sait plonger dans les gouffres,
> Lis-moi, pour apprendre à m'aimer;
>
> Ame curieuse qui souffres
> Et vas cherchant ton paradis,
> Plains-moi! . . . Sinon, je te maudis![16]

sets up the terms of a relationship in which love and sympathy co-exist with moral lucidity – 'sans se laisser charmer' – with distance, and in which the poet and his reader are both embarked with total seriousness in a quest for a 'paradis'. In such perspective, there is a call to others in the very anguish with which a poet such as Baudelaire stakes his all in his attempt to penetrate and redeem life. One could say of Baudelaire what he says of Poe, 'Il a beaucoup souffert pour nous', or what Maistre says of the innocent 'Il souffre pour vous, si vous le voulez'. Not this time necessarily in a 'Christian' perspective, but with a sense that each man 'engages' mankind, in more ways than Sartre meant, in that the quality of his success makes it more possible for others to try, indeed makes it imperative for others to try. If you believe that there is such a thing as a *life* of the spirit, it creates a responsibility for you not to allow what others made vigorous to become degraded. The survival of a world in which integrity can exist is in each man's hands.

We are also very close, talking of Baudelaire in this way, to Coleridge's sense that there is an 'air', a freedom of the spirit, which superior minds breathe, and to which only quality of soul gives access. It is Baudelaire's greatness that out of the gloom of his life he should have made access to that superior air possible, not only for himself, but for his readers.

Thus, whether he sings the erotic ecstasy which for a while opens up the sky:

> Cheveux bleus, pavillon de ténèbres tendues
> Vous me rendez l'azur du ciel immense et rond . . .[17]

or the horror which slams it shut like a lid:

> Partout l'homme subit la terreur du mystère,
> Et ne regarde en haut qu'avec un oeil tremblant.
>
> En haut, le Ciel! ce mur de caveau qui l'étouffe . . .
> . . .

Le Ciel! couvercle noir de la grande marmite
Où bout l'imperceptible et vaste Humanité.[18]

the 'joie calme' which his verse elevates you to make you breathe the superior ether which is inhabited by the heroes and poets of Dante's Limbo. In the surrounding hemisphere of darkness, a fire, by its purifying intensity, becomes light, recreates the azure of the sky. It is no accident that, commenting on Delacroix's painting of the ceiling of the Luxembourg Library, Dante's and Virgil's encounter with the poets of antiquity in the first circle of Hell, Baudelaire should trace the theme back to its origins. He quotes from Pier Angelo Fiorentino's translation:

'Nous ne laissions pas d'aller, tandis qu'il parlait; mais nous traversions toujours la forêt, épaisse forêt d'esprits, veux-je dire. Nous n'étions pas bien éloignés de l'entrée de l'abîme, quand je vis un feu qui perçait un hémisphère de ténèbres. Quelques pas nous en séparaient encore, mais je pouvais déja entrevoir que des esprits glorieux habitaient ce séjour.

'– O toi, qui honores toute science et tout art, quels sont ces esprits auxquels on fait tant d'honneur qu'on les sépare du sort des autres?

'Il me répondit' – Leur belle renommée, qui retentit là-haut dans votre monde, trouve grâce dans le ciel, qui les distingue des autres.

'Cependant une voix se fit entendre: 'Honorez le sublime poëte; son ombre, qui était partie, nous revient.'

'La voix se tut, et je vis venir à nous quatre grandes ombres; leur aspect n'était ni triste ni joyeux. . . .

Baudelaire goes on to quote Dante describing how Virgil showed him Homer, Ovid, Horace and Lucan, gathering around him, and how the five poets received him in their midst 'de sorte que je fus le sixième parmi tant de génies'. He thus comments on Delacroix's painting of this:

. . . Je m'attache surtout à l'esprit de cette peinture. Il est impossible d'exprimer avec la prose tout le calme bienheureux qu'elle exprime, et la profonde harmonie qui nage dans cette atmosphère. Cela fait penser aux pages les plus verdoyantes du *Télémaque*, et rend tous les souvenirs que l'esprit a emportés des récits élyséens. Le paysage . . . circulaire, est peint avec l'aplomb d'un peintre d'histoire, et la finesse et l'amour d'un paysagiste. Des bouquets de lauriers, des ombrages considérables le coupent harmonieusement; des nappes de soleil doux et uniforme dorment sur les gazons; des montagnes bleues ou ceintes de bois font un horizon à souhait *pour le plaisir des yeux*. Quant au ciel, il est bleu et blanc, chose étonnante chez Delacroix; les nuages, délayés et tirés en sens divers comme une gaze qui se déchire, sont d'une grande légéreté; et cette voûte d'azur, profonde et lumineuse, fuit à une prodigieuse hauteur . . .[19]

Such are the heights to which 'Elévation take the speaker, and take you, reader:

> Au-dessus des étangs, au-dessus des vallées,
> Des montagnes, des bois, des nuages, des mers,
> Par-delà le soleil, par-delà les éthers,
> Par-delà les confins des sphères étoilées,
>
> Mon esprit, tu te meus avec agilité,
> Et comme un bon nageur qui se pâme dans l'onde,
> Tu sillonnes gaiement l'immensité profonde
> Avec une indicible et mâle volupté.
>
> Envole-toi bien loin de ces miasmes morbides;
> Va te purifier dans l'air supérieur,
> Et bois, comme une pure et divine liqueur,
> Le feu clair qui remplit les espaces limpides.[20]

A fire there conquers surrounding darkness, the 'miasmes morbides', the 'ennuis' and the 'vastes chagrins/Qui chargent de leur poids l'existence brumeuse': on the level of art, in an immediate, deeply satisfying way: 'Tout l'être intérieur, dans ces merveilleux instants, s'élance en l'air par trop de légéreté et de dilatation, comme pour atteindre une région plus haute'.[21] But also, as a premonition to the spirit of what lasting 'grace' could be, and how worthwhile it might be to try and conquer it.

Notes

(For a list of abbreviations used, see p. 00.)

INTRODUCTION

1. FM, pp. 176–7.
2. FM, p. 21.
3. FM, p. 40.
4. FM, p. 41.
5. FM, p. 47.
6. As Charles Mauron has done with *Le Spleen de Paris*, in *Le Dernier Baudelaire*, Paris, José Corti, 1966.
7. Written on Philoxène Boyer's *Album*, JOPR II, p. 140.
8. CG III, p. 267.
9. *Journal des Débats*, 4 July 1887.
10. See on contemporary opinion A. E. Carter, *Baudelaire et la Critique Française, 1868–1917*, University of South Carolina Press, 1963.
11. 'Baudelaire, à Paul Bourget', *Lettres chimériques*, Paris, Charpentier, 1885, pp. 278–84.
12. 'Une Réforme à l'Académie', JOPR I, p. 215.
13. 'Le Songe d'Athalie', in *Promenades littéraires*, 2nd series, Mercure de France, 1906.
14. Verlaine, *Oeuvres posthumes II* in *Oeuvres complètes*, Paris, Messein, 1913, pp. 8–9.
15. Nadar, *Charles Baudelaire intime*, Paris, Blaizot, 1911.
16. 'Charles Baudelaire, sa vie et son oeuvre', in Crépet et Pichois, *Baudelaire et Asselineau*, Paris, Nizet, 1953, pp. 65–6.
17. 18 Février 1866, CG V, p. 279.
18. F. W. Leakey, *Baudelaire and Nature*, Manchester University Press, 1969, p. 124.
19. *Préface* to *Les Fleurs du Mal*, ed. Pelletan et Helleu, 1917.
20. *Introduction* aux *Ecrits intimes* de Baudelaire, ed. Point du Jour, 1946, p. LVII.
21. Paul Bourget, *Essais de psychologie contemporaine*, Paris, Plon-Nourrit, 1901, p. 6.
22. Turnell, *Baudelaire, a Study of his Poetry*, London, Hamish Hamilton, 1953, p. 108.
23. 'Sur mes contemporains', AR p. 325.
24. 'Choix de maximes consolantes sur l'amour', JOPR II p. 3.
25. 'A Poulet-Malassis', CG III pp. 178–9.

26. 'Sur mes Contemporains', AR p. 325.
27. 'Sur les *Liaisons Dangereuses*', JOPR I p. 331.
28. 'Exposition Universelle de 1855', CE pp. 220–1.

PART ONE (A)

CHAPTER 1

1. Arthur O. Lovejoy, 'On the Discrimination of Romanticisms', in *Essays in the History of Ideas*, Johns Hopkins Press, 1948; reprinted in *English Romantic Poets, Modern Essays in Criticisms*, ed. M. H. Abrams, London, Oxford, New York, Oxford University Press, 1960. Quotations are from this edition.
2. Ibid., p. 11.
3. Ibid., p. 13.
4. Ibid., p. 14.
5. Ibid., p. 20.
6. See Marcel Raymond, *Jean-Jacques Rousseau, La quête de soi et la rêverie*, Paris, José Corti, 1962, pp.159–63.
7. See Mario Praz, *The Romantic Agony*, trans. Angus Davidson, Oxford University Press, 1933. He also goes in for a complicated 'genesis' of the term 'romantic'.
8. Baron d'Holbach, *Système de la Nature*; trans. as *Nature and Her Laws: as Applicable to the Happiness of Man Living in Society, Contrasted with Superstition and Imaginary Systems*, from the French of M. de Mirabaud, in 2 vols.; London, James Watson, 1834, Vol. I, Part 1, Chapter i, p. 18.
9. *Boyle's Free Enquiry into the Received Notion of Nature*, quoted in Dr Johnson's *Dictionary* at the end of the word 'Nature'.
10. Sade, *Idées sur les romans*, 1800.
11. F. Engels, *The Condition of the Working-Class in England in 1844*, London, Allen and Unwin, 1892, p. 4. This contention is largely supported by modern historians, such as E. J. Hobsbawn, *Industry and Empire*, London, Weidenfeld and Nicolson, 1968; E. P. Thompson, *The Making of the English Working Class*, London, Gollancz, 1963; Klingerer, *Art in the Industrial Revolution*, London, Carrington, 1947. For specific points see J. H. Plumb, *England in the Eighteenth Century*, Penguin, 1950, p. 77, and Charles Knight, *A Popular History of England*, Vol. 8, Chapter 26. The contention must however be set in the perspective of differences between France, England, and Germany, as they are discussed for example in G. Lukács' *The Historical Novel*, London, Merlin Press, 1962.
12. FM, p. 34.
13. Ibid., p. 40.
14. *The Correspondence of Robert Southey with Caroline Bowles*, ed. Edward Dowden, 1881, p. 52.
15. M. H. Abrams, 'English Romanticism: The Spirit of the Age', in *Romanticism Reconsidered*, selected papers from the English Institute, edited with a foreword by Northrop Frye, New York and London, Columbia University Press, 1963, p. 54.

NOTES

16. Northrop Frye, 'The Drunken Boat', in ibid., p. 14.
17. Jones, *The Egotistical Sublime, A History of Wordsworth's Imagination*, London, Chatto and Windus, 1960 – Jones is talking of Wordsworth's misuse of Rousseau's term, the 'general will'.
18. Hazlitt, *Lectures on the English Poets and the Spirit of the Age*, London and Toronto, J. M. Dent, 1910, p. 161.
19. Ibid., p. 253.
20. John Jones, op. cit., p. 200.
21. *Table Talk*, 31 July, 1832.
22. Reported by De Quincey, 'Essay on Style' in *Collected Writings* Vol. X; quoted by John Jones, op. cit., pp. 195–6.
23. See Harold Bloom, *The Visionary Company, A Reading of English Romantic Poetry*, London, Faber, 1962, p. 129.
24. 'M.W.'s mind is obtuse, except as it is the organ and receptacle of accumulated feelings: it is not analytic, but synthetic'. Hazlitt, *Lectures . . .*, p. 257.
25. My access to them is through Albert Béguin, *L'Ame romantique et le rêve: Essai sur le romantisme allemand et la poésie française*, Paris, José Corti, 1963 (1st ed. 1937); especially the chapter called 'L'Unité Cosmique', pp. 67–72.
26. Hazlitt here again brilliantly underlines this contradiction: 'They were for bringing poetry back to its primitive simplicity and state of nature, as he (Rousseau) was for bringing society back to the savage state: so that the only thing remarkable left in the world by this change, would be the persons who had produced it.' *Lectures . . .*, p. 163.
27. Quoted by H. Bloom, *The Visionary Company*, p. 123.
28. *The Prelude, or Growth of a Poet's Mind*, ed. Ernest de Selincourt, Oxford, Clarendon Press, 1959 (2nd ed. revised by Helen Darbishire, 1965), 1805–6 version, X, ll. 136–58, pp. 374–6. All further references to *The Prelude* will be to the 1805–6 version unless otherwise indicated.
29. Ibid., l. 186, p. 378.
30. Ibid., XIII, ll. 366–7, p. 502.
31. Lukács, *La Théorie du roman*, trans. by Lucien Goldmann, Paris, Gonthier, 1962, pp. 46 and 78.
32. Auerbach, *Mimesis, The Representation of Reality in Western Culture*, trans. from the German by Willard R. Trask, Princeton University Press, 1953, p.463.
33. Alexander Welsh, *The Hero of the Waverley Novels*, New Haven and London, Yale University Press, 1963, p. 28. The 'moral' status given to that stability is shown by a quotation Welsh gives from the *Morning Chronicle* of 2 Feb 1815; 'It is to the cultivation of the moral qualities that England is indebted for her power and influence. For the want of them France may be mischievous, but she will never be great.'
34. Coleridge, 'Essay on Poesy or Art', *Biographia Literaria*, ed. J. Shawcross, 2 vols, Oxford University Press, 1907, Vol. II, p. 258,
35. Northrop Frye, 'The Drunken Boat', op. cit., pp. 14ff.
36. Bloom, *The Ringers in the Tower, Studies in Romantic Tradition*, Chicago and London, University of Chicago Press, 1971.
37. To Thomas Moore, 1821, quoted in ibid., p. 80.

38. 'Feelings of a Republican on the Fall of Bonaparte', in *The Poetical Works of Percy Bysshe Shelley*, ed. William Rossetti, London, E. Moxon, Son & Co., 1887, p. 431.
39. 'The Triumph of Life', ibid., p. 609.
40. Bloom, *The Ringers in the Tower*, p. 84.
41. 'Lines written on hearing the News of the Death of Napoleon', *Poetical Works*, p. 524.
42. Such as, for instance, *Une Ténébreuse affaire*, *La Duchesse de Langeais*, *La Paix du ménage*, the beginning of *La Femme de trente ans*.
43. 'Le 15 Mai 1796, le général Bonaparte fit son entrée dans Milan à la tête de cette jeune armée qui venait de passer la pont de Lodi, et d'apprendre au monde qu'après tant de siècles César et Alexandre avaient un successeur.' *Romans et nouvelles*, ed. Henri Martineau, Paris, Pléiade, 1952, II, p. 25.
44. Mme de Staël, *De L'Allemagne*, Paris, Hachette, 5 vols, 1958–60, Vol. II, pp. 131–3.
45. *The Philosophical Lectures of S. T. Coleridge*, ed. Kathleen Coburn, London, Pilot Press, 1949, XII, pp. 343–4.
46. Merleau-Ponty, 'L'Existentialisme chez Hegel', *Sens et non-sens*, Paris, Nagel, 1948, pp. 115–16.
47. Bloom, *The Visionary Company*, op. cit., especially pp. 132–9.
48. JOPR I, p. 306.
49. Crépet et Pichois, *Baudelaire et Asselineau*, p. 85. Baudelaire is thought to have adhered to the Blanqui–Raspail–Proudhon tendency.
50. A Ancelle, 5 Mar. 1852, CG I, p. 152.
51. A Nadar, 16 May 1859, CG I, p. 319.
52. Rude, *Confidences d'un journaliste*, Paris, Sangnier, 1876, p. 176.
53. JI, p. 57.
54. AR, p. 418.
55. JOPR I, p. 237.
56. JOPR I, pp. 242–4.
57. As G. Hartmann would say. See 'Romanticism and Anti-Self-Consciousness', in *Beyond Formalism. Literary Essays 1958–1970*, New Haven and London, Yale University Press, 1970, pp. 298–310.
58. CE, p. 384.
59. CE, p. 385.
60. CE, p. 385.
61. CE, pp. 381–2.
62. CE, p. 380.
63. AR, pp. 194–5.
64. See poems LIV and LXXXIV.
65. AR, p. 366.
66. JI, p. 56.
67. JI, p. 57.
68. 'La Guerre Civile', draft for a prose poem.
69. JOPR III, p. 12. On Sade and Baudelaire, see Georges Blin, *Le Sadisme de Baudelaire*, Paris, José Corti, 1948, and on 'la littérature du Mal' in the eighteenth century, see M. A. Ruff, *L'Esprit du Mal et l'esthétique baudelairienne*, Paris, Armand Colin, 1955.

70. JOPR III, p. 215–16.
71. *Prelude*, IX, ll. 289–92, pp. 328–30.
72. JI, p. 73.
73. See Albert Béguin, op. cit., p. 68.
74. Maistre, *Les Soirées de Saint-Pétersbourg, ou Entretiens sur le gouvernement temporel de la Providence*, Paris, La Colombe, 1960, pp. 56–7. See also p. 272.
75. 26 Juin 1860, CG III. p. 125. He adds, characteristically: 'Remarquez bien que je ne renonce pas au plaisir de changer d'idée ou de me contredire'.
76. AR, pp. 96–7.

CHAPTER 2

1. Northrop Frye, 'The Drunken Boat', in *Romanticism Reconsidered*, p. 13.
2. Cowper, *The Task*, I, ll. 749–53. It is around this sense of vegetable nature and natural man, that Professor F. W. Leakey's remarkable study, *Baudelaire and Nature*, is built.
3. Lamartine, 'Le Vallon', *Méditations poétiques*, in *Oeuvres poétiques*, Paris, Pléiade, 1963, p. 20.
4. To Desnoyers, CG I, p. 323.
5. Wordsworth, *Poetical Works*, ed. E. de Selincourt, Oxford, Clarendon Press, Vol. II, 1940, p. 139.
6. 'A Celle qui est trop gaie', FM pp. 283–4.
7. AR, p. 294.
8. CG I, pp. 321–3. See on this J. Massin's chapter, 'Les Légumes Sanctifiés', in *Baudelaire entre Dieu et Satan*, Paris, René Julliard, 1945.
9. Rousseau, *Oeuvres Complètes*, ed. Bernard Gagnebin and Marcel Raymond, Paris, Pléiade, 1959, Vol. I, pp. 13–24.
10. *Rêveries du promeneur solitaire*, ibid., p. 1079.
11. *Prelude*, III, ll. 590–6, p. 102.
12. AR, p. 37.
13. *Prelude*, V. ll. 354–7.
14. AR, p. 37.
15. Ibid.
16. 'De l'Essence du rire', CE p. 383.
17. *Prelude*, II, ll. 266–7, pp. 56–8.
18. JOPR I, p. 251.
19. AR, pp. 59–60.
20. *Prelude*, II, ll. 269–73, p. 58.
21. FM, p. 28. See Georges Poulet's comments in *Etudes sur le temps humain*, Paris, Plon, 1949, pp. 328–9.
22. JI, p. 88.
23. CE, p. 374.
24. To his mother, CG I, p. 164.
25. JI, p. 82.
26. JI, p. 53.
27. *Prelude*, VII, ll. 311–14, 1850 version, p. 239.

28. JI, p. 69.
29. *Prelude*, XII, ll. 207–19, p. 466.
30. 'Essay, Supplementary to the Preface of 1815' (quoted in Abrams (ed.), *Romanticism Reconsidered*, p. 67).
31. 'William Blake and his Illustrations to the *Divine Comedy*', *Essays and Introductions*, London, Macmillan, 1961, pp. 120–1.
32. JI, p. 97.
33. 'Sur les *Liaisons Dangereuses*', JOPR I, p. 330.

CHAPTER 3

1. Marx, *Le 18 Brumaire de Louis Bonaparte*, Editions sociales, 1969, p. 43. These few quotations from Marx are given in their French translation because some of the words in French (such as *à rebours*) show the relation to French literature better than would their English translation.
2. Stendhal, *Mémoires d'un touriste*, 12 Sep 1837, Paris, Champion, 1932.
3. Walter Benjamin, *Charles Baudelaire: a Lyric Poet in the Era of Capitalism*, translated from the German by Harry Zohn, London, NLB, 1973, p. 101.
4. Marx, *Le 18 Brumaire* . . . , p. 44. See how Géralde Nakam relates these texts of Marx to Flaubert in 'Le 18 Brumaire de *l'Education sentimentale*', Mars–Mai 1969, in *Europe: Flaubert*, Sep, Oct, Nov 1969, Paris.
5. Marx, *Les Luttes de classe en France: 1848–1850*, Editions sociales, 1967, p. 64.
6. Ibid., pp. 66–7.
7. *The Class Struggles in France, 1848–1850*, Marx and Engels: *Selected Works* in 2 vols, Moscow, Foreign Language Publishing House, 1951, Vol. I, pp. 160–1.
8. *The Eighteenth Brumaire of Louis Bonaparte*, Marx and Engels: *Selected Works*, Vol. I, p. 307.
9. Walter Benjamin, op. cit., p. 73. Stanza quoted is from FM, p. 178.
10. Benjamin, op. cit., pp. 32–3.
11. *The Eighteenth Brumaire* . . . , p. 307.
12. Lukács, 'Reification and the Consciousness of the Proletariat', in *History and Class-Consciousness, Studies in Marxist Dialectics*, London, Merlin Press, 1971.
13. Cassirer, *The Problem of Knowledge: Philosophy, Science and History since Hegel*, trans. William H. Woglom and Charles W. Hendel, New Haven and London, Yale University Press, 1950.
14. Ibid., p. 1.
15. Ibid., p. 11.
16. Ibid., p. 12.
17. Ibid., p. 17.
18. Ibid., p. 18.
19. Northrop Frye, *A Study of English Romanticism*, New York, Random House, 1968, p. 15.

NOTES

20. Marx, quoted in Lukács, op. cit., p. 86.
21. Ibid., p. 88.
22. Ibid., p. 89.
23. Ibid., p. 100.
24. Ibid., p. 101.
25. FM, p. 143.
26. FM, p. 40.
27. Lukács, op. cit., p. 109.
28. FM, p. 141.
29. Robert Langbaum, *The Poetry of Experience, the Dramatic Monologue in Modern Literary Tradition*, New York, Random House, 1957.
30. Rousseau, *L'Emile*, L. II, Paris, Editions sociales, 1958, p. 52.
31. AR, pp. 95–6.
32. Lukács, op. cit., p. 89.
33. Ibid., p. 91.
34. Ibid., p. 97.
35. Ibid., p. 107.
36. C. F. Volney, *La Loi naturelle, ou catéchisme du citoyen français*, complete critical edn., 1793 and 1826 texts Gaston-Martin, Paris, Colin, 1934.
37. Rousseau, *L'Emile*, p. 183.
38. E. Burke, *Vindication of Natural Society: or, a View of the Miseries and Evils arising to Mankind from any Species of Artificial Society, Works*, ed. F. C. and J. Rivington, London, 1808, Vol. I, pp. 35–6.
39. Ibid., p. 62.
40. See the *Discours sur les fondements de l'inégalité par les hommes*.
41. Burke, *Reflections on the Revolution in France*, ed. with an introduction by C. C. O'Brien, London, Pelican Classics, 1968, p. 92.
42. *Prelude*, X, ll. 430–40, p. 392.
43. Maistre, *Considérations sur la France, suivies par l'Essai sur le principe générateur des constitutions politiques*, Lyon, J. B. Pélagaud & Co., 1852, pp. 145–6.
44. Burke, *Reflections . . .*, pp. 119–20.
45. Ibid., p. 182.
46. Rousseau, *Contrat social*, II, 7, Paris, Rieder et Cie, 1914, p. 183.
47. Lukács, op. cit., p. 136.
48. Ibid., pp. 136–7.
49. Ibid., p. 128.
50. Ibid., p. 129.
51. One can use as models of this ethos Renan's *L'Avenir des sciences*. Cassirer stresses the continuity of this ethos with the Enlightenment. He talks of Buckle's *History of Civilization* and Lecky's *History of the Rise and Influence of the Spirit of Rationalism* (1865) as in agreement with Voltaire's view that 'progress in enlightenment and general understanding is the real, indeed the only, criterion of the development of a civilisation.' Next to that, Buckle placed the technical and material advance which followed as a simple consequence of the advancement of science. It was to this advancement that, in Baudelaire's time, the idea of progress was most frequently linked.

52. CE, pp. 226–7.
53. Benjamin, op. cit., p. 116. 'He (Baudelaire) envisioned blank spaces which he filled with his poems. His work cannot merely be categorized as historical, like anyone else's, but it is intended to be so and understood itself as such'.
54. 'Notice' to *Les Fleurs du Mal*, Calmann-Lévy edition of *Oeuvres complètes*, 1869, pp. XXXVII and XXVI.
55. Letter to Tisserand, 28 Janvier 1854, JOPR I, pp. 85–6.
56. Lukács, op cit., p. 98.
57. Ibid.
58. Ibid., p. 104.
59. Ibid., p. 109.
60. Cassirer, op. cit., p. 175.
61. Ibid., p. 244.
62. Auguste Comte, Letter to Valat, 8 Sep 1824; see Lévy-Bruhl's *La Philosophie d'Auguste Comte*, 2nd edn, Paris, F. Alcan, 1905, p. 270.
63. Cassirer, op. cit., pp. 245–6.
64. Taine, *Histoire de la littérature anglaise*, Paris, Hachette et Cie, 1863, I, IXff.
65. T. R. Malthus, *An Essay on Population* in 2 vols, London and New York, J. M. Dent & Sons, 1958 (reprint), p. 6.
66. It is an image which Charles Du Bos applies to Stendahl's sentences, in *Approximations*, Paris, Fayard, 1965 (reprint): 'Les membres de le phrase ne s'additionnent pas, ne se commandent pas d'une manière rigoureuse et apparente; chacun d'eux est un coup de feu tiré par un tireur individuel, et c'est seulement parce que tous les tireurs tirent sur la ligne du combat que le lecteur perçoit un crépitement ininterrompu.' 'En lisant *le Rouge et le noir*', p. 265.
67. Maistre, *Les Soirées de Saint-Pétersbourg*, p. 143 and 141.
68. JI, p. 99.
69. Maistre, *Les Soirées de Saint-Pétersbourg*, p. 306.
70. Maistre, *Considérations sur la France*, p. 67.
71. *Biographia Literaria*, p. 83.
72. Quoted by Joseph Vouga, *Baudelaire et Joseph de Maistre*, Paris, José Corti, 1957, p. 27.
73. JI, p. 64.
74. JI, p. 16.
75. See AR, pp. 89–91.
76. JI, p. 54. When planning to write about the great dandies of his age, Baudelaire had placed Maistre among them.
77. CE, pp. 187–8.
78. PA, pp. 274–5.
79. AR, pp. 97–100.
80. JI, pp. 12–13.
81. FM, pp. 85–6.
82. Bourget, *Essais de psychologie contemporaine*, p. 10.
83. For the source of the image in Hegel, see Frederic Jameson, *Marxism and Form, Twentieth-Century Dialectical Theories of Literature*, Princeton University Press, 1971, pp. 369–73.

84. *The German Ideology*, edited with an Introduction by C. J. Arthur, London, Lawrence and Wishart, 1970, Part I, p. 47.

CHAPTER 4

1. Blake to George Cumberland, 12 Apr 1827, *Poetry and Prose*, edited by Geoffrey Keynes, Nonesuch Press, 1939, p. 927.
2. Robert Langbaum, *The Poetry of Experience*, p. 22. See also Northrop Frye's *Fearful Symmetry: a Study of William Blake*, Princeton University Press, 1947, Chapter I: 'The Case against Locke'.
3. Goethe, *Faust*, Part I, 'Faust's Study'; translated by C. F. MacIntyre, Norfolk, Connecticut, New Directions, 1949, p. 60.
4. An Eckermann, 2 Aug 1830, Goethe's *Gespräche*, V, p. 175, discussed in Cassirer, *The Problem of Knowledge . . .*, 'The Idea of Metamorphosis and Idealistic Morphology: Goethe', pp. 137–50.
5. 'Entwurfe einer vergleichenden Anatomie', *Naturwiss. Schriften*, VIII, 73ff. Quoted in Cassirer, op. cit., p. 144.
6. *Prelude*, II, ll. 215–19, 1850 version, p. 55.
7. Lukács, *History and Class Consciousness*, p. 135.
8. Northrop Frye, *A Study of English Romanticism*, p. 13.
9. Quoted by Raymond Williams, *Culture and Society, 1780–1950*, London, Chatto and Windus, 1958, p. 26.
10. 'The Romantic Artist', ibid., pp. 32ff.
11. *Communist Manifesto*, in Marx and Engels: *Selected Works*, Vol. I, p. 35.
12. Hazlitt, *Lectures on the English Poets . . .*, p. 203.
13. See Walter Benjamin, *Charles Baudelaire*, p. 171.
14. *Prelude*, X, ll. 273–4, p. 382.
15. 'Bénédiction', FM, p. 28.
16. See JI, Fusées X.
17. See especially R. Vivier, *L'Originalité de Baudelaire*, 1st ed., 1927, reprinted Bruxelles, Palais des Académies, 1952 and 1965; and J. Pommier, *Dans les chemins de Baudelaire*, Paris, José Corti, 1945.
18. FM, p. 31.
19. Defined by Lukács as the third kind of meaning of the word 'nature' in the Romantic period, *History and Class Consciousness*, p. 136.
20. Ibid.
21. See Béguin, *L'Ame romantique . . .*, pp. 68–72.
22. 'Savez-vous pourquoi j'ai si patiemment traduit Poe? *Parcequ'il me ressemblait.* La première fois que j'ai overt un livre de lui, j'ai vu, avec epouvante et ravissement, non seulement des sujets rêvés par moi, mais des PHRASES pensées par moi, et écrites par lui vingt ans auparavant'. To Théophile Thoré, circa 20 June 1864, CG IV, p. 277. My italics.
23. *The Complete Tales and Poems of Edgar Allen Poe*, The Modern Library, New York, Random House, 1938, p. 610.
24. AR, p. 95.
25. Poe, op. cit., p. 611.
26. Ibid., p. 608.

27. 'Alchimie de la douleur', FM, p. 150.
28. CE, pp. 445–6.
29. 21 Jan. 1856, CG I, p. 370.
30. Poe, op. cit., pp. 675–6.
31. CE, pp. 333–4. My italics. Also: 'M. Rousseau tombe dans le fameux défaut moderne, qui naît d'un amour aveugle de la nature, de rien que la nature; il prend une simple étude pour une composition.' CE, p. 336.
32. CE, pp. 143–4.
33. CE, pp. 332–3.
34. Maistre, *Soirées de Saint Pétersbourg*, p. 57.
35. JI, p. 40.
36. See also in this perspective of the creation of a 'super-nature' studies of Diderot's possible influence on Baudelaire: especially Jean Pommier's *Dans les chemins de Baudelaire* and G. May, *Baudelaire et Diderot critiques d'art*, Geneva, Droz, 1957.
37. Mallarmé, 'Variations sur un sujet', *Oeuvres complètes*, ed. Henri Mondor, Paris, Pléiade, 1961, pp. 365–6.
38. Ibid., p. 364.
39. PPP, p. 55.
40. 'Les Plaintes d'un Icare', FM, p. 355.
41. 'Théophile Gautier', AR, p. 161.
42. 'Dialectic of the Marriage of Heaven and Hell', in *The Ringers in the Tower*, p. 55.
43. On these two poems see Bloom, *The Visionary Company*, pp. 178–9.
44. '*The Immortality Ode*', *The Liberal Imagination*, Viking Press, 1942, reprinted in Abrams (ed.), *English Romantic Poets*, pp. 132–3.
45. *Prelude*, X, ll. 764–5, p. 410.
46. Ibid., ll. 769–70.
47. Ibid., l. 417, p. 390.
48. See Ruskin, *Lectures on Architecture and Painting, delivered at Edinburgh in November 1853*, London, Smith, Elder and Co., 1854. It is entertaining to see that Ruskin argues that a square leaf could be ugly – that the tulip-tree, which has square leaves, 'loses much beauty in consequence', (p. 27). Whereas Poe chooses the tulip-tree, precisely because of the unusual shape of its leaves, as 'the most magnificent tree' he has ever seen, to decorate the entrance to his ideal landscape in *Landor's Cottage* (op. cit., p. 619).
49. CE, pp. 95–6.
50. CE, pp. 91–2.
51. CE, p. 276.
52. CE, pp. 108–9.
53. CE, pp. 434–5.
54. CE, pp. 439–40. The same ideal is expressed in 'Tout Entière':
    Et l'harmonie est trop exquise,
    Qui gouverne tout son beau corps,
    Pour que l'impuissante analyse
    En note les hombreux accords.
55. He praises Barbier who 'dans un langage enflammé' proclaims 'la sainteté de l'insurrection de 1830' and sang 'les misères de l'Angletere et de l'Irlande', despite 'ses rimes insuffisantes': 'l'art fut désormais insépara-

ble de le morale et de l'utilité', even though there was at that time the siren's song of a '*voluptuosisme* armé de mille instruments et de mille ruses'. AR, pp. 184–5.
56. AR, p. 184.
57. AR, pp. 294–7.
58. I do not want to take the space to argue a case brilliantly proved by Professor Ruff, in Parts III, IV and V of *L'Esprit du Mal et l'esthétique baudelairienne*, Paris, Colin, 1955. His study, conducted along *chronological lines*, shows the continuous oscillation, in Baudelaire's life and thought, from high to low, but also the continuity of a core of feeling: 'Dans l'ordre de la foi comme dans l'ordre de l'esthétique, il y a chez Baudelaire une oscillation. Mais ni dans l'un ni dans l'autre elle n'obéit à un rythme égal et régulier. Des deux côtés il y a une base fixe que Baudelaire n'abondonne jamais complètement, même quand il cède momentanément à l'attraction contraire. L'esthétique de "l'âme" et de la "naïveté" est toujours la sienne, celle de l'art pour l'art ne doit jamais être comprise sans cette restriction au moins mentale.' (p. 185). See also the discussion of "L'Ecole Païenne" pp. 233–4 and that of the 'Exposition Universelle de 1855', pp. 265–8.
59. AR, p. 471.
60. JOPR III, pp. 189 and 195.
61. JOPR III, pp. 187–8.
62. Are God and Nature then at strife,
That Nature lends such evil dreams?
So careful of the type she seems,
So careless of the single life.
'In Memoriam', LV. In *The Works of Alfred Tennyson*, London, Strahan & Co., 1872, Vol. IV, p. 84.
63. AR, p. 185.
64. History and Class-Consciousness, p. 137.
65. Ibid., p. 139.
66. Ibid., pp. 139–40.

PART ONE (B)

1. Hegel, *Werke* I, pp. 173–4. Quoted by Lukács, 'Reification and the Consciousness of the Proletariat', *History and Class-Consciousness*, p. 141.
2. See René Wellek, 'Romanticism Re-examined', in Northrop Frye (ed.), *Romanticism Reconsidered*, esp. pp. 129–30, where Romanticism is described as being essentially 'the concern for the reconciliation of subject and object, man and nature, consciousness and unconsciousness'.

CHAPTER 5

3. Rousseau, *Oeuvres complètes*, Paris, Pléiade, 1954, Vol. I, pp. 1045–8.
4. See Marcel Raymond, *Jean-Jacques Rousseau, La quête de soi et la rêverie*, esp. pp. 177–85.

5. 'Tintern Abbey', *Poetical Works*, II, p. 260.
6. 'Frost at Midnight', *The Complete Poetical Works of S. T. Coleridge*, ed. E. H. Coleridge, 2 vols, Oxford, Clarendon Press, 1912, Vol. I, pp. 240–1.
7. *Prelude*, V, ll. 404–9, p. 158.
8. *Biographia Literaria*, Vol. I, p. 184.
9. *The Statesman's Manual*, quoted by I. A. Richards, *Coleridge on Imagination*, London, Kegan Paul, 1934, pp. 52–3.
10. Quoted by Walter Pater, *Appreciations*, London, Macmillan, 1889, p. 73.
11. *Complete Poetical Works*, I, pp. 364–5.
12. *Poetical Works*, IV, p. 467.
13. Ibid., p. 464.
14. Jones, *The Egotistical Sublime*, p. 32.
15. Quoted by John Jones, ibid., p. 26.
16. *Anima Poetae*, ed. E. H. Coleridge, London, Heinemann, 1895, p. 184.
17. 'Dejection Ode', ll. 56–66, *Complete Poetical Works*, I, p. 365.
18. 'Intimations of Immortality', ll. 140–53, *Poetical Works*, IV, p. 283.
19. *Notebooks* . . . , ed. Kathleen Coburn, 3017, 1958.
20. PA, pp. 33–4.
21. Verlaine, *Oeuvres poétiques complètes*, ed. Y.-G. Le Dantec, Paris, Pléiade, 1962, p. 196.
22. FM, p. 135.
23. FM, p. 136.
24. Richard, *Poésie et profondeur*, Paris, Le Seuil, 1955, p. 148.
25. PPP, pp. 11–12. My italics.

CHAPTER 6

1. Walter Benjamin, *Charles Baudelaire* . . . , p. 148.
2. *Prelude*, V, ll. 619–29, p. 170.
3. Ibid., VIII, ll. 84–101, p. 268. See also ll. 101–19.
4. 'Intimations of Immortality' ll. 62–5, *Poetical Works*, IV, p. 281.
5. Ibid., ll. 119–21, p. 282.
6. Ibid., ll. 126–9, p. 283.
7. FM, p. 141.
8. FM, p. 34.
9. FM, p. 47.
10. Benjamin, op. cit., p. 141.
11. See ibid., pp. 140–2, esp. note 68.
12. See ibid., p. 142.
13. *Sens et non-sens*, p. 25.
   *Baudelaire's word in 'Correspondances': 'une mystérieuse et *profonde* unité'.
14. *Prelude*, VIII, ll. 428–36.
15. *The Complete Philosophical Works of Sigmund Freud*, trans. James Strachey, London, Hogarth Press, 1955, Vol. XVIII, pp. 24–33.
16. Notably in Proust. Involuntary memory, the 'breath of prehistory' surrounding the object, as Walter Benjamin calls it, is Proust's attempt to

recreate, on an individualistic level, by seeking for 'profondeur' in the past rather than in the meeting between consciousness and nature, the 'aura' that was lost in Baudelaire's time. One could also discuss Mallarmé's notion of 'suggestiveness', Bergson's concept of 'grâce', in this perspective.
17. FM, p. 149.
18. Benjamin, op. cit., p. 147.
19. *Our Mutual Friend*, Book I, Chapter eleven: 'Podsnappery'.
20. FM, p. 142.
21. Merleau-Ponty, *Sens et non-sens*, p. 30.
22. See Part Three of this work.
23. *Aurélia*, in Nerval, *Oeuvres*, Paris, Pléiade, 2 vols, 1961, I, pp. 366–7.
24. *A la recherche du temps perdu*, Paris, Pléiade, 1962, Vol. II, p. 760.
25. FM, p. 262.
26. T. S. Eliot, quoted by P. Quennell, 'Baudelaire and the Symbolists', *Criterion*, Jan 1930, pp. 357–8.
27. PPP, pp. 163–4.

CHAPTER 7

1. Kleist, quoted in Thomas Mann's *Doctor Faustus*.
2. *The Logic of Hegel*, translated from the Encyclopaedia of Sciences by W. Wallace, 2nd ed., Oxford, 1904, pp. 54–7. Both quotations are to be found in G. Hartmann, 'Romanticism and Anti-Self-Consciousness', in *Beyond Formalism*, pp. 300–1.
3. PA, pp. 3–5.
4. CG II, pp. 276, 283 and 286.
5. JOPR I, pp. 226–31.
6. JI, pp. 21–2.
7. Milton's Satan, whom Baudelaire hails as the ideal type of virile beauty, was also, in Blake, the agent of energy.
8. 'Théophile Gautier', AR, p. 172. For a fine discussion of how pain becomes transmuted into joy in Baudelaire, see Du Bos's commentary on 'Recueillement', in *Approximations*, 5ème Série, pp. 1022–3.
9. FM, p. 71.
10. 'Le Vieux Saltimbanque', PPP, pp. 43–4.
11. *Prelude*, VII, ll. 598–619, p. 256.
12. FM, pp. 98–9.
13. *Prelude*, XIII, ll. 53–65, p. 482.
14. FM, pp. 173–4.
15. 'With every step he took, with every thud of his foot on the granite of the pavement, there leapt up as though out of the earth a Mr. Golyadkin precisely the same, perfectly alike, and of a revolting depravity of heart. And all these precisely similar Golyadkins set to running after one another as soon as they appeared, and stretched in a long chain like a file of geese, hobbling after the real Mr. Golyadkin, so there was nowhere to escape from these duplicates – so that Mr. Golyadkin, who was in every way deserving of compassion, was breathless with terror; so that at last a

terrible multitude of duplicates had sprung into being. . . .' 'The Double' in *The Eternal Husband and other Stories*, trans. Constance Garnett, Heinemann, 1917, pp. 232–3.
16. 'Le Gouffre', FM, p. 354.
17. Hegel, *Phenomenology of Mind*, translated with an Introduction and Notes by J. B. Baillie, London, Allen and Unwin, 1931, p. 237.
18. *Biographia Literaria*, I, p. 202.
19. *Salon de 1859*, CE, pp. 274–5.
20. *Notes nouvelles sur Edgar Poe*, NHE, p. xv.
21. *Le Peintre de la vie moderne*, AR, pp. 64–5.
22. *Werke I*, pp. 173–4. Quoted by Lukács, 'Reification . . ., *History and Class-Consciousness*, p. 141.
23. FM, p. 54.
24. FM, p. 59.
25. AR, pp. 159–60.
26. *Le Peintre de la vie moderne*, AR, pp. 65–6.
27. *Biographia Literaria*, II, p. 10.
28. Wordsworth, *Poetical Works*, II, p. 399.
29. *Biographia Literaria*, II, pp. 49–50.
30. Ibid., p. 50.
31. Ibid., pp. 39–40.
32. Ibid., pp. 19–20.
33. Quoted in ibid., p. 51.
34. AR, p. 165.
35. See Northrop Frye, 'The Drunken Boat', in *Romanticism Reconsidered*, esp. pp. 14 and 22.
36. FM, p. 366.
37. PA, p. 52. For a discussion of Baudelaire's use of language, see J.-P. Richard's fine article in *Poésie et profondeur*, pp. 161–2.
38. AR, p. 165.
39. Hubert, *L'Esthétique des 'Fleurs du Mal', essai sur l'ambiguité poétique*, Genève, Pierre Cailler, 1953, p. 62.
40. FM, p. 180.
41. See J. D. Hubert, op. cit., esp. first chapter.
42. Quoted by E. and J. Crépet, *Charles Baudelaire*, Paris, Messein, 1907, pp. 242–3. The passage comes from an article in the *Musée des Deux Mondes*, 1 Sep. 1876. It was re-used in a short story, 'Dux', *Bonshommes*, Paris, Charpentier, 1889.
43. CG II, 11 Feb. 1859, pp. 265–6.
44. FM, pp. 175–6.
45. T. S. Eliot, 'Baudelaire', in *Selected Essays*, Faber, 1951, p. 426. Erich Auerbach has finely analysed how Baudelaire combines a sublime tone with images, vocabulary and occasional rhythms of the low and the trivial. See 'The Aesthetic Dignity of the *Fleurs du Mal*', in *Scenes from the Drama of European Literature, Six Essays*, Meridian Books, 1959.
46. 'Michael', ll. 46–8. *Poetical Works*, II, p. 82. Quoted by Coleridge, in *Biographia Literaria* as an example of successful pastoral poetry.
47. FM, p. 178.
48. *Prelude*, VII, ll. 655–8, p. 258.

49. Ibid., ll. 658–61.
50. Ibid., ll. 707–11, p. 260.
51. PPP, pp. 41–3.
52. Letter to Fernand Desnoyers, 1855, CG I, p. 323.
53. JI, p. 9.
54. FM, p. 170.

CHAPTER 8

1. *The Waste Land, a Facsimile* ... ed. Valerie Eliot, London, Faber and Faber, 1971. I take the liberty not to reproduce the bars crossing off the lines.
2. *Prelude*, XI, ll. 171–80, pp. 438–40. My italics.
3. FM, p. 167.
4. FM, p. 345.
5. *Biographia Literaria* I, pp. 166–7.
6. Eliot, op. cit., p. 69.
7. Ibid., p. 67.
8. FM, p. 233.
9. 'Reification and the Consciousness of the Proletariat', op. cit., p. 140.
10. *Phenomenology of Mind*, p. 239.
11. *Prelude*, X, ll. 916–18, p. 420.
12. Ibid., X, ll. 922–4.

PART TWO

CHAPTER 9

1. Théodore de Banville, *Lettres chimériques*, Paris, Charpentier, 1885, pp. 278–84.
2. Baudelaire, article on *Les Martyrs ridicules* (Lettres Chimériques, Paris, Charpentier, 1885) AR, p. 425.
3. Letter of 7 Apr 1855.
4. Letter of 9 Dec 1856.
5. Letter to Vigny, 12 or 13 Dec 1861.
6. From an article intended for *Le Pays*, 1857, which owing to the prosecution of the *Fleurs* did not appear until 1860. Reprinted in *Poésie et Poètes*, A. Lemerre, 1906, pp. 97–123.
7. The most authoritative studies are, beside the Crépet-Blin ed. of *Fleurs du Mal*, Corti, 1942, reprinted 1950, rehandled by G. Blin and C. Pichois 1st vol. 1968; Prince Ourousoff, *Le Tombeau de Baudelaire*, Paris, 1896; L. F. Benedetto, 'L'Architecture des *Fleurs du Mal*' in *Zeitschrift für französische Sprache und Literatur*, Vol. 39, 1912; R. Vivier, *L'Originalité de Baudelaire*, Bruxelles, Palais des Académies, 1927, reprinted 1952; A. Feuillerat 'L'Architecture des *Fleurs du Mal*', Studies by Members of the French Department of Yale University, *Yale Romanic Studies*, No.

XVIII, New Haven and London, 1941; R.-B. Chérix, *Essai d'une critique intégrale: Commentaire des 'Fleurs du Mal'*, Genève, Cailler, 1949; M. Turnell, *Baudelaire: a Study of his Poetry*, London, Hamish Hamilton, 1953; M. A. Ruff, *L'Esprit du Mal et l'esthétique baudelairienne*; L.-J. Austin, *L'Univers poétique de Baudelaire*, Paris, Mercure de France, 1956; D. J. Mossop, *Baudelaire's Tragic Hero, a Study of the Architecture of 'Les Fleurs du Mal'*, Oxford, Oxford University Press, 1961. See also E. Starkie's appendix, 'The Architecture of the *Fleurs du Mal*', in *Baudelaire*, London, Faber and Faber, 1957, pp. 569–74; M. A. Ruff, in *Revue d'Histoire littéraraire de la France*, 1930, on 'L'Architecture des *Fleurs du Mal*', pp. 51–69 and 393–402; and Marc Séguin, 'Génie des *Fleurs du Mal*', Paris, Messein, 1938.
8. Vivier, op. cit., p. 78.
9. Feuillerat, op. cit., p. 67.
10. *Salon de 1846*, CE, p. 92.
11. CE, p. 103.
12. Along guide-lines traced by M. A. Ruff in his 1930 articles.
13. CE, p. 99.
14. CE, p. 110.
15. CE, 105.
16. On this see M. A. Ruff's 'Postface' to the Pauvert edition on the *Fleurs du Mal*, 1957.
17. Letter to Victor de Mars, spring 1855. Victor de Mars was to publish 11 poems of Baudelaire's in the *Revue des Deux Mondes*. Quoted by Feuillerat, op. cit., pp. 38–9.
18. FM, p. 152.
19. Ibid., p. 119.
20. Feuillerat, op. cit., pp. 79–80.
21. See Th. Gautier's Préface to the 1868 edition of the *Fleurs*, and M. A. Ruff's *Baudelaire, l'homme et l'oeuvre*, Paris, Hatier, 1955, pp. 110–14.
22. CE, p. 97.
23. CE, p. 120.
24. CF. 'Tout entière'. . . . 'Pour que l'impuissante analyse/En note les nombreux accords'. FM, p. 91.
25. CE, pp. 112–13.
26. Turnell, op cit., pp. 224–5.
27. Austin, op. cit., p. 153.
28. Pommier, *La Mystique de Baudelaire*, Les Belles Lettres, 1932.
29. Austin, op. cit., p. 54.
30. Ibid., p. 112.
31. Blin, *Baudelaire*, Paris, Gallimard, 1939, pp. 193–207.
32. Ruff, *L'Esprit du Mal* . . . , p. 289.
33. Ibid., p. 314.
34. Reliquat du Dossier des *Fleurs du Mal*, FM, p. 437.
35. Quoted by L.-J. Austin, op. cit., p. 299. Mallarmé, *Oeuvres complètes*, p. 872.
36. FM, p. 60.
37. FM, p. 263.

38. FM, pp. 213–14.
39. *Les Fleurs du Mal*, ed. Michel Lévy, 1868, pp. 37–8.
40. FM, p. 49.
41. Ibid.
42. FM, pp. 52–3.
43. FM, p. 54.
44. FM, p. 59.
45. FM, p. 40.
46. FM, p. 30.
47. Ibid.
48. FM, p. 54.
49. FM, p. 59. My italics.
50. Martin Turnell cannot think why it should come where it does, nor indeed why it should be there at all.
51. FM, p. 60.
52. FM, p. 63.
53. FM, p. 69.
54. FM, p. 64.
55. FM, p. 67.
56. FM, p. 64.
57. FM, p. 76.
58. FM, p. 73.
59. FM, p. 74.
60. FM, p. 79.
61. FM, p. 65.
62. FM, p. 71.
63. Au détour d'un sentier une charogne infâme
    Sur un lit semé de cailloux,

    Les jambes en l'air, comme une femme lubrique,
    Brûlante et suant les poisons,
    Ouvrait, d'une facon nonchalante et cynique
    Son ventre plein d'exhalaisons . . .
64. FM, p. 72.
65. FM, p. 81.
66. FM, p. 82.
67. FM, p. 87.
68. FM, p. 88.
69. FM, p. 54.
70. FM, p. 55.
71. FM, p. 58.
72. FM, p. 41.
73. 'Le Mauvais Moine', FM, p. 44.
74. 'De Profundis Clamavi', FM, p. 73.
75. 'Semper Eadem', FM, p. 89.
76. FM, p. 56.
77. With Marie it happens in 'Chant d'automne':

    'Ah! laissez-moi, mon front posé sur vos genoux,

> Goûter, en regrettant l'été blanc et torride,
> De l'arrière-saison le rayon jaune et doux!' (FM, p. 119.)

78. FM, p. 89.
79. FM, p. 91.
80. FM, p. 93.
81. FM, pp. 100–1.
82. FM, p. 103.
83. FM, p. 118.
84. FM, p. 156.
85. Reliquat de Dossier des *Fleurs du Mal*, 'Notes et Documents pour mon avocat', FM, p. 435.
86. FM, p. 105.
87. FM, p. 117.
88. FM, p. 45.
89. FM, p. 107.
90. 'Le Serpent qui danse', FM, p. 69.
91. FM, p. 106.
92. FM, p. 59.
93. FM, p. 94.
94. FM, p. 156.
95. FM, pp. 152–3.
96. FM, p. 162.
97. FM, p. 163.
98. FM, p. 151.
99. This is also true of Madame Bovary, on whom Flaubert passes this comment: 'Etant de tempérament plus sentimentale qu'artiste, cherchant des émotions, et non des paysages.'
100. FM, p. 155.

CHAPTER 10

1. FM, p. 194.
2. FM, pp. 191–2.
3. PPP, pp. 129–30.
4. PPP, p. 107.
5. PPP, pp. 94–5.
6. PPP, p. 99.
7. FM, p. 279.
8. FM, p. 319.
9. 'Prométhée délivré', JOPR, p. 238.
10. Ibid., p. 240.
11. 'Théophile Gautier', AR, pp. 157–9.
12. *Les Drames et les romans honnêtes*, AR, p. 284.
13. AR, p. 285.
14. 'A Arsène Houssaye', PPP VI.
15. *L'Art philosophique*, AR, p. 119.

PART THREE

CHAPTER 11

1. 'Du Vin et du haschisch' was published in the *Messager de l'Assemblée*, 7, 8, 11 and 12 Mar 1851. Towards 1857, Baudelaire started rehandling the material: he wrote 'Le Poëme du haschisch' and 'Un Mangeur d'opium' which were eventually published under the title *Les Paradis artificiels*, 2 June 1860. The 1869 editors joined 'Du Vin et du haschisch' to their edition of *Les Paradis artificiels*.
   The larger, mature work, is that which concerns us, because Baudelaire's insight into drugs is so much deeper there, extended to more of life; also, because it is there that the translation from De Quincey's *Confessions* first appears. However, we must keep open the option to draw upon 'Du Vin et du haschisch' were relevant. Despite the shift in perspective from one work to the next, the early essay shades and complements, rather than contradicts, the later one.
2. 'Théophile Gautier', AR, pp. 149–50.
3. 'Quelques caricaturistes français', CE, pp. 417–18.
4. CE, p. 413.
5. *Salon de 1859*, CE, p. 284.
6. Valéry, 'Situation de Baudelaire', *Variétés* II, *Oeuvres* I, Paris, Pléiade, 1957, pp. 598–13; T. S. Eliot, 'From Poe to Valéry', New York, Harcourt Brace, 1948. Also of great use are W. T. Bandy, 'New Lights on Baudelaire and Poe', *Yale French Studies*, No. 10, pp. 65–9; C. P. Cambiaire, *The Influence of Edgar Allan Poe in France*, New York, Stechert, 1927; Charles du Bos, 'Poe and the French Mind', *Athenaeum*, 7 Jan 1921, pp. 26–7 and 14 Jan 1921, pp. 54–5; Y.-G. Le Dantec, 'Baudelaire traducteur', *Le Correspondant*, 25 Dec 1931, pp. 895–908 and 10 Jan 1932, pp. 98–112; Georges Poulet, 'L'Univers circonscrit d'Edgar Poe', *Les Temps Modernes*, CXIV–CXV, June–July 1955, pp. 2179–204; and Patrick F. Quinn, *The French Face of Edgar Poe*, Carbondale, Southern Illinois University Press, 1957.
7. Poe, in *The Complete Tales and Poems*, p. 231, and Baudelaire, NHE, p. 337.
8. On this subject of breathing in Baudelaire, see the fine chapter 'Le Souffle chez Baudelaire', in Jean Prévost's *Baudelaire, Essai sur l'inspiration et la création poétique*, Paris, Mercure de France, 1953 (reprinted 1963).
9. *Literary Essays of Ezra Pound*, London, Faber and Faber, 1960, p. 157.
10. *Le Peintre de la vie moderne* was written between November 1859 and February 1860. *Les Paradis artificiels* were written or rewritten between 1858 and 1860.
11. *Edgar Allan Poe, sa vie et ses ouvrages*, JOPR I, p. 293.
12. PA, p. 195.
13. AR, p. 60.
14. PA, p. 162.
15. AR, pp. 70–1.
16. AR, p. 71.

17. AR, pp. 71–2.
18. AR, p. 109.
19. *Confessions of an English Opium-Eater*, De Quincey's *Collected Writings*, new and enlarged edition by David Masson, 14 vols, London, A. & C. Black, 1890, Vol. III, pp. 390–1.
20. PA, p. 114.
21. '... Les soleils mouillés/De ces ciels brouillés/Pour mon esprit ont les charmes/Si mystérieux/De tes traîtres yeux/Brillant à travers leurs larmes ...' The word 'mystérieux' is the same in both, and so is the sense of a land of heart's desire where there is no separation between the world outside and the world inside.
22. FM, p. 116.
23. JI, p. 61.
24. AR, p. 83.
25. PA, pp. 33–4.
26. PA, p. 319.
27. PA, p. 319.
28. 'A quoi bon la critique?', *Salon de 1846*, CE, p. 87.
29. AR, p. 203.
30. AR, pp. 203–4.
31. Each was written without the knowledge of the others.
32. The very words he adds to his translation from De Quincey.
33. AR, p. 206.
34. *Salon de 1859*, CE, p. 298. The italics are mine.
35. 'Théophile Gautier', AR, p. 159.
36. 'Exposition universelle de 1855', CE, p. 251.
37. 'Du Vin et du haschisch', PA, p. 214.
38. *Salon de 1859*, CE, pp. 280 and 283–4.
39. 'Le Poëme du haschisch', PA, pp. 52–3, pp. 376–7.
40. *Salon de 1859*, CE, p. 274.
41. JI, p. 24.
42. PA, p. 51.
43. PA, p. 51.
43. 'Le Cygne', FM, pp. 167–9.
44. The same rhythms and rhymes too: Andromaque could rhyme with 'baraques' and 'flaques', and 'Fûts/confus' is in fact the same rhyming as 'Pyrrhus/Hélénus'.
45. My italics.
46. *Salon de 1859*, CE p. 279.
47. AR, p. 106. My italics.
48. *Salon de 1846*, CE, p. 144. My italics. See also 'Le Confiteor de l'artiste': 'Nature, enchanteresse sans pitié, rivale toujours victorieuse, laisse-moi! Cesse de tenter mes désirs et mon orgueil! l'étude du beau est un duel où l'artiste crie de frayeur avant d'être vaincu.'
49. *Du Vin et du haschisch*, PA, p. 215.
50. FM, p. 225.
51. JI, p. 38.
52. *Richard Wagner et 'Tannhäuser'*, AR, p. 206.
53. *Le Peintre de la vie moderne*, AR, p. 71.

54. From what I say in this chapter on Baudelaire's sense of imagination, it should be clear that I very much disagree with the conclusions which G. T. Clapton reaches in his study of Baudelaire and De Quincey:

> ... Baudelaire a voulu faire plus [que traduire fidèlement], mêler ses propres impressions à celles de De Quincey. Ici il faut s'avouer surpris. La contribution de Baudelaire à la psychologie du mangeur d'opium et à ses rêves, ses constructions imaginatives, ses révélations, est extrêmement mince ... Baudelaire ... se borne à faire ça et là un petit commentaire moral et tant soit peu prêcheur sur certains aspects très généraux de la nervosité du malade, commentaire qui souligne si l'on veut, les obsessions du traducteur lui-même, ses luttes et ses remords, mais qui n'ajoute rien à la littérature proprement dite de la maladie qu'il examine. On pourrait même affirmer ... que Baudelaire, malgré sa connaissance de l'opium, n'avait pas une très grande expérience des rêves causés par l'opium.... Baudelaire ne semble pas inondé de cette abondance de matière rêvée et s'attache plutôt, par préférence ou par impuissance, aux observations morales qu'il fait ou qu'il souligne ... ... (Baudelaire) ne possédait pas l'imagination somptueuse de De Quincey. Les heures de rêverie silencieuse qu'il a passées n'étaient guère traversées de vastes cortèges d'images comme chez De Quincey mais de conceptions purement égoïstes calquées sur des souvenirs littéraires et bornées à certains motifs. Car l'imagination de Baudelaire était entravée par des préoccupations d'un autre ordre. Elle n'avait ni la force ni la souplesse nécessaires pour effacer les douleurs de sa vie quotidienne et pour lui offrir une consolation vraiment durable. Elle se débattait plutôt dans le cercle étroit de ses propres obsessions. En ce sens, cette imagination est toujours restée presque exclusivement personnelle.

G. T. Clapton, *Baudelaire et De Quincey*, Paris, Les Belles Lettres, Etudes françaises, October 1931, 26th *cahier*, pp. 117–20. Such a sense of imagination as Clapton exhibits here seems to me shallow and 'Romantic' in the pejorative sense of the word.

CHAPTER 12

1. JI, p. 58.
2. *The Affliction of Childhood, Collected Writings*, Vol. I, p. 48.
3. *Confessions ...*, *Collected Writings*, Vol. III, pp. 315–16.
4. JI, p. 85.
5. PPP, p. 89.
6. *Introduction to the World of Strife, Collected Writings*, Vol. I, pp. 59–60.
7. *Confessions ...* , p. 392.
8. PA, p. 116.
9. PA, p. 115.
10. *Confessions ...* , p. 394.
11. 'For opium (like the bee, that extracts its materials indiscriminately from roses and from the soot of chimneys) can overrule all feelings into a compliance with the master-key'. Ibid., p. 393.

12. Ibid., pp. 409–10.
13. Ibid., p. 446.
14. 'Infant Literature', *Collected Writings*, Vol. I, pp. 121–2.
15. *Confessions* . . ., pp. 392–3. How spurious this 'means of consolation' is one realises by confronting this with texts that try to face the reality of poverty: Engels' *Conditions of the English Working-class* in 1844; Mrs Gaskell's *Mary Barton*; or Charles Kingsley's *Alton Locke* – to mention but a few major ones.
16. PPP, pp. 170–2.
17. FM, pp. 210–11.
18. 'Du Vin et du haschisch', PA, p. 205.
19. PA, p. 215.
20. PA, p. 231.
21. PPP, pp. 76–7. These two paragraphs were revised in 1864, under the impact of 'The Man of the Crowd'. The quotation from La Bruyère was used by Poe as the epigraph to his story, and the word 'prostitution', though Baudelaire's own word, may have been inspired by the behaviour of the old man in the story. He is continuously looking for customers and takes an obvious erotic delight in being mixed in the crowd. He reminds one of Sartre's Autodidacte in *La Nausée*.
22. 'Les Tentations, ou Eros, Plutus et la Gloire', PPP, p. 67.
23. JI, p. 92.
24. It is confirmed by Prévost's chapter on 'sympathy' in Baudelaire, *Baudelaire, Essai sur l'inspiration et la création poétique*.
25. De Quincey's *Collected Writings*, Vol. XIII, pp. 334–5.
26. There is an instructive episode in which he tells how his brother and himself made themselves governors of imaginary islands. They were also at that time waging war against Lancashire factory boys. And De Quincey says that the anguish of reality was as nothing compared to that which responsibility to his 'moonshine' world gave him: 'Long contemplation of a shadow, earnest study for the welfare of that shadow, sympathy with the wounded sensibilities of that shadow under accumulated wrongs, these bitter experiences, nursed by brooding thought, had gradually frozen that shadow into a rigour of reality far denser than the material realities of brass or granite.' Op. cit., Vol. I, p. 92 'Introduction to the World of Strife'.
27. *The Affliction of Childhood*, *Collected Writings*, Vol. I, pp. 47–8.
28. *L'Oeuvre et la vie de Delacroix*, AR, pp. 27–8.
29. JI, p. 8.
30. JI, pp. 79–80.
31. *L'Homme des foules*, NHF, p. 56.
32. 'Les Foules' PPP, pp. 33–4. The two prose poems which follow, 'Les Veuves' and 'Le Vieux Saltimbanque' are beautiful illustrations of what Baudelaire states here.
33. *Le Peintre de la vie moderne*, AR, pp. 61–2.
34. FM, pp. 178–9. Italics mine.
35. JI, p. 7.
36. Maistre, *Les Soirées de Saint-Pétersbourg*, 8th *Entretien*, pp. 256–8.

37. JI, p. 32. My italics.
38. JI, p. 13.
39. *Soirées de Saint-Pétersbourg*, p. 258.

CHAPTER 13

1. FM, p. 257.
2. *Suspiria*, 1845 Blackwood edn., pp. 483–484.
3. Poe, *The Complete Tales and Poems*, p. 649.
4. Nerval, *Oeuvres*, I, p. 359.
5. FM, p. 261.
6. PPP, pp. 54–5.
7. *Collected Writings*, Vol. I, p. 42.
8. *Suspiria*, 1845 Blackwood edn., pp. 483–484.
9. FM, p. 262.
10. Mallarmé 'Les Fenêtres', *Oeuvres complètes*. p. 33.
11. PA, pp. 17–18.
12. PA, 66–7.
13. JI, p. 34.
14. It is interesting to notice that T. S. Eliot's Narcissus (in 'The Death of St Narcissus') is more like Baudelaire's, than like Valéry's:

    By the river
    His eyes were aware of the pointed corners of his eyes
    And his hands of the tips of his fingers . . .

    although this image:

    First he was sure that he had been a tree
    Twisting its branches among each other
    And tangling its roots among each other.

    is amazingly similar to the image from Valéry's 'Narcisse':

    L'arbre immense vers l'arbre étend ses membres sombres
    Et cherche affreusement l'arbre qui disparait.
    Mon âme ainsi se perd dans sa propre forêt . . .
15. *Aurélia, Oeuvres*, I, p. 364.
16. Ibid., p. 385.
17. It would be fascinating to follow what happens to this Ulysses myth in T. S. Eliot's 'Death by Water' in the original drafts of *The Waste Land*, and in Pound's first *Canto*.
18. Nerval, op. cit., p. 364. See also p. 412.
19. De Quincey, *Collected Writings*, Vol. III, pp. 209–11.
20. Ibid., p. 230.
21. Ibid., p. 231.
22. Nerval, op. cit., p. 1170.
23. Ibid., p. 1094.

24. *Collected Writings*, Vol. III, p. 434.
25. Ibid., p. 443.

CHAPTER 14

1. 'Le Joueur généreux', PPP, p. 104. This poem follows 'La Fausse monnaie'.
2. 'Le Jeu', FM, p. 188.
3. PA, pp. 57–60.
4. *Collected Writings*, Vol. III, p. 394.
5. PA, p. 24. My italics except for the word *'hasard'*.
6. PA, p. 139.
7. *The English Mail-Coach, Collected Writings*, Vol. XIII, p. 330.
8. *Confessions, Collected Writings*, Vol. III, p. 433.
9. FM, p. 156.
10. PA, 132–3. My italics.
11. Ibid.
12. PA, p. 68.
13. PA, p. 238.
14. Quoted by Charles du Bos, 'Meditation on the life of Baudelaire', *Baudelaire, a Collection of Critical Essays* ed. H. Peyre, Englewood Cliffs, N.J., Prentice-Hall, 1962, p. 45.
15. 'Au Lecteur', FM, p. 21.
16. PA, p. 227.
17. PA, p. 65.
18. 'A Madame Aupick', 11 Janvier 1858, CG II, p. 120.
19. JI, pp. 45–6.
20. JI, p. 44.
21. *L'Oeuvre et la vie de Delacroix*, AR, p. 18.
22. AR, p. 32.
23. 'L'Horloge', p. 77.
24. Nerval, *Correspondance, Oeuvres*, Vol. I, p. 1110.
25. PA, p. 224.
26. Balzac, *Melmoth réconcilié, Oeuvres complètes*, Vol. IX, Paris, Pléiade pp. 296–7.
27. CE, p. 379.
28. PA, pp. 64–5.
29. PA, p. 61.
30. PA, p. 66.
31. PPP, p. 14.
32. JI, p. 93.
33. JI, p. 25.
34. *Conseils aux jeunes littérateurs*, AR, pp. 274–5.
35. PA, p. 69.
36. JI, p. 87.
37. FM, p. 384.
38. 'Reification and the Consciousness of the Proletariat', *History and Class-Consciousness*, p. 181.
39. See Lukács's analysis, ibid., pp. 159–86.
40. Ibid., p. 158.

NOTES

41. *Collected Writings*, Vol. XIII, pp. 350–1.
42. See Hillis Miller's discussion of 'Achilles and the Tortoise' in the essay on De Quincey, in *The Disappearance of God: Five Nineteenth-Century Writers*, Cambridge, Mass., Harvard University Press, 1963, pp. 53–5. See also Lukács's discussion of the rigid dialectics of the Eleatic philosophers, op. cit., p. 180.
43. Tennyson, *In Memoriam*, II, in *Works*, Vol. IV, p. 7.
44. 'L'Horloge', FM, p. 157.
45. Lukács, op. cit., p. 180.
46. *Suspiria de Profundis, Collected Writings*, Vol. XIII, pp. 338–9.
47. *The English Mail Coach, Collected Writings*, Vol. XIII, pp. 271–2. My italics.
48. JI, p. 78.
49. JI, p. 39.
50. JI, p. 40.
51. *The English Mail-Coach*, pp. 311–12. My italics.
52. Ibid., p. 313.
53. Bergson, *Essai sur les Données immédiates de la conscience*, 1889.
54. *The English Mail-Coach*, pp. 315–16.
55. Ibid., p. 329.
56. Ibid., p. 320.
57. Ibid., p. 321.
58. Ibid., p. 325.
59. Ibid., p. 317.
60. Quoted by Lukács, op. cit., pp. 158–9.
61. Nerval, *Oeuvres*, I, p. 362.
62. W. B. Yeats, *Collected Poems*, London, Macmillan, 1958, p. 293.
63. *Confessions* . . . , *Collected Writings*, Vol. III, pp. 355–6.
64. *The Affliction of Childhood, Collected Writings*, Vol. I, p. 43.
65. *Collected Writings*, Vol. III, p. 444.
66. Ibid., p. 292.
67. 'Vision of Life', in *Suspiria, Collected Writings*, Vol. XIII, p. 350.
68. *Un Mangeur d'opium*, PA, pp. 161–2.
69. *Suspiria*, pp. 347–8.
70. Ibid., pp. 346–8.
71. PA, p. 179.
72. Poulet, *Etudes sur le temps humain*, Paris, Plon, 1949, pp. 278–307. The first version of De Quincey's *Confessions* had been made available in translation by Musset in 1828.
73. Poulet underlines the fact that the image of the 'excentric circles' is not explicitly there in Goethe. He suggests that Gautier thus develops Goethe's implicit metaphor in the light of the undulatory theory of light which had just been confirmed by Fresnel's discoveries (pp. 300–1).
74. *Le Panthéon, peintures murales*, September 1848, and *L'Art Moderne*, p. 70. Quoted by Poulet, pp. 298–9.
75. *Revue de Paris*, Mars 1852. Quoted by Poulet, p. 299.
76. Poe, *The Power of Words, The Complete Tales and Poems*, pp. 441–2.
77. PA, p. 124.
78. JI, p. 103. See on this Pierre Emmanuel, *Baudelaire*, Paris, Desclée de Brouwer, 1967, collection: 'Les Ecrivains devant Dieu', pp. 96–7.

79. Maistre, *Les Soirées de Saint-Pétersbourg* . . . , pp. 165–6.
80. 'Du bonheur et du guignon dans les débuts', AR, pp. 268–9. This text is an early one (1846): as such, it is clearly more optimistic in mood than *Les Paradis artificiels*. But the continuity of the images is most striking. The poem 'Le Guignon' (traditionally difficult to interpret) was written in 1851. It links 'Du Bonheur et du guignon . . .' to the later meditations on fate and freedom, testifying to the permanence of Baudelaire's preoccupation with the subject.
81. FM, p. 46. The poem is made up of the translation of two fragments, one from Longfellow ('A Psalm of Life'), the other from Gray's 'Elegy written in a Country Churchyard'. It seems to me impossible to understand the disparity between quatrains and tercets unless the tercets (in which Gray's values are entirely transformed) are seen as the baneful result of the failure of the quatrains.
82. 'Le Vierge . . . , *Plusieurs sonnets*, Pléiade Mallarmé, pp. 67–8.
83. Beckett, *Proust*, New York, Grove Press, 1966, p. 49.
84. 'Bénédiction', FM, p. 9.
85. 'L'Ennemi', FM, p. 16.

CONCLUSION

1. *Soirées* . . . , op. cit., pp. 220–2.
2. Ibid., pp. 287–8.
3. Charles du Bos makes beautiful points about this, quoting Paul Bourget. See his 'Méditation sur la vie de Baudelaire', *Approximations*, pp. 183–237.
4. Maistre, op. cit., p. 298.
5. Pierre Jean Jouve, *Tombeau de Baudelaire*, Paris, Le Seuil, 1958, pp. 16–18.
6. Ibid., p. 16.
7. The 'satanic' aspect of Baudelaire has been so extensively explored that I will take the reader's knowledge of it for granted. For a fine, short statement of it, see especially P. J. Jouve again, pp. 18–29.
8. JI, p. 38.
9. 'Fleurs du Mal'. FM, p. 226.
10. *Soirées* . . . , op cit., p. 222.
11. Ibid., p. 223.
12. Ibid., p. 273.
13. Ibid., p. 316.
14. Ibid., p. 315.
15. Letter to Madame Paul Maurice 24 May 1865.
16. FM, p. 337.
17. 'La Chevelure', FM, p. 63.
18. 'Le Couvercle', FM, p. 345.
19. *Salon de 1846*, CE, pp. 115–17.
20. FM, p. 32.
21. 'Théodore de Banville', AR, pp. 353–4.

Bibliography

I. BIBLIOGRAPHICAL WORKS

In chronological order. Only the more significant ones have been retained.

Peyre, H., *Connaissance de Baudelaire*, Paris, José Corti, 1951.
Bandy, W. T., *Répertoire des écrits sur Baudelaire*, Madison, 1953.
Pichois, Claude, 'Esquisse d'un état présent des études sur Baudelaire', *L'Information littéraire*, Jan.–Feb. 1958, pp. 8–17.
Carter, A. E., *Baudelaire et la critique française, 1868–1917*, Columbia, University of South Carolina Press, 1963.
Bandy, W. T., Patty, S., and Hoy, P. C., *Bulletin baudelairien*, Vanderbilt University, Nashville, Tennessee, 1965 (continuing W. T. Bandy's work; see above).
Austin, L.-J., 'Etat présent des études sur Baudelaire', *Forum for Modern Language Studies*, Vol. III, No. 4, St Andrews University, October 1967, pp. 352–69.
Cargo, R. T., *Baudelaire Criticism 1950–1967. A Bibliography with Critical Commentary*, University of Alabama Press, 1968.
Pichois, Claude, 'Pour une prospective baudelairienne', *Etudes Littéraires*, Vol. I, No. 1, Université de Laval, Apr. 1968, pp. 125–8.
Pichois, Claude et Kopp, R., *Compte-rendu des publications des années Baudelaire et nouvel état présent*, Neuchâtel, Éditions de la Baconnière, 1969.
Trottman, P. M., *French Criticism of Charles Baudelaire, Themes and Ideas, 1918–1940*, Ann Arbor, University Microfilms, 1971. Continues Carter (No. 4); available on microfilm or xerox.
Pichois, Claude, 'Le dossier Baudelaire', in *Romantisme*, No. 8, Flammarion, 1974, pp. 92–102.

On specific works, see the excellent bibliographies of the José Corti editions of FM, JI and PPP. The Baudelaire Bibliography (over 20,000 titles) has been assembled over the years by W. T. Bandy and is in the 'W. T. Bandy Center for Baudelaire Studies', Vanderbilt University, Nashville, Tennessee.'

II. EDITIONS OF BAUDELAIRE'S COLLECTED WORKS

(In Chronological order.)

Oeuvres complètes, definitive edition, with a Foreword by Théophile Gautier, Paris, Michel Lévy, 'Bibliothèque contemporaine':
  I.   *Les Fleurs du Mal*, 1868.
  II. *Curiosités esthétiques*, 1868.
  III. *L'Art romantique*, 1869.
  IV. *Petits poëmes en prose – Les Paradis artificiels – La Fanfarlo – Le jeune enchanteur*, 1869.

Oeuvres complètes, edited by Jacques Crépet in collaboration with Claude Pichois for the last volumes, 19 vols, Paris, Conard. (This is the standard edition, and a masterpiece of scholarship and dedication.)
  Les Fleurs du Mal, 1922.
  Curiosites esthétiques, 1923.
  L'Art romantique, 1925.
  Petits poëmes en prose, 1926.
  Les Paradis artificiels – La Fanfarlo, 1928.
  Histoires extraordinaires, 1932.
  Nouvelles histoires extraordinaires, 1933.
  Aventures d'Arthur Gordon Pym, 1934.
  Euréka, 1936.
  Histoires grotesques et sérieuses, 1937.
  Juvenilia - Oeuvres posthumes – Reliquiae, 3 vols, 1939–1952.
  Correspondance générale, 6 vols, 1947–1953.
  There are doubts as to whether Baudelaire would have arranged his artistic and literary criticism under the headings *'Curiosités esthétiques'* and *'Art romantique'*, and some editions of the collected works, unlike Crépet's, have arranged it in chronological order.

Oeuvres complètes, first edited by F. F. Gautier then by Y.-G. Le Dantec, Paris, NRF, began to appear in 1918, never completed. It has become:

Oeuvres complètes, edited and annotated by Y.-G. Le Dantec édition révisée, completed and annotated by Claude Pichois, Bibliothèque de la Pléiade, 5th edition, revised 1968. New ed. in 2 vols presented and annotated by Claude Pichois, Vol. I 1975, Vol. II 1977.

Oeuvres complètes, in chronological order, ed. Claude Pichois, 2 vols, Paris, Le Club du Meilleur Livre ('Le Nombre d'or'), 1955.

Oeuvres complètes, ed. Yves Florenne, centenary edition, 3 vols, Paris, Club francais du Livre. Yves Florenne has substituted a doubtful chronological order of composition for the chronological order of publication, and used for FM the 1857 instead of the 1861 text.

Oeuvres complètes, ed. Marcel Raymond, Lausanne, La Guilde du Livre, 1967.

Oeuvres complètes, ed. with preface and notes by Marcel A. Ruff, Paris, Le Seuil, Collection l'Intégrale, 1967.

III. INDIVIDUAL WORKS

a. *Les Fleurs du Mal*
Les Fleurs du Mal, ed. J. Crépet and G. Blin, Paris, José Corti, 1942, reprinted 1950. The Conard edition of FM (No. 13) was based on the 1861 text, posthumously established by Gautier and other friends of Baudelaire to include eleven new poems. The authority of this text being more and more in doubt (Le Dantec had rejected it for his NRF edition), and J. Crépet being dissatisfied with his work, he issued this. It is a first-class edition, further improved and extended by G. Blin and C. Pichois, again at José Corti. The first volume, including text, variants and documents relative to the trial, was published in 1968. The next two, to include comments are still due for publication.
Les Fleurs du Mal, Les Épaves, Les Sylves, avec certaines images qui ont pu inspirer le poète, ed. J. Pommier and C. Pichois, Paris, Club des Libraires de France, 1959, reprint, A. Ballard, 1967.
Les Fleurs du Mal, ed. Antoine Adam, Paris, Classiques Garnier, 1961.
Les Fleurs du Mal, a facsimile of the 1857 edition, Genève, Slatkine Reprints, 1968 (on Jean Pommier's suggestion).

b. *Petits poèmes en prose*
Petits poèmes en prose, ed. H. Lemaitre, Paris, Classiques Garnier, 1958.
Petits poèmes en prose, edited with an Introduction and Notes by Melvin Zimmerman, Manchester University Press, 1968, French Classics.
Petits poèmes en prose, critical edition by R. Kopp, Paris, José Corti, 1969.

c. *Journaux intimes*
Journaux intimes, critical edition by J. Crépet and G. Blin, Paris, José Corti, 1949. This is also Crépet improving on his Conard work, and, like the Corti FM, is a remarkable piece of editing.

d. *Les Paradis artificiels – La Fanfarlo*
Les Paradis artificiels, ed. C. Pichois, Paris, Club du Meilleur Livre, 1961. Reprinted in 1964 in Livre de Poche.
Un Mangeur d'opium, [Avec le texte parallèle des] 'Confessions of an English Opium-Eater'; [et des] 'Suspiria de profundis' de Thomas de Quincey;

critical edition by Michèle Staüble-Lipman Wulf, Neuchâtel, La Baconnière, Langages-Etudes baudelairiennes VI–VII, Paris, Payot, 1976.
La Fanfarlo, ed. and annotated by C. Pichois, Monaco, Éditions du Rocher, 1957.

e. *Criticism, translations, etc.*
Le Salon de 1845 de Charles Baudelaire, a critical edition with introduction and notes by André Ferran, Toulouse, éditions de l'Archer, 1933.
Le Salon de 1846, ed. David Kelley, Oxford University Press, 1975.
Selected Critical Studies of Baudelaire, ed. D. Parmée, Cambridge University Press, 1949.

Baudelaire critique d'art – Curiosités esthétiques, poèmes oeuvres, diverses lettres, Editions Bernard Gherbrant, Paris, Club des Libraires de France, 1956.
Critique littéraire et musicale, ed. C. Pichois, Paris, Armand Colin, 1961.
Curiosités esthétiques – L'Art romantique, ed H. Lemaitre, Paris, Classiques Garnier, 1962.
Critique d'art, ed. C. Pichois, 2 vols, Paris, Armand Colin, 1965.
Edgar Allan Poe, sa vie et ses ouvrages, edited by W. T. Bandy, Toronto, University of Toronto Press, 1973.

f. *Correspondance*
Lettres inédites aux siens, ed. Philippe Auserve, Paris, Grasset, 1966.
Correspondance, ed. and annotated by C. Pichois with the collaboration of Jean Ziegler, Paris, Gallimard, 1973. Bibliothèque de la Pléiade, Vols 247 and 248. Includes Auserve's edition of 1966 (corrected), Crépet's of 1947–1953, plus many unpublished letters.

g. *Documents*
Carnet, facsimile reproduction, édition de la Sirène, 1920.
Dessins de Baudelaire, facsimile reproduction (Jacomet), with a notice by J. Crépet, Paris, Gallimard, 1927.
Bibliothèque Nationale – Charles Baudelaire – Exposition organisée pour le centenaire des Fleurs du Mal, Paris, 1957.
Album Baudelaire, iconography ed. Claude Pichois, Paris, Gallimard, 1974.

IV. TRANSLATIONS INTO ENGLISH

Les Fleurs du Mal – Petits poëmes en prose – Les Paradis artificiels, translated by Arthur Symons, London, Casanova Society, 1925.
Poems – a Translation of 'Les Fleurs du Mal', by R. Campbell, London, 1952.
'The Voyage' and other Versions of Poems by Baudelaire, by Robert Lowell, illustrated by S. Nolan, London, 1968.

For a list of translations from the Prose Poems, see R. Kopp's edition of the *Petits Poèmes en prose*. Translations of other works likely to be of use are, in chronological order:

The Mirror of Art; Critical Studies by Charles Baudelaire, edited by J. Mayne, London, Phaidon Press, 1955.
Hyslop, L. B. and F. E., *Baudelaire, a Self-Portrait*, London and New York, 1957.
Baudelaire as a Literary Critic, Selected Essays introduced and translated by L. B. Hyslop and F. E. Hyslop, Jr, the Pennsylvania State University Press, University Park, Pennsylvania, 1964.
The Painter of Modern Life and Other Essays by Charles Baudelaire, edited by J. Mayne, London, Phaidon Press, 1964.
Art in Paris, 1845–1862, Salons and Other Exhibitions, reviewed by Charles Baudelaire, edited by J. Mayne, London, Phaidon Press, 1965.

V. BIOGRAPHICAL WORKS

In alphabetical order of authors.

Asselineau, Charles, *Charles Baudelaire, sa Vie et son Oeuvre*, Paris, Lemerre, 1869.
Billy, André, *La Présidente et ses amis*, Paris, Flammarion, 1945.
Cladel, Léon, 'Dux', *Bonshommes*, Paris, Charpentier, 1879.
Crépet, Eugène, *Charles Baudelaire, Oeuvres posthumes et Correspondances inédites*, with a biographical study by ..., Paris, Quantin, 1887.
Crépet, Eugène, *Charles Baudelaire*, a biographical study by Eugène Crépet, revised by Jacques Crépet, followed by Asselineau's *Baudelairiana*, Paris, Léon Vanier, 1906. (This is a mine of documents and the basis of all later biographies, unfortunately not available commercially.)
Crépet, J. et Pichois, Claude, *Baudelaire et Asselineau*, Paris, Nizet, 1953.
Feuillerat, A., *Baudelaire et sa mère*, Montréal, Variétés, 1944.
Feuillerat, A., *Baudelaire et la Belle aux cheveux d'or*, Paris, José Corti, 1944.
Mouquet, J. et Bandy, W. T., *Baudelaire en 1848*, Paris, Emile-Paul, 1946.
Nadar, F., *Charles Baudelaire intime*, Paris, Blaizot, 1911.
Pichois, Claude, *Baudelaire à Paris*, photographed by Maurice Rue, Paris, Hachette, Albums Littéraires de la France, 1967.
Pichois, Claude, *Baudelaire – Etudes et témoignages*, Neuchâtel, Editions de la Baconnière, 1967.
Pichois, Claude, et Ruchon, F., *Iconographie de Charles Baudelaire*, Genève, Pierre Cailler, 1960.
Porché, F., *La Vie douloureuse de Charles Baudelaire*, Paris, Plon, 1926. Revised and augmented as: *Baudelaire, histoire d'une âme*, Paris, Flammarion, 1945, reprinted 1967.
Porché, F., *Baudelaire et la Présidente*, Genève, Editions du Milieu du Monde, 1941; reprint, Gallimard, Paris, 1959.
Starkie, Enid, *Baudelaire*, London, Faber and Faber, 1957 and New York, New Directions, 1958.

VI. CRITICAL WORKS ON BAUDELAIRE

Apollinaire, G., 'Baudelaire dans le domaine public', *Nord-Sud*, 15 Mai 1917.
Apollinaire, G., 'Préface' à l'*Oeuvre poétique* de Baudelaire, Paris, Mercure de France, Bibliothèque des Curieux, 1917.
Aragon, L., *Chroniques du Bel Canto*, Genève, Skira, 1957, pp. 171–81.
Arnold, P. *Le Dieu de Baudelaire*, Paris, Savel, 1947.
Auerbach, E., 'The Aesthetic Dignity of the *Fleurs du Mal*', *The Hopkins Review*, IV, 1. Autumn 1950. Reprinted in *Scenes from the Drama of European Literature, Six Essays*, Meridian Books, 1959.
Austin, L.-J., *L'Univers poétique de Baudelaire*, Paris, Mercure de France, 1956.
Bandy, W. T., *Baudelaire Judged by his Contemporaries, 1845–1867*, New York, Publications of the Institute of French Studies, 1933, and Paris, José Corti.
Bandy, W. T., and Pichois, Claude, *Baudelaire devant ses contemporains*, Monaco, Editions du Rocher, 1957.
Bandy, W. T., and Pichois, Claude, *Baudelaire devant ses contemporains*, Paris, Union générale d'édition, 1967, Coll. 10/18, revised ed. of the prededing.
Bandy, W. T., 'Baudelaire et Edgar Poe: Vue rétrospective', *Revue de littérature comparée*, 41, 1967, pp. 180–94. A similar article was printed in RHLF in 1967, special number on Baudelaire.
Banville, Th. de, 'Note sur les *Petits Poëmes en Prosé, Le Boulevard*, 31 Aug. 1862.
Banville, Th. de, 'Charles Baudelaire', in *Petites études, mes souvenirs*, Paris, Charpentier, 1885.
Banville, Th. de, 'XXXVIII, Baudelaire, à Paul Bourget', in *Lettres chimériques*, Paris, Charpentier, 1885.
Barbey d'Aurevilly, J., 'Les Fleurs du Mal', to be published in *Le Pays*, 1857. The article was suppressed because of the prosecution of the book, and included in *Poësie et Poëtes*, Paris, A. Lemerre, 1906.
Barbey d'Aurevilly, J., 'M. Charles Baudelaire', in *Les Oeuvres et les hommes*, III, 1862.
Barrès, Maurice, 'Méditation spirituelle sur Charles Baudelaire', *L'Aube*, Juin 1896.
Barrès, Maurice, 'La Folie de Charles Baudelaire'. *Les Taches d'encre*, Nov.–Déc. 1884, reprinted Paris, Les Ecrivains réunis, 1926.
Bataille, Georges, 'Baudelaire mis à nu: l'analyse de Sartre et l'essence de la poésie', *Critique*, 8–9 Janv.–Fév. 1947, pp. 3–27.
Bataille, Georges, *La Littérature et le mal: Emily Bronte – Baudelaire – Michelet – Blake – Sade – Proust – Kafka – Genet*, Editions de Minuit, 1957.
Baudelaire et son rayonnement, Table Ronde, 232, 1967. Articles by Pierre Emmanuel, Stanislas Fumet, Christian Dedet, Xavier Tilliette, Henri Lemaitre, Enid Starkie ('Baudelaire et l'Angleterre', 51–70), Albert Sonnenfeld, Yvan Christ, etc.
Baudelaire, Actes du colloque de Nice, 25–7 Mai 1967, Annales de la Faculté de Lettres et Sciences humaines de Nice, 1968.

Baudelaire, Revue d'Histoire Littéraire de la France, Apr.–June 1967, reprinted by the Publications de la Société d'Histoire littéraire de la France, Armand Colin, 1967.

Béguin, Albert, *L'Ame romantique et le rêve: Essai sur le romantisme allemand et la poésie française*, Paris, José Corti, 1937, reprinted 1963.

Béguin, Albert, 'Baudelaire et l'autobiographie', *Poésie 45*, 28, Oct.–Nov. 1945, pp. 51–7.

Benedetto, L. F., 'L'Architecture des *Fleurs du Mal*', *Zeitschrift für französische Sprache und Literatur*, Vol. 39, 1912, pp. 18–70.

Benjamin, Walter, 'Uber einige Motive bei Baudelaire', *Illuminations*, Frankfurt, Suhrkamp Verlag, 1961, pp. 201–54.

Benjamin, Walter, *Charles Baudelaire: a Lyric Poet in the Era of Capitalism*, translated from the German by Harry Zohn, London, NLB, 1973.

Bennett, J. D., *Baudelaire, a Criticism*, Princeton University Press, 1944, 2nd ed., Princeton and London, 1946. (Connections between 'Le Cygne' and Eliot's 'What the Thunder said' and *Gerontion*, pp. 103–4.)

Blanchot, Maurice, 'L'Echec de Baudelaire', *L'Arche*, 24 (pp. 80–91) and 25 (pp. 97–107).

Blanchot, Maurice, *La Part du Feu*, Paris, Gallimard, 1949, pp. 137–56.

Blin, Georges, *Baudelaire*, Paris, Gallimard, 1939.

Blin, Georges, *Le Sadisme de Baudelaire*, Paris, José Corti, 1948.

Blin, Georges, 'Les Fleurs de l'impossible', *Revue des Sciences Humaines*, 127, 1967, pp. 461–5.

Bonnefoy, Yves, *L'Improbable*, Paris, Mercure de France, 1959. ('*Les Fleurs du Mal*', pp. 35–48.)

Bopp, L., *Psychologie des Fleurs du Mal*, 4 vols, in 5 vols, Geneva, Droz, Publications romanes et françaises, 1964–69.

Bourget, Paul, *Essais de psychologie contemporaine*, Paris, Lemerre, 1885, reprinted Plon-Nourrit, 1901. Definitive edition Plon, 1926, Vol. 1, pp. 2–33.

Brunetière, C., *Nouveaux Essais de Littérature contemporaine*, Paris, Calmann-Lévy, 1895.

Bush, William (editor), *Regards sur Baudelaire*: Actes du colloque de London (Canada), the Department of French, the University of Western Ontario, 1970. Communications by W. T. Bandy . . . (and others). Ed. William Bush, with the collaboration of J. C. Vilquin. Situations, No. 29, 1974.

Butor, Michel, *'Les Paradis artificiels'*, *Essais sur les modernes*, Paris, Editions de Minuit, 1960, reprinted in Collection Idées, Gallimard, 1964.

Butor, Michel, *Histoire extraordinaire, Essai sur un rêve de Baudelaire*, Gallimard, 1961.

Chérix, R.–B., *Essai d'une critique intégrale: Commentaire des 'Fleurs du Mal'*, Genève, Pierre Cailler, 1949.

Chisholm, A. R., *Towards Hérodiade. A Literary Genealogy*, Melbourne University Press, 1934.

Clapton, G. T., 'Balzac, Baudelaire and Maturin', *French Quarterly*, June 1930, pp. 66–84 and 97–115.

Clapton, G. T., *Baudelaire et De Quincey*, Paris, Les Belles Lettres, Etudes françaises, Octobre 1931, 26th *cahier*, 122 pp.

Clapton, G. T., *Baudelaire the Tragic Sophist*, London and Edinburgh, Oliver and Boyd, 1934.

Claudel, Paul, *Positions et propositions*, 2 vols, Paris, Gallimard, 1928–34.
Coléno, Alice, *Les Portes d'ivoire, métaphysique et poésie*, Paris, Plon, 1948.
Crépet, Jacques, 'Baudelaire et Delacroix', Preface to a reprint of Baudelaire's study on Delacroix, Paris, P. Kieffer, 1928.
Crépet, Jacques, *Propos sur Baudelaire*, ed. and annotated by C. Pichois, Foreword by Jean Pommier, Paris, Mercure de France, 1957.
Croce, B., *Poesia e non poesia, note sulla letteratura europea del secolo decimonono*, Bari, Laterza, 1923, pp. 252–65.
Decaunes, Luc, *Charles Baudelaire*, Paris, Seghers, 'Poètes d'aujourd'hui', No. 31, 1963.
Deux années d'études baudelairiennes, suppl. to *Studi francesi*, No. 39, 1969.
Du Bos, Charles, 'Méditation sur la vie de Baudelaire', *Approximations*, 1st series, Plon, 1922; 'Introduction a *Mon coeur mis à nu*', 5th series, Corréa, 1932. Both reprinted in *Approximations* (7th series), Paris, Fayard, 1965.
Eliot, T. S., 'Baudelaire', *Selected Essays*, London, Faber and Faber, 1951
Eliot, T. S., 'Baudelaire in our Time', *Essays Ancient and Modern*, London, Faber, 1936.
Emmanuel, Pierre, *Baudelaire*, Paris, Desclée de Brouwer, 1967, Collection 'Les Ecrivains devant Dieu'.
Etudes baudelairiennes, Neuchâtel, A la Baconnière, Coll. Langages:
 I. No. 9.
 II. 1971. Contains unpublished material, including Baudelaire's translation of *Hiawatha*, etc., and important critical studies.
 III. 1973. *Hommage à W. T. Bandy*. Foreword by de Jean Pommier and 19 studies by Baudelaire scholars.
 IV—V. 1973. *Lettres à Charles Baudelaire*, ed. Claude Pichois with the collaboration of Vincenette Pichois.
 VI–VII., 1976. See section IIId.
L'Esprit créateur, special number on Baudelaire, Vol. 13, No. 2, 1973. Eight studies on Baudelaire.
Europe 456–7, articles on Baudelaire to commemorate the centenary year of his death (1967) by Raymond Jean, Max-Pol Fouchet, Charles Mauron, etc.
Fairlie, Alison, 'Some Remarks on Baudelaire's "Poème du haschisch"', *The French Mind, Studies in Honour of Gustave Rudler*, Oxford, Clarendon Press, 1952.
Fairlie, Alison, *Baudelaire: 'Les Fleurs du Mal'*, London, Edward Arnold, 1960, reprinted 1963, 1965.
Ferran, André, *L'Esthétique de Baudelaire*, Paris, Hachette, 1933, reprinted 1967.
Feuillerat, Albert, 'L'Architecture des *Fleurs du Mal*', Studies by Members of the French Department of Yale University, Yale Romanic Studies, New Haven and London, Yale University Press, 1941, pp. 221–330.
Fondane, B., *Baudelaire et l'expérience du gouffre*, Paris, Seghers, 1947.
Fumet, Stanislas, *Notre Baudelaire*, Paris, Plon-Nourrit, 1926.
Gautier, Th., 'Notice aux *Fleurs du Mal*', Michel Lévy edition, *Oeuvres complètes*, 1868.
Gide, André, 'Preface aux *Fleurs du Mal*', *Incidences*, Paris, 1924, NRF.
Gilman, Margaret, *Baudelaire the Critic*, New York, Columbia University Press, 1943. (Also several useful articles in the *Romanic Review*.)

Gourmont, Rémy de, 'Baudelaire et le Songe d'Athalie', *Promenades Littéraires*, 2ème série, Paris, Mercure de France, 1906.

Grava, A., *L'Aspect métaphysique du mal dans l'oeuvre littéraire de Charles Baudelaire et d'Edgar Allan Poe*, University of Nebraska Studies, new series No. 15, 1956.

Guillain de Benouville, P., *Baudelaire, le trop chrétien*, Foreword by Charles du Bos, Paris, Grasset, 1936.

Hamburger, Michael, *The Truth of Poetry. Tensions in Modern Poetry from Baudelaire to the 1960s*, Weidenfeld and Nicolson, 1969.

Hubert, J.-D., *L'Esthétique des 'Fleurs du Mal'*, Genève, Pierre Cailler, 1953.

Huyghe, René, et al., *Baudelaire*, Paris, Hachette, 1961, Collection 'Génies et Réalités'.

Huysmans, J.-K., *A Rebours*, Paris, Fasquelle, 1884.

Hyslop, L. B. (editor), *Baudelaire as a Love Poet and other Essays commemorating the Centenary of the Death of the Poet*, Pennsylvania State University Press, 1969.

Jakobson, Roman, et Lévi-Strauss, Claude, '"Les Chats" de Charles Baudelaire', *L'Homme*, Janv.-Avril 1962, pp. 5–21.

Jouve, P. J. *Le Tombeau de Baudelaire*, Neuchâtel, La Baconnière, 1942.

Jouve, P. J., 'Le Spleen de Paris', *Mercure de France*, 1er Nov. 1954, pp. 32–9, reprinted as an Introduction to the *Oeuvres complètes* at the Club du Meilleur Livre.

Kahn, Gustave, *Charles Baudelaire, son oeuvre, document pour l'histoire de la littérature française*, Paris, Edition de la Nouvelle Revue Critique, 1925.

Kelley, D. J., 'Deux aspects du *Salon de 1846* de Baudelaire: la dédicace Aux Bourgeois et la Couleur', *Forum for Modern Language Studies*, Oct., V, n° 4, pp. 331–46.

Kelley, D. J., '"Modernité" in Baudelaire's art criticism', in *The Artist and the Writer in France*; Essays in honour of Jean Seznek; edited by Francis Haskell, Anthony Levi and Robert Shackleton, Oxford, Clarendon Press, 1974, pp. 138–52.

Laforgue, Jules, 'Notes sur Baudelaire', *Mélanges postumes,* Paris, Mercure de France, 1903, and in *Dragées*, La Connaissance, 1920, pp. 133–56.

Laforgue, R., *L'Echec de Baudelaire*, Paris, Denoël, 1931.

Leakey, F. W., *Baudelaire and Nature*, Manchester University Press, 1969.

Leakey, F. W., 'Baudelaire: The Poet as Moralist', in: *Studies in Modern French Literature*, presented to P. Mansell Jones by Pupils, Colleagues and Friends, edited by L. J. Austin, Garnet Rees and Eugene Vinaver, Manchester University Press, 1961, pp. 196–219.

Leconte de Lisle, '*Les Fleurs du Mal*', *La Revue Européenne*, 1er Déc. 1861.

Le Dantec, Y.-G., 'Baudelaire traducteur', *Le Correspondant*, 25 Dec. 1931, pp. 895–908, and 10 Jan. 1932, pp. 98–112.

Le Dantec, Y.-G., 'Sur le poème en prose', *Revue des Deux Mondes*, 1st Oct. 1948, pp. 760–6.

Lemonnier, L., 'Sainte-Beuve et Baudelaire', *Revue Hebdomadaire*, IX, 17 Sept. 1924, pp. 431–52.

Lemonnier, L., *Les Traducteurs d'Edgar Poe en France de 1845 à 1875: Charles Baudelaire*, Paris, Presses Universitaires, 1928.

Lemonnier, L., *Edgar Poe et la critique française*, Paris, Presses Universitaires, 1928.
Lemonnier, L., *Enquêtes sur Baudelaire*, Paris, Crès, 1929.
Mansell-Jones, P., *Baudelaire*, Cambridge, Bowes and Bowes, 1952 (and New Haven University Press).
Mansell-Jones, P., *The Background of French Poetry*, Cambridge University Press, 1951
Mansell-Jones, P., 'Poe, Baudelaire and Mallarmé: a Problem of Literary Judgment', *Modern Language Review*, XXXIX, July 1944.
Maritain, Jacques, *Frontières de la poésie*, Paris, Rouart, 1935.
Maritain, Jacques, *Situation de la poésie*, Paris, Desclée de Brouwer, 1938.
Massin, J., *Baudelaire devant la douleur*, Paris, Sequana, 1944. (The first essay only is on Baudelaire).
Massin, J., *Baudelaire entre Dieu et Satan*, Paris, René Julliard, 1945.
Mauriac, F., *De quelques coeurs inquiets: Petits essais de psychologie religieuse*, Paris, Société littéraire de France, 1919.
Mauron, Charles, *La Dernier Baudelaire*, Paris, José Conti, 1966.
May, Gita, *Baudelaire et Diderot critiques d'art*, Genève, Droz, and Paris, Minard, 1957.
Michaud, Guy, *Message poétique du Symbolisme*, Paris, Nizet, 1947, in Vol. I: *L'Aventure poétique*, pp. 43–80: 'Baudelaire poète moderne'.
Milner, Max, *Le Diable dans la littérature française de Cazotte à Baudelaire, 1762–1861*, 2 vols, Paris, José Corti, 1960.
Milner, Max, *Baudelaire, enfer ou ciel, qu'importe!*, Paris, Plon, 1967, coll. 'La Recherche de l'absolu', Vol. 24.
Mossop, D. J., *Baudelaire's Tragic Hero, a Study of the Architecture of 'Les Fleurs du Mal'*, Oxford University Press, 1961.
Mother Mary Alphonsus, *The Influence of Joseph de Maistre on Baudelaire*, Bryn Mawr, 1943.
Murry, J. M., 'Baudelaire', in *Countries of the Mind*, 1st series, Collins, 1922, reprint, Oxford University Press, 1931.
Noejgaard, Morten, *Elévation et expansion, les deux dimensions de Baudelaire*, Odensee University Press, 1973.
Peyre, Henri (editor), *Baudelaire, a Collection of Critical Essays*, Englewood Cliffs., N.J., Prentice-Hall, 1962.
Pia, Pascal, *Baudelaire par lui-même*, Paris, Le Seuil, 1952, coll. 'Les Ecrivains de toujours'.
Pommier, Jean, *La Mystique de Baudelaire*, Paris, Les Belles Lettres, 1932, reprint Genève, Slatkine Reprints, 1967.
Pommier, Jean, *Dans les chemins de Baudelaire*, Paris, José Corti, 1945.
Poulet, Georges, 'Baudelaire', in *Etudes sur le temps humain*, Paris, Plon, 1949.
Poulet, Georges, 'L'Univers circonscrit d'Edgar Poe', *Les Temps Modernes*, CXIV–CXV, June–July 1955, pp. 2179–204.
Poulet, Georges, 'Baudelaire', in *Les Métamorphoses du cercle*, XIV, Paris, Plon, 1961.
Poulet, Georges, 'Baudelaire et la critique d'identification', *Parragone*, 214, 1967, pp. 18–37.

Poulet, Georges, *Qui était Baudelaire?*, A critical essay by ——, with documentary notes by R. Kopp, Geneva, Skira, 1969.
Preuves 207, Baudelaire et la critique d'art, Paris, 1968. Articles by P. Schneider, J. Starobinski, G. Picon, M. Raymond, etc.
Prévost, Jean, *Baudelaire, Essai sur l'inspiration et la création poétique*, Paris, Mercure de France, 1953, reprinted 1963.
Proust, Marcel, 'A propos de Baudelaire', *Nouvelle Revue Française*, June 1921, reprinted in *Chroniques*, Paris, Gallimard, 1927.
Proust, Marcel, *Contre Sainte-Beuve*, Paris, Gallimard, 1954.
Quennell, Peter, *Baudelaire and the Symbolists*, London, Chatto and Windus 1929.
Raymond, Marcel, *De Baudelaire au Surréalisme*, Paris, José Corti, 1953, reprinted 1940, 1963.
Raynaud, E., *Baudelaire et la religion du dandysme*, Paris, Mercure de France, 1918.
Raynaud, Ernest, *Charles Baudelaire*, Paris, Garnier, 1922.
Reynold, Gonzague de, *Charles Baudelaire*, Paris et Genève, Crès, 1920.
Riffaterre, Michael, *Essais de stylistique structurale*, presented and translated by Daniel Delas, Flammarion, 1971, coll. 'Nouvelle bibliothèque scientifique'.
Rhodes, J. A., *The Cult of Beauty in Charles Baudelaire*, 2 vols, New York, Institute of French Studies, Columbia University, 1929.
Richard, J.-P., 'Profondeur de Baudelaire', in *Poésie et profondeur*, Paris, Le Seuil, 1955, pp. 93–162.
Rivière, Jacques, *Etudes*, Paris, NRF, 1911, reprinted 1948.
Ruff, M. A., *L'Esprit du Mal et l'esthétique baudelairienne*, Paris, Armand Colin, 1955, reprinted by Slatkine Reprints, 1972.
Ruff, M. A., *Baudelaire, l'homme et l'oeuvre*, Paris, Hatier-Boivin, 1955, coll. 'Connaissance des Lettres', reprinted 1966, 1967.
Ruff, M. A., 'Baudelaire et le poème en prose', *Zeitschrift für französische Literatur*, Jan. 1967, pp. 116–32. Reprinted as Introduction to the PPP, Garnier-Flammarion, 1967.
Ruff, M. A., 'Postface', *Les Fleurs du Mal*, Paris, Pauvert, 1957.
Sainte-Beuve, 'Des prochaines élections à l'Académie', 20 Jan. 1862, *Le Constitutionnel*, reprinted in the *Nouveaux lundis*, Michel Lévy, 1863.
Sartre, J.-P., 'Baudelaire', Introduction to the *Ecrits intimes*, Paris, Editions du Point du Jour, 1946. Reprinted as *Baudelaire*, Paris, Gallimard, 1947.
Soupault, Philippe, *Baudelaire*, Paris, Les Editions Rieder, 1931.
Spronck, Maurice, *Les Artistes littéraires*, Paris, Calmann-Lévy, 1889.
Studi francesi, Supplemento al No. 39, 1969: *Deux années d'études baudelairiennes* (July 1966–June 1968). With a Foreword by Antoine Fongaro and an 'Introduction' by L.-J. Austin.
Suarès, André, *Trois grands vivants: Cervantès, Tolstoï, Baudelaire*, Paris, Grasset, 1937.
Swinburne, Algernon Charles, Article on Baudelaire in *The Spectator*, 6 Sep 1862, reprinted in *The Complete Works of* ——, Bonchurch Edition, edited by Sir Edmund Gosse and Th. J. Wise, New York, Russell and Russell, 1968, Vol. XIII, pp. 417ff., dated 1861.

Symons Arthur, *Charles Baudelaire, a Study*, London, Matthews, 1920.
Tabarant, A., *La Vie artistique au temps de Baudelaire*, Mercure de France, 2ᵉ ed., 1963.
Thibaudet, Albert, *Intérieurs: Baudelaire, Fromentin, Amiel*, Paris, Plon, 1924.
Thierry, E., Articles on 'Baudelaire', *Moniteur Universel*, 14 July 1857 (Mentions Dante). Reprinted in Vol. I of the Lévy *Oeuvres complètes*.
Tombeau de Baudelaire, Le, Ouvrage collectif précédé d'une Etude sur le texte des 'Fleurs du Mal', commentaire et variantes publiées par le Prince Alexandre Ourousof, suivi d'oeuvres posthumes ou inédites de Charles Baudelaire, et d'un essai iconographique, Paris, Bibliothèque artistique et littéraire, 1896.
Turnell, Martin, *Baudelaire, a Study of his Poetry*, London, Hamish Hamilton, 1953.
Valéry, Paul, 'Situation de Baudelaire', *Revue de France*, 15 Sept. 1924, reprinted in *Variétés II, Oeuvres I*, Paris, Pléiade, 1957, pp. 598–613.
Verlaine, Paul, 'Baudelaire', *L'Art*, 16 Nov. 1865, reprinted in *Oeuvres complètes, Oeuvres posthumes* II, Paris, Albert Messein, 1919–20.
Vivier, R. *L'Originalité de Baudelaire*, 1st ed. 1927, reprinted 1952, then *Nouveau tirage revu par l'auteur de la réimpression en 1952, avec une note, de l'édition de 1927*, Bruxelles, Palais des Académies, 1965.
Vouga, J., *Baudelaire et Joseph de Maistre, Essai*, Paris, José Corti, 1957.
Weinberg, B., *The Limits of Symbolism, Studies of Five Modern French Poets*, University of Chicago Press, 1960.
Zilberberg, Claude, *Une lecture des Fleurs du Mal*, Tours, Mame, 1972, coll. 'Univers sémiotiques'.
Zola, Emile, 'Compte-rendu de l'édition Lévy', *Le Gaulois*, 19 Aug. 1869.

VII OTHER WORKS USED FOR THIS STUDY

Abrams, M. H. (editor), *English Romantic Poets, Modern Essays in Criticism*, London, Oxford, New York, Oxford University Press, 1960.
Abrams, M. H., *Natural Supernaturalism*, Oxford University Press, 1971.
Arnold, Matthew, *Culture and Anarchy*, in *The Complete Prose Works of* ———, edited by R. H. Super, University of Michigan Press, 1965.
Auerbach, E., *Mimesis, The Representation of Reality in Western Culture*, translated from the German by Willard R. Trask, Princeton University Press, 1953.
Bachelard, Gaston, *L'Eau et les rêves: Essai sur l'imagination de la matière*, Paris, José Corti, 1941.
Bachelard, Gaston, *La Poétique de la rêverie*, Paris, Presses Universitaires de France, 1960.
Balzac, H. de, *Oeuvres complètes*, 10 vols, ed. Marcel Bouteron, Bibliothèque de la Pléiade, 1951–66.
Bandy, W. T., *The Influence and Reputation of Edgar Allan Poe in Europe*, Baltimore, Edgar Allan Poe Society, 1962.
Beach, J. W., *The Concept of Nature in Nineteenth-Century English Poetry*, New York, Macmillan, 1936, and Pageant, 1956.

Bertrand, Aloysius, *Gaspard de la nuit*, Paris, La Colombe, 1962, coll. Littérature et Tradition.
Blake, William, *The Poetical Works of* ——, with an Introduction and Textual Notes by J. Sampson, Oxford University Press, 1958.
Bloom, Harold, *The Visionary Company, A Reading of English Romantic Poetry*, London, Faber, 1962.
Bloom, Harold, *The Ringers in the Tower, Studies in Romantic Tradition*, Chicago and London, University of Chicago Press, 1971.
Bonaparte, Marie, *Edgar Poe: Etude psychanalytique*, with a Foreword by Sigmund Freud, 2 vols, Denoël et Steele, 1933.
Bowra, C. M., *The Romantic Imagination*, Cambridge, Mass., Harvard University Press, 1949.
Boyle, R., 'A Free Enquiry into the Vulgar Notion of Nature', and 'An Enquiry into the Final Causes of Natural Things', in *The Philosophical Works of* ——, abridged, etc., by Peter Shaw, London, 1738.
Brierre de Boismont, *Des Hallucinations*, Paris, Baillière, 1845.
Burke, E. *Reflections on the Revolution in France*, edited with an Introduction by C. C. O'Brien, Pelican Classics, 1968.
Burke, E., *Works*, edited by F. C. and J. Rivington, London, 1808, Vol. 1
Byron, George Gordon, Lord, *Poetical Works*, London, Oxford University Press, 1967.
Cambiaire, C. P., *The Influence of Edgar Allan Poe in France*, New York, Stechert, 1927.
Carlyle, Thomas, *Sartor Resartus*, London, World's Classics, 1902.
Cassirer, Ernst, *The Problem of Knowledge: Philosophy, Science and History since Hegel*, translated by William H. Woglom and Charles W. Hendel, New Haven and London, Yale University Press, 1950.
Coleridge, S. T., *The Philosophical Lectures of* ——, edited by Kathleen Coburn, London, Pilot Press, 1949.
Coleridge, S. T., *Complete Poetical Works*, edited by E. H. Coleridge, Oxford, Clarendon Press, 1912.
Coleridge, S. T., *Anima Poetae*, edited by E. H. Coleridge, London, Heinemann, 1895.
Coleridge, S. T., *Biographia Literaria*, edited by J. Shawcross, Oxford University Press, 1907, 2 vols.
Coleridge, S. T., *The Notebooks of* ——, edited by Kathleen Coburn, New York and London, 1957–61.
Crocker, L. G., *Nature and Culture. Ethical Thought in the French Enlightenment*, Baltimore, Johns Hopkins Press, 1963.
Darwin, Charles, *The Origin of Species by Means of Natural Selection*, London, John Murray, 1917.
Darwin, Erasmus, *The Temple of Nature: or, the Origin of Society*, London Jones, 1803.
De Quincey, Thomas, *Collective Writings*, new and enlarged edition by David Masson, 14 vols, London, Adam and Charles Black, 1890.
Dickens, Charles, *Our Mutual Friend*, London, Odhams, with Illustrations by Phiz.
Dostoevsky, F., *The Double*, in *The Eternal Husband and Other Stories*, translated by Constance Garnett, Heinemann, 1917.

Eliot, T. S., 'From Poe to Valéry', New York, Harcourt Brace, 1948. Reprinted in *To Criticize the Critic and Other Writings*, London, Faber and Faber, 1965.

Eliot, T. S., *The Waste Land, a Facsimile and Transcript of the Original Drafts, including the Annotations of Ezra Pound*, edited by Valerie Eliot, London, Faber and Faber, 1971.

Engels, F., *The Condition of the Working-Class in England in 1844*, London, Allen and Unwin, 1892.

Europe, Flaubert, annales du colloque Gustave Flaubert tenu à l'occasion du centenaire de 'L'Education Sentimentale', 25–8 Apr. 1969, Sept.–Oct.–Nov. 1969, Les Ecrivains français réunis.

Flaubert, G. *L'Education Sentimentale*, in *Oeuvres*, Paris, Bibliothèque de la Pléiade, 1951–52, Vol. II.

Freud, Sigmund, *Beyond the Pleasure Principle*, in *The Complete Philosophical Works*, translated by James Strachey, London, Hogarth Press, 1955, Vol. XVIII.

Frye, Northrop (editor), *Romanticism Reconsidered*, Selected Papers from the English Institute, edited with a Foreword by ——, New York and London, Columbia University Press, 1963.

Frye, Northrop, *A Study of English Romanticism*, New York, Random House, 1968.

Greene, E. J. H., *T. S. Eliot et la France*, Etudes de Littérature étrangère et comparée, 29, Paris, Boivin, 1951.

Hartmann, Geoffrey, *Beyond Formalism. Literary Essays 1958–1970*, New Haven and London, Yale University Press, 1970.

Hazlitt, William, *Lectures on the English Poets and The Spirit of the Age*, London and Toronto, J. M. Dent, 1910.

Hegel, G. W. F., *The Phenomenology of Mind*, translated with an Introduction and Notes by J. B. Baillie, London, Allen and Unwin, 1931.

Hegel, G. W. F., *Philosophy of History*, Dover Publications Inc., 1956.

Heisenberg, *La Nature dans la physique contemporaine*, Paris, Gallimard, 1962, coll. Idées.

Hills, W. and Bloom, Harold (editors), *From Sensibility to Romanticism*, Essays presented to Frederick A. Pottle, New York, Oxford University Press, 1965.

Holbach, P.–H. Baron d', *Système de la Nature, ou des Lois du monde physique et du monde moral*, 2 vols, London, 1770. Translated as *Nature and her Laws: as Applicable to the Happiness of Man Living in Society, Contrasted with Superstition and Imaginary Systems*, from the French of M. de Mirabaud, in 2 vols, London, James Watson, 1834.

Jameson, Frederic, *Marxism and Form, Twentieth-Century Dialectical Theories of Literature*, Princeton University Press, 1971.

Johnson, Samuel, *Dictionary*, London, 1765.

Johnson, Samuel, *The History of Rasselas, Prince of Abyssinia*, edited by R. W. Chapman, Oxford, Clarendon Press, 1927.

Jones, John, *The Egotistical Sublime, a History of Wordsworth's Imagination*, London, Chatto and Windus, 1960.

Kermode, Frank, *The Romantic Image*, Routledge and Kegan Paul, 1957.

Kojève, Alexandre, *Introduction à le Lecture de Hegel*, Paris, Gallimard, Bibliothèque des Idées, 1947.

Lamartine, Alphonse de, *Oeuvres poétiques*, Paris, Bibliothèque de la Pléiade, 1963.
Langbaum, Robert, *The Poetry of Experience, the Dramatic Monologue in Modern Literary Tradition*, New York, Random House, 1957.
Laprade, V. de, *Le Sentiment de la nature chez les modernes*, Paris, Didier, 1868.
Lévi-Strauss, Claude, *Race et histoire*, Paris, Plon, 1952.
Lukács, George, *La Théorie du roman*, transl. by Lucien Goldmann, Paris, Gonthier, 1962.
Lukács, George, *The Historical Novel*, London, Merlin Press, 1962.
Lukács, George, *History and Class-Consciousness, Studies in Marxist Dialectics*, translated by Rodney Livingstone, London, Merlin Press, 1971.
Maistre, Joseph de, *Lettres et opuscules inédits*, 2 vols, Paris, A. Vaton, 1851.
Maistre, Joseph de, *Considérations sur la France, suivies par l'Essai sur le principe générateur des constitutions politiques*, Lyon, J. B. Pélagaud & Co., 1852.
Maistre, Joseph de, *Les Soirées de Saint-Pétersbourg, ou Entretiens sur le gouvernement temporel de la Providence*, Paris, La Colombe, 1960, coll. 'Littérature et tradition'.
Maistre, Joseph de, *The Works of* ——, selected, translated and introduced by Jack Lively, London, Allen and Unwin, 1965.
Mallarmé, Stéphane, *Oeuvres complètes*, Paris, Bibliothèque de la Pléiade, 1961.
Malthus, T. E., *An Essay on Population*, 2 vols, London and New York, J. M. Dent and Sons, E. P. Dutton & Co, Inc., 1914, reprinted 1958.
Marx, Karl, *Le Dix-huit Brumaire de Louis Bonaparte*, Editions sociales, 1969.
Marx, Karl, *Les Luttes de classe en France: 1848–1850*, Editions sociales, 1967.
Marx, Karl, *The German Ideology*, edited with Introduction by C. J. Arthur, London. Lawrence and Wishart, 1970, 2 vols.
Marx, Karl and Engels, F., *Selected Works in Two Volumes*, Moscow, Foreign Languages Publishing House, 1951.
Merleau-Ponty, Maurice, *Sens et non-sens*, Paris, Nagel, 1948.
Miller, Joseph Hillis, *The Disappearance of God; Five Nineteenth-Century Writers*, Cambridge, Mass., Harvard University Press, 1963.
Mornet, D., *Le Sentiment de la nature en France de J.-J. Rousseau à Bernardin de Saint-Pierre: Essai sur les rapports de la littérature et des moeurs*, New York, Burt Franklyn n.d., reprinted from the 1907 Paris edition.
Nerval, Gérard de, *Oeuvres*, ed. Albert Béguin and Jean Richier, 2 vols, Paris, Bibliothèque de la Pléiade, 1961.
Pater, Walter, *Appreciations*, London, Macmillan, 1889.
Poe, Edgar Allan, *The Complete Tales and Poems*, The Modern Library, New York, Random House, 1938.
Pope, A., *Essay on Man*, in *The Poems of* ——, Twickenham Text, edited by John Butt, London, Methuen, 1963.
Praz, Mario, *The Romantic Agony*, translated by Angus Davidson, Oxford University Press, 1933.
Praz, Mario, *The Hero in Eclipse in Victorian Fiction*, translated by Angus Davidson, Oxford University Press, 1956.
Proust, Marcel, *A la recherche du temps perdu*, ed. Pierre Clarac and André Ferré, 3 vols. Paris, Bibliothèque de la Pléiade, 1962.

Quinn, P. F., *The French Face of Edgar Poe*, Carbondale, Southern Illinois University Press, 1957.
Raymond, Marcel, *Jean-Jacques Rousseau: la quête de soi et la rêverie*, Paris, José Corti, 1962.
Reynold, M., *The Treatment of Nature in English Poetry from Pope to Wordsworth*, Chicago, 1896.
Richards, I. A., *Coleridge on Imagination*, London, Kegan Paul, 1934.
Rimbaud, Arthur, *Oeuvres complètes*, Paris, Bibliothèque de la Pléiade, 1954.
Rousseau, J.-J., *Oeuvres complètes*, 4 vols, Paris, Bibliothèque de la Pléiade, 1959–69.
Ruskin, J., *Edinburgh Lectures: Lectures on Architecture and Painting* delivered at Edinburgh in November 1853, London, Smith, Elder & Co., 1854.
Sade, Donatien Alphonse François de, marquis, *Idées sur les romans*, 1800, reprinted with a Preface by Frederic Prince, 1945.
Shelly, Percy Bysshe, *The Poetical Works of* ——, edited by William Rossetti, London, E. Moxon, Son & Co., 1887.
Staël, Madame de, *De L'Allemagne, nouvelle édition publiée d'après les manuscrits et les éditions originales, avec des variantes, une introduction, des notices et des notes par le comtesse* J. de Pange *avec le concours de* S. Balayé, Les Grands Écrivains de la France, 5 vols, Paris, Hachette, 1958–60.
Starobinski, J., *Jean-Jacques Rousseau: la transparence et l'obstacle,* Paris Plon, 1957.
Stendhal, (Henri Beyle), *Oeuvres complètes*, 2 vols, Paris, Bibliothèque de la Pléiade, 1952–55.
Stendhal, *Mémoires d'un touriste*, 3 vols Paris, Champion, 1932.
Stovall, F., 'Poe's Debt to Coleridge', *University of Texas Studies in English*, No. 10, July 1930.
Swedenborg, E., *Angelic Wisdom*, London, Swedenborg Society, 1931.
Swedenborg, E., *Heaven and Hell*, id.
Swedenborg, E., *Compendium of Swedenborg's Theological Writings*, id., 1939.
Tennyson, Alfred Lord, *In Memoriam*, in *The Works of* ——, London, Strahan & Co., 1872, Vol. IV.
Toussenel, A., *Le Monde des oiseaux: Ornithologie passionnelle*, 2 vols, Paris, E. Dentu, 1864–66.
Van Tieghem, P., *Le Sentiment de la nature dans le préromantisme européen*, Paris, Nizet, 1960.
Verlaine, Paul, *Oeuvres poétiques complètes*, ed. Y.-G. Le Dantec, Paris, Pléiade, 1962.
Voisine, J., *Jean-Jacques Rousseau en Angleterre à l'époque romantique: les écrits autobiographiques et la légende,* Paris, Etudes de Littérature étrangère et comparée, 31,1956.
Volney, C. F., *La Loi naturelle, ou catéchisme du citoyen français*, a complete critical edition, 1793 and 1826 texts, Gaston-Martin, Paris, Colin, 1934.
Ward, Anthony, *Walter Pater: The Idea in Nature,* London, MacGibbon & Kee, 1966.
Welsh, Alexander, *The Hero of the Waverley Novels*, New Haven and London, Yale University Press, 1963.

Williams, Raymond, *Culture and Society, 1780–1950*, London, Chatto & Windus, 1958.
Willey, B., *The Eighteenth-Century Background: Studies on the Idea of Nature in the Thought of the Period*, London, Chatto & Windus, 1940.
Wimsatt, W. K., *The Verbal Icon: Studies in the meanings of Poetry* [with] two preliminary essays written in collaboration with Monro C. Beardsley, Lexington, [Kentucky], Noonday Press, 1960, (essay on the Structure of Romantic Nature Imagery, pp. 103–16).
Wordsworth, W., *The Prelude*, edited by Ernest de Selincourt, 2nd edition revised by Helen Darbishire, Oxford, Clarendon Press, 1965.
Wordsworth, W., *The Poetical Works of*, edited by E. de Selincourt, 5 vols, Oxford, Clarendon Press, 1940.
Yeats, W. B., *Collected Poems*, London, Macmillan, 1958.

Index

Abrams, M. R., 19, 58
Apuleius, 242
Aristotle, 49
Asselineau, 7, 27, 28
Atala, 15
Aubigné, Agrippa d', 13
Auerbach, 23
Austen, Jane, 18
Austin, Prof. L.-J., 157–9, 161, 162, 179, 286

Baader, Franz von, 21, 75, 76
Balzac, H. de, 13, 24, 48, 50, 66
Balzacian, 178, 189–93 *passim*, 200, 217, 235, 249, 256–61 *passim*
Banville, Th. de, 6, 147, 155
Barbey, d'Aurevilly, 148
Barrès, M., 6
Beckett, S., 284
Béguin, A., 32, 75, 78
Benedetto, L. F., 150
Benjamin, W., 43, 47, 60, 82, 105–13 *passim*
Bergson, H., 269
Berlioz, 213
Bernardin de Saint-Pierre, 13, 39
Blake, 21, 24, 41, 66, 70, 72, 80, 119, 148
Bleak House, 50
Blin, G., 60
Bloom, H., 24, 27, 80
Boileau, 13
Bonald, 32
Bosch, 4
Bourget, P., 68
Boyle, 17, 76
Breton, A., 73

Breughel, 4, 77
Brothers Karamazov, The, 144
Browne, Sir Thomas, 213
Burke, E., 32, 55–7 *passim*, 128
Burkean, 163
Byron, 13, 18, 23, 24, 25, 27, 47, 73, 74, 116, 184

Calonne, A. de, 131
Callot, J., 2
Carlyle, 52
Cassirer, E., 48–9, 62–3
Cavalcanti, G., 204
Cézanne, 109, 112
Chamisso, 43
Champfleury, 29
Chateaubriand, 16, 18, 27, 73, 135
Chénier, A., 18
Cladel, L., 131
Claudel, P., 261
Clough, A., 126
Coleridge, S., 21, 23, 25, 26, 29, 65, 72, 73, 74, 94–9, 100–4 *passim*, 114, 115–16, 121, 123–8, 136, 137–41 *passim*, 195, 220, 234, 250, 294
Comédie humaine, 13
Comte, A., 49, 63–64
Condorcet, 19
Constant, Abbé, 12
Constant, B., 18
Cooper, F., 133
Corbière, T., 113
Cowper, 34
Crime and Punishment, 61
Croce, B., 5
Cruickshank, 84

INDEX

Dante, xi, 3-4
Dantean, 130, 137, 184, 190, 199, 241, 247-9, 286, 295
Darwin, Ch., 49, 63, 86
Delacroix, E., 150-6 *passim*, 160, 200, 214-17 *passim*, 235, 247, 257-8, 295-6
De Quincey, Th., 19, 112, 199, 200, 203, 204-23, 224-37, 241-52, 253-5, 263-83, 286
Desbordes-Valmore, M., 9
Descartes, 92
Desnoyers, 35
Dickens, Ch., 275
Diderot, 13, 27, 28, 31
Divine Comedy, 5
Dostoevsky, F., 120
Du Bellay, 171
Du Bos, Ch., 105, 177, 184
Dupont, P., 10, 30

Eliot, T. S., 13, 73, 113, 132, 137-44, 202, 203, 286, 287
Eschenmayer, 21

Fénelon, 92
Feuillerat, A., 148-9, 150, 151, 152, 157
Fichte, 87
Ficino, 246
Flaubert, G., 19, 32, 44-7, 105, 112, 142, 200
Freud, S., 110
Frye, N., 24, 34, 49, 58, 86, 144

Gautier, Th., 61, 64, 117, 128, 163, 166, 183, 200, 212, 280, 281
Gide, A., 8
Godwin, W., 19
Goethe, 21, 71, 74, 205, 280
Gourmont, R. de, 7
Goya, 84
Guys, C., 200, 204-9

Hartmann, G., 58
Hazlitt, W., 19, 20-1, 22, 23, 40-1, 73
Heart of Darkness, 119

Hegel, 26, 32, 49, 80, 87, 89, 105, 115, 121, 122, 143
Heine, H., 116
Holbach, baron d', 17, 76
Hölderlin, 73, 74
Hubert, J. D., 130
Hugo, V., 3, 60, 116, 150, 151, 217, 246
Huysmans, J.-K., 6, 43, 68

Janin, J., 116
Jarry, A., 3
Jeffrey, F., 19, 73
Johnson, Dr. S., 17, 76
Jones, J., 20, 97
Jouve, P. J., 162, 291

Kant, E., 48-9, 58, 62
Keats, J., 74, 183
Kieser, 21
Kleist, 115

La Bruyère, 232
Laclos, Ch. de, 13
Laforgue, 7, 9, 73, 113
Laforguian, 180, 219, 286
Lamartine, 34, 47-8, 60, 72, 184-5
Langbaum, R., 52, 71
La Rochefoucauld, 37
Lautréamont, 73
Lawrence, D. H., 232-3
Leakey, F. W., Prof., 7-8, 27, 85
Lemaître, J., 6
Le Père Goriot, 46
Liszt, 213
Locke, 70
Lovejoy, A., 15, 16
Lukács, 22, 48-50, 54-8 *passim*, 61-4 *passim*, 83, 87-8, 142, 263, 281, 288

Maistre, J. de, 1, 8, 13, 32-3, 56, 64-6, 78, 238-40, 283, 288-94
Mallarmé, S., 78-9, 113, 121, 161, 284, 286
Malthus, 63-4
Mars, V., 147

INDEX

Marx, K. (and Marxist), 43–58 *passim*, 50, 69, 72, 73, 80
Merleau-Ponty, M., 109
Mill, J. S., 19, 49
Miller, H., 274–5
Millet, F., 37
Milton, 23–6 *passim*, 117,
    Miltonic, 129, 143, 148
Misanthrope, Le, 16
Molière, 29, 135, 201
Montaigne, 15, 93, 219
Mossop, D., 157, 165
Murillo, 2
Musset, A. de, 122

Nadar, O., 1, 7
Napoléon, I, 18, 20, 24, 43, 45, 47
Napoléon III, 45, 47
Nerval, G. de, 112, 184, 242, 243, 247–52 *passim*, 258, 280
Newton, 70. *Newton*, Blake's, 66
Nietzsche, F., 29
Novalis, 15, 105

Oken, 21
Our Mutual Friend, 111, 120, 144
Ovid, 219

Pascal, 13, 59, 105, 232, 260, 261, 289, 293
Passavant, 21
Petrarch, 177
Plato, 29, 49, 141
Pléiade, 13
Plotinus, 139, 140
Poe, E. A., 61, 74, 75–80 *passim*, 86, 116, 121, 179, 200, 202–4, 205, 212, 214, 216, 232, 236, 242, 243, 247, 248, 274, 280, 281, 288, 293, 294
Pommier, J., 158, 163
Pope, 15
Poulet, G., 275, 280
Poulet-Malassis, 147
Pound, E., 13, 204, 219
Proust, 112–13, 193, 277, 284
Praz, M., 16

Rabelais, 15, 16
Racine, 3, 13, 218
Raphaël, 84
Raymond, M., 16
Rembrandt, 1, 84
Richard, J.-P., 103, 130
Richter, J.-P., 15
Rimbaud, A., 73, 86, 87–8, 113, 242, 286
Ritter, 21
Robespierre, 3, 28, 56
Ronsard, 173, 174, 218
Rousseau, J.-J., 13, 15, 16, 20, 22, 27, 28, 29, 31, 33, 34, 36–7, 40, 53–7 *passim*, 91–6, 100–4 *passim*, 105, 123–4, 250, Jean-Jacques 254
Rude, M., 28
Ruff, M. A., Prof., 147, 151, 159, 160, 163, 286
Ruskin, J., 84

Sade, marquis de, 13, 18, 31, 32, 37, 42, 184
Sainte-Beuve, 7, 13, 73, 116, 184
Saint-John Perse, 202
Saint-Just, 55
Sand, G., 37, 40, 42
Sarte, J.-P., 8, 9, 32, 288, 294
Schelling, 21, 75, 76, 77, 78, 127
Schiller, 15, 57, 75, 78, 87
Schlegel, 15
Scott, Sir W., 74, 205
Sénèque, 29
Sense and Sensibility, 18
Shakespeare, 15, 16, 82, 127, 128
Shelley, 19, 23, 24, 25, 27, 73, 74
Smith, A., 72
Southey, R., 19
Spenser, 16
Staël, Madame de, 15, 25, 29, 45, 58
Stahl, 55
Steffens, 21
Stendhal, 13, 16, 18, 22–5 *passim*, 47, 64, 66–7
Swedenborg, 242
Swift, 41
Swinburne, 6, 148

Symons, A., 6

Taine, 63–4
Tasso, 16
Tennyson, 86, 116
Toussenel, 77
Trilling, L., 81
Turnell, M., 9, 157–8, 286

Valéry, P., 127, 203, 246, 259, 286
Verlaine, P., 7, 101, 113
Vigny, A. de, 147, 184–5
Villiers de l'Isle-Adam, 68
Virgil, 218, 219, 295
Volney, 19, 55
Voltaire, 3, 13, 33, 55

Wagner, J. J., 21

Wagner, R., 200
Warton, 15
Wellek, R., 58
Williams, R., 72
Winter's Tale, 128
Wordsworth, W., 15, 17, 18, 20–7 *passim*, 31, 34–42, 52, 54, 56–8 *passim*, 70–4 *passim*, 80–3 *passim*, 94–9, 100–4 *passim*, 105–10 *passim*, 112, 114, 118–127 *passim*, 134–5, 137–9 *passim*, 143, 228–9, 287

Young, 12

Zola, E., 61